Hello, God—It's Me Again

To: Lori, my sister in Christ. May you ever feel the presence and love of God in your life. Your example challenges all who know you.

All my love
Tammy
14 July 2014

K. THOMAS GREENE

Hello, God— It's Me Again

The Musings of a Wholly Man

Angel Books

Angel ✶ Books

an imprint of

THE INTERMUNDIA PRESS, LLC
Warrenton, Virginia

A DELAWARE COMPANY

Hello, God—It's Me Again: The Musings of a Wholly Man

© 2014 by K. Thomas Greene. All rights reserved.
Published 2014.
Printed in the United States of America.
ISBN 978-1-887730-38-9

To order additional copies of this book, contact:

THE INTERMUNDIA PRESS

www.intermundiapress.weebly.com

and

www.amazon.com

*This book is dedicated
to the memory of my beloved mother,*

Helen Greene.

*For twenty years, she fought alongside
the other 2.4 million people
with Parkinson's disease and their caregivers,
with dignity and a gentle love
that even today encourages all who knew her.*

FOREWORD

I recently heard Martin Cruz Smith, the author of *Gorky Park* and other
best-selling novels, being interviewed on NPR by Diane Rehm. They
were discussing Smith's Parkinson's disease.

"When did you first realize you had it?" asked Rehm.

Smith said it was about a dozen years ago, when he was preparing to go
to a dinner with a friend. The friend noticed he was dragging a foot and one
of his arms was hanging sort of limply, and commented on it.

Smith said he hadn't been aware.

"You'd better see a doctor," said the friend. "Those are signs of Parkinson's."

At the dinner that evening, Smith watched an older man who was known
to have Parkinson's disease. He was slouched over at the table and had a hard
time getting food to his mouth.

Smith said he was miserable all evening, because he knew he was looking
at his own future.

Tom Greene's Parkinson's began with numbness in his fingers. He had
been heavily rear-ended on a highway in Memphis, and the numbness had followed soon after. He was a minister, and soon began noticing quirky little
problems when he was up in front of his congregation. Sometimes his voice

wouldn't function normally. Other times he would begin to shake and couldn't stop.

Eventually he had to retire on disability pay several years before he would normally have stopped working.

Tom's problems since then have been multiple, as they often are in people with Parkinson's. His speech grew progressively harder to understand. His body often trembled. Sometimes he shook all over. Walking became more and more difficult.

Eventually, Tom allowed the doctors at Duke University to implant an electrical stimulator in his brain. It helped to send messages to his legs, so that his walking became easier. Sometimes it improved the quality of his speech, but not a lot. I have often had to say when we were talking on the phone, "Tom, I'm sorry, but I missed that. Could you repeat it for me?"

But Tom has never been a quitter. After his and his wife's divorce, he met a woman named Trudy. He told her about his problems and what a bleak future he had to offer her, but Trudy was already in love with him and said that she would marry him. I was serving a church in New York at the time, and flew down to perform their ceremony in a beautiful little glass chapel in a wooded park outside of Hot Springs.

A couple of years later, Trudy sold her home in Arkansas, and she and Tom renovated his parents' old home in Lenoir, North Carolina, and moved into it. Trudy, who had been an administrator in Arkansas, started a catering business. Tom didn't want to become useless, so he began writing the meditations in this book, hoping that they would some day find their way into the hands of others who were suffering from a debilitating disease.

Even writing was not easy for him. Some days his mind wouldn't cooperate. He would begin a thought and not be able to conclude it. Even the physical act of writing was difficult for him. But he struggled valiantly onward until he had completed enough daily meditations to fill this book.

The tensions of his life are easily visible in the meditations: his yearning for physical vigor and wholeness and his having to settle for ever-changing physical limitations; his wanting his spirit to soar like a great balloon and his acceptance of the gravity imposed upon it by his clumsy, ailing body. These are the tensions that anyone with a serious affliction experiences almost daily—tensions that regrettably define most of their existence.

Frankly, it is painful for me to read these pages, because I can feel the tensions so palpably, and, having been with Tom at various times both before and after the onset of his Parkinson's, know how they express themselves in his daily life. Here is a man who once played baseball well enough to have turned pro and now has to think before he makes a single step; a man who once bounded spiritedly over the mountains of western North Carolina and now has trouble getting out of bed; a man who once spoke eloquently from the pulpit of the churches he pastored and now has difficulty making his speech understood; a man who once sang and danced and cavorted like a leprechaun and now can only do these things in his imagination.

But Tom is stalwart. I tell him he is one of my two great heroes.

The other is an old friend, Dr. William H. Hull, once my provost at Samford University, who has been struggling with ALS, or Lou Gehrig's disease, for the past five years, and who for at least two of those years has been unable to speak or move any part of his body so that he must be totally cared for 24/7, yet has continued, with the aid of a highly specialized computer, to write books and papers.

These men—Bill and Tom—are like Superman made powerless by contact with kryptonite, the mysterious mineral from his home planet that always rendered him helpless. Superman never stopped being Superman, even when some evildoer managed temporarily to halt him with a piece of kryptonite. And Bill and Tom have not been destroyed or silenced by the extreme diseases that have attacked their bodies.

Tom's handicap will reveal itself from time to time in these devotionals. Sometimes, he speaks of it directly. Other times, it is evident in some missed connection in a thought that he is trying to express. But always the shining spirit of the man comes through, glowing like a beacon to guide us to the truth he is attempting to exhibit.

The very title of the book is vintage Tom: "Hello, God—it's me again." In all the years I've known him, Tom has been a man of genuine prayer and spirituality. Like Job in the Old Testament, he continues to depend on the deity who ironically seemed to be absent while the Parkinson's was taking over his body. And his little prayers at the ends of the meditations are priceless insights into Tom's sincere and irrevocable relationship to the Almighty.

Different meditations will appeal to different people. Some are specifically about Parkinson's and its problems, whereas others are more general in nature. Some are geared to people with physical ailments, and others are for those who have something to offer the handicapped. But all of them are reminders of our human frailty, something those of us whose bodies haven't yet betrayed them tend to forget. As we age, even those of us who aren't bedeviled by Parkinson's or ALS or cancer or some other dreaded disease realize more and more each day that we are skating on thin ice.

The trick of life at this point, as Tom indicates, is to live increasingly close to God, so that we too murmur many times a day, "Hello, God—it's me again." It involves getting to the place where we hardly have a thought or experience a problem with our bodies that doesn't shunt us instinctively toward the deity. Tom has already reached this plateau. Now he's trying to help others achieve it too.

I find his thoughts edifying, and believe other readers will too—especially those with an intractable physical problem of some kind and those who are charged with their care.

John Killinger
AUTHOR, PREACHER, AND THEOLOGIAN

ACKNOWLEDGEMENTS

*I*t is with the humblest of hearts that I thank so many of you who have played such an integral part in my life. Yet, I would be remiss if I did not thank a few key people who have shown us through their "life stories" that God is with us on our spiritual journey.

Dr. John and Anne Killinger, who are fighting their own battle with an uninvited guest (cancer), are a constant source of encouragement. I was patiently and lovingly guided through the rough water of writing.

Dr. Gardner C. Taylor, friend, brother, and spiritual guide, led me through a "legion" of questions and thoughts on the scriptures and insights of others.

Others who were instrumental in seeing this project through were my publisher, Eric Killinger, and Betty Pruitt, who through her labor of love, helped lay the foundation.

And to all of those who have allowed me entrance into your lives, your joys, and your heartbreaks for over thirty years, I thank you. I am blessed . . .

Day 1
Really Listening

Then a cloud overshadowed them. A voice came out of the cloud and said, "This is my Son, whom I love, listen to him" (Mark 9:7).

HOW MANY TIMES HAVE YOU heard someone say, "Did you hear me?" or, "Are you listening to me?" Is there a way for our minds and hearts not to be distracted by all the goings-on of the world around us? We who have Parkinson's disease are easily distracted by the fact that we have to be single-minded in our day-to-day living, because in order to get through the day we have to concentrate on one thing at a time to be deliberate. We have to remind ourselves, for example, to lift up our feet and take a full stride, not slide and shuffle our feet. When we don't listen, we receive a great many miscues, and more times that not we fall.

The questions that must be asked are, "How do you go from an absurd life to an obedient life, from a deaf life to a listening life?" We become anxious, nervous, tense, and upset; and when we do that, we don't listen. And we don't listen because we are so anxious that we don't have space to listen. We can't let the voice of God come in. And God's voice is saying, "You are with me always, and all I have is yours." We must try to listen to that again and again. For when we listen, we can hear and receive a great deal of direction for our lives from God.

To be able to listen, we must create a space in which we can hear the voice that says, "You are my beloved son; you are my beloved daughter; you are my favored son; you are my favored daughter. All that is mine is yours." That is hard to imagine, knowing the state of disobedience in which we find ourselves so many times What it boils down to is this: Jesus is saying, "All that I say is for you to hear; all that I know is for you to know; all that I do is for you to do." He continues and says, "Nothing that the Father gave me do I hold back from you." Really listen, so as not to forget. That's a real but rewarding discipline.

PRAYER: O God, we hear your Spirit telling us to be quiet so that we can hear your plans for uncluttering our lives. It is so easy to sit quietly with our minds dwelling on so many other things other than a word from you. Enable us, once we hear the quietness of your voice, to heed without any hesitation. Amen.

⊰ ◇ ⊱

Day 2
Being Renewed by Prayer

I will be like the dew to Israel; she shall blossom like the lily, he shall strike the root like the forests of Lebanon (Hos 14:5).

PEOPLE WITH PARKINSON'S DISEASE BECOME fatigued at different times during the day. It is at these times when there seems to be no reservoir of energy, no container from which to pull the needed energy to overcome the fatigue and all its companions. Following a rest or short nap, the Parkinson's patient is able to carry on with the day's activities. It can be compared to prayer. There are times when we are spiritually fatigued and in need of some additional spiritual energy.

We grow silent, which leads us to suspect that prayer is acceptance. Without prayer there would be less acceptance. A person who prays is one who stands with his hands open to the world. The one praying is confident that God will show himself in the things we experience each day—nature that surrounds us in the people we meet, in the situations we run into. We trust that the world holds God's secret within it, and we expect that secret to be shown to us. Prayer creates that openness where God can give God's self to humanity. Indeed, God wants to give God's self; God wants to surrender to the man and woman that God has created. He or she might be seen as doing all that they can to take the excuses used to keep God at arm's length from our prayer closets.

Those who allow God to enter, however, experience an openness that is not automatic. It does not simply come of itself. It requires our confession. We must confess to being broken vessels, weak, limited, and even sinful. Whenever we pray, we confess that we are not God's but rebellious folk who want to keep their freedom and that we wouldn't want to lose that. We realize that we haven't reached our goal yet, and, in all honesty, we never will reach it in this life. We admit that we must constantly stretch out our hands and wait again for the gift that gives new life.

PRAYER: Our gracious heavenly Father, you desire to be with us more than we do with you, and deep down we know that is not right. Please forgive us. We are also aware of the fact that many times our arms are not reaching out in acceptance to you and others. Instead of outreaching we are holding ourselves tightly appearing as though we are keeping others away from that acceptance. Forgive us, O God. In the name of Jesus, we pray. Amen.

⸺◈⸺

Day 3
Doing the Right Thing

Mary answered, "I am the Lord's servant. Let everything you've said happen to me" (Luke 1:38).

HAVE YOU EVER GIVEN MUCH thought to Mary, the mother of Jesus, and what she did? I don't mean the placid, gentle, calm, even-tempered, watered-down version of children's church school lessons. We can only guess what unique attributes she had that she was chosen to be blessed among women. It would be rather difficult to imagine what went through her mind and soul at the words of the angel Gabriel. Instead of saying, "No," or, "Pass," and running in the opposite direction as fast as her legs would carry her, this remarkable, humble young girl, this bearer of God's precious son, had the audacity to say, "Let it happen," or, in the words of the gospel writer, "I am the Lord's servant. Let everything you've said happen to me." These are the words of a young girl whose only thought was how to serve, or how to fulfill her vocation as handmaiden of the Lord.

What a remarkable position in which to find oneself. This is obedience in the face of mystery. It is service in the face of misunderstanding. It is a yes, when a no would have been understandable. With Mary's eyes leading the way, we too are invited to say yes to God's often mysterious call.

We have no way of knowing the consequences of our yes when we respond to God's call, whatever that might be. Ours could be an understandable no in light of all the trouble and misunderstanding it might bring. But like Mary's, ours should be a yes.

The yes that is represented here is not a flippant yes; one that cannot be of our own making. This yes can only be a response to faith and more times than not like is made with trembling and uncertainty to God's insistent call. It is not made in order to protect, to have fame, or to be successful; it can only be made based on trust in the One who has called.

A yes like this calls for courage of relinquishment, a willingness to let go of the world lived in before God's call, and to enter into the mysterious world of the unfolding of God's will.

> **PRAYER:** Father in heaven and on earth, giver of life and joy: give to us the courage of Mary. Even when the way is not as clear as we would like, give us the courage like that that this teenaged girl had as she said yes to being part of the greatest love and enterprise the world has ever witnessed. In the name of Jesus, we pray. Amen.

Day 4
The Naked Truth

I can guarantee this truth: whatever you failed to do for one of my brothers or sisters, no matter how unimportant they seem, you failed to do for me (Matthew 25:40).

HEN JESUS WAS ASKED WHICH was the greatest commandment, his initial response really wasn't that much of a surprise. But when he gave the second one, you could say that he kicked the proverbial hornet's nest. I'll bet that you could see ears perk up and hear a murmur that arose within the crowd and began to crescendo.

I can hear them now. Can't you? "He doesn't mean that Samaritan whose wheat field meets my corn field." "Surely he doesn't want me to help that guy, or that family." Yes, Christ died for them, too. Is it not the same in our modern day world? "He was not asking us to reach out to that woman who admits herself in rehab, or the man in the checkout lane being ill-tempered and impatient, or this farmer with a leathery face, or the alcoholic lying in the ditch by the side of the road passed out from too much booze." Jesus Christ died for them, too.

One of the first questions that I imagine being discussed was, "Who is my brother?" Jesus claims each and every one of us are brothers and sisters. He was giving us the example to follow that did not quite make it to our acceptability.

It is essential that we accept all without reservation—those we normally accept, those we normally don't, and those we question. There is before us an absolute necessity to join together with all our sisters and brothers. Our hearts need to grow to the point at which we are all one, regardless of whether others are thrust into our arms or not.

PRAYER: Father, help us to do more than just talk about helping others. May our words have conviction to say what we will do and then may have the drive to follow through. Amen.

Day 5
What Was I Thinking?

Lazarus was the reason why many people were leaving the Jews and believing in Jesus (John 12:11).

THE EIGHTH OF AUGUST IS the birthday of my deceased son, Thomas. He would have been twenty-eight. I can't help but think about him and that day twenty-eight years ago. We went to the doctor, who sent us to the hospital where we walked the hallways of Rex Hospital in Raleigh until his mother's water broke. We were the only ones in delivery, so all the nurses on duty were helping. The doctor and I discussed the book I was reading, C. S. Lewis' *The Last Night of the World*. Then, with the help of the forceps, Thomas was delivered and hurried out of the room.

We didn't even get to hold him; he was having a problem and was taken to Pediatric Natal Intensive Care. When they let me see him, he was hooked up to every kind of machine they had. The problem had something to do with the cord wrapped around his neck, causing his lungs not to start inflating on their own. They assured us that he would be okay and that their actions were simply precautionary. When I was finally able to hold him, I could not and still cannot put into words the feelings that washed over me. Who could imagine that twelve short years later my Thomas would be dead. Never in a million years would I have dreamed, let alone guess, that when I told him good night that night in August that it would be the last time we would speak.

What kind of father was I to think so much about my aloneness, my loss, and so much less of Thomas? I remember seeing his body for the first time lying there motionless in the coffin and crying out from my shattered heart, "Thomas, come back!" I waited for him to open his eyes, but he didn't.

Now, I realize that my "come back," was quite selfish. Who in their right minds, having experienced ultimate peace and bliss, want to return to this place? It was for my own sake. It was sometime later, speaking of wishing many times over to be able to see his face, to be able to touch him, talk with him, that I realized I never raised a very important question.

If such a return were possible, would it be good for him? I wanted him back as an ingredient in the restoration of my past. The truth of the matter is, I'm not too sure that I couldn't ask for anything worse. Having gone through death, to come back, and then at some later date have all his dying to do over again? Although in history, Stephen holds claim to being the first Christian martyr, I believe Lazarus had the rawer deal.

PRAYER: Father, I ask that you help me live my life in such a way that those I live amongst and those I meet will come to believe in Jesus Christ, because of it. Amen.

Day 6
Courage Like You've Never Seen

When he came closer to the city, he began to cry (Luke 19:39, 41).

E READ IN THE GOSPELS that our Lord steadfastly, resolutely set his face toward Jerusalem. He went up to the city knowing he was going to die there, and that takes courage. If we knew that we were going to die as we went into a particular city, we would find a way to bypass it and put as much distance as we could between us and them. But to know that and go anyway, who else but Jesus could have done that? As soon as Jesus announced his intentions, Thomas declared, "Let us go up also and die with him." He saw clearly that if Jesus went to Jerusalem, he would be killed. And Thomas, who should be admired for his candor rather than blamed for his doubts, blurted out what all the others were afraid to say, that Jesus was going up to Jerusalem to accomplish his death. He could have run away but he didn't. He faced the deadly business head on, and that takes courage.

Have you ever thought what it meant to Jesus to know what this fateful journey would do to his friends? He knew it would be their undoing. We don't like to put pressure of this sort on people we love. We'd rather protect them than expose them, reassure them rather than test them beyond their limit of courage and devotion. He knew he would stretch them to the breaking point, such that Peter would deny him, Judas would betray him, and they all would forsake him. We can imagine something of what their failure meant to them; but think of what it meant to Jesus to put to the wall those whom he loved so deeply.

And there was Mary, his mother. Think of what going up to Jerusalem was to do to her. He was put to death on a hill, and her love followed him to the place of crucifixion. Simeon's prophecy to Mary was fulfilled: "You shall be pierced to the heart," he had said. But think what it meant to Mary's son to bring such pain upon his mother. He went to Jerusalem, knowing it was going to do that to her. No wonder he had to set his face like flint to take the first dreadful step toward Judea amid all the distractions and trappings he experienced. And the quality of his courage was that being aware of it all, and still carrying the weight of all the pain he was to bring to others on own his spirit, he still went up to Jerusalem. It makes our courage pretty superficial, doesn't it?

PRAYER: Lord, we so quickly forget the price paid for our salvation. We so conveniently dismiss the courage it took for Jesus to go to Jerusalem and the pain that he knew he would bring upon family and disciples. Help us not to settle for a courage that is insipid but rather for one that is bold and alive. Amen.

Day 7
Wrinkles

Now, Abraham and Sarah were old, advanced in years (Genesis 18:10).

I GET A CHUCKLE EVERY TIME I see a picture of someone who has had plastic surgery. Especially when they're shown in before and after shots, and the after shot makes them look as though they had seen a monster. They are the ones who, if their skin was pulled any tighter, would be looking out their navels. Their relentless pursuit to do whatever it takes no matter the cost to remain young looking is, in the end, to no avail: gravity always wins out, and when they are done, the advances they might have made drop them right back to where they were when dealing with a third or fourth chin and furrows on their face around their eyes. Their endless search for that magical whatever to keep one looking younger than one's years has been desired for many years. Remember the main purpose of the voyage of Ponce de Leon to America was to find the "fountain of youth," but it was not anywhere to be found. This certainly has not deterred those folk whose desire is to never look their true age. I think the latest advertisement claims that the latest beauty product can give you back ten years.

One of the common causalities of Parkinson's disease is the loss of muscle control in the face, which plays a big part in one's ability to show expression. People with PD go about their daily activities expressionless. Often times they are mistakenly accused of being mad or not caring about a subject matter, which is certainly not the case. One little boy asked my son, "Why does your papa always look angry?" to which he replied, "He's saving all his smiles for the old people and us."

Herbert Spencer had no wrinkles on his forehead and certainly was not in need of any Botox injections. George Elliot asked him about it one day, expressing surprise that there were no lines on his forehead. Spencer said that there were none because he was not puzzled. George Elliot replied that this was the most arrogant statement she had ever heard. Look at what God accomplished through two elderly people: Sarah, who was beyond the way of the woman, and Abraham, who was as good as dead. So the next time you look at that face and contemplate ridding yourself of the signs of age, think again. When you look in the mirror and see your face, love it, wrinkles and all. Think for a moment: you get wrinkles around your eyes when you smile a lot and around you mouth if you laugh a lot, and on your forehead if you're puzzled. Wrinkles are signs, not only of a maturing face, but of a youthful spirit, and a brain humble enough to be puzzled, remembering all the while that God can and wants to use us for the kingdom, wrinkles and all.

PRAYER: O merciful God, we need your forgiveness for messing up these bodies you have given us by filling in the cracks and wrinkles with silicon and plastic injections. May we be content with what we have and give us courage to show off our wrinkles. We have enjoyed every one of them, for Christ's sake. Amen.

⊰◯⊱

Day 8
Seeing Is Believing

The ax is now ready to cut the roots of trees. Any tree that doesn't produce good fruit will be cut down and thrown into a fire (Luke 3:9).

WE READ ABOUT THE POSITIVE, loving virtues of Christianity; and if they are true, then it would logically follow to say that all Christians are obviously nicer than all non-Christians. But one need not look too far to realize that that is not true. Let's be reasonable. If one claims to have been converted and that conversion brings with it no improvement in that person's outward actions, that is, if they continue to have the same characteristics as before—spiteful, negative, angry, envious, snobbish, harboring a non-forgiving spirit—then we must suspect that person's conversion was more imaginative than real. One can claim to have new insights, better feelings, a greater interest in religion, but these remain only empty words unless they make our day-to-day behavior better.

I can hear someone admonishing me now, saying that I am not supposed to judge. It is true: the scriptures do contain some words that tell us that to judge is dangerous and warn us to remember that we will be judged as we have judged. I take issue, however, with those who say that judging has no part in a believer's life. The fact is that Christians are faced with having to make quite a few judgments each day. To fail to do so could have dire consequences with their non-action. Alongside the verses of scripture they may use to support their claim, I suggest other verses that tell us to be careful about how we judge.

Jesus himself gave us the direction of how to judge. He told us to judge others by their fruits. Just as an apple tree bears apples and a date tree, dates, we wait and make our judgment upon seeing the fruit the tree bears. A tree known by its fruits is "the proof in the pudding." As neither an apple tree can produce dates nor dates produce apples, the life of a Christian will produce the fruit of God's spiritual kingdom.

This is not to advocate that Christians are without blemish. When we Christians behave wrongly—and we will—when our lifestyles are in the opposite direction of heaven, then we bring great harm to Christianity. Our actions make Christianity unbelievable to those who are in another world of their own. And it can happen without our suspecting it. Someone recalled wartime posters that were prominently displayed throughout the city during World War II. The posters read, "Careless Talk Costs Lives." It is equally true that careless lives cost talk. Our careless lives give the outside world plenty of ammunition to talk about and put down religion, providing grounds for talking in a way that throws doubt on the truth of Christianity itself.

What does the fruit in your basket say about you and the life you are living?

PRAYER: Gracious Father, be with us and hold us in your loving hand. Protect us so that the things we say and do will bring glory to you and will build up your church. Amen.

Day 9
How Clean Is Your Religion?

Create in me a clean heart, O God, and renew a right spirit within me
(Psalm 51:10).

SOME MIGHT BE SURPRISED AT the emphasis in the title on "clean" religion, with the implication being that there can be such a thing as dirty, polluted, or corrupt religion. Unfortunately, there can be, as history clearly reveals. The tragedy is that when religion goes bad, the effect is worse than no religion at all.

Even our vocabulary reveals a universal yearning for inward cleansing. "Clean up your act," we tell those who scoff at our standards in the world of politics, business, the media, and religion. "Come clean" is what we say to those who are being interrogated daily on our TV screens. We need to hold one another accountable at all times, because with a closer look we will realize that the seeds of corruption we clearly see in others lurk in our own hearts. It is the inner cleansing to which Jesus gave priority. It is when "Clean up your act" and "Come clean" are not judgments on others but are a divine Word to us that we get to the heart of the matter. "Create in *me* a clean heart, O God, and renew a right spirit within *me*."

This cleansing power enters the human soul and society to purify and keep us on the right track. Throughout the Bible, it is assumed that every human being needs this cleansing and renewing power. It speaks of a living God, who wills a life of harmony, love, creative energy peace, and purity for the family God created in the image of God. True religion wears no blinkers but sees what is wrong in others and in us. The pollution is there and cannot be ignored. True religion carries the news of the cleansing power.

This is the function of real religion: the cleansing water, the healing stream. But it still can become polluted. It is terribly true. "How can this be?" you might ask. The corruption of the good can be seen when the external forms, rituals, and codes of behavior become more important than our internal relationship to God.

Another way this corruption invades our lives is when the lust for worldly wealth and power goes with it. Clean religion demands a strict accounting of all we hold in trust for God. It steers clear of empire building, whether that of the proud medieval bishop or of the equally arrogant modern televangelist.

The risen Christ is the one who can give and keep giving to us the clean religion that he represents. He is the one who renews a right spirit within us. This clean religion for which we yearn—a religion of the heart, an uncomplicated, a sincere religion, one we share in word and deed and for others—this clean religion is a gift to pray for every day. We open our hearts, with their load of regrets and anxieties, to God and we hear the changing words in answer to our prayer: "I will; be clean."

PRAYER: Father, create in us clean hearts and renew a right spirit within us. Amen.

<hr>

Day 10

Expecting

Lazarus was the reason why many people were leaving the Jews and believing in Jesus (John 12:11).

WHEN A COUPLE HEARS THE doctor's words, "You are going to have a baby," everything moves into baby mode. Expecting a baby changes everything. The mother starts looking after herself better—after all, she is eating and caring for two now. The excitement is somewhat muffled until you begin to tell family and friends that you are with child; then the mother-to-be begins showing, and you start hearing, "You are going to have a baby, that's great." But nine months is a long time to wait, to expect. You might find yourself asking questions about the life growing inside of you. Some you can express, and others are so personal that you can't. This verse of scripture is somewhat like that.

Doesn't this verse leave you with a vivid picture of God's people (you and me and the rest of creation) standing on tiptoe, waiting with great anticipation for the kingdom to be revealed?

Looking forward to today, tomorrow, and the rest of our lives, we might easily become frustrated as we see little change for the better in ourselves, our situations, or in those we love. Our dear Lord understands. Our groans, our sighs, and our tears are heard. Our struggles, like childbirth, can be exhausting.

"Be encouraged!" Paul writes, "The Spirit also intercedes for us with sighs too deep for words." Paul goes on to say that all things work together for the good of others who love God. So we cannot be overcome.

Begin the day with the desire to live as God's child, expecting that the Spirit will be very close to you and that all your needs are known. Now watch the adventure unfold as you walk through your day.

If we can see our days—our lives—as an adventure, we can look forward with anticipation to what God will do through us and all of creation.

> PRAYER: Thank you, ever-renewing God, that we can expect great things to happen when we walk with you each step of the way. Amen.

Day 11
I've Had It!

So Jesus said to them: "Let's go to a place where we can be alone for a while."
Many people were coming and going, and Jesus and the apostles didn't even
have a chance to eat (Mark 6:31).

WHEN OUR DAYS ARE TOO busy, we hope that the telephone won't ring. We find ourselves thinking or saying out loud, "If one more person asks me to do one more thing, I'll simply collapse."

Need we to assume, however, that when God calls, it is with the intention of giving us more work to do? Every call isn't a call to service. God, like human beings, might call just to keep in touch, to see how we're doing.

In the Old Testament, the story is recounted that Elijah was at a low point in his prophetic life. He had had it. He was only wise enough to know Jezebel had put a price on his head, and he surely could use some needed sleep. God knew he also needed some food and Elisha to take over some of his responsibilities. God called, not to increase his work, but to tell him how to lighten his load. Elijah, who had been waiting to die, found that he could carry on and that he was not alone in the fight with the worshipers of Baal.

Everyone, even ministers and especially those folk who look after others with Parkinson's, needs a break. When they get that time off, it helps make them ready to start again and realize that they are not alone in their role as caregivers. There are others out there ready to help lighten their load.

Sometimes God's call is to tell us to share our burdens with others. Sometimes we're instructed to let others take over. We have to listen carefully to hear whether God is saying, "Go, labor on," or, "Come, rest a while."

> **PRAYER:** God, help us be neither lazy nor workaholics. Call us to join you in the rhythm of the kingdom and what is best for your kingdom and for us. Amen.

Day 12
Perfection—Impossible?

You, therefore, must be perfect, as your heavenly Father is perfect (Matthew 5:48).

HOW MANY TIMES HAVE YOU failed to attempt something because you already had it in your mind that it was impossible, and you hadn't even tried the first time? Yet one cannot go through life and never be faced with the dilemma of attempting something or not, especially trying to be perfect. Would not a more preferred way to approach this be not to think about possibility or impossibility? We have to face it, this being perfect; there is no getting around it. We must face it and do the best that we can. This applies to all that we encounter: in-line skating, scuba diving, trekking through the mountains, hang-gliding, or attempting to button your shirt when your fingers and hands are not working due to arthritis or Parkinson's disease. The attempt needs—no, must—be taken. We are caught up in how amazingly wonderful it is what we can do when we have to.

Let us be warned that following such an achievement, we cannot sit back on our laurels. We realize when expected to be as Christ—perfect—that it will not be attained by merely human effort. One must seek and ask for God's help. And yes, I will confess that there are times that even after you have asked for assistance, it seems to be so long in coming and then not to full realization. With each failure, we ask for forgiveness, pick ourselves up, and go at it again. It would appear that where God firsts moves us is not in the direction of our request but rather to the power of always trying again. This process shows and trains us in the habits of the soul which are the most important. The illusions about ourselves are cured, but we're also taught to depend upon God.

When we learn the important lesson that we cannot be depended on, even on our best days, we need not despair. Even when life tumbles in on us for whatever reason, our failures are forgiven. With that said, we can be warned that the only fatal thing is to sit down content with anything less than perfection.

PRAYER: Almighty God, Father, the call to perfection as you are perfect is not an easy one to hear or even accomplish. After all, we're not fully complete as you are. Therefore, we ask that you help us through your Holy Spirit to enter into Christ and become as Jesus was, is, and forever shall be: fully human, fully divine, fully yours that we attain the perfection of your image as we should. It is in his name that we pray. Amen.

⸺⟨○⟩⸺

Day 13
How Long Must I Wait?

"For I know the plans I have for you," declares the Lord, "plans to prosper you and not to harm you; plans to give you hope and a future" (Jeremiah 29:1).

IT IS EASY FOR US TO sit on the sidelines and complain because God is taking God's own sweet time about answering our prayers. Why doesn't God provide the solution? After all it is God. And there's the rub. The secret is not how long it takes God to answer our prayers, but rather that God knows what is best for us. It is amazing how many times we are guilty of thinking that we know more about what is ended and the timing than the Almighty does. I can imagine God and all the angels laughing so hard that their halos hurt when they watch our meager attempts to play God and how full of ourselves we become.

To illustrate this point, all one needs to do is to look at the life of Nelson Mandela, who recently passed away. The life of this giant of a man was movingly shown in a recent movie, *Invictus*. It depicted the segment of his life in which he challenged the South African rugby team to win the World Cup, which was being played in South Africa. He thought that this would help to begin the healing of his country. It did, and they won.

Mandela spent twenty-seven years in prison because of the hope he had for a new South Africa, and he believed that hope could become a reality. Close to the end of his prison stay, he was allowed visitors. His only daughter was allowed to see him. On one of her visits, she carried with her the granddaughter Nelson had never seen. Mandela's daughter had waited until her father could name her. He was so happy not only to hold her but to name her as well. Her name is Zaziwe, an African word for hope. He called her Hope, he said, "Because during all my years in prison, hope never left me—and now it never will."

Caregivers for Parkinson's patients understand when one says that worry is automatic. A concerted decision needs to be made daily as to what attitude will prevail: decisions to be truthful, to wait with patience, no matter how long the shadows or dark the night. We will be advised to let hope live and let worry die. There are times when worry almost convinces us, but we need to decide to keep it waiting. And that decision colors and shapes the whole of our living.

PRAYER: Our gracious Father, grant unto us a spirit of hope so that our future does not seem to be a closed door or darkened tunnel. Help us to keep hope alive. In the name of the one who is our hope, Jesus Christ, our Lord. Amen.

Day 14
All from Neglect

Don't neglect the gift which you received (1 Timothy 4:14).

THESE WORDS OF ENCOURAGEMENT AND advice were issued to this new, young preacher. The writer of this letter shared with Timothy the things that he would need in order to have a successful ministry.

Guidelines were given on how to deal with the leaders in the church and the church itself. Paul tells Timothy to watch out for sinful people and to live a godly life so the church would accept and follow his example.

This letter also contained warnings, one that is our text for today. As I pondered these words, I realized that I did not know of a person who did not have at least one gift. If everyone has a gift, then what's the problem that keeps the church from being as effective now as it was then?

Is it that we don't want a gift?

Is it that we don't believe we have a gift?

Is it that we wanted a different one?

Is it that we believe that we deserve a gift?

Is it that we think we can handle more than one?

I know folk who are so obsessed with gifts and with who has what and how many, that they miss opportunity after opportunity to use their gift(s) to touch someone's life for good. They treat gifts like the Boy Scouts who check off their steps in order to obtain a merit badge: once done, it's earned.

Even with all the warnings of future persecution(s), having to contend with phony preachers and false teachers, the writer of the letter to Timothy not only warns of troublemakers in the church but also encourages Timothy to hold fast to his gift, to teach the truth in the sure and certain hope that they would follow his example.

PRAYER: Father, give us the courage to hold fast to the teachings that can bring us closer to you and to our brothers and sisters. And help us not to neglect our own gifts. Amen.

Day 15
Manifested Glory

Have the same attitude that Christ Jesus had. Jesus, although he was in the form of God and equal with God, did not take advantage of this equality. Instead, he emptied himself by taking on the form of a servant, by becoming like other human beings, by having a human appearance (Philippians 2:5–7).

REMEMBER THE STORY OF JESUS' arrest? A large group of soldiers (the Gospel of John indicates that it was a cohort, or about 480 men) and religious leaders (or their servants) was a huge force that made its way through the darkness of night to arrest this one simple carpenter from Nazareth. Although Jesus had eleven disciples, who had earlier said that they would die with him—they ran as fast as they could from fear of meeting the same fate—as well as a legion of angels at his beck and call, he chose not to call on their assistance in disbanding the group that came to arrest him. Jesus chose to be handed over to them without any retaliation. It is that moment, when Jesus is abandoned by family and friends and totally alone, that he is handed over. Thus begins his passion.

Jesus, meeting the crowd, asked, "Whom do you seek?"

"Jesus of Nazareth," came the reply.

"I am he." This is not the first time we have heard these words. They echo all the way back from God's appearance to Moses through the burning bush that was not consumed. "I am who I am . . . I am the one" (see Exodus 3:1–14). The words of Jesus, *I am he*, carried with them the glory of God. Strictly speaking, Jesus was not being handed over to the soldiers, but already we see the glory of God being handed over to us. While we were receiving Jesus, God revealed that he embraces Christ's passion as well as resurrection.

"The Son of Man," Jesus says, "must be lifted up as Moses lifted up the serpent in the desert, so that everyone who believes may have eternal life in him" (John 3:14–15). He is lifted up in glory, so the cross—which at first is a sign of life gone wrong and laws disobeyed—becomes a sign of hope. Suddenly, we realize that the glory of God, the divinity of God, is bursting through in Jesus' passion precisely when he is most victimized.

PRAYER: Our heavenly Father, forgive us for the many times we obstruct your plan to bring us life and bring it more abundantly. We miss out on so much when we think that life can only be lived our way. Help us to see through to the heart of your son, Jesus, who lived and lives among us and through his death provided and provides for us a way of salvation. Help us to live in that strength. In his name, we pray. Amen.

⸺◆○◆⸺

Day 16
Help Me Understand

Martha told Jesus, "Lord, if you had been here, my brother would not have died (John 11:20).

ANY FOLK HAVE EXPERIENCED TRAGEDY IN their lives. Some of those who haven't might do so at some point. One soon discovers that no matter the "cause," the "when," or the "where," the questions always find their resting place in the word "why." And upon whatever level it falls, and at what age one may be for whatever reason it happens, it always comes back to *why*: Why did something like this happen? We hear the words from Mary and Martha about their brother Lazarus, who, they said in bitter disappointment, would not have died if Jesus had arrived sooner. Yes, we can point to a minute bit of belief (v. 22). There was faith, but there was also frustration. There was love, but there was also puzzlement. There was that great unanswered question: *Why?*

If Jesus is alive and active, then why did God allow this to happen? This is not a question of doubt; it is, rather, a faith question. It is the cry of a wounded believer. Someone wrote that a person could suffer anything, if he or she knew that what he or she was going through had meaning.

Each of us must find one's own answer, one's own meaning, for the many things that happen in our lives. One thing I learned in the loss of my son is that God is present, not off in some ivory castle far removed from the tragic scene.

This was not some fly-by-night occurrence. This was a story with real people with real names and real emotion that touch Jesus' heart. Mary, Martha, and Lazarus were friends. Isn't it a comfort to know that whatever tragedy we are in, whether it be death, a diagnosis of Parkinson's disease, or cancer; or you are financially bankrupt; or you lose your job that Jesus knows our names. How strengthening to know that he loves us that much. Christ walks with us through the valley of the shadow of death, transforming the way of tears into the valley of rejoicing. I have seen it repeatedly in the faces of those in the midst of tragedy and marveled at the strength of weakness with God. Why? I don't know. But I do know that Christ understands you and what you are going through. He has been there himself. No tragedy can or will separate us from the love of God.

I can hear Jesus. Can't you? "Lazarus, come out!"

And there was great rejoicing!

PRAYER: Father, our voices join the many voices throughout history that seek and yearn for the answer to the question, "Why?" Give us peace and patience to wait for your answer. But until then, help us to be at work for your kingdom. Amen.

Day 17
Praying through Clenched Teeth

I want you to know, brothers and sisters, that the good news I have spread is not a human message (Galatians 1:11).

YOU HAVE WORKED MANY YEARS toward your dream. You did everything you were supposed to do when the schedule and directions called for it. Everything was perfect until the doctor threw his hat on the jigsaw puzzle you were putting together: "I'm sorry, but you have Parkinson's disease." You noticed that you were struggling to get enough air to breathe. Suddenly you were outside your body, hearing but not hearing. You were there but you weren't. The shock of the announcement was starting to sink in. You thought of a thousand things at once: your family and friends, our family and friends, your work, your employer, your dream.... Your dream. Then it hits you like a ton of wet noodles: you will never realize your dream. How did you feel when you heard those words? Shock? Anger? Bitterness? Hurt? Denial?

Saul was responding to the preaching of Stephen and Philip, whose sermons were simply that your background or your nationality didn't matter, as long as you put your trust in God and believed that God sent God's Son, Jesus Christ, into the world to save humankind. But for Saul, it did matter. His anger was directed toward those young preachers, who were telling the people that what Saul's great-grandfather, his grandfather, his father, and he himself believed was being unraveled. He was angered by this group of followers of Jesus of Nazareth, who opened the arms of God wider than ever. For them, Jew and Gentile were the same. Saul, however, had spent a great deal of his life trying to be true to God, trying to keep the candle of faith burning in a dark and pagan world.

It is one thing to know something; it's another thing to really know it. He knows it, and he does not know it; and the battle that is fought between knowing and really knowing is fierce. It is sometimes called the struggle from head to heart. I know that the longest trip we ever have to make is the trip from head to heart, from knowing to knowing; and until that trip is complete, we are in great pain. We might even lash out at others.

So what about your dream? If you truly can't reach your dream, dream another dream.

> **PRAYER:** Heavenly Father, walk alongside us as we make our journey from head to heart. We need your companionship. Prevent us from wasting the remainder of our lives away because of unrealized dreams. We are grateful that you already have something in mind for us to do. Give us ears to hear, in Jesus' name. Amen.

⸺◈⸺

Day 18
Recapturing Wonder

Oh the wonder of it all.
The wonder of it all.
Just to think that God loves me.

— From a song

I LIKE THIS QUOTATION: "As civilization advances, the sense of wonder declines." Isn't that a great quotation? Such decline is an alarming symptom of our state of mind. Humanity will not perish for want of information but from want of appreciation. The beginning of our happiness lies in the understanding that life without wonder is not worth living. What we lack is not a will to believe but a will to wonder.

So I turn again and again to the scriptures to retrieve the sense of wonder. The scriptures help us bind our fragmented selves together. They help us to recognize ourselves in all manner of terrible and marvelous complexity. The scriptures affirm that there are constants, despite the change and decay in all that we see around us. One of the constants is a particular question that is asked in every generation: "Who am I?"

The scriptures help to answer that question. As we identify with the various characters, we help to build ourselves. We may not be able to slow down the accelerating changes in the world around us, but we are free to react to them in our own ways, changing not only ourselves but also whatever it is we react to. We are surrounded by disillusioned, frightened, and zealous people who have forgotten that they can cooperate with change by telling their stories because they have neglected it as their prime vehicle for truth.

> PRAYER: Our heavenly Father, only you can show us the way to our true being. You alone can answer the questions we have about our existence and the purpose for our being here at this particular place and time. Unstop our ears so we can hear you clearly. Remind us that one thing we need to do is to go out in our backyards tonight and stand there for a while gazing at the stars realizing how small we really are. In the name of Jesus, we pray. Amen.

Day 19
Rewind—One More Time

He who has ears to hear, let him hear (Mark 4:9).

HAVE YOU EVER THOUGHT ABOUT how we communicate? It certainly doesn't make our "top ten" list of things to spend our time thinking about. My skills in communication have been greatly hampered because of Parkinson's. I have to slow down, breathe deeply, and be deliberate and conscious of everything I am trying get across. I am aware that when I am tired, I either speak too softly or very fast. I have noticed that, when someone does not understand what I am saying, they start to look for something that will provide them with a means of escape. The sad part is that instead of rushing out of the room, a simple statement such as, "I'm sorry, I missed that," or, "Could you repeat what you just said, I'm sorry I didn't understand you" is more beneficial. The remarkable thing is that when someone

HELLO, GOD—IT'S ME AGAIN

has the courage to speak out, I don't commit hari-kiri, and the world continues to spin.

The next obvious question is, "How do I communicate with God? Is it like the dramatic Damascus road experience of Saul? Or when Elijah heard God's whisper in the cave where he was hiding from Jezebel and Ahab? Or is it similar to when God opened the mouth of Balaam's donkey to speak?" Along my life's journey, God has led me and spoken to me through gentle nudges. Nudges, because I have gotten so busy that I might forgot to pray, or maybe God wanted me to do something for someone, and I didn't hear.

This presents a big challenge for us. It implies that the grace of God interrupts those times we have not prayed. Maybe we haven't taken the time to listen and see if we have a part in what God is wanting to do. These interruptions are directed at us not to do something alone but rather to what God wants us to do.

Then the questions are: Will we stop? Do we see? Will we join with God in this concept?

The grace of God does not pressure us into service. There is no forcing us. Here is only the nudge, the call, the invitation: God invites us to respond. We are told to serve and to give. We are all called away from our pride and the world's captivity to be willing to serve the needy. Because we can't predict these nudges of God, we must learn to live more openhandedly and prepare for an exciting spiritual journey filled with the gentle nudges. Who knows what we will hear and where the journey will take us?

> **PRAYER:** Our gracious and holy God, help us to pay the attention that is due you such that we don't have to make you repeat yourself. Give us ears to hear. Amen.

Day 20
Confession and Forgiveness

God is faithful and reliable. If we confess our sins, he forgives them and cleanses us from everything we've done wrong (1 John 1:9).

HOW MANY ARGUMENTS, CONFLICTS, AND wars are the result of the arrogance of one not willing to muster up the courage to forgive. I believe that courage is the one element indispensable to forgiveness, for forgiveness hinges on our willingness to confront our demons and admit our failures. Without it, all of our efforts to face the issues of today—such as racial equality, disarmament, and prison reform—although laudable, can breed an insidious form of self-righteousness. It is when we rarely search our own souls to see where our sins collided with others. We don't face that because we lack the moral courage to admit our kinship between us, that though my sins may be of a different nature, they still injure others and myself, as well.

So we have confession and forgiveness, two strands of discreet energy intertwined because each cannot live without the other. The same strength we call on to accept our own falsity is also the source for the wisdom we receive to accept the shortcomings and failures in others.

Our failures and disappointments with others can serve to harden the misunderstandings between us or to clarify what we must do if we are to live together as sisters and brothers. Failures are not without value, not redeemable. Not that we experience them but how we redeem them is the factor that determines if they have somehow served a greater purpose.

How many arguments, conflicts, wars and deaths could have be been prevented? How many innocent lives would be spared if enemies only sat down together and confessed their less than noble inclinations to one another?

Do you think that any of the eighty conflicts being fought today around the world could be resolved by warring sides, admitting that neither one has any moral superiority over the other? And that the more than 700 billion dollars, spent annually on their madness, could better serve the people of the world by helping bring healthcare, food, water, education, and medicines? I wonder if there are any voices that have enough courage, humility rather than arrogance, to resolve the differences between them.

Compassion is rooted in our shared sense of need. Forgiveness is grounded in our shared sense of contrition. In forgiveness we come face to face with our own failures of will. We accept them, confess them, and repent of them. It is only then that we redeem them and are transformed into seeing ourselves in others and extending to them the very understanding we want so much to receive from them. That is the idea is caught up in the words of Peter Ustinov who said once, "Love is an endless act of forgiveness, a tender look that becomes a habit."

> **PRAYER:** God, thank you for your willingness to mediate the trouble in our lives and to make things right. Your Spirit is the comforter. Thank you for your Spirit. Amen.

—◄○►—

Day 21
Don't Forget

I knew that you are a merciful and compassionate God, patient, and always ready to forgive and to reconsider your threats of destruction (Jonah 4:13).

THE TEXT FOR TODAY IS the reason Jonah gave for not obeying God and going straightaway to Nineveh. Rather, he went in the opposite direction but didn't reach his destination because a big fish, which God had prepared, swallowed him. We are "majoring on the minors" when we worry as to what kind of fish it was. One thing I do know is that Jonah's sour attitude gave the fish a terrible tummy ache, causing the fish to vomit Jonah up onto the shore. We really shouldn't worry whether the fish was a whale or even what kind of fish it was.

Jonah said, "I knew that you are a merciful and compassionate God, patient, and always ready to forgive." Isn't it a comfort to know that we don't have to worry about God being vengeful or unforgiving, not holding a grudge, or that

God is unloving. Wow, that's a comfort isn't it, to know that the holy, all powerful God chooses to deal with us through mercy, compassion, and love rather than through vengeance?

It is sad to hear Jonah complaining all through his written record, ignoring his vocation, and being saddened in his heart when the Ninevites repented and were saved from God's wrath and destruction. I know quite a few preachers, myself included, who would have loved to be a part of this occasion and especially hear the response to their efforts. God even provided for Jonah some comfort when he made a plant to grow, covering Jonah from the hot sun as he observed what was happening in Nineveh.

Here we have in Jonah an angry, unhappy, madman who was more upset about his plant dying than he was about the grand miracle that God was preforming when 120,000 people in Nineveh, as well as their animals, were saved from God's judgment, and that God was willing to care for them all. Think of how much God cares for you and me. I don't know what happened to Jonah after the city repented. Did he ever come around to love the people of Nineveh and experience happiness at their response? We don't know what became of Jonah. But the miracle was not with Jonah; it was with the people of Nineveh who repented. We join with them in praising and thanking God for their deliverance. It is an incredible story.

PRAYER: Father, help our spirits not to be hampered by the negativism such as that which possessed Jonah. Help us to increase our sensitivities toward all wayward folk. Amen.

Day 22
Selling Our Courage

Then the Lord spoke his word to Elijah. He asked, "What are you doing here, Elijah" (1 Kings 19:9)?

HAVE YOU EVER BEEN DOWN in the dumps and you read or heard something that caused the windows of your soul to be flung wide so as to witness the glory of God? For that short time, you have the chance to glean from it whatever it is that God wants you to hear, or you can sit nonchalantly and never experience the fullness of it. It might be a reminder that you are not alone. Or maybe you have been agonizing over a decision that needs to be made. And it could be something that is missing in your relationship with God or with another person. Whatever the situation, we know that we have been, figuratively speaking, in the presence of God. That moment becomes a holy moment and will be etched in our hearts forever.

For me, it came about three weeks after being told that I had Parkinson's disease. I came across a statement that was made years ago by Helen Keller, who said, "Above all, we must never, never, never feel sorry for ourselves." The statement gave me pause, and I wondered why was she so certain, so adamant? Then came the answer to my own question. It was because she knew what we all have discovered: that feeling sorry for ourselves does not make our troubles go away but steals the one essential quality we need to deal with them. It robs us of our courage. We must never feel sorry for ourselves because self-pity costs too much. We must pay for it with our fortitude. And that is a price none of us can afford.

O friend, never strike sail to a fear! Come into port greatly, or sail with God the seas.

— Ralph Waldo Emerson, *"Heroism"*

PRAYER: God, thank you for your love and the extra courage you give to us that keeps us from feeling sorry for ourselves. When we do get down at times remind us to put our habituation in contrast with Jesus on the cross. That will change our perspective. Amen.

Day 23
Are You Satisfied?

I'm not saying this because I'm in need. I've learned to be content in what-ever situation I'm in (Philippians 4:10).

A FRIEND OF MINE WAS BEING interviewed for the position of pastor in a mountain church in North Carolina. He had just received a description for the vacant position. It was amusing to see where the governing board's interests were settled, what they thought were important areas of ministry. What it boiled down to was that he was expected to be an expert in all kinds of things, from being a good preacher and able pastor to knowing something about music, as well as an ability to relate well with young people, etc. Thinking about what was expected of ministers of God by their congregants, it became increasingly clear that the deepest desires were for the minister to be an all-encompassing expert in all kinds of things!

We then wrote our own list. Instead of calling it a job description, we called it a "covenant" between the pastor and the church. In it, the church made vows to the pastor, who in turn would make vows to the congregation. It was well done and has been used as a model for other churches since we first wrote it. We added a few items of our own, such as the pastor must be able to meet sorrow without despair, difficulty without defeat, success without pride, etc. In other words, he or she is one who can cope with the list's items, but does not have to do it alone. If she or he attempted to carry out these vows alone, that person would come up short. We all need help each and every day.

Paul clams this very thing, as today's text attests: "I've learned to be content. . . . I can do all things." He had found the secret of becoming an expert: Jesus. Jesus can make a woman or a man an expert and a specialist in every circumstance of life because he fills each circumstance with his presence.

I wonder what God's list would look like, especially when compared to ours.

PRAYER: Father, you continually raise up your faithful to the glory of holiness. In you, love kindles in us the fire of the Holy Spirit. Amen.

Day 24
Rubbing Elbows with God

He is the one who fills your life with blessings so that you become young again like an eagle (Psalm 103:3).

I HAVE HAD THE JOY OF taking hot-air balloon rides (my sister and her husband own a couple). Also, I have been allowed to fly a glider. In both cases, they are non-motorized flying machines that have no means of powering themselves. With a balloon, you unpack it, pulling it the length from basket to top of the balloon. There are a couple of people holding onto the rope to keep it from rolling over and used when the balloon begins its descent.

After connecting the correct ropes to the basket, a burner is hooked onto its resting harness. The balloon is inflated using a large fan, until there is enough air to start heating in the balloon by giving the burner a couple of blasts. Once the air inside the balloon is heated, it begins to rise. Once the balloon is in its upward position, another blast from the burner causes the balloon to rise. You cast off; and up, up, up you go. Now, the landings can be a little bit tricky at times, but they can also be a lot of fun.

There is a difference with the glider. You simply hook the glider to a motorized tow. Once the plane climbs to around 4,000 feet, you are cut loose, and you take advantage of thermals. If you hit a cool thermal you will start your descent; if you hit a heated thermal, however, you can glide higher and farther. So you play the currents up and down to achieve your destination. The landings are usually very smooth. On my flight, I reached over 6,000 feet and was aloft for about forty-five minutes. Would I do it again? Yes, every chance I could. Some say that those two flying machines, especially gliders, are the closest you can get to actually flying like a bird. I hear you skeptics, giving us a rerun of that old adage, "If God had meant for man to fly, he would have given him wings"—my dad would be the first one to say it.

But I tell you, I have never in my life ever experienced such peace, calm, tranquility, such silence, and quietness that it almost hurts. The calmness that flooded my spirit is beyond words. There was no doubt that God was there. I don't think it's too big a step to go as far as to say it was redemptive. Looking at scripture, I saw that each time birds are mentioned, the Bible talks about their wings being a shelter that protects, renews, and at times they give their own in order that we might have it. I couldn't see God, but I felt God. It really was like rubbing elbows with God.

> **PRAYER:** Father, we want to soar; we want to be healed of our hurts and pain. Use us as you will to get the word out to believers and unbelievers alike. Amen.

⋯⋯⋯◁◯▷⋯⋯⋯

Day 25
Peace, Peace, God's Peace

I will offer you peace like a river (Isaiah 66:12).

WE HEAR PEOPLE SAY HOW much they long for peace of mind in their lives. They look at their lives, and all they see is chaos and turmoil. What they are actually saying when talking about peace is that they want or need a break from the hustle and bustle of day-to-day living.

Those who long for peace of mind should know what they mean by it, because there is more than one kind. A group that had a felt need to accomplish this were the Stoics. Zeno founded the Stoics around 300 BC. They attempted to have peace of mind by making themselves invulnerable—untouchable—to either joy or pain, denying themselves both agony and ecstasy. Someone once said of the Stoics that they made life a desert and called it peace.

The prophet Isaiah, on the other hand, speaks of the peace of the river, which is often tortured and turbulent as it seeks to make the wilderness glad and the desert rejoice and the rose to blossom. This peace of Isaiah is one of being comforted by God, who also will come with fire to judge. We are reminded of the still waters to which he promises to lead us. When you are at peace, are you thinking of the desert or the river? Are you asking for death?

Or are you asking for life?

PRAYER: Father, give us clarity of mind and vision so we might sing in one voice: "I've got peace like a river in-a my soul." Amen.

◄○►

Day 26
Loving God as Well

For I am about to create a new heaven and a new earth, the former things shall not be remembered or come to mind (Isaiah 65:17).

GOD WANTS US TO LOVE God. That's the vulnerability of God. Dietrich Bonhoeffer, that great German theologian/preacher who was hanged during World-War II for his part in a plot to assassinate Hitler, wrote while in prison, "Guilt is the idol hardest to break down." To be honest, I had never thought of it that way. It opened a totally new way at looking at guilt. I know people who are overwhelmed with grief. They want and need to rid themselves of their guilt for their spiritual and physical well-being.

And yes, we can make an idol out of guilt. Guilt can be an idol, and we may find ourselves holding onto it and even clinging to it. You go over past events, somehow hoping that by rethinking them they might become good events, but you already know that that doesn't work. Trying to rethink our past into a good past not only doesn't work, but it also makes the guilt greater. It is a very difficult challenge to let go of all this, because our particular past is ours and is true for us. It is our unique history. Even though you sometimes don't like it, you cannot change it. Thus, it becomes like an idol that you must carry with you at all times. But the guilt must go; otherwise, you are indirectly competing with God. God says, "I have always loved you, and I love you now. I want to give you my love." And we respond by saying, "You can't love me, God, because I'm so bad. By thinking about my past I will prove to you that I am beyond forgiveness." God then shows us Jesus on the cross, and we begin to understand the depth of God's love.

PRAYER: Thank you, dear God, for making all things new, for making us new. Once we have been made new, you can better use us for your kingdom's sake. Amen.

────◆◇▶────

Day 27
How Can We Be Afraid?

Be strong and courageous! Don't tremble or be terrified, because the Lord your God is with you wherever you go (Joshua 1:9).

I ASKED MY OLDER BROTHER TO take me to the movie, to which he promptly said, "No!" That is, until I reminded him that I knew he went someplace Mom and Dad would not have approved. Needless to say, I was able to meet some of my friends at the movie. After sitting through the double feature horror movies, we waited outside for our rides. We discussed the movies, and, although no one would admit it, they frightened us. Then I noticed, we brave souls were all closely huddled under the streetlights. No one would admit to being scared, even the two that ran to their rides. All I know was that I saw the horror characters wherever I looked. One jumped behind the ticket booth and another behind the popcorn maker. Everywhere I looked, I thought I saw them. I was quite scared. I remember how terrified I was when they turned off the lights, except for the one that separated me from the four streetlights between me and our car, which was from the upcoming attractions marquee. Beyond that, it was pitch dark. I looked around for my brother and recognized his silhouette as he leaned against a light pole talking with a girl from school. He motioned to me to go to our car. Was he crazy? My heart started pounding faster, my palms became soaked, and my mouth was drier than a desert wind.

I assessed my surroundings and broke into a run toward the first street light. I made it alive and out of breath, but assured that the demons of the darkness would not bother me as long as I was in the light. So I was slow getting to the edge of the darkness where it seemed to have beaten the light back. Then I heard footsteps getting faster and faster. I knew what was about to happen. I had just watched it happen on the big screen: I was going to get caught and be killed. My mind was not giving me any help. It was at that moment that I made a decision about the familiar psychological example we humans have as an option we'll have to make in any given situation: "fight or flight." As the sounds got closer to me, I chose flight and broke into a run toward the car, when I heard a deep growl. Then I felt something grabbing at my arm. Shaking free of its grasp, I fell to the ground. I was scared so badly that I couldn't speak or make any sound for help or mercy. I looked up and saw Lucifer himself! My brother bent double laughing. We immediately engaged in a little tussling before getting in the car and going home. Occasionally, on the ride home he would break the silence with a little chuckle and, "You should have seen your face," or, "I have never seen you run that fast."

Here we have a plea not only for mercy but a word of encouragement for the children of Israel to obey the words Moses and Joshua were giving them. If only I had known then what I know now, I might still have been a little scared, but I could have been strong, courageous, not trembling or terrified because the Lord God is my constant companion.

PRAYER: Thank you, dear God, for making all things new, for making us new. Once we have been made new, you can better use us for your kingdom's sake. God, we need your help in the midst of our lives, of our being your followers because of all the evil that surrounds us that is both real and imagined. With you we can do anything because you are our creator God who loves us and protects us. Knowing that, O God, help us not to be afraid. Amen.

Day 28
Yes, You Can

There is something being done on earth that is pointless. Righteous people suffer for what the wicked do, and wicked people get what the righteous deserve (Ecclesiastes 8:14).

OW MANY TIMES HAVE YOU failed to attempt something because you already had it in your mind that it was impossible, and you have not even tried the first time? Yet, one cannot go through life and never face this dilemma, especially hoping for perfection. Would not a more preferred way to approach this be not to think about possibility or impossibility? We must face it, this being perfect; there is no getting around it. We must face it and do the very best that we can. This applies to all that we encounter; in-line skating, scuba diving, trekking though the mountains, hang-gliding, or attempting to button your shirt or blouse when your fingers and hands are refusing to co-operate due to arthritis or Parkinson's disease. The attempt needs—no must—be taken. We are caught up in how amazingly wonderful what we can do when we have to is.

Having experienced something in which the outcome was not quite as positive as you hoped, the next words out of your mouth should not be, "That's not fair." But sometimes we find out our waning energies are due to something else other than our dilemma: Energy wanes as the day progresses. At the end of the day, I am exhausted. My energy has abandoned me and I sit there wondering if I helped or complicated the problem. All I know is that I feel like I've been ridden hard. Mentally and emotionally I have been drained dry. Yes, it is true that Parkinson's could be blamed for this depletion of energy. When that happens it is called being "off-time," meaning that my meds are no longer effective in helping me until I build up the meds in my system. My feeling this way is due in part to the fault of Parkinson's, but the rest could be blamed on a very intense and draining counseling session I had with a member of my congregation. He was beside himself as to what to do. He was "not sure that they were going to make it."

Our discussion covered several problems he was experiencing. First, there was a forced transfer in his work (he would either accept the transfer or take an unemployment check); then, his weight and diabetes were out of control. He and his wife were in financial difficulty—his wife was content working at a blue-collar job barely making minimum wage, even though she had a masters degree in her field of study.

He was so negative about everything. Convinced that God had forgotten him in his situation, he proceeded to tell me how he believed that the writer of the book of Ecclesiastes was right when he said, "Vanity, vanity, all is vanity," and that all he should do is to sit back and simply respond as life passed him by.

I shared with him my belief that if you go into a situation thinking how bad, empty, and dry it's going to be, it probably will be that way. If, however, you believe and trust that God's presence can transform a bad situation into a blessing, God's resourcefulness, creativity, and ability to turn a tragedy into a triumph might surprise you. Knock the "t" off "can't" and what do you have? You see, the choice is God's and yours. What will it be?

> **PRAYER**: Father of the positive, we come to you with all of our negativity to be transformed into your likeness through the death and resurrection of our Lord Jesus Christ. Thank you for providing this. Amen.

⸻◁○▷⸻

Day 29
Pardoning

As far as the East is from the West, so far has he put our transgression from us (Psalm 130:12).

ARE YOU MOVED, AS I AM, as to how many times God forgives us over, and over, and over again? If we return to God with repentant hearts after we have sinned, God is always there to embrace us and let us start afresh. "Merciful and gracious is the Lord, slow to anger and abounding in kindness" (Psalm 103:8).

That's a comfort to know, but what about repeat offenders who are deliberate in the committing of their offenses. It certainly doesn't do much for building the trust factor between two people. In fact, I now recognize my reluctance to forgive someone who has really offended me, especially when it happens more than once. When an offence is repeated, I begin to doubt the sincerity of the one who asks forgiveness. Then when it happens again for a second, third, or fourth time, my reluctance turns to skepticism and disbelief. But we need to have no fear that God is that way at all. There is no evidence in the scriptures that can lead one to believe that God keeps score. God does not count. God just waits for us to come to *ourselves* and return home. God waits for our return, without resentment or desire for revenge. God wants us back home.

We must believe that God forgives the evilest of evil. If God can and will forgive those more vile than we, God can and will forgive us. Maybe that's the bottom line. It seems hard for us to forgive others, because we do not fully believe that we are forgiven. If we could fully accept the truth that we are forgiven and do not have to live in guilt or shame, we would be free. Our freedom would help us to forgive others seventy times seven. By our not forgiving, we are bound to a desire to get even, and that leads to losing our freedom.

A forgiven person forgives.

> **PRAYER:** Our heavenly Father, our hearts are overwhelmed when comparing your love and forgiveness to our love and forgiveness. Yours is so unconditional with no hidden agenda. Usually, ours come with a multitude of conditions and many hidden agendas. Help us to be more like Jesus, in whose name we pray. Amen.

Day 30
The Power of His Touch

*Jesus reached out, touched him, and said, "I'm willing. So be clean!" Imme-
diately, his skin disease went away, and he was clean* (Matthew 8:3).

HAVE YOU EVER THOUGHT MUCH about your hand and what it can
do? It is a powerful instrument, and that power can be used in two
ways. There is the touch that is therapeutic: wiping away tears or
holding one that is hurt or dying, for instance. Not only can such touch heal,
but it also brings love and value to a person. There is also the touch that brings
lust or violence. Its purpose is to hurt and destroy. The same hand does both.
What makes the difference is what is in the heart. It is the heart that determines which one of the hands it will be. The touch is a definite extension of
the heart and brain of a person. The tenderest sensory nerves of a human being
are in the hand and go directly to the brain.

We need not look very far to see the importance of touch in our culture
and lives. If it is lacking in our lives, we first need the Christ's touch that re-
stores the powerful force we call "love." We need to allow Jesus to touch us
with his own transforming, strengthening hand, allowing him the opportunity
to work through us and then to use our touch of therapeutic love to help others to have more of that love.

The Bible has several stories of the power of touch. One story has a man
asking Jesus to heal him, who could have dispensed with a quick, "Now be
thou clean," without breaking his stride. Instead of recoiling, the Savior took
a step forward, and the Greek says that he did not just touch him—he clasped
him. What makes his even more than powerful still is the man was a leper.

Jesus touched the blind, the sick, the prostitutes, the outcasts, and healed
their infirmities, physically as well as emotionally. Don't forget the time when
Jesus touched the man a second time for him to have his sight restored. I like
this story because we all need in our lives a second touch of Jesus. The Bible
tells us that Jesus came into people's lives again and again and touched them,
helping them to positively live their lives with a loving and healing touch.

Then there is the story of Mary in the garden on that first Easter morning,
when Jesus tells her not to touch him. "Mary there is more to come, much

more: more love, more awe, more mystery, more wonder, more of life, more to come. Don't clinch it now; I haven't seen the Father yet."

We can give a second touch of encouragement to people in our workplace and those we meet each day who are struggling and fearful. By our hand, we can give love to Jesus by giving it to the least of these and know that he will accept our love.

PRAYER: Thank you, O Father, for the touch of your hand on us. May we follow your example and use the power of our touch to show people the way to you. In Jesus' name, we pray. Amen.

⟨○⟩

Day 31
The Virtue of a Vow

I will keep my vows to the Lord in the presence of all his people (Psalm 116:14).

THERE ARE SEVERAL THINGS ONE can do on a rainy, messy day: curl up and read a good book, write some letters, make phone calls, send out emails, or clean out that closet you've been putting off doing since the turn of the century. One thing I enjoy on such a day is to get in front of the TV with a bowl of popcorn and a Pepsi and watch a good classic western like *Shane*, Gary Cooper in *High Noon*, or Kirk Douglas and Burt Lancaster in *Gunfight at the O.K. Corral*. And is there anyone better to call on to bring justice to the Wild West and to right the right the wrongs of the west than John Wayne or Clint Eastwood? In a lot of these movies, contracts, promises, pledges, and vows are made with the shake of a hand, which is as good a seal as any.

Have you ever made a vow? Vows are common in the Bible. In the beginning, the word meant an oath paid to the emperor and to the country on the part of a citizen. In our coming together to worship we pledge our loyalty and fidelity to Christ as the source and norm of our Christian life. Then we give meaning to the phrase of Paul to "put on" Christ: to take on the character of the person with whom we are identified. We are called, therefore to put on the character of Christ, to take the whole pattern of his life and spirit for our own. Someone once put it this way:

> A Christian is ordinarily defined as 'one who believes in Jesus Christ' or as 'a follower of Jesus Christ.' Such a person might more adequately be described as one who counts oneself as belonging to that community of people for whom Jesus Christ—his life, words, deeds, and destiny—is of supreme importance as the key to understanding of themselves and their world. He is the main source of the knowledge of God and humanity, good and evil, the constant companion of the conscience, and the expected deliverer from evil.

When we observe communion and baptism we are vowing something to God.

Many people pass through life without ever making a serious vow at all. There is no calling of the mind to halt and no dedication of the spirit to bigger things, never a pledge or promise or commitment made to God committing oneself to an act of service.

What is a vow? A vow is an attempt to capture the high serious moments—to make it one of the things that are permanency of the soul's life. When there comes an unusual moment of higher vision and desire when something in our inner lives stirs and lifts us above the routine, above the trivialities and superficiality of things, we become aware of the greatness of life and the dignity of our personal being.

I believe it was in John Bunyan's *Pilgrim's Progress* that Pilgrim cries out to those whose faith had faded and who doubted whether there was a celestial city: "Did we not see it from the top of Mount Clear?" What would we do in life without those moments and places of clarity and vision?

> **PRAYER:** Father, we know in our heart of hearts that you are here with us even when the darkness tries to overwhelm us. Remind us of the vows we made when we walked through the light so we will be able to continue our journey when in the darkness. Amen.

Day 32
Having Parkinson's Disease

Awake and strengthen what remains and is on the point of earth (Revelation 3:2).

SEVERAL YEARS AGO, I LISTENED AS A preacher friend of mine said that God was to be found in the dreaded diseases as much as in the sunset. I believed that, but it was an intellectual statement. Now I have had to ask if I can say that of myself, which is a much greater test.

How does one prepare to become an invalid and to die, whether we're talking of other people or oneself? It is something that we rarely talk about. There is the elementary duty of making one's will, which is no more a morbid occupation than taking out life insurance.

There is an even deeper level of seeking to round off one's account, of ordering one's priorities and what one wants to do in the time available—a bucket list, if you will. That list would contain those things that you want to see or accomplish before you die. It is times like these that we can clearly see how much time we waste or have wasted. It is a time we are faced with, whether we have reduced what has been entrusted to us as trivial or as life shaping. When I was told that I had Parkinson's disease, my first reaction was, of course, shock. The next one was, I need to get ready.

In fact, preparing to becoming an invalid and even for death is not the otherworldly exercise stamped upon our minds. Rather, for the Christian it is preparing for "eternal life," which means really living a more abundant life. That life is begun, continued—though not ended—now. This also points to the fact that this is a question of quality, not quantity. How long we have here and in what condition we find ourselves is purely secondary. You see, preparing for quality of life and dying with dignity means learning really to live, not just concentrating on keeping oneself alive. It means living it up, becoming more concerned with contributing to and enjoying what matters most: giving the most to life and getting the most from it, while it is being offered.

PRAYER: Heavenly Father, grant us the courage and stamina to strengthen what we have left, so as to be able to continue living the abundant life that you provide for us. Help us to live boldly. In the name of Jesus, we pray. Amen.

⟨○⟩

Day 33
A Poor Sort of Memory

As long as I'm still alive I think it's right to refresh your memory . . . so I will make every effort to see that you remember these things (2 Peter 1:13).

IT'S A POOR SORT OF memory that only works backwards." The White Queen in *Alice in Wonderland* spoke these words. She explains how sometimes she lives backward and so remembers forward. For example, her finger bleeds before a thorn pricks it. This way of thinking certainly gets complicated. I passed a street person in New York City wearing a cardboard piece that read, "Can anyone tell me who I am?" Having lost his memory, he had no identity. He had no name, no past, no history, and little sense of self. If he found a memory he would have recovered a person—not only a past, but a present as well.

Memories allow us to work forward and backward in shaping the nature of our faith. For example, how would we know we were lost without an Eden to remember a paradise regained. Without this sort of history, there is no faith, for these words form the story of faith; and there is no hope, for hope is rooted in memory, remembering that we had our being in the eternal heart that was to love us into life. This sense of belonging to God is something we bring with us.

We are strangers and pilgrims on the earth, and here we have no continuing city. Many writers attempt to interpret what one already knows and had already experienced. They speak of the music with which people are born, remembering the eternal voices that call from far away the reality of our lives.

There is an old story in which fallen Lucifer is asked what he missed most

44

of the life he knew when he was in heaven. Lucifer replies, "The sound of trumpets in the morning." Whether what we miss is the sound of trumpets or not, we all miss something, for the Father has made us so that our hearts are restless until they rest in him.

The divine nostalgia is the best sort of memory. It is not the poor sort that only works the more backward we go.

It is a poor sort of memory to work forward; it brings us to heaven by reminding us of home. In the end there is only one sickness. It is homesickness.

PRAYER: God of all life, cause us to have memory that is ever trained on you, a memory that moves in all directions, not just backward. One that remembers how we are held by the greatest love the world has ever known. Equipped with that good sort of memory, let us live life positively, moving forward in the advancement of our Christian lives and of your kingdom. In your holy Son's name, we pray. Amen.

Day 34
What the World Needs . . .

He told the innkeeper, "Take care of him. If you spend more than that I'll pay you on my return trip" (Luke 10:35).

I REMEMBER FROM MY HIGH school days a popular song that carried a powerful message in its words, "What the world needs now is love, sweet love." It is a message that if we had the courage and unselfish nature to comply with it, this world would be a better place. We get a glimpse of God's kingdom being a restive place with common people armed with God's blessing doing their best to redeem an imperfect world. It is not something we sit back and wait for, but something we get into to and create.

We can see that faith compels action that in turn deepens faith. When we combine attitude and action, faith and works, we—according to Harry Emerson Fosdick—let our conscience get the better of our desires. This is realized each time we let these acts glimmer in our lives. Our acts of mercy, kindness, sacrifice, or conscience to others along with compassion, override those negative items that try to put us under lock and key. In short we can experience the blessed life as we turn the world upside down.

Sadly, we have evidence all around us that show these wonderful words are not heeded. We believe that there are alternative plans. Oh we're good people not bad people going through our rituals. But remember the words of Zechariah when asked by the Hebrew people if they should thank God for the restoration of the Temple. He said to them, never mind your rituals; if you truly want to be closer to God, try "showing kindness and mercy to one another" (Zech 7:9). Advice is not loved, but this lasting piece of advice stands on its own feet. It reminds us of those unsung heroes among us who show their thanks to God in the quality and conscience of the work that they do. They are those who throw themselves into the task of restoring dignity, decency, and hope to our inner cities. They are the police and firefighters who risk life and limb rushing into collapsing buildings to try and save a life. And then there are those burrs under our saddles, whose concern is human justice and who accept the responsibility of resisting ill-conceived policies, immoral laws, and encourage us to do the same.

Wherever we refuse to remain silent in the face of the pain of another human being, wherever angels make possible what devils make necessary, where soft we blow upon the embers of compassion to warm a steely cold and troubled world, the blessed life is coaxed into being because it is here that we are truly being agents of God on earth. Søren Kierkegaard, the great theologian/philosopher, wrote that to love another person is to help them love God.

The world does indeed need love, sweet love, but we also need to "try a little kindness" to show the world God. Kindness—love—neighbor—God: a good place to start.

> **PRAYER:** Dear lover of our souls, your love is abundant, unconditional, free, and sufficient for all of us. Thank you. In Jesus' name, we pray. Amen.

Day 35
Giving out of Empty Pockets

As Jesus sat facing the Temple offering box, he watched how much money the people put into it. . . . This widow in her poverty has given everything she had to live on (Mark 12:41–43).

JESUS SPOKE MORE ABOUT MONEY than heaven and hell together and more about it than anything else except the kingdom of God. Out of thirty-nine parables, he spoke on money in one of every seven verses in Luke. I believe we can say with confidence that for Jesus, money is an important part of the life of the believer. Are you surprised? I'm not speaking of the advocates of a prosperity mindset, who say the size and amount of God's blessings depend on the amount of your check.

A minister friend and I were at lunch one day when a member of his church came up to our table and asked, "Preacher, when are we supposed to tithe, before or after taxes?" To which my friend said, "I guess God will take it when and whereever he can get it." There was a strange silence before we exchanged goodbyes and the person left. I pondered this odd luncheon encounter. My mind traveled to Jesus' story of the widow who gave all she had: two mites, or pennies; all she had, she placed in the offering box. We don't know how long Jesus watched, but it must have been a bird's eye view of what the people placed in the offering box. Evidently, there were some heavy hitters that walked by with their offerings. But this widow came by and dropped two coins in the box. Her actions caused Jesus to break the silence with some very strong words. She gave all she had to live on, which was a step of faith. Or did she know something that the people around her didn't? What would cause someone to give up everything he or she had to live on?

Could she know who this carpenter really was? Or, was she just trusting in God and God's love to provide for her. Whatever the case, her actions caused Jesus to say that she had given more than all the others because she given all.

Did she hear what Jesus said? For that matter, who heard what Jesus had to say? I don't know about you, but I have always wanted to add a Hollywood ending to the story. I want Jesus to run after her, give her pennies back to her and say something like, "You have shown the right example and gave all; but you can't afford it, so take it back and here's a little extra." No, Jesus remained still. If we look closely at the scriptures, we see that Jesus never stood in the way of someone and his or her sacrifice. He allows people to give, and he takes it and uses it for the kingdom. We don't know what he did after he and his disciples left the Temple. If he did anything, he might have taken her food or helped her some other way. One thing is clear: don't expect Jesus to get in the way of you and your sacrifice.

What have you given lately?

> PRAYER: Father, you are quite clear on what we are to give. The thing you want most of all is our love and commitment to you and our brothers and sisters. Grant us the courage to move forward and give of our finances as well. Amen.

Day 36
Hear the Quietness?

One handful of peace and quiet is better than two handfuls of hard work and of trying to catch the wind (Ecclesiastes 4:6).

PEACE AND QUIET. AT TIMES, we set ourselves up for all the noise. While we were in the hospital having our second child, my oldest son, Thomas, was staying in the home of some friends from our church who already had five children of their own. When the two older boys were together, they were quite loud and active. They played, and they played hard and rough, willing to explore anything. Things would settle down, and one of them would do something to pick at the other, and they would be at it again. They were just being boys. All they really needed was an IV drip of Ritalin to soothe the moment. It would help them not to be so excitable. After several hours of non-stop action, Thomas approached the mother and said, "Miss Betty, sometimes my mama and papa let me play by myself." He had had enough action for one day.

Can you see that in your life as well? We become so busy taking care of a family member with Parkinson's or other illness, or doing church work, that we become exhausted from all the time we are working and trying to gain God's acceptance and love. We can get so exhausted at this task. Sometimes, we get to the point that we have had all the action and activity we can stand and we need a space in which to be quiet. Maybe it's a closet or a prayer room or chapel. Like Thomas, we all need that time alone so we can center and settle down, a place where we can be play or be quiet, kneel and be alone with God. Be careful, for a beautiful and delicate moment can happen—a moment of grace—when we realize that there is nothing we can do to earn God's love.

Take time, and you might be surprised to learn that God loves you for who you are, not for what you are doing. Works are not part of the equation. God accepts us without our first being made right with him. Let me be among the first to remind you that you *cannot* catch the wind.

> PRAYER: Father God, you tell us to be quiet, to be still and know that you are God. Please help keep all the distractions that prevent this from happening away from us so we can glory in your presence. Amen.

◄◇►

Day 37
What Is Life?

Remember, my life is only a breath (of wind); and never again will my eyes see anything good (Job 7:7).

THE AUTHOR OF ECCLESIASTES ASKS IN gloomy dejection, "What is life?" As we sometimes do, he found life bitter and futile. He believed that he had tasted everything, yet concluded, "All is vanity and a striving after wind" (Eccl 2:17). He voiced very much the same question that Job did, "Why is . . . life [given] to the bitter in soul" (Job 3:20)?

When you are told that you have Parkinson's, after getting over the shock of having this thief to deal with, you probably have the same question that those ancient writers had. I know I did and still do at times. Life has given us a bitter style of existence for the rest of our lives. Will God be there to see us through? Will we feel and know God's presence? Will God be instrumental in helping to find ways to better handle PD? What about new medications that allow for more normalcy to be experienced, possibly even a cure? All we know is that all the dreams and plans we had are now stalled and in need of revamping. But not before issuing question after question seeking some kind of answer as to why this drastic change is hitting us right between the eyes.

Life is a gift we sometimes appreciate as little as the proverbial Christmas tie! Endless rounds of feverish priorities can make our lives stark and meaningless rather than glorious and full. We want to scream or groan, "O God, all I'm doing is 'trying to catch the wind.' Forgive me. Help me!"

C. S. Lewis has said that in Ecclesiastes we get a clear picture of human life without God. It might drive us at last to discover the truth: the need for God's presence in our lives. This is a vital part of what we celebrate on Pentecost: the wind or the breath of God, which is the presence of God the Holy Spirit, offers meaning and purpose, joy and power to our new life.

> **PRAYER:** Wind of God, you have taught us to lead new lives in Christ! You have filled our existence with meaning. You have come into our jungle of despair and laid out a path of joy. You are our light and our salvation. Amen.

Day 38
Why Give?

They gave from their surplus wealth, but she gave from her want (Mark 12:44).

GIVING FROM YOUR WANT, RATHER than from your wealth, is the great challenge of the gospel. It is a challenge at this point for it to happen. You have to take a risk and become vulnerable, which means having to trust someone else. Trust is something we don't walk around town giving to everyone we meet. Trust comes more easily if there has been no betrayal or hurt, but there are very few that have not felt the sting of mistrust and betrayal.

Not so with the one I would suggest, and that is God Almighty. If we would take the time to critically examine our lives we would probably find that we were most generous during periods of wealth. We give some money, some of our time, and some of our thoughts to God and to others, but we make sure that enough money, time, and thought remain to maintain our own security. Have we really trusted God? Have we given God a chance to show us boundless love and that God can be trusted?

Many of the desert fathers and early church leaders took vows of poverty. When Ignatius of Loyola was converted to Christianity, he left on a pilgrimage to the Holy Land. He also went in total poverty, begging for food and shelter along the way, never keeping anything for himself. Ignatius believed he would be better off and would be able to experience his total dependence on God. He wanted to live what he had come to know in prayer, that God showers us with greater love than a mother for her child.

Giving up my last thought is as important as giving up the last coin. The fact that we are so full of ideas, plans, worries, and fears shows that we are still trying to secure our own future and do not fully trust God. When God becomes our only concern, then we are truly poor, can listen, and can be guided to wherever we are called. God sees high potential and usability in the poor, because they are free to listen and follow.

PRAYER: Our gracious Father, help us not to be bound by the trappings of the world. Instead, help us become more dependent on you because you have never hurt us or betrayed us. Rather you chose to give up heaven and come to earth and live so that we could have not only an example to follow, but also the power of your Spirit to help us to no longer try it on our own. In the name of Jesus, we pray. Amen.

⊸◇⊷

Day 39
I Don't Deserve It

But the householder replied to one of them, "Friend . . . am I not allowed to do what I choose with what belongs to me? Or do you begrudge my generosity?" So the last will be first, and the first, last (Matthew 10:13–16).

A WOMAN ONCE REMARKED TO A famous novelist, "God has no reason to forgive me." She was right; except that God loved her, and love is the reason beyond reason, the immorality of grace, which is the highest form of morality. And scripture carries on every page this sweet unreasonableness. Says the returning prodigal, "I am no more worthy to be called your son." Of course! Yet the father calls for the best robe, shoes, and the ring of sonship. One disciple complained to our Lord of the extravagance of a woman who anointed his feet with perfume. The action was wasteful. The perfume could have been sold and the money given to the poor. No doubt! Except that in the economy of heaven, extravagance is a necessity and reason is sometimes a barrier to grace. The "nicely calculated less or more" reveals a mercenary spirit that does not understand Christ.

And that's the gospel: Equal pay for unequal work. What trade union could endure it? Negotiate, not from strength, but from weakness. Strike a hard bargain and end up with only what you bargained for, when what God wanted to give you was "good measure, pressed down, shaken together, and flowing over." Demand what you deserve, and you may never discover how much you missed. Claim your rights, and you may never learn how wrong you were. Insist on justice, and you will never know the mercy that was offered you. Win at all costs, and you may never understand that the loser takes all. Seize what is yours, and you will never possess what is God's. For God's only reason for loving us is that God loves us. And what a divine reason that is!

PRAYER: Heavenly Father, we give you thanks for the love you choose to freely give to us. Whether we are the last or the first, whether unworthy or unreasonable, we are truly grateful for all you have done and continue to do in and for our lives through Jesus Christ, in whose name we pray. Amen.

———◦———

Day 40
The Strength of a Child

Beloved, let us love one another, for love is of God; and he who loves is born of God and knows God (1 John 4:7).

BEFORE MUHAMMAD ALI WAS DIAGNOSED with Parkinson's, he would increase the hype of the heavyweight championship boxing match, trying to intimidate his opponent by chanting, "I am the greatest." Without getting into a debate as to the validity of his statement, I would like to offer some others who could vie for the title "The Greatest" without ever landing the first punch.

What made people like Mother Teresa, Albert Schweitzer, Gandhi, and Martin Luther King Jr. a cut above the societies in which they lived was the fact that they gave us the greatest gift any one of us could give: themselves.

They lived on the edge and gave from their little to make a lot.

When someone is diagnosed with Parkinson's, that person immediately thinks that because of his or her condition there is nothing to contribute to the world in which that person lives; that the liabilities beginning in life will far outweigh the positive. So why even make an effort? Not so. The fact of the matter is that through the different dynamics of how we live with our disease, we can very easily be the greatest gift we have to give. The fact that we are as much as what we do serves to liberate us to do more and give our world the greatest gift we have: ourselves, as limited as that might be.

God is love, and the greatest gift God can give us is that love. And our response to this gift of love is to give the greatest gift we can: give to God our love. It has been called the bond of perfection; it is old and it is new. It is the greatest commandment, and it is all the commandments because it fulfills all law. It enables one to become holy without any exterior disciplines, any laborious arts of fasting, small reaches for glory through grace's heart, without any other arms save that of love. It is that grace that encourages us to love God for himself and our neighbors for God. At first we may take into consideration God's acts; but once we have tasted the goodness of God, we love the spring offered for its own excellence. This movement begins with passion from passion. The next step would be to reason, from thanking to adoring, from sense to spirit, from consideration of ourselves to a union with God, and God's is the image and little representation of heaven: it is beatitude in picture or, rather, the infancy and beginning of glory.

> **PRAYER:** Dear God, instill in us the desire to be the greatest in your kingdom. We know that in order for that to take place we have to become a servant willing to serve even those who are low in life. Help those of us who have that desire to grow in number so that what is in heaven is also on earth. Amen.

Day 41
Where to Find God's Hope

Then you will have deeper insight. You will know the confidence that he calls you to have and the glorious wealth that God's people will inherit (Ephesians 1:18).

HOPE. SOUNDS GREAT, DOESN'T IT? But where can we find reason for hope today? Countries that once were friendly to America are friendly no longer, and what makes this a threatening problem is that these are folk are reactionary zealots and are willing to die; after all, the sacrifice of himself would send him right next to Allah. He thinks nothing of walking or driving into a crowded market with a bomb strapped to himself or to the vehicle and then to detonate it, killing many innocent people. It doesn't matter the number of women and children that it will impact or the number of those who will die. He had to do this to "help Allah in purging the land of the infidels."

Some of these so-called friends are also sitting on stockpiles of nuclear weapons or the capability to build them. These radicals hijack planes, and use them as missiles to their targets. They zeroed them in on their targets of both World Trade Center towers, the Pentagon, and yet another that crashed on a hillside in Pennsylvania, their goal being to kill as many non-Muslims (especially if they are American) as they can. So they become bolder and use any crowded market places full of innocent civilians, cars, and police stations as targets by their suicide bombers. People are not only afraid of traveling outside our borders, but also for some that fear has crept into traveling domestically, as well. It shows the evil side of life. Terrorism cheapens life. We can see at any time on any television channel the eyes of those who really know what despair is like. So is this what we are left with—despair, not hope?

If we look back at scripture, some folk come away shocked to learn that not a lot has changed. Soldiers commandeered anyone to carry their packs. Tax collectors charged what they wanted. They only had to be sure that the Romans got their share first. Bandits beat up travelers. Riots flared between rival religions. Innocent victims were crucified on trumped-up charges.

In this setting, Paul writes that God calls us to hope. It isn't that Paul had blinders on with regard to what was going on around him. No, it is that Paul saw something else. Along with the scales falling from his eyes before his conversion, we see that now the eyes of his heart are open, too. He saw God working on a deeper level with great power. What Paul saw with his natural eyes was insignificant. All along, God's children were (and are) receiving an inheritance, and the Holy Spirit was (and is) its guarantee, its down payment. God boldly calls us also to hope. God sent the Son not to take away our suffering but to fill it with his presence and his hope.

PRAYER: Lord, open the eyes of our hearts that we may see you at work in our lives and in our world. Amen.

Day 42
More Like the Father

At once the Spirit brought him into the desert, where he was tempted by Satan for forty days (Mark 1:12–13).

FOLLOWING JESUS' BAPTISM, LUKE WRITES that the Spirit led him into the desert to be tempted by Satan for forty days. Not to make light of all that was going on between Jesus and Satan or to lessen the seriousness of these transactions, this could be seen as a test between immediate and delayed gratification. Let me illustrate. I know two brothers, both of whom like M&Ms candy. One brother eats the entire pack rather quickly, whereas the other brother takes his time eating only two to three M&Ms at a time, taking a week or so to finish the pack. Each time they had a pack, they had a decision to make: immediate or delayed gratification. The three offers that Satan made to Jesus were, in fact, basically a choice between whether Jesus would settle for immediate or delayed gratification.

Do you want catch the people's attention in order to feel their pats on your back? Then turn the stones to bread. But once you stop making the bread, the crowds will leave as quickly as they came. Do you want to be noticed and become famous? Then jump from a tower so that everybody can see you, and you can be on television because you're so influential, so important. Do you want to be able to wield your power? Kneel before me and I will give you supreme authority over everything you see. But Jesus said, "No," because he knew God's way was not just to experience immediate gratification but rather *the* way. God's way is the lifting up of the poor, the humble, the poor of heart, the meek, and peacemakers.

Here we have not only a self-portrait of Jesus but also a reflection that is of the Father because Jesus said, "Who sees me sees the Father." If you read the Beatitudes, you see Jesus' face and through his face you see the love of his Father. Humble. Poor. Meek. Peacemaker. One hungry for justice and peace. It is so important for you see, that Jesus wants you to be more and more like that. That's the reflection of God that appears in flesh among us. That is our way and that's the way to *glory*.

> **PRAYER:** To be more like you and your Son is our plea, O God. We are aware of what that entails but only in part. Give us eyes to see and ears to here so that we can be better able to respond to the call to discipleship. In the name of Jesus, we pray. Amen.

———◇———

Day 43
Remember When. . . ?

I call to remembrance my song in the night: I meditate within my heart; and my spirit makes diligent search (Psalm 77:6).

HOW MANY TIMES HAVE YOU heard someone say about babies or young children, "You had better enjoy them now; they will be up and out of here before you know it." This is one of those bits of wisdom we know, but we don't know. We respond, in our minds, "This will never happen to me. I plan to enjoy every minute with my children." Then *life happens*—work, meetings, doctor's and dentist's appointments, sports, music lessons, maybe school work, whatever—they rob our plans for the time we meant to spend with them.

You know what I'm talking about. One day, it comes crystal clear. You go to bed and awaken to a nest that lies empty. We say, "It seems like only yesterday that we were changing diapers and tucking you in bed after prayers and now. . . ." All of the voices that issued that bit of wisdom come back to haunt us. In shock, I confess, it actually happened to me.

When my boys were little, they would occasionally manage to get their hands on one of my books from my library and proceed to personalize it according to their tastes. Needless to say, when I first found it, I was a bit agitated, and there was always a reckoning. But no amount of fussing or reprimands would undo what had been done. They really didn't understand the gravity of the moment. To them, paper was paper, whether it was a blank sheet in a book or a loose sheet lying on the desk. It was a done deal.

Now when I open the book and find scrawled or half-formed letters announcing, "This is papa's book," I find that there are no feelings of anger or frustration, and I'm not upset at all. Memories of times long gone return, and they fill me with tenderness. They are children for only a short time and we find ourselves, soon enough, wondering where the time went; it was so short. How quickly we lose them! How was I to know that some of the things that upset me would one day become the shining of remembered days?

PRAYER: Dear God, thank you for the memories of the many times you have shone us your love. Forgive us for those times we have impeded your kingdom's work. We ask that you remember something we did to bring a smile to your face as you remember with us. Amen.

Day 44
They Look Just Like Their Parents

Let's make them in our own image (Genesis 1 36).

EOPLE CAN FIND A GREAT deal of amusement if they happen to be visiting with both families of a newborn baby, especially if they begin to compare the different parts of the newborn. "Look, doesn't she have her mother's eyes?" "Just look at those fingers; they're his father's. I will wager you that he is going to play the piano."

The comments will go on and on, even negatively. You may wonder if someone watching this fiasco is tallying up which part belongs to which family. I have been present at some doozies, and some of them were way out in left field, whereas others were right on target. My hillbilly granny would warn us: "You had better be careful so you don't 'mark' that child," or, "You had better be careful or you'll have a child that will be or do the exact same thing you did (or said)." I know when my boys were coming up they reinforced these beliefs. When they were rambunctious and into everything, not doing what they were told, they were their mother's side of the family, little devils for sure. But on the occasions when they were well behaved, using proper manners, acting the way little gentlemen should, they were no doubt from my side of the family.

When I left a thirteen-year pastorate and moved to Dallas, Texas, to start up a new international ministry, it caused my dad to pull me aside and ask, "Tommy what did you do to get God mad enough to send you to Texas?"

I had friends and colleagues who said they thought I was nuts to do this, the major reason being that those people I would be working with were ultra-fundamentalists and my theology was not as extreme as theirs. "How are you going to be able to work with them when we are poles apart?" they asked.

My response was that I would look for the common scarlet thread that we were all created with and begin working from there. That point of commonality was the spark of God that created us: the "image of God." That image levels the playing field on which we practice our Christian faith. I know some folk at both extremes that never reach that cooperative point because of their belief that those who don't agree with their way of believing still smells of fire and brimstone, which means they are not eager to find that commonality running through the pages of scripture and overflowing into our lives. Jesus put it another way by giving us only two commandments to follow. We are to be busy fulfilling them: to love God with our entire being and our neighbor as ourselves. That is the spark. That is what it means to be created in God's image. Who knows? Maybe when we get it right, we might hear someone say, "Look, he has his Father's heart."

> **PRAYER:** Father, we thank you for giving us your Son, Jesus Christ. We thank you that he died on the cross for us and that we can all be united, remembering that there is a spark of God in each of us. Enable us to find that sense of commonality to serve you in spirit and in truth. Amen.

Day 45
There Will Be Consequences

And as for that, in the good soil they are those who, hearing the word, hold it fast in a honest and good heart, and bring forth fruit with patience (Luke 8:15).

*W*E LIVE IN A WORLD that is difficult and stubborn, and our experiences confirm this. In spite of our tedious and careful planning, things do not always work out.

Things do not just happen. In some situations there is order, and those things occur almost automatically. For example, forgiving someone who has wronged and hurt us. When this occurs and we forgive the person who has wronged us, we can rest assured that our hearts will be free of any bitterness. When there is no coercion or guilt in our serving others but rather our service is motivated by love, we ourselves will be blessed. When the driving force for our giving is out of a deep love rather than out of any expectation of receiving anything in return, freely with a generous heart, we will receive it freely. We will grow in spiritual wisdom when we become women and men of prayer. And our lives will be quite fruitful when we live in obedience to God's will.

But we need to be careful that we do not think that things follow only in the spiritual realm. If we take time for solitude and renewal, we will be refreshed. If we care for our souls, our bodies will also be blessed.

If our day is spent in purposefully living, we will also have power over the night and receive a good night's rest as well. Good actions have good consequences. Good seed produces good fruit.

The sad part of this analogy is that we oftentimes focus too much on our results, on the end rather than the journey. We want to harvest the fruit we have neither planted nor cared for. We want to be blessed without walking the road of obedience. We want to experience well-being without caring for our own bodies. We want inner peace without being honest and transparent.

Yet we can have what we want. But this will involve some sowing and watering. It will involve doing what is right ahead of what suits us. It may well involve walking the seemingly long road of faith and obedience rather than taking shortcuts to grasp the promised goal.

PRAYER: Father, instill in us the deep yearning to be your children, readying ourselves for the life you would have us live. Give us the courage and perseverance to live it daily. Amen.

⊷◇⊶

Day 46
What Seems to Be the Problem?

In my distress I cry to the Lord, that he answer me: "Deliver me oh Lord, from, lying lips, from deceitful tongue. Too long have I had my dwelling among those who hate peace. I am for peace: but when I speak, they are for war" (Psalm 12:6–7)!

GOSSIP. IT HURTS WHEN WE hear it and hurts even more when we can't do anything about it. We are enticed to add to the problem by buying it, watching it on television, and reading it. The magazine racks are filled with tabloid gossip from the *National Enquirer* stories to the ones in "Israel Snoops" (my imaginative title), each trying to outdo the other for a larger readership. And it doesn't matter if the stories aren't true; just let them have two lines of truth to three full pages of writing only half or less truths, just enough to keep them out of court. Peace and harmony are all we want.

Now life is made more complicated because we face the fact that we cannot clear everything up. There are people we encounter every day with whom we just are not at peace. And every episode does not end happily ever after. We search for a happy resolution; no matter how hard we try, that peace and harmony for which we yearn might be a while in coming. We have lived as Jesus said: "Love your enemies. Be kind to those who hate you. Bless those that curse you" (Luke 6:27–28). That didn't work. We attempted to "do for other people everything you want them to do for you" (Luke 6:31). Still no go. We have prayed for resolution and peace. We have gone into our closets and admitted our faults and shortcomings before God and sought forgiveness and reconciliation. We have even talked about and confronted the problem, but disharmony, uncertainty, and even distrust live on. The relationship remains difficult, and it seems that the harder we try to make things right, the worse they become.

People often find this to be true, especially in the times when the difficulty lies in not really knowing what the problem actually is. These are symptoms, but the opportunity to be able to discuss them heart-to-heart is not afforded us, leaving us living a life lacking in insight and openness and therefore a lack of resolution.

We see in this just how fragile we are and how broken our world is. When met with this situation, we can only bring and place our difficulties and painful circumstances into the hands of the Master. We wait then for another day when he presents us with new opportunities to make peace, knowing all along that such an opportunity can only be God's precious gift.

PRAYER: All-powerful God, You in your infinite wisdom and power provide for us the tools and the emotions or lack of emotions to live at one with others that we meet. Thank you for loving us enough to help us see the problem and to correct it for your glory. Amen.

Day 47
Not Them, Too!

In this way you show that you are children of your Father in heaven. He makes his sun rise on people whether they are good or evil. He lets the rain fall on them whether they are just or unjust (Matthew 5:45).

JESUS SHOWS US THAT TRUE that love, the love that comes from God, makes no distinction between friends and foes, between people who are for us and people who are against us, people who do us a favor and people who do us ill. God makes no distinction. God loves all human beings, good or bad, with the same unconditional love. This all-embracing love Jesus offers us, and he invites us to make this love visible in our lives.

If our love, like God's love, embraces foe as well as friend, we have become children of God and no longer children of suspicion, jealousy, violence, war, and death. Our love for our enemies shows to whom we really belong. It shows our true home.

There you have it: The love of God is an unconditional love, and only that love can empower us to live together without violence. When we know that

God loves us deeply and will always go on loving us, whoever we are and whatever we do, it becomes possible to expect more of our fellow men and women than they are able to give, to forgive them generously when they have offended us, and always to respond to others' hostility with love. By doing so we make visible a new way of responding to our world problems.

Whenever, contrary to the world's vindictiveness, we love our enemies, we exhibit something of the perfect love of God, whose will is to bring all human beings together as children of one Father. Whenever we forgive instead of letting fly at one another, bless instead of curse one another, tend one another's wounds instead of rubbing salt into them, hearten instead of discourage one another, give hope instead of driving one another to despair, hug instead of harass one another, welcome instead of cold-shoulder one another—in short, whenever we opt for and not against one another, we make God's unconditional love visible, we are diminishing violence and giving birth to a new community.

> PRAYER: Father God, save us from ourselves. We are often to ready to hear the benefits we receive from you and to realize that they are not ours alone, especially your love that is not reserved strictly for us but for all people. Save us, O Lord. In the name of Jesus, we pray. Amen.

———◇———

Day 48
When God Says No

But he told me: "My kindness is all you need" (2 Corinthians 12:9).

WE HEAR THIS STORY. MANY OF us have uttered the same words with the same outcome. It is the story of Paul's "thorn in the flesh" that he asked God on three different occasions to remove.

There is no certainty as to what exactly Paul was talking about, but that has not quieted those who have "the ear of God" and know the answer to every question in scripture. The answers range from being serious to being silly.

Will we ever know what it was this side of Jordan? I am not sure, and I can only speak for myself. What I know for certain is that God has not answered my prayer, which is almost verbatim of Paul's. You can almost see the words of his prayer dripping with disappointment, depression, and even despair. All we have here is Paul going through his daily routine with an ailment of which he could not rid himself that was causing him great distress and making his ministering more difficult.

People with cancer, MS, and Parkinson's know what I am talking about. Our illness makes us weary, and causes us to skirt the edge of despair. We, like Paul, have asked for God to remove this from us, and God has said, "No." Let's say honestly that this not a word that I want to hear. I would prefer, "You're okay. You're well."

Grace has to mean more than God's unmerited favor. It means God's presence, God's gift of God's self. More than anything else it necessitated learning how to go down like a swimmer in the water to discover it.

The saints remind us that we live in a sea of love, God's love, and if we learn how to let ourselves down, we will discover buoyancy that holds us up. Thus the answer to Paul's and our request is, "No I will not remove it"; for God tells Paul, "My power is strongest when you are weak."

To which Paul answers, "I accept weakness, mistreatment, hardship, persecution, and difficulties suffered for Christ. It's clear that when I'm weak, the power of Christ rests upon me."

The next time we are dancing with depression and despair because of our personal "thorns in the flesh," we might hear God's words echoing throughout the chambers of our heart, "My grace is sufficient." God's kindness is all we need.

PRAYER: Father God, only you can take away our "thorn in the flesh." If you choose not to grant us our request, then give us the acceptance of your presence. Amen.

Day 49
The Power of Little Things

Who despised the day when little things began to happen will rejoice
(Zechariah 4:10).

THERE ARE ALL KINDS OF people that have received a message of doom. Their existence will be made up of a short normal life until the illness makes one completely helpless. When we realize that there is no getting better, we must resign ourselves to a life that is cut off much too early. For we know that life demands more from any person than a handful of lyrics and promises left unkempt. This gave me pause, and I took time to look back at my life. Certainly my childhood was rather predictable. I know in my heart of hearts that if I have been privileged to catch a more comprehensive glimpse of life than many other people, it is because I have stood on the shoulders of my parents, who did all they could to help make my life mean something.

Little things can be so powerful. Sometimes they can literally save a person. As I watched and ministered to people who were sick from Parkinson's to cancer of various parts of their bodies, to people with AIDS and Alzheimer's, I ministered to myself—but not to the same degree as to the others—I soon found out something about people. We find in our increasing helplessness that it was inevitable more and more things should and would vanish from our lives. Someone once wrote that so much can wither away from the human spirit, and yet the great gift of the ordinary day remains. The stability of the small things of life, which yet remain in their constancy, are the greatest.

It happens time after time that women and men find salvation in the things of every day. This means that a man's sanity and life, when faced with the problems of feelings of doubt, anxiety, sorrow, and indecision must seek the best remedy. There is nothing which so saves a man's sanity and life as simply going on with the ordinary, routine things of life. To sit down in the midst of regrets and do nothing but worry is fatal. Ordinary duties during these times are what help us to go on. If we are to make life tolerable for ourselves and for others, we must learn something of the virtue of eternity, and our best teacher for that is Jesus himself.

Prayer: Father God, you have made it that we have a choice to follow you or to fight with you. We are a capable people, but we can also be quite foolish. But you are patient with us, and we soon realize our ignorance. Thank you for that patience. Have mercy on us, O God. Amen.

Day 50
Letting God Love You

Look at it this way: At the right time, while we were still helpless, Christ died for ungodly people (Romans 5:8).

A FAMILY IS OUT FOR A drive on a Sunday afternoon. It is a pleasant afternoon and they relax at a leisurely pace down the highway. Suddenly the two children begin to beat their father on the back: "Daddy, Daddy, stop the car! There's a kitten back there on the side of the road!"

The father says, "So there's a kitten on the side of road. We're having a drive."

"But Daddy, you must stop and pick it up."

"I don't have to stop and pick it up."

"But, Daddy, if you don't, it will die."

"Well, then it will have to die. We don't have room for another animal. We have a zoo already a the house. *No more animals.*"

"But Daddy, are you going to just let it die?"

"Be quiet, children; we're trying have a pleasant drive."

"We never thought our Daddy would be so mean and cruel as to let a kitten die."

Finally, the mother turns to her husband and says, "Dear, you'll have to stop." He turns the car around, returns to the spot and pulls off the side of the road. "You kids stay in the car. I'll see about it." He goes out to pick up the little kitten. The poor creature is just skin and bones, sore-eyed, and full of fleas. When the kitten sees his hand reaching down for him, bristles with th last bit of its energy, bearing tooth and claw. *Ssss!* The father picks up the kitten by the loose skin at the neck, brings it over to the car and says, "Don't touch it. It's probably got leprosy."

Back home they go. When they get to the house the children give the kitten several baths, about a gallon of warm milk, and intercede, "Can we let it stay in the house tonight? Tomorrow, we'll fix a place in the garage."

The father says, "Sure, take my bedroom; the whole house is already a zoo." Several weeks pass. Then one day, the father walks in, feels something rub against his leg, looks down, and there is the kitten. He reaches down toward the kitten, carefully checking to see that no one is watching. When the kitten sees his hand, it does not bare its claws and hiss; instead, it arches its back to receive a caress. Is that the same kitten? No, of course not: It's not the same hissing kitten on the side of the road. And you and I know what makes the difference.

Not too long ago, God reached out a hand to bless my family, friends, and me. When God did, I looked at God's hand. It was covered with scratches. Such is the hand of love, extended to everyone, especially those who are scarred or bitter.

PRAYER: Heavenly Father, thank you for your persistence. Help us to fall into your extended hands. You have bathed us in your love; you have fed us and given us drink; you have held us; you healed our hurts; and you have caressed us. Now we are at one with your Spirit and with one another. In the name of Jesus, we pray. Amen.

Day 51
What's the Purpose of the Inner Life?

So faith, hope, and love remain, but the greatest of these is love (1 Corinthians 13:13).

HAVE YOU EVER PERFORMED A task or something out of habit and then one day ask yourself, "Why am I doing this? When did it all start and why?" It is easy for us to fall into the trap of forgetting the reasons why we do certain things. And so we begin to lose our way.

We might have a particular game plan and a certain way to accomplish it. We have every little detail all scoped out. We are so busy maintaining those plans that we forget what we were seeking to achieve in the first place. In others words, it is very easy for us to be diverted, and we are good at it.

This is the same truth that plays into the exercise of the discipline of the inner life. The desire to be still might spring out of the need to reevaluate our life and its direction. But once we have tasted the initial fruit of our quest and have gained some new insight, we easily become distracted. We thus fail to press for deeper change. And the discipline to be still takes on all kinds of dimensions. In fact, we can become preoccupied with stillness for stillness's sake.

In this stillness, the purpose remains that of love and charity. I am not suggesting that the exercise of the discipline of stillness should not serve to help us to reevaluate, gain new strength for the deepening of our self-understanding, give new depth to our prayers, and deepen our intimacy with the Great Lover who calls us to new life. The discipline of the inner life can serve these and many other purposes.

But in the final analysis, the discipline of the inner life is to be utilized in order that we might love and serve more generously and purposefully. If we forget to maintain this important purpose, the fruit that springs from our inner life will be unripe. It will not only be sour to others, but it will leave a bitter taste in our own mouths.

PRAYER: Our most loving Father, forgive us for not cleaning all the clutter from our hearts so that there is more room for your presence and work in our lives. Enable us to get rid of the unneeded clutter that we will not be distracted and can have some special time in getting to know each other better. Amen.

◦

Day 52
Listening to Which Voice

He was in the wilderness forty days, tempted by Satan (Mark 1:13).

I LOVED TO WATCH CARTOONS when I was growing up. I still love them: the old ones, the good ones—not today's computer generated attempts to show talent. I enjoy watching those that not only sought to entertain but to teach as well. They exposed young viewers to a sampling of the fine arts, paintings, and operas that have lasted hundreds of years. Now we have noise disguised as music coming through headphones from different sources that do not teach and celebrate the fine music—opportunities to excel in the fine arts are the first to feel the cuts of the school's budget because, once again, there is more money at the end of the month, so the arts budget is cut, if not totally wiped out. But not the golden calf of athletics; they, more times than not, escape the cuts unscathed. The cartoons were one place where the fine arts were introduced, and inspired, and elevated children.

I was introduced to a lot of the cartoon classics while watching them. I can still see Bugs Bunny directing the rotund operatic tenor in the *Marriage of Figaro*. I especially enjoyed the ones when the character was found in a dilemma or situation in which a decision between the right and wrong way to respond had to be made. Suddenly appearing on each shoulder was a small replica of the character—one dressed in "heavenly" garb with a harp and the other in "hellish" garb and a pitchfork. They would banter back and forth between each other trying to convince the character to choose one or the other's side.

Our Lord was faced with the same dilemma when he had a face-off with Satan himself. His dilemma was much like the cartoon characters in that the voice speaks from above and from within and whispers softly or loudly: "You are my Beloved, on you my favor rests." It certainly is not easy to hear that voice in a world filled with voices that shout out: "You are no good, you are ugly, you are worthless, you are despicable, you are nobody, unless you can demonstrate the opposite."

These negative voices are so loud, so plentiful, so persistent, that it is easy to believe them. That's the great trap. It is the trap of self-rejection. I believe the greatest trap we must avoid is not success, not popularly, not power, but self-rejection. Success, popularity, and power can, indeed, be a great temptation, but their seductive power often comes from the way they are a part of the much larger temptation to self-rejection. When we have come to believe in the voices that call us worthless and unbelievable, then success, popularity, and power are easily perceived as attractive solutions.

So turn on a Looney Tune, and see what you can learn.

PRAYER: Father, grant us to hear your your voice above all others and to respond to your call. We ask in the name of Jesus Christ our Lord, who has already defeated Satan and won the victory. Amen.

◀◯▶

Day 53
Preparing to Go

From that time on Jesus began to inform his disciples that he had to go to Jerusalem. There he would have to suffer a lot because of the leaders, chief priests, and scribes. He would be killed (Matthew 16:21).

FROM THE MOMENT THAT JESUS "set" his mind to go to Jerusalem, his determination to face his suffering and even his death was unparalleled. He chose to face it directly. Jesus also asks that his disciples follow his example in the same manner. He doesn't pull any punches in telling them that there would not be easy future for himself or his disciples.

They would be tortured and die for their part in spreading the gospel—tradition and myth have it that all of the disciples met with a tragic death except for John. Jesus went against the human inclination to avoid suffering and death, but his followers realized that it was better to face up to the truth.

Suffering and death were along the narrow road traveled by Jesus. Although Jesus chose the way of suffering and death, he does not glorify them. Neither does he call them beautiful, good, or something to be desired. Jesus does not call for heroism or suicidal self-sacrifice. No. Jesus invites us to take a close look at reality: the reality of our existence and the harsh reality as to the way to new life. The core message of Jesus is that joy and peace can never be reached by bypassing suffering and death, but only by going right through them.

We can deny the reality of life, or we can face it. When we face it with the eyes of Jesus, we discover that where we least expect it, something is hidden that holds a promise stronger than death itself. Jesus lived his life in the trust that God's love is stronger than death and that death therefore does not have the last word.

> **PRAYER:** Our gracious heavenly Father, whose power over death is undeniable, enable us, we pray, to walk through the pain and suffering that the world gives, following your Son, to the other side where there is joy and peace. For without his leading the way, we would be unable to come out victorious but defeated. Amen.

Day 54
Staying Found

Too restless . . . looking for (union with God) was right in front of my nose and I couldn't see it.

HILE I WAS LOOKING THROUGH some files, I came across a sermon ("A Whale of a Problem") that someone had preached. The major player in this sermon was good ol' Jonah. You remember the tenderhearted, obedient, selfless, compassionate, and lover of all humankind especially the people of Nineveh. Actually, he was the prophet of God who loathed the Ninevites, and on his journey in the opposite direction was swallowed by a large fish. Jonah had such a sour disposition that he gave that fish a terrible tummy ache, and when the fish could take it no longer vomited that sourpuss of a prophet onto the beach.

Jonah did not like his new assignment, so he tried to run away and get lost. That causes one to ponder. Is our day-to-day living one in which we are trying to get lost, or are we trying to be found? Are our actions trying to add to our disguise, or what? I am afraid to say but I believe that too often we are hiding, trying not to be found.

And all that is true. My mind is scattered with things, not because of my work, but because I am detached, and I do not attend first of all to God. On the other hand, I do not attend to him because I am so absorbed in all these objects and events. I have to wait on his grace. But how stubborn and slow is my nature, and why do I keep confusing myself and complicate things for myself by useless twisting and turning?

What I need most of all is the grace to really accept God as God gives the divine self to me in every situation. "He came unto his own and his own received him not."

PRAYER: Good shepherd, you have some wild and crazy sheep in love with thorns and brambles. But please don't get tired of looking for us! I know you won't, for you have found us and all we have to do is stay found. Amen.

Day 55
I Sure Could Use a Drink

Jesus answered her, "Everyone who drinks this water will become thirsty again. But those who drink the water that I give will never become thirsty again" (John 4:14).

WE WERE HIKING ON THE trails that run parallel to the Blue Ridge Parkway. We had not planned to take a trail, but I felt great and the weather was beautiful. We had hiked a fairly good clip, at last for me, when someone in the group complained, "I am dying of thirst." The statement spread like wildfire. We all were thirsty and getting thirstier by the minute. We turned around and headed back to our cars. Some of our company started getting giddy and making silly statements such as, "My horse (or kingdom) for a drink of cold water," as we approached the spring of water. Those who were ready to give up their kingdoms for water broke into a jog and then into an outright run for the prize. Each one of us took our turn to go to the water; each slaked his or her thirst with the cool mountain water. Some had so much that when they moved, you could hear the movement of the water in their stomachs.

Have you ever been extremely thirsty? If you have experienced a deep thirst, you know how wonderful refreshing cool water can be. As you know, we can live for a number of days without food but only several days without water. Remember Jesus meeting with the Samaritan woman at Jacob's well? She was searching for something to quench her thirst: for water that was both life-giving and life-sustaining. She came to the answer of her search when she recognized her thirst, and that thirst was a thirst for God. It was to this thirst that Jesus offered living water and the promise that her thirst for God could be satisfied.

If we have not experienced this thirst of the body, we all have experienced the thirst for God. We have a desire to know and be known by our Creator. Within this desire to know and be known by this one who made us and loves us, however, God is often ignored, denied, and buried under an avalanche of other dreams and interests. Then some tragic or traumatic event occurs that causes us to desire God once again. We know that a real life is impossible without the companionship of the one who first gave us the gift of life and who sustains us even now. We then have to admit that we need living water, we need what only God can give us if we are to really live.

Today, Jesus still offers living water, a way and a companionship that can quench our thirst for God. The role we play here is to recognize the deep need for God within us and offer hospitality to the one who seeks to fill and satisfy that need. We join with the psalmist, our souls thirst for God. The good news we share is that through Jesus Christ our thirst can be satisfied.

> PRAYER: Father, our souls thirst for you. Help us to realize that our lives will always be less than what they can be as long as we fail to take time to stop and take a long drink of you, the living water. Amen.

⎯⎯⎯ ◁ ◇ ▷ ⎯⎯⎯

Day 56
Through the Darkness

Out of the depths I cry to you, O Lord (Psalm 130:1).

YOU DON'T HAVE TO HAVE Parkinson's to be a PD caregiver of one who has come face to face with the empty darkness of loneliness. They have, however, experienced from time to time some degree of uncertainty that comes with being grasped by the hands of the shadows of loneliness and pulled into a space of nothingness, that place where dreams come up empty and hope is lost and we feel totally isolated and have no companionship.

In thinking about the darkness of loneliness, one can see that there are two distinct types. The first loneliness is the emotional loneliness where people are needed. We need family, we need friends, we need home, we need encouragement, and reassurance. When all of those needs have been satisfied, then we see that there is still another loneliness.

The second loneliness requires something more than any characters of the first loneliness can provide. The second loneliness is our answer to God, who calls us to a deep and personal intimacy, and it is an intimacy that is quite demanding. The loneliness calls for us to let go of things that are effectively very satisfying to us, such as anything emotional or intellectual. We must grow to realize and to trust that this deeper loneliness is not to be overcome, but lived. We must live with trust, must learn to try to say, "Yes, I am lonely, but this particular loneliness sets me on the road to intimacy with God. It does not pull me away from God or my deepest self, but brings me closer to the source of love in the depths of my being."

It is very important for us to welcome the fullness of this second loneliness because it goes back to the oldest mystical traditions of spiritual life and prayer life. The "dark night of the soul" is another expression of the second loneliness. In a way, this loneliness pushed us to know personally the true God. When we touch the darkness, we know that God cannot be owned, neither can God be grasped in the affections of the human heart, because God is greater than my heart and God is greater than my mind. And our hearts are grateful, for that is what is needed to overcome and to live the life we were meant to live.

> **PRAYER:** Jesus, you know well what we talk about regarding loneliness, You experienced it first hand on the cross where you took all of our sins upon yourself and where even God turned his back on you. You know and you can help us know how to come through the depths of our darkness as stronger persons and more deeply in love with you and our heavenly Father. Thank you for going through the darkness first and filling it with your light. Amen.

Day 57
Telling One Who Already Knows

The Father knows what you need before you ask him (Matthew 6:8).

WHEN SOMEONE SAYS THE WORD *pray* or *prayer*, my mind goes immediately to two images, both from childhood. One is of Dürer's drawing of the praying hands; the other one is the Sunday school picture of Jesus in the Garden of Gethsemane praying in agony just before his arrest and death. Those two objects and knowing and learning from folk I consider to be "prayer warriors" (you know the who they are—they can pray you in and out of places you never thought possible). Equipped with all of the above tools, I began my journey of learning about prayer.

Praying is not wishful thinking or an escape from reality. It is not self-negation; neither is it wanting something magical to happen. It is not surrendering to words of defeat and despair, such as "I am despicable and lowly and am in desperate need of God's help." One can breathe a bit easier knowing that prayer is not that way at all but rather is the opposite.

Prayer is self-assertion, not self-abnegation. It is to say, "I need to live fully and purposefully and for that to be accomplished I need wisdom, direction, and encouragement from a source beyond myself." Prayer faces the real world; it is not world-denying. The true practice of prayer brings our whole world and all our struggles and issues into dialogue with the one who persistently and unconditionally loves us.

Prayer seeks wisdom, not simply answers. It looks for courage, not simply help. It seeks for the gift of persistence, not simply quick solutions.

Prayer means being true to ourselves. It involves acknowledging what is really happening to us. But it wisely recognizes that we ourselves don't have all the answers. This has nothing to do with an unhealthy self-negation. It is simply acknowledging our own limitation, and that has everything to do with a healthy realism.

> **PRAYER:** Father, help us to look on prayer in a more positive way, acknowledging the negative aspects of only praying for individual concerns. Help grow us beyond the childish way of praying selfishly. Amen.

Day 58
Hearing with All of Our Being

Jesus said to her, "Mary" (John 20:16).

I HAVE BEEN KNOWN BY several different names—no, I am not trying to elude the Feds. When I was growing up my friends called me Tom, and my family called me Tommy. These were the names I went by. I felt safe and secure when I heard either one. But when I am in the throes of some minor misunderstanding or some misdeed and hear my mother or dad say *Kevin Thomas Greene*, I immediately sought a safe haven. I knew I had been found out or told on or something major had happened and had my name on it. Hearing your name can bring on a myriad of emotions, good and bad, glad and sad, grace and judgment.

When Jesus calls Mary by her name, he is doing much more than speaking the word by which everybody knows her, for her name signifies her whole being. Jesus knows Mary of Magdala. He knew her story: her sin, her virtue, her fears, her love, her anguish, and her hope. He knows every part of her heart as he does with each of us. Nothing in her or in us is hidden from him. He even knows us deeper and more fully than we know ourselves. Unlike when my parents uttered my full name and I knew that I had been had, when Jesus utters Mary's name, he is bringing about a profound event. It feels like being wrapped up in a big warm blanket. Mary suddenly feels that the one who truly knows her truly loves her. We can have that same event take place in our lives. Jesus knows everything about us. He even understands us when we lash out at him for allowing our bodies to fall prey to a dreaded disease. All we need do is to listen to Jesus uttering our name, and we know that we are not alone. He is with us to fill the suffering we experience from our sin and with Parkinson's, and he promises to see it through.

Aren't we always wondering if people know every part of us, including our deepest, most hidden thoughts and feelings, and really do love us. Often we are tempted to think that we are loved only as we remain partially known. We fear that the love we receive is conditional. We might say to ourselves, "If they really knew me, they would not love me." But when Jesus calls Mary by name, he speaks to her entire being. She realizes that the one who knows her most deeply does not flee from her, but instead offers her unconditional love.

What a healing moment this encounter must have been! Mary feels at once fully known and fully loved. We too can feel such a feeling.

PRAYER: Our dearest heavenly Father, you want to show us how much you love and care for us unconditionally. Help us to accept it unconditionally. Forgive us for our unbelief. It's just difficult to grasp that you could love people like us. Another reason is that many of us don't even love ourselves. Give us eyes to see the little things you do for us that show us the enormity of your love. Thanks! In the name of Jesus, we pray. Amen.

Day 59
Can We Get Away from God?

Where can I go to get away from your Spirit? Where can I run to get away from you (Psalm 139:7)?

WE BELIEVERS ARE A SHALLOW LOT. Oh, we're not bad people. How could we be? After all, we have found God. We attend church on a regular basis, and some of us even get involved in various ministries that the church supports. We become busy with what my papa would call piddling with our faith; just along the fringes: not too involved, not too committed, just enough to be able to get in the game. Who cares that it is in the nosebleed section or in the outfield bleachers. We walk around, convinced that we have the brass ring of religion in hand whereas all along we are spiritually bankrupt, convinced that we have fooled all who might know us. So why even question it? After all we've found God.

If indeed we have, what kind of God is God? A subjective God of beauty, truth, and goodness inside our heads? Or is God a formless life-force, surging through us, a vast power that we can tap 24/7. But we don't; rather, if we look closely, we see that our direction is away instead of toward God. May be the reason we find ourselves drawing back is because we discover that God is alive pulling at the other end of the rope. There comes a moment when people who have been dabbling in religion draw back. Supposing we really found God? We never meant it to come to that; worse still, what if God had found us?

Yet we find ourselves too frequently trying to find diversions to keep from encountering God on an intimate basis. Even though we have said that we want to have this relationship, when it comes to the bottom line, we would rather be on the fringe where too much is not expected of us. Those times when there is no escape, we often draw back. There are times when we draw back and ponder whether we will continue along the Christian journey.

PRAYER: Heavenly Father, help us to see the importance of stopping and to quit running in the wrong direction. Amen.

Day 60
Don't Give up on. . . ?

The potter was at his working wheel. Whenever a clay pot he was working on was ruined, he would rework it into a new clay pot the way he wanted to make it (Jeremiah 18:3).

THERE ARE TIMES IN MY day-to-day living when life seems to be too much to bear. It takes great effort to put one foot in front of the other. Soon one is recalling the "good old days," when life was easier and simpler. But a then a memory—some tragedy, some traumatic event, some death—jolts us back into reality, and we remember that the good old days had their share of heartache and heartbreak. We remember that the scriptures never promised that our lives would be free from any predicament in which we find ourselves. We travel back to today and we see children dying from hunger, our prisons are overflowing, there's scandal after scandal, fighting unwinnable wars, economic chaos, record foreclosures of homes, and bankruptcies. These events cannot stand against a burning faith, even when that faith is an evil and perverted one. It is almost as ineffective as a umbrella in a tornado. The only way in which we can overcome our impotence and save our civilization is by the discovery of a sufficient faith. Goodness we must have, but the way to goodness is to find our peace, in the love of God, who as the source of goodness, makes us know that even we are not really good. This is the peace that passes all understanding.

The danger that we have in our time consists in the fact that ours is a "cutflower civilization." The cut flowers are as pretty as they can be and no matter how much Miracle Grow or other tricks of the trade we put on them, they die. They will die, and they die because they are severed from their sustaining roots. We are living to maintain the dignity of the individual apart from the deep faith that people—male and female—are made In God's image and therefore precious in God's sight.

We have been given a task, the task of helping to make this world a decent world for our modern technological society. No matter how many times we need to start over with new clay, let us be that clay for God to mold and fashion into the vessel God wants us to be. This cannot be done without convictions. Convictions cannot be nourished apart from their religious roots, and the religious roots cannot be nourished without Christ showing and teaching us through his word and his church.

> **PRAYER:** Father, we need your hands to fashion and mold us after your will. Create in each of us a hunger and thirst after your righteousness so we will be enabled to complete our task and then hear your words, "Well done my good and faithful child." Amen.

Day 61

No Guarantees

Now faith is being sure of what we hope for and certain of what we do not see (Hebrews 11:1).

HOPE IS NOT A GUARANTEE OF complete satisfaction. It is a kind of power, an inner power to believe that life can get better—not perfect, just better. In fact, we are better equipped to keep our commitments if we come to terms with the likelihood that some things don't change.

Let's think for a moment about things that don't change. You used to be twenty-five; now you're forty-five. You can't go back. No use hoping. You've had a mastectomy and lost a breast; you can't take it back. Your husband has incurable erotic burnout; he won't ever be as attractive, as young as the suave charmer at your office. Your wife is a messy housekeeper and a lousy cook, and she just doesn't think those things are important, even though they mean a lot to you. She probably isn't going to change. Your children have flown the coop and left you at home with your workaholic husband. They won't come back to stay unless they are shaky financially. And you hope against all hope that it is not for an extended stay for both of your sakes. Your parent has Alzheimer's and the time of lucidity is growing shorter and shorter.

Hope that things can change is not a blank check drawn on earthly perfection. Coping with whatever arises might be a realistic way of hoping for what can be. Goodness, the world would be more pleasant to live in and less of a struggle if we had more guarantees, but that is not our way.

> PRAYER: Father, grant us the proper perspective so that we do not spend valuable time hoping where there is no hope or getting back in our lives that which once was. Rather empower us to expend those energies and efforts of hope on the important things here and now. Amen.

Day 62
If Only . . .

Not that I complain of want, for I have learned in whatever state I am to be content. I have learned the secret of facing plenty and hunger, abundance and want, I can do all things in him who strengthens me (Philippians 4:11–13).

E OFTEN ENGAGE OURSELVES IN playing the "if only" game, and some of us have become pros at playing it. It is a rather simple game. We participate by finishing the sentence, "If only. . . ." "If only I had a different job." "If only I had stayed in school longer." "If only I had married someone different." "If only I didn't have health problems." "If only my children had turned out differently." "If only my circumstances were different, then things would be a whole lot better." "If only. . . ." "If only. . . ."

When we approach circumstances this way, there is a strong tendency for our lives to be less productive. Because when we play the "if only" game, we are blinded to what is good in our present situations, consistently shifting our responsibility to something or someone "over there." It's not almost like giving the blame for our circumstances to someone else—it is blaming others! And it's not fair to them.

It would be far more truthful—not to mention, beneficial—if we were to admit that it was our own bungling that got us into the circumstances we find ourselves. Refuse to play the "if only" game and turn to the question, "What is God's plan for me in this situation?" It is not where you are that matters. It is how you live wherever you are.

The most relevant issue is not a change of circumstances—"if only"—but rather a change of self. A changed self is one that faces all of one's excuses and game playing and assumes the responsibility for what one makes of life.

Are you playing "if only" now?

PRAYER: It is so amazing, dear God, to read how much of our lives is supposed to be free of any anxiety, or worry, or fear, because you are our all powerful God who loves us so unconditionally and wants nothing but the best for us. Amen.

Day 63
What Do We Need?

Surrender yourself to the Lord, and wait patiently for him (Psalm 37:7).

ONE WONDERS, SEEING THE MASSES scurrying along like a mindless army of ants, what they are thinking. Sometimes I enjoy looking, watching and imagining that each one has a comic page's balloon over someone's head, and I am the writer, creating their conversations and thinking. Some of them are really good, and I have a chuckle. Others, I imagine, are unhappy to be going to their all-too-familiar cubicles. No matter their mindset, each and everyone of them will soon be swallowed up in the activity of the day. You look into their eyes and you see nothing, an empty void. Why?

Unfortunately, we live in a society that more often than not assigns a person's worth on the basis of how much money he or she has in the bank or how full each one's Palm Pilot or BlackBerry or iPad might be. At the end of the day, traveling for home, overstuffed briefcases crammed full of work that was not dealt with leaves a feeling that nothing of value was accomplished and makes its presence known. We need something, but what? What are we looking for, and are we looking in the right places?

I believe the answer can be found in leisure. Yes, leisure, not more activity like a swarm of bees. There is a tremendous need in each of our lives to cultivate leisure—*otium sanctum*, a holy leisure. That need issues a call to our world for effort, deepening, change, and transformation. I am not simply advocating for a special project of self-transformation or that I must "work on myself." If that was all there was to it, it would be better to forget it. Just to go for walks, live in peace, let change come quietly and invisibly on the inside.

If anyone is like me, we can identify with the fact that we do have a past to break with, an accumulation of inertia, waste, wrong, foolishness, not junk, a great need of clarification, of mindfulness, or rather of no mind: a return to genuine practice, right effort, the need to push on to the great doubt, need for the Spirit. Our need is for that holy free time that can only be what we require for the restoration of our spirit to be at one with God.

PRAYER: It is so amazing, dear God, to read how much of our lives is supposed to be free of any anxiety, or worry, or fear, because you are our all powerful God who loves us so unconditionally and wants nothing but the best for us. Amen.

◄ ○ ►

Day 64
Transacting the Business of the Soul

He touched my mouth with it (burning coal) . . . your guilt has been taken away, and your sin has been forgiven (Isaiah 6:7).

WHILE AT THE TRAPPIST MONASTERY IN Gethsemane, Kentucky, I attended Mass at 6:00 A.M. every morning, though I was not allowed to partake of Holy Communion. I did not understand everything that was being said because the words of the Mass were in Latin. My limited mastery of Latin, however, did not keep me from being able to follow the activity going on in front of me. One thing was certain: I, even as a spectator, was part of something special, something bigger than me, than all of us. I was witnessing something "holy" unfolding before my very eyes. Even from my vantage point, I, too, was caught up in this holy moment receiving a hint of God. I left it somehow different each day. The feeling was one of peace, a place where I was loved and cared for, a place where I was encouraged to reach my potential, the place where I belonged. There was still a sense of something missing.

This brought to mind Jesus' story of the prodigal son, who after having wished his father dead traveled to that far-off country where he learned the true nature and the fickleness of so-called friends. The son, Jesus said, knew something was missing, and it was in the pigsty where he came to himself. This young pig farmer returned home to his father. That is exactly what we need: a wake-up call, a coming to our self before we can go home. We now know what that something that was missing. I don't know about you, but I find at times a need to come to myself. Knowing that caused me to wonder how "prodigal" am I? What was needed was the return to the One who loves, who oftentimes is silent—a return to the holy, to the merciful, to the One who is all!

Oh, how the world needs—oh, how I need—to go beyond, to leave everything and press forward to the end and to the beginning, to the ever-new beginning that is without end. How our souls cry out to obey God on the way through life's journey in order to reach the One in whom I have begun, who is the way and the end and is also the beginning.

> **PRAYER:** We pray that we don't burn any more daylight but rather return home, return to the Father and meet all that life throws our way with confidence, peace, and joy. Amen.

Day 65
How Shall I Pray?

At the same time, the Spirit also helps us in our weakness because we don't know how to pray for what we need (Romans 8:26).

FOR THOSE WHO ARE SERIOUS about prayer and want to go deeper, they can find it difficult at times—what St. John of the Cross called the "dark night of the soul." Or it can be as simple as a child's prayer—now I lay me down to sleep. Prayer can be difficult one minute and simple the next. It can be a paradox.

Prayer is surrounded by difficulties. The difficulties sometimes are compounded when the situations and circumstances that touch the event are so clouded with complexity and ambiguity that we are not clear on how to pray.

We are literally confused. The most obvious is the lack of prayer. Most of us are eager to pray when there is a crisis or an emergency, but that is pretty much the extent of it. What follows the sporadic use of prayer is how to pray for particular situations. For example, should I pray that God would heal the person that is terminally ill or take them home where they would suffer no longer. Do we pray that the one who has abused and killed children would be caught and punished, or do we pray for their conversion and extend forgiveness.

Prayer is hard. How do you pray? Someone—I think it was Mother Teresa—said, "If you find it hard to pray, you can say, 'Come Holy Spirit.'" With those words, combined with Paul's words in Romans 8:26, we can receive wisdom from the Holy Spirit to instruct us as to how to pray.

We might find that we are led to pray in very general terms: *Do as you see best in this situation, O God.* Other times, we might find ourselves praying that God would fill the situation with his presence and assurance. Yet at other times, our prayers are running over with boldness and full of faith: *We thank you ahead of time for your merciful and gracious hand on our family member.*

The Holy Spirit can encourage, lead, and inspire us in many ways. There might be inspiration in those times during which we realize that we are praying in ways that we had not thought or anticipated. Then, on the other hand, the inspiration might come in the form of perseverance, the gift of love, or wisdom in guiding us how to pray.

When we experience the moving of the Holy Spirit, we come to realize how impossible it is try and bound the Holy Spirit into any boxes we have. Acknowledging that the Holy Spirit is light, power, and wisdom, we must realize that when we open ourselves up to the Holy Spirit, we are opening ourselves up to all that God might do. And isn't that where we want to be?

> **PRAYER:** Dear Father, enable us to pray as we ought with your Spirit's presence, for Christ's sake. Amen.

Day 66

From Darkness to Light

Once you lived in the dark, but now the Lord has filled you with light. Live as children who have light. Light produces everything that is good (Ephesians 5:8–9).

I HAVE EMBARKED ON A NEW venture: I am teaching myself how to paint. No, I don't mean by numbers and there will be no junior Van Goghs or Picassos produced from my brushes—I have too much admiration for them to insult them by thinking that I will produce any paintings of the caliber of the masters. I am going at it as a means to provide me an escape from the skirmishes of the day. Painting will provide me an escape, and it will be fun. Most of the masters paid a high price for their work. They faced poverty and hunger and braved all kinds of hardships in order to show us how the world around us looked through their eyes. They have left our world their gifts of beauty. It is amazing to see through their eyes the depth and richness of the objects that they were painting. They left us a little of themselves in each of their paintings. We should be thankful.

One such artist was a young man whose name was Rembrandt. Rembrandt probably had no plans of addressing himself to future centuries through his self-portraits. As he aged and experienced the reality of emotion instead of merely studying its surface signs, however, he used his face to convey a deeper meaning. He pitilessly portrayed the slow ruin of his own flesh, reflecting the tides of skepticism and courage, melancholy and calm that made their way through him. In so doing, he captured the universal, describing not only his pilgrimage but also that of all humanity toward a final peace with this world and with God. All around him were the Calvinists advocating a strict and stern God, but Rembrandt saw things differently. He believed in a God who was loving and forgiving, the polar opposite of the Calvinist's God with their strict morality of life. That belief was foreign to him, and he did not ridicule it. He ignored it.

One of Rembrandt's best gifts that he left to the world of art was his use of light. His art casts a vivid light on certain selected causes. Those, who for him were the best and greatest, were given that light, and Rembrandt leaves all the rest in shadow or unseen. His earliest known dated painting was *The Stoning of Stephen*. Painted at age nineteen, Rembrandt includes his head just above the kneeling saint. A belief in active rather than passive Christianity was central to Rembrandt's intense faith. He expressed this idea in the painting, *Descent from the Cross* (1633), by portraying himself next to the right hand of the dead Christ. He knew that Christ died for his sins. It is a place we could be ourselves as well. It's quite a special gem, isn't it?

> **PRAYER:** Father, you have provided so much beauty in our world; forgive us for abusing it. Open our eyes so that we can catch as much of that beauty as we can. Father, we also ask that you help us to find the gift you have given each one of us that we might use it to the advancement of your kingdom. Amen.

Day 67
Underdog

"I can't walk in these things (speaking of Saul's armor)," David said to Saul. "I've never had any practice doing this," so David took off all those things (1 Samuel 17:39).

WHEN I WAS GROWING UP, I enjoyed watching cartoons (still do, as you might recall). One of my favorites was an unlikely hero who fought and defeated villains of all shapes and sizes. When he was not off doing good, he was known around town as the "humble shoeshine boy." He flew through the skies in a red costume and blue cape with a yellow "U" on his chest, delivering the people of his city from the villains. Whether fighting or while flying, his famous line was, "There's no need to fear—Underdog is here." In most trying situations, his name was not only Underdog, he *was* the "underdog." That is also where you can find God: with the underdogs of our world, including those that the world has cast aside as weaklings. I enjoyed watching Underdog prove them wrong; he met the challenge. Look at another underdog.

Goliath was ten feet tall; wore a bronze helmet, a bronze coat of arms weighting 125 pounds, bronze shin guards; and carried a bronze javelin (the head of the javelin was fifteen pounds of iron).

David was a stick who carried five smooth stones, a shepherd's bag, and a sling.

If you were a betting person, on whom would you put money on: Goliath or David? Have you ever wondered why they stayed out in that barren wasteland to hear the insults of Goliath? May be they thought that if they waited long enough he would get tired and go home. Whatever reason, it was clear the armies of the Philistines had the advantage. The story tells one of the character and leadership of a leader in times of crisis. As soon as Saul heard David say that he was willing to fight the enemy, he sent for him, and his bearers began dressing David in his armor until he told them to stop. Saul's armor was too heavy and bulky for David. He said in essence, "I can't use this. I am not used to it and can hardly move in it." He could have broken out with a song from the Broadway musical, *Golden Rainbow*, "I've Got to Be Me." All joking aside, they took the armor off him, and he was already giving God the thanks for the victory. There was David, a shepherd boy with only a sling and five smooth stones (why five?) going out to meet this big braggart, knowing in his heart God's deliverance. And God did deliver, and David was a hero.

David couldn't be Saul. He had to be himself. He couldn't be his brother Eliab. He had to be himself. He could not be his father. He had to be himself. That self was unencumbered. No one expected David to win, except David and God. Hooray for the underdog!

Jesus takes the underdog mentality to a higher level: *If you want to be master, you must be a servant.* The world doesn't understand, but we do. God loves us and will deliver us from all the Goliaths in our lives. Hooray for the underdog!!!

PRAYER: Father, thank you for taking care of all our Goliaths and granting us the victory. I claim that deliverance before it happens, as did David. Amen.

<hr/>

Day 68
Making Peace

Make peace with your sister or brother, and then come back and offer your gift (Matthew 5:24).

THE SCRIPTURES ARE CLEAR: we should love our enemies, and pray for those that persecute us. From the mouth of Jesus to John, we are encouraged to be at peace with all we meet. John even goes as far as to say that if you can't say that you love God and hate your fellow man, then you are a liar. It also causes me to wonder if they knew some of the people I know. This tough admonishment shakes your spiritual bones, for there are still many people whom I am trying to like. Remember the bumper sticker that reads, "God loves you and I'm still trying?" Scripture does indeed encourage us to love them, but with some of these people it takes a great deal of effort just to make the "like" stage because I am not fully at peace with them.

With any relationship or friendship, one can look back over the years of those friendships, encounters, and confrontations and realize that there are still small wounds caused by anger, bitterness, and resentment that lie hidden in my heart. When we bring to mind all whom we personally know or about whom we have heard or read, we have the tendency to divide them between those who are for us and those who are against us, those whom we like and those we do not like, those whom we want to be with and those whom we try to avoid at all costs.

We must let go of all these divisive emotions and thoughts, so that we can truly experience peace with God and with all God's people. This means an unrestrained willingness to forgive unconditionally and to let go of old fears, bitterness, resentment, anger, and lust in order to find reconciliation.

> **PRAYER:** Our Father in heaven, we think we are closer to peace than we are. Help our souls to win the battle, and let there be peace in our hearts. Then help us to busy ourselves with making peace with our brothers and sisters. Let there be peace on earth, and let it begin me. This task completed, we can go about our day in the confidence that you will accept our gifts. In the name of Jesus, we pray. Amen.

◄◇►

Day 69
Bad Duty

God is faithful and reliable. If we confess our sins, he forgives them and cleanses us of any thing we've done wrong (1 John 1:9).

ONE OF THE MOST UNPOPULAR virtues of Christians can be found in the words, "You should love your neighbor as yourself." Unpopular looking through Christians morals, we discover that "your neighbor" includes "your enemy." And there we are, up against this reluctant duty being taught and shone by Jesus of forgiving our enemies.

Forgiveness means, "cleansing your soul of the bitterness of what might have been, what should have been, and what didn't have to happen." Someone has defined forgiveness as "giving up all hope of having had a better past." What is past is past and there is little to be gained by dwelling on it.

You can hear a chorus of voices agreeing in harmony that forgiveness is a good idea. A good idea, until they have something to forgive. Then let forgiveness become the topic of discussion and you are greeted with howls of anger. That is not to say that those voices belong to people who believe this virtue to be too difficult; rather, it is an act that they find contemptible. How could you ask me to forgive a colleague that took my idea and presented it as hers? And what about the drunk driver who hit my car and killed my little girl? I wonder how you'd feel about forgiving them, if you were in that situation?

So do I. It causes me to stop and ponder my reaction. It is akin to those instances in which Christianity instructs me not to deny my faith, even to save myself from being tortured to death. I wonder at those times what I would do if and when it came to that point. I am not professing these to be my words and that they should be followed as an example. Rather, I'm trying to suggest that this Christian virtue can be found at home in the scriptures. And if I dare to look, I will see there, right in the middle of it, "Forgive us our sins as we forgive those that sin against us." There is a suggestion that we are not offered forgiveness on any other terms.

PRAYER: Father, you tell us that the most important thing we can do is to love you with all our heart, soul, mind, and to love our neighbor as ourselves. Grant us the will to want to make our part happen. Protect us from the evil one, who tells us that you will not forgive us all our sin; and remind us gently that the Spirit tells us something more. Thank you! In Jesus' name, we pray. Amen.

Day 70
The Gift That Keeps on Giving

This is the kind of fasting I have chosen: Loosen the chains of wickedness,
untie the straps of the yoke, let the oppressed go free and break every yoke.
Share your food with the hungry, take the poor into your house, and cover
them with clothes when you see them naked (Isaiah 58:8–9).

EVERY ONE OF US HAS virtues engaged in the act of giving at one time or another. It can be a tremendous joy and blessing, or it can become a dreaded hassle. We procrastinate until it is absolutely the latest possible time to have the gift. This process is made more complicated when the person you are buying for is one of those folk who already have everything one could possibly want and then some. The act of buying a gift for such a person causes the act of giving to be downgraded, to become nothing but a chore. This brings up the question: How do you go about buying the right gift? It is my thought that the better you know someone, the easier it is to buy for him or her. What do I mean? One of the first things we do is to examine the appropriateness of the gift. For example you would not purchase a fur coat for someone who is a diehard member of the animal activists group, PETA. These two sides of how or what to buy someone come into conflict.

I know both sides of this dilemma. At one time or another, I have found myself in one or the other group. How do you handle your gift giving? Are you one of those people who live positively, joyously, and rejoice in the opportunity of God using you to bless someone? The flip side is people who look at life more negatively and rob the event of every possibility for a blessing or joy this could bring to others. Which raises the question: What would you bring to others? Would the gift cause the recipient to exclaim, "Thank you, this is just what I wanted"; "Yes! Yes! Yes! This will be perfect in our living room"; or, "Thanks mama and papa, I have been wanting this for a while." What would you give to someone who has everything? Take it a step further and ask, "What would you give to God?"

As believers, we are called upon not to live our lives as the world says we should. We should be different. PDers have to live life as being limit-filled. For example: one day, people understand every word you speak, and the next they are nodding their heads in frustration for not being able to understand you, instead of saying, "What?" they just sit there with that deer-caught-in-the-headlights look. See what I mean? The limit-filled life finds itself getting in the act of giving as well. To start with, we see these limitations as God's possibility. We see our frailty as God's strength. Our mortality becomes the instrument of his immortality.

Paul considers our mission to be right. Our mission is to live in terms of the gift of the cross; the attributes being self-denial, self-emptying, forgiving, serving, and loving. Sounds like an echo of the words and actions used by a carpenter from Nazareth. We learn through experience that Christians are not exempt from the trials of the day; that friends will desert you; and we are called to live a redeemed life. In this place, God can once again tell the story of the sacrificial love of his Son. You see, a gift to a human being in need is the kind of gift that pleases God the most. It is God's nature to be more concerned about God's children than about God's self, and especially about those who have the greatest need. A person is called to die for the Lord who died for us, and they die by living for Jesus.

PRAYER: Father, may our gift to you of a broken spirit and a contrite heart be acceptable to you. Amen.

⟨◇⟩

Day 71
There It Is

Now we see a blurred image in a mirror. Then we will see very clearly (1 Corinthians 13:12).

HAVE YOU EVER MET PEOPLE whom you would like to buy for their worth and then sell them for what they think they are worth? There's a lot of money to be made out there in the world, if one could do that. I don't know about you, but for me it seems that our world is getting more and more cocky, that people think they are invincible and that if it happens, we have to do it.

Even though this may be true in part, we are responsible, special creatures in God's world tasked with the dreaming, creating, and doing. Our job is extended through our caring and sharing to shape the world by building human community.

After all, being created in the image of God brings with it the call for us to take the creative initiative. This does not give us the okay to be passive, sitting around waiting for life to happen to us. Even with these responsibilities, it doesn't mean that it all depends on us, and for certain no solo efforts are expected. Rather, we need cooperation and human partnership. And yet more is needed than human partnership.

This human partnership is required. We're not alone in fulfilling these responsibilities. God does not give us a task and then abandon us; God joins with us. The fact of the matter is that God is already at work in our world, even though this is mainly a hidden and mysterious work.

In the midst of life's busyness and challenges, we often do not see this hidden work of God. But often afterward, with the eyes of faith we can see that God has provided, that God has made a way, and that God has gone and goes before us.

PRAYER: Father, infuse us with the power of your Spirit so that we may be at one with you and one another that we may accomplish the creative work you would have us to be about. Amen.

⚬

Day 72
Love Rather Than Hatred

Love is patient and kind; love is not jealous or boastful. . . . Love bears all things, believes all things, hopes all things, endures all things (1 Corinthians 13:4, 7).

WHEN MY MOTHER WAS LIVING, she loved working among her flowers and helping to make things grow, as was evident by all the flower beds in her and dad's yard. You couldn't leave without her walking with you through the different beds and telling their stories, and you certainly could not leave without a clipping or a root with instructions on how to plant and watch it grow. In the evening, you would find her out walking among them taking in their gifts of beauty and fragrance. As she strolled through her flowers, she would stop occasionally to pull an unwanted weed trying to sneak into her flower beds. It was at this time that she also gave each of her flowers and plants their nighttime drinks of water to those that needed it. She loved her flowers and plants and would say, "A gift; they are a gift." Mother worked in her flowers until PD stopped her, but even PD couldn't stop her from being able to supervise and instruct whoever was with her what she wanted done.

It takes time to grow healthy, beautiful plants. I can hear her saying, "Everything has a time." Paul is both poetic and eminently practical. One person even imagined using the qualities listed in verses 4–7 as the basis for a practical questionnaire and guide as a positive resource for those getting married. The session would go through the subject of love. It would start with self-evaluation, such as how patient have I been, how kind, and how irritable and resentful.

To sow love is to be actively patient and kind and to work against our own selfishness and irritability. Love as a feeling is wonderful. Love as a verb is hard work, but in the long run, it is an awesome power.

PRAYER: Loving God, help me feel love, especially in difficult relationships. Amen.

Day 73
Still a Pain in the ...

In my distress I cry to the Lord, that he answer me: "Deliver me O Lord, from lying lips, from deceitful tongues. . . . Too long have I had my dwelling among those who hate peace. I am for peace: but when I speak, they are for war" (Psalm 120:1–2, 6–7)!

ONE OF THE DIFFICULTIES THAT WE face in life is the fact that we cannot clear everything up. There are people we encounter every day with whom we just are not at peace. And every episode does not end in "happily ever after." We search for a happy resolution no matter how hard we try. We have prayed for resolution and peace. We have gone into our closets and admitted our faults and shortcomings before God and sought forgiveness and reconciliation. We have even talked about and confronted the problem, but disharmony, uncertainty, and even distrust live on. The relationship remains difficult, and it seems that the harder we try to make things right, the worse things become.

Oftentimes, the difficulty is that we really don't know what the problem actually is. There are symptoms, but to be able to discuss it heart-to-heart is not an opportunity afforded us, which leaves us living a life lacking in insight and openness and thereby a lack of resolution.

We see in this just how fragile we are and how broken our world is. When met with this situation, we can only bring and place our difficulties and painful circumstances into the hands of the Master. We wait then for another day when God presents us with new opportunities to make for peace knowing all along that such an opportunity can only be God's precious gift.

PRAYER: Father, make me an instrument of your peace: where there is hatred, let me sow love. Where there is injury, pardon. Where there is doubt, faith. Where there is despair, hope. Where there is darkness, light. Where there is sadness, joy. Amen (part of a prayer of St. Francis of Assisi).

Day 74
Have Your Eaten Yet?

Jesus told them, "I have food that you don't know about" (John 6:32).

WHAT ARE WE HUNGRY FOR? Could it be for God? This nourishment comes through God's presence in the spirit of Jesus Christ and that is where we partake of God. We must absorb God's teaching, God's character, God's mind, and God's ways; we must appropriate the virtue there is in God, "Till his mind becomes our mind and God's way our ways; till we think somewhat as God would do if God were in our place; and we can be and do what without God we could not be or do; and this because God's power has passed into us and become our power," until, like Paul, we see ourselves as being "in Christ" and see all things in relation to him. That means God is of the ordinary stuff of every day if we only have eyes to see.

God is a roving God, the guest who comes for dinner, invited or uninvited. God does not always knock at the door. Sometimes God breaks in and enters, quietly and without shame. God stands lovingly and laughing by the desk of the atheist who is writing a book to prove that God does not exist. Into the lives of people who will not or cannot call God by name God comes in disguise, taking on any name they are capable of speaking. And though we resist God, God is very hard to discourage. Before giving up, God will have recourse to strong measures. If God cannot ravish you alive with beauty, God is not beyond catching you in a foxhole. God is the father who knows no rest till the prodigal child falls at the Almighty's feet and says, "Father"; God cares little for statistics such that the one lost sheep is more valued than the "ninety-nine." So God can be perceived in every word that proceeds from the mouth of the Lord as God shapes and claims our lives by being present in God's world and word.

> PRAYER: Our heavenly Father, thank you for your patience with our hardheartedness and our lack of commitment and staying power. You have given us the power to be like Christ, who can restore us to right relationship with you and put the pieces of our

fragmented lives together. You and you alone are the only who can right this wrong. In the name of Jesus, we pray. Amen.

⎯⎯◁○▷⎯⎯

Day 75
Sorrow

Even while laughing, a heart can ache, and joy can end in grief (Proverbs 14:13).

PAIN IS A SPECIFIC HURT. Sadness is a condition of being in low spirits. Grief is deep anguish or remorse. All are poured into sorrow through the generous repository where nourishment and healing may be found. I remember sorrow in the eyes of a family member who kept secrets, whose inner truth I never came to know. There is the anguish of bereaved people gathered at the gravesides of loved ones in Afghanistan, Iraq, and in New York City whose wounds are imprinted on our lives and reflected our sorrow. Looking over your own experience, acknowledging, naming, and embracing our sorrows might yield fresh strength and wisdom for living out our days.

I saw in my visits with my mother, who was diagnosed with Parkinson's disease, the gradual takeover of her body and the unfolding of the unique character of her disease. Exploring my own emotional and spiritual turmoil, I faced my struggles to find new skills to sustain our communication to the last. I learned how to "listen to the garble." I would assist my dear sister, who served as primary caregiver to our mother. There would be times that I fed her, read to her, shared family stories, and sang to her. We would listen to music together and communicate the best we could. There is much that I regret about the disease and what a wasting it was of her in those years, but I am grateful too for the use we made of that time, salvaging so much even when we both were losing so much. Things changed once I was diagnosed with Parkinson's.

Here, I thought was the primary example of a stewardship of sorrow, tending it, not wallowing, but conserving that it might remain available to nourish ourselves and others. We can all tell stories of our own individual daily battles with our illness. Whether it be cancer, diabetes, Parkinson's, cerebral palsy, heart disease, or any of the other numerous illnesses that are robbing us of living a normal lifestyle. Someone wrote in a journal about their fight with cancer in such a way that I felt a kinship with the writer. We were comrades in our daily sorties. The writer related,

> I will bring the fear into my heart, to meet the pain and fear of that openness, to embrace it, to allow it. This is the severing that we were all the time constantly changing. Realizing that brings the wonderment at life. Just when I hear the birds outside my window, or drive through the countryside, it gladdens my heart and nourishes my soul. I feel such joy. I'm not trying to "beat" it; I am allowing myself into it, forgiving it. My illness; I'm alive. I sailed into it, forgiving it. I'm still very moved to do what I have to do to try and beat this thing at its own game and not let it get the better of me. I will go on, not with anger and bitterness, but with a determination a joy.

As we grieve losses and suffer heartbreak, sorrow might darken and enrich our lives, and in some way not yet understood, allow self pity, make our fate accessible as vocation, and increase our compassion for others.

PRAYER: Father, It is so easy to throw in the towel, throw our hands up, and give up when the pain, stress, and anxiety seem to overwhelm us, and we believe that we cannot make it through the storm. Help us to realize that we are not alone in the battle, that you stand by our side, shoulder-to-shoulder, helping us to see the journey through the storm. Thank you for your love, compassion, and concern as we face the journey together. Amen.

Day 76

Memories

Do this to remember me (1 Corinthians 11:24).

WE FOLK WITH PARKINSON'S HAVE A short memory at times. We become battle weary with the ongoing daily sorties from our enemy, the uninvited guest, that we forget that God is alive, that God loves us unconditionally, and that God is active in our lives. We cannot stand up alone against the guerilla warfare that is relentlessly being waged against us. We are distracted and unable to be single-minded as the apostle Paul encourages us to live, even if we have PD.

When our attention is turned to remembrance, it brings us to a mood of worship that cannot be denied, and that worship turns to the very heart of the Christian faith. To discover it is to discover the act of worship that defines us more than any other discipline. It speaks to us of the power of memory as a means of grace. In our remembering what can occur is an act of worship. The act we bring from the past is brought into the present so that we will be confident to go into the future equipped to face whatever the future holds. These words join memory and hope. Paul saw it at once by remembering, "You tell about the Lord's death until he comes."

This holy time reminds us from where we have come. It helps us discover who we are. Such an act of remembering forms the person who moves into the future with confidence. It reminds us that we aren't forgotten. We are guilty of forgetting what God has done. God and all his blessings, though we may not realize it at times, are quite active in the day-to-day lives of those who have eyes to see and ears to hear.

Even when we gather around the Lord's table and share the loaf and the fruit of the vine, we gather to pray and worship. No words have to be spoken; the act of remembering is for many one of the most eloquent moments of life. This is why memory is so important. It reminds us that we are not alone, not by a long shot. Remember, when we go to bed at night perhaps we should count our gifts instead of counting sheep.

PRAYER: Dear Father, help us not to forget your wondrous deeds for us and your many blessings upon us. Sometimes we forget, allowing ourselves to get too busy and not notice your presence. Forgive us, dear Father. Help us to realize that each time we remember, Christ is brought back to fill the present with his presence. In his name, we pray. Amen.

Day 77
It Cost How Much?

The Kingdom of God is like a merchant who was searching for pearls. When he found a valuable pearl, he went away, sold everything he had, and bought it (Matthew 13:45–46).

IF WE HEAR, REALLY HEAR, from the depths of our hearts God's knocking and wake to the adventure of experiencing the world in the Father's presence, we will not turn back. We should hold onto it, for embarking into a conscious awareness of and intimacy with God is the great treasure of life.

Like the merchant who found the pearl of great price who went and sold all he had to buy the pearl. Could Jesus have been referring to those priceless moments when we discover the voice of God calling out to us, summoning us to a new creative experience with him? He tells us bluntly that if we buy the pearl, it will cost us everything; but the pearl is worth it. The merchant didn't think twice about his decision.

It's the gleam of the pearl, the lure of the Spirit, that sees us through everything that pulls us back and makes us doubt our decisions and wonder why we're doing this.

We need to catch the tiniest sparkle of it, the desire to be united with God's presence in the midst of our moments. We are quite a distance away from achieving it, but we still have the audacious hope burning within. God has ignited the finest flame for us and is cupping the divine hands around it so as not to let it be extinguished. If you have it you can feel the great tenderness that guards us.

PRAYER: Dear God, help the scales of this world fall from our eyes so that we can see the real price that has been paid. Enable us to see the true value of our treasure and give us the willingness and the courage to sell everything and buy it. Amen.

---◀◦▶---

Day 78
No More Time?

Be still then . . . and know that I am God (Psalm 46:10).

IT SEEMS THAT WHEN WE think we can go no faster or add anything else to our overcrowded schedules, we find a little white space in the margins of the year into which we can put another something. We run around like a bee visiting flower after flower, gathering nectar from one plant and then another, nonstop it seems. Let's face it. We are a very busy people, and our schedules being what they are have little or no room for anything spiritual because that might take up too much time, and you already know how busy you are.

Meditation, contemplation, silence: you have got to be kidding! Where's the time for it—and we wonder why there are so many visits scheduled for the therapist and the huge monthly pharmaceutical bills? Yet, if we are truthful, we know deep inside what is needed: inner stillness. Inner stillness is necessary if we are to be in control of our faculties and if we are to be able to hear the voice of the Spirit speaking to us.

There can be no stillness if we can't control the busyness of our day to day living. We have to learn to say "no" in order for us to have time to experience stillness. Without discipline, there can be no stillness, and the discipline of external silence can help us toward that inner tranquility that is at the heart of authentic religious experience.

In meditation, we take steps to achieve this stillness. We calm our bodies and our emotions, then gradually allow the mind to become single-pointed. Stillness within one individual can affect society beyond measure.

PRAYER: Our Heavenly Father, we need you to quiet our tumultuous lives. Enable us with the courage to say "no" in order to be able to say "yes." We realize that life is really no life without the stillness that puts our lives in order and perspective. Thank you for your desire to be with us and for the measure you took to show us. We are indeed humbled. In the name of Jesus, we pray. Amen.

—◇—

Day 79
Added Protection

God has commanded his angels to guard you in all your ways (Psalm 91:11).

The Lord opened the servant's eyes and let him see. The mountain was full of fiery horses and chariots around Elisha (2 Kings 6:17).

NO ONE NEEDS TO BE reminded of these words better than those who are trying to live the life God wants them to live. In the text today, we are reminded of God's promise never to leave or forsake us. God promises to take care of and deliver us from struggles, loneliness, and fear. That is a great comfort. Now we mustn't try and stuff God into our small box; God is much larger than our doubt-ridden hearts. We must hold to the vastness of God's promises for protection remembering the Almighty's faithfulness.

As much as we may desire it, God does not take us out of the world but helps us live in it. And it is through prayer that we become aware of this. During times of prayer it is easy to sense a protective presence of God and the angels amid destruction, fears, temptations, and doubts. At those times we can feel surrounded by a universal—even a cosmic—goodness, gentleness, kindness, and acceptance. Some have said that they feel it is as if large wings of angels keep them safe. That being the case, they can feel it as a sort of protective cloud covering them. It is hard to describe this experience against the danger of a seductive world. But this protection is very soft, gentle, and caring. It is not the protection of a wall or an armor or metal screen. It is more the protection of a hand on our shoulder, or a kiss to our forehead, or smiling eyes looking at us. We are not taken away from the dangers. We are not lifted out of this seductive world. We are not removed from being stomped on and screamed at; noisy distractions always demand our attention and never seem to get tired of bothering us. Still, there is the hand, those lips, and eyes that I see and feel with my heart and by which I know that I am safe.

PRAYER: Heavenly Father, we are so thankful that you came to earth so as to provide us with the protection that we would need to live in the world. We thank you that you help to quiet the noisy distractions that are always trying to undo our relationship with you. Continue to empower us so we can emerge victorious. In the name of our added protection, Jesus Christ, we pray. Amen.

Day 80
Me? Sacrifice?!

Don't forget to do good things for others and to share what you have with them. These are the kinds of sacrifices that please God (Hebrews 13:16).

MY YOUNGEST SON, JOHN ARTHUR, IS IN the theatre. He had the role of Riff in *West Side Story* on Broadway and has a role in the new musical from London entitled *Matilda*. I remember very clearly the miles we traveled for auditions, callbacks, and lessons. You could sense the anticipation and excitement going from one audition to another, to be part of such an opportunity auditioning and meeting so many like-minded people with similar dreams and hopes. Many have sacrificed greatly in order to follow their dreams.

What would they be willing—what would *you* be willing—to do to make the yearnings and the passion of your heart a reality? What about your friends and colleagues? Is there anything you would sacrifice in order for a friend, a family member, or a colleague to see their dream come true? Would you put your dreams on hold or maybe even give them up for someone else to be happy who might otherwise not have such an opportunity?

What do you think about this story? Nearly 500 years ago, two young friends in Germany, Albrecht Dürer and Franz Knigstein were struggling to become artists. Both had raw talent but few funds. They decided one would work to support the other until his university education was completed; then the other would sell his paintings to finance his friend's education.

They drew lots to decide which one would attend school first. Dürer went to school and Knigstein went to work. After years of study and hard work, Dürer was selling his paintings, and he returned to keep his part of the bargain. Only then did he realize the great price his friend had paid. Knigstein's delicate and sensitive fingers had been ruined by years of rugged manual labor. Although he had to abandon his artistic dreams, he rejoiced in his friend's success.

One day when Knigstein was kneeling with his rugged, gnarled hands intertwined in prayer; Dürer quickly sketched the hands of his friend and completed the drawing of what we now call the "Praying Hands."

Today art galleries the world over feature many works of Albrecht Dürer, but the peoples' favorite is the "Praying Hands," inspired by his friend.

Even though it has been disproved, isn't that a wonderful story? "See, upon the palms of my hands, I have written your name" (Isa 49:16).

> **PRAYER**: Dear God, what sacrifice! What unselfishness! But you already know about that, don't you? You even saw it outside a city gate hanging on a cross, and you showed it to us again in an empty tomb. Are we willing to sacrifice even just a little time for God and others? Amen.

Day 81
Letting Go

But let your will be done, rather than mine (Matthew 26:39).

THERE IS A LARGE PART OF ME that wants to do my will, realize my plans, organize my future and make my decisions. Even though I have attempted it before, I had the same results. My world was upended and I had to go to God for help and deliverance from all of my miscues. I searched for peace and joy, and I knew the right direction to follow to get them. Still, I know that true joy comes from letting God love me the divine way, whether that is through illness or health, failure or success, poverty or wealth, rejection or praise. We also come to recognize that this stage cannot be achieved overnight. It takes a maturation that a great many believers are reluctant to give up. We still like to be in control. I find myself guilty of putting things in Gods hands, only to find myself pulling it back out of God's hands. It is hard for me to say, "I shall gratefully accept everything, Lord, what pleases you. Let your will be done." But I know that when I truly believe my Father is pure love, it will become increasingly possible to say these words of the heart. To be able to say these words entails a great deal of trust and faith.

Charles de Foucauld was considered a martyr by the Roman Catholic Church. Living as a Cistercian Trappist in almost complete seclusion, he wrote a prayer of abandonment that expresses beautifully the spiritual attitude that I wish I had. I still pray it even though the words do not yet fully come from my heart.

"Father, I abandon myself into your hands. Do with me what you will. Whatever you may do, I thank you. I am ready for all. I accept all. Let only your will be done in me and in all your creatures. I wish no more than this, O Lord, into your hands I commend my spirit. I offer it to you with all of the love of my heart. For I love you, Lord, and so need to live, to surrender myself into your hands without reserve, and with confidence beyond all questioning because you are my Father."

PRAYER: Dear God, let us join Charles de Foucauld in his prayer of letting go. Amen.

Day 82
Do You Smell That?

They have noses, but they cannot smell (Psalm 115:7).

MY BROTHER AND I WOULD make our annual trip in the Fall to the County Fairgrounds to watch the midway for our agricultural fair come to life. We would watch as the carnies assembled the game booths and the rides, transforming the area into acres of blaring music and colorful, flashing lights. The lights raced around the outline of each ride, hoping to lure one to come and ride them. The game booth operators would hawk their challenge to any passersby who felt lucky. Then came what used to be my favorite part: the food The air was filled with the smell of green peppers, sausages, and onions cooking, cotton candy, popcorn, peanuts, corn on the cob, corn dogs, and French fries. All of the food etched its unique smell into the night air.

I said it used to be my favorite, because Parkinson's has caused my sense of smell to be deadened. There would be no more literal enjoyment of the fair smells, no more being moved by the beautiful aroma of a rose, no more pleasure from the enticing fragrance of a lady's perfume. The sense of smell did not go all at once, but slowly and slightly.

I will admit that I have to fight from becoming resentful because of this robbery of my sense of smell. There would still be, "Something sure smells good." "I can hardly wait to eat, especially if this tastes as good as it smells." I have to deal with my resentment or the temptation to be sad and miserable each time someone says something about an enticing smell. Now, I just have to enjoy all my favorite smells the same way I enjoy my granny and my mom's cooking: through the delicious plate of memories of those wonderful times.

> **PRAYER:** Our Gracious Father, we are in need of your presence, so we will, with the help of your Holy Spirit, replace our feelings of resentment with feelings of acceptance and love. May the smell of our sacrifices and offerings be pleasing and acceptable to you. In Jesus' name, we pray. Amen.

Day 83
Doing What We Are Told

You have also obeyed me in everything I commanded you (Joshua 22:2).

THE WRITER OF THE BOOK OF Proverbs writes, "the fear of God is the beginning of wisdom" (Prov 1:7). By "beginning," did he mean the thing where wisdom begins or the chief thing in wisdom? I believe it to be the latter. It is what philosophy refers to as "the numinous." Numinous is the feeling of awe that comes to every woman and man at some time or other. That eerie feeling of being present with something that is beyond our world. A presence that something mysterious is "wholly other" than ourselves. If we agree with the thinkers of our day, then we would have to agree with their assessment that this mysterious feeling is the raw material of all religion.

Jesus is the one who has made it possible for a relationship with the Father, a friendship that says we can come before God with childlike confidence and boldness. But a warning must be sounded at this point: familiarly can breed contempt, which in turn can lead to an insensitive heart. One of life's great troubles is when we do not take God's demands seriously. We are guilty of choosing either to ignore his commands or forget them as if they didn't matter.

When we treat God's demands trivially, our disobedience has us taking our own way. We are not so much breaking God's law as we are breaking God's heart.

One thing that reduces the times we treat God and others so lightly and keeps us from doing many wrong things is simply the fear that our actions would wind up hurting those we love. In remembering how thoughtlessness and our disobedience hurt the heart of God, then we would dread to disobey God.

> PRAYER: Father, help us to walk daily with our eyes on you and not to forget that when we take our eyes off of you we hurt you and a great many other folk. Amen.

Day 84
No Darkness Allowed—Only Light

The light came into the world. Yet, people loved darkness rather than the light because their actions were evil (John 3:19).

HAVE YOU EVER PONDERED, *really* pondered, the words of our Lord Jesus recorded in Matthew 5:16 which reads, "let your light shine before others so that they may see your good works and give glory to your Father in heaven?" Are these words grounds for a religious arrogance to be lorded over others? Absolutely not. Are these words unattainable for us believers? Is the task too big? After all, there is only so much light one can let shine.

Is there more to it than that? Does letting our light shine encompass peace? I believe it does. It starts with our being at peace with God. For when we are at peace we are in service to God, a service in that our peace is a reflection of the divine peace. God does not let us use this peace for a time and then pull it away. No, not only does God give us this peace, but God leaves this peace with us in hopes that we will use it in our part of the world as a love message from God, like the lightning bug in the dead of night. The lightning bug's light does not blind the world because its light is not that strong. But to our surprise it breaks though the darkness to remind everyone who sees its little glow that God is watching over us and being afraid has no place in the believer's life.

Don't be surprised if you catch yourself humming the tune to the children's song that I invite you to break out into song now. Here are the words:

> *This little light of mine,* ⎫ 3x
> *I'm gonna let it shine.* ⎭
>
> *Let it shine, let it shine, let it shine.*

PRAYER: Father, thank you for the "light." We need you to let us know and understand that you are here with us in all your love, mercy, and glory. For when our confidence is in you, we too want to sing and let our little light shine. Amen.

Day 85
Like the Eagle

He does not faint or grow weary.... They who wait for the Lord shall renew their strength; they shall run and not be weary; they shall walk and not faint (Isaiah 40:19, 31).

WHILE AT THE TRAPPIST MONASTERY IN Gethsemane, I had walked up a hill and was looking out over the forest and pastures of the monastery, contemplating. As I sat there, there soon glided over my head an eagle. It was high in the sky and as I sat there in the silence watching it go up and down and side to side, I heard a voice. It said one word: "kettering." At first, I was startled, wondering if all the quiet solitude had gotten to me and that it was causing me to hear things. Could it be the voice of God, or was I just imagining it? As it turned out, it was none of these, but one of the monks, Brother Luke, walking up behind me. I looked at him rather quizzically because he was speaking to me. This was my first time at the monastery, and I thought they limited the amount of conversation they had with others. It is an atmosphere of silence they are to keep. We sat there together not speaking but watching the eagle as another one soared into the picture, both riding the currents of air effortlessly.

We sat there for a while before he spoke again. Kettering is when the eagle soars with wings fully outspread to catch the full force of the air currents. They were literally floating on air, very rarely, if at all, flapping their wings. Once in a while, the eagle shifted its tail feathers to change direction. After a few more moments, I turned and Brother Luke was back at the bottom of the rise we had to climb. He turned, waved, and then was gone. Our quiet time together caused my mind to rush to today's scripture. No one that I know of has ever gotten through life without some degree of weariness of spirit—and I include believers in that number as well—someone who has been so weak that he or she was unsure of taking the next step. None of us are, have, or will be exempt from this feeling of weariness.

I have not been able walk long distances or ride my bike for some time. I wanted to because I enjoyed it. It gave me time to be with God. It has been several months, and I am excited because I rode my bike two miles and walked another mile without falling or crashing. Boy, did it feel great. I hope all of you can take Isaiah's words to heart. The key is, "those who wait on the Lord," and I for one at times have little patience. I want it done yesterday, thank you very much. Wait. It's a holy wait, but look at the benefits we receive from waiting on the One who knows what we need, how much we need it, and when we need it. Let us soar together even if our feet don't leave the ground. Our hearts will effortlessly ride the currents of the Spirit and soar the heavens.

> **PRAYER:** Father, how gracious you are to us. Your care and provision are beyond words. We find renewed hope, love, and strength in your promise. Thank you for making it and for doing it. You are faithful! Amen.

⸺◁○▷⸺

Day 86
God's Part in Prayer

You are the one who hears prayers. . . . You are the one who forgives our rebellious acts. Everyone will come to you. . . . O God, our savior, the hope of all the ends of the earth . . . those who live at the ends of the earth are in awe of your miraculous signs. The hands of the morning sunrise and evening sunset sing joyfully (Psalm 65:2–3, 5, 9).

HETHER YOU ARE ON YOUR knees, sitting with your head bowed, eyes open, eyes closed, looking down, or looking up, most all of us are saying prayers. We are trying to get in touch with God.

There are a great many people who kneel down to say their prayers. They are trying to get into touch with God. But if these persons are Christian, they know what's prompting them to pray is also God—God, so to speak, inside them.

But they also know that all of their real knowledge of God comes through Christ, the man who was God, that Christ is standing beside, helping them to pray, praying for them. You see what is happening? God is the thing to which they are praying, the goal that they are trying to reach. God is also the thing inside them that is pushing them on: the motive power. God is also the road or bridge along which they are being pushed to that goal. So that the whole threefold life of the three-person being is actually going on in that ordinary little bedroom where an ordinary person is praying his or her prayers. The person is being caught up into a higher kind of life—what some call Zoë, or spiritual life. That person is being pulled into God by God, while still remaining himself or herself.

> **PRAYER:** O God, you call us to yourself by calling us into prayer with, through, and in you. Bring us to new life as we pray in secret and together. In Jesus' name, we pray. Amen.

Day 87
Turning up the Volume

Let the person who has ears listen (Matthew 11:15)!

THE TITLE OF TODAY'S DEVOTION IS inspired by that all too familiar Verizon television commercial that brags about the great reception they get, no matter where the guy in the black-rimmed glasses goes. He always asks, "Can you hear me now?" The same question can be put to everyone. Can you hear me now? For the unbeliever, deciding whether or not to follow Jesus, can you hear me now? For the believer who is deciding whether or not to give God all that they are and ever hope to be, just having a closer walk with him, can you hear me now?

Every person with Parkinson's disease could also utter these words. You see,

THE MUSINGS OF A WHOLLY MAN

PD has a tendency to make the vocal chords less responsive. Our speech becomes softer because the vocal chords bow out, making our speech garbled and allowing air to escape without sounding. The softness of our voice is due to the fact that we do not breathe deeply from our diaphragm; thus the voice softens even more. It is also common for us not to breathe deeply, which can lead to other health risks, like pneumonia.

Another factor that comes to play on our speech is the DBS (Deep Brain Stimulator) surgery. At least for me it has affected my speech in all the ways mentioned earlier, and I catch myself asking, "Can't you hear me?" Even our caretakers find it hard to understand us, and we folk with PD are pretty adept at knowing the answer to the question simply by looking at the expression on their faces.

This leaves us folk with PD with a few questions to answer: (1) Do we consult a speech therapist and work hard on our speech (Lee Silvermann is an excellent source and has created a program just for folk with Parkinson's)? (2) Do we ignore the confused looks on people's faces as if there isn't a problem, leaving both them and us frustrated and disappointed?

Let's take this to a higher plane and hear Jesus asking the questions as well as giving the answers. "Can you hear me now, telling you I am with you; telling you I will never leave you; that I love you and it hurts me to see you suffering; that I will fill your pain and suffering with my presence? You are not alone, never ever alone."

PRAYER: Thanks be to God for our Lord Jesus Christ, the great physician, and all his children: doctors, nurses, and researchers who are trying to find a cure for PD. Thanks to all of them, faithful ones. Amen.

Day 88
Do You Care?

Turn all your anxieties over to God, for he cares for you (1 Peter 5:7).

IT'S NOT ALWAYS EASY TO ride the carousel of our dreams with our hands tight upon the reins of our painted horse while all who are around us are grabbing for the brass ring. Could that be what Jesus was referring to when he encourages us to hunger and thirst after righteousness? Hunger in this instance is the unmet desire—or more to the point, choice to render a desire unmet—as a good way of being right with God. In hunger he intimates, we deepen our appreciation for what we have by heightening our awareness of what it means to do without what we've long taken for granted. Just ask anyone who has Parkinson's disease or a broken leg.

Jesus is teaching us to be hungry. Live more simply than you have to, if only just a bit. Put your relationship right with God by putting your relationship right with others. And put yourself in relationship with others by putting yourself second and them first. Allow yourself a little less so others might have a little bit more. Buy one less Christmas present and give the money to the poor. Watch one less television show and give a little time to your children. Pray for others before you pray for yourself. Cut out a meal this week, or maybe just a snack and use your savings to pick a few groceries for the local food pantry. Volunteer some time there. Visit the neighbor whom no one else can stand. Walk to work tomorrow for the sake of the air you breathe, let alone some exercise. Maybe you can follow one man's habit to take a cold bath once a week if only to remind yourself that you're *not* among the billions, who by necessity do so every night.

Navigating through this unfamiliar territory is difficult at first, like trying to find our way through a strange room at night. Here we are not accustomed to our new surroundings, having more doubt than trust, but with a little patience trust and doubt switch places and trust commands more territory.

The words of Tennessee Williams put flesh to the bone of what we are trying to say here. It is told that on his deathbed he said, "Redemption happens when a person puts himself aside to feel deeply for another."

PRAYER: Father, help us to grow a caring heart so we can brighten someone else's life better. Amen.

---◆〇◆---

Day 89
In the Hands of the Master

Your steadfast love, O Lord, endures forever. Do not forsake the work of your hands (Psalm 138:8).

THERE WAS A MAN AND A woman whose life together began after a long courtship, so sweetly and without blemish, whereas yet another couple's courtship was riddled with problems from the very beginning. Both couples had the world by the tail and lived life to the fullest. Then life started happening. Their businesses failed, she got sick, and his mother became ill. They had a lot to contend with. One couple handled the rough places well and maneuvered around them safely and without a great deal of stress, but the other couple didn't handle their rough places as well. And as is so often the case, they grew resentful and bitter as they grew older. With time, their image of an ideal life was disturbed because painful historical, political, personal, family, or financial realities broke through.

Your pain, seen in the light of a spiritual journey, can be interpreted. The great art is to gradually trust that life's interruptions are the places where you are being molded into the person you are called to be. I heard a potter say in reference to the passage in Jeremiah 18:

> You see, all the different pottery, we all have the same starting point: a chunk of clay. Without it, there would be no vessels. Interruptions are not disturbances of your way to holiness, but rather are places where you are being molded and formed into the person God calls you to be. You know you are living a grateful life when whatever happens is received as an invitation to deepen your heart, to strengthen your love, and to

broaden your hope. You are living a grateful life when something is taken away from you that you thought was so important and you find yourself willing to say, "Maybe I'm being invited to a deeper way of living."

PRAYER: O Lord, mold me and make me after your will. Amen.

◄○►

Day 90
It's Not Fair

For he makes his sun rise on the evil and on the good, and sends the rain on the just and unjust (Matthew 5:45).

IT ASTONISHES ME THAT BELIEVERS sometimes complain that a particular occurrence isn't fair in their lives. The tremor in the hands of a surgeon can cause him to reevaluate his career. A diva has to give up the opera because her voice has too many holes in it. A preacher has to give up the pulpit because people can no longer understand him. It's not fair, but all one needs to do is to read the scriptures. People should know better than to expect life to be fair. It causes one to wonder, have they not read the Psalmist, Job, Isaiah, and Jeremiah? One also pauses when remembering that in the short history of the Christian faith, there is the cross. Have folk forgotten that the symbol of the cross is the symbol of human suffering? When people's expectations of fairness are disappointed, a sense of grievance and resentment occasionally erupts. It might even cause them to start to have a pity party, feeling sorry for themselves, and there is no energy gained in that. Self-pity robs us of our courage, deprives us of the very fortitude we need to deal with life's injustices.

Life is not fair, but it can be splendid, and it is made so by those who refuse to yield to self-pity and keep their courage so as not to cast away the hero in their souls. Miguel de Unamuno caught its sense perfectly when he wrote, "May God deny you the peace that He may give you glory."

118

PRAYER: Life can change so quickly and for the worst, and we wonder, *Why did this happen to me? I'm a good person. What about all the riffraff out there who seem to get all the breaks?* Then we remember that you love everyone and wish no one to perish. God, give us your heart and spirit in the name of Christ, we pray. Amen.

——◇——

Day 91
Once upon a Time

Blessed are those who receive help from the God of Jacob. Their hope rests on the Lord their God (Psalm 146:5).

I will look up towards the mountains (Psalm 121:1).

WHEN I WAS GROWING UP, children's books mostly began with, "Once upon a time," and concluded with, "And they live happily ever after," exempt of problems, frustrations, and disappointments. My goodness, what a fantasy!

We are often faced with having to resolve problems over and over again. After solving one, we restart down the road of "happily ever after," and suddenly we crash and burn, one challenge after another. When I lived in Arkansas, my morning walks or bike rides concentrated on the distance of the ride. I did not have to exert a great deal of effort because the terrain was mostly flat with a small hill here and there. But since moving back to North Carolina, the walks and rides have become a bit more demanding because Lenoir is at the foothills of the Blue Ridge Mountains. You can imagine the challenges of terrain: you got it, more hills. Steeper ones are more demanding, calling on more body effort, and causing more strain on the leg muscles.

Can you imagine how flabby our spiritual lives would become if our lives were pitfall-free, always smooth, never a challenge or problem to face?

As the muscles in my legs are strengthened from my walking and bike riding, so the challenges and problems I have to face day-to-day keep me aware of the avenues and channels left open by God. They are there to give an opportunity to respond to the challenge. If we listen to the challenges we face, we will be strengthened and guided by the divine presence of God, whose company reminds us that we don't have to face the challenges alone. Life might not mean trouble just "once upon a time," but it can be lived, "happily ever after" through the grace, mercy, and joy that Jesus Christ gives.

> **PRAYER:** Father, you are the God of peace and provision. Keep sending us the little hills to climb, those challenges us that keep us alive, growing, and moving. We want to keep growing in our service to you and to our neighbors, as well as to our enemies. Amen.

Day 92
The Great One

Of all the people ever born, no one is greater than John the Baptizer (Matthew 7:11).

HERE WE HAVE THE STORY OF John the Baptizer, who is said to have been the forerunner of the Messiah. Radiating vitality and speaking with flaming syllable and burning word, John moved through wilderness wearing clothes of camel hair and living on an acetic diet of locusts and wild honey. He boldly announced that Jesus was there to take away the sin(s) of the world.

Then came the birthday of King Herod, and when Salome asked for the Baptizer's head, John was captured and put in Herod's dark prison. A condemned man awaiting his execution, the Baptizer wanted to know that his preaching, "Repent, for the kingdom of God is at hand," was not just empty words and that his introduction of Jesus as "the Lamb of God that takes away the sin(s) of the world," was not a hoax. He sent his people to ask Jesus if he indeed was the one or whether there was to be another.

The question is understandable. Perhaps John could hear the executor sharpening his scimitar. He wanted the light of sun and stars, not flickering shore lights. He had lost the cadence and music of the Jesus way. But the question, "Are you the real thing?" is somewhat embarrassing. Imagine such a thing being filed away in John's credentials for all the people of subsequent centuries to read. Yet that little vignette touches our human hearts. Half of us are always on the Mount of Transfiguration, whereas the other is half in the shadowed valley.

As I grow older, I value a fundamental honesty that is willing to face up to life's dissonances as well as its harmonies. The kingdom of God is made up of a wonderful company of joyous possessors and tormented seekers. Which are you?

By no means do I wish to create the impression that one goes through life always hovering on the edges of doubt, fear, and tentativeness, unwilling and unable to make firm commitments to act. One of the great hallmarks of an authentic Christian life style is the willingness and courage to risk adventure, seeking no security save the garrisoning of grace.

> PRAYER: Father, help us to be more like the Baptizer who, when faced with doubt and waning hope sent to Jesus for his answer. What he found was reason not to give up hope. There he found the answer that renewed his hope and the courage enabled him to face Herod's sword. Help us to learn that with you there is always hope, no mater how dark our dungeon might become. Amen.

————◄ ◇ ►————

Day 93
Fanned into Flame

I strive to keep my conscience clear before God and man (Acts 24:16).

SHAME IS A FLAME FROM THE glowing embers of our original fire. You remember that time when we first became believers, and we felt that we could change or save the world. We even felt like we could take on the devil and all his minions singlehandedly by sunset, thank you very much. Fresh from a victory or two, we were hit with the reality as it raises its ugly head, and we had no other choice than to realize that we couldn't do it alone. We were shocked and caught off guard to realize that there were actually some people who didn't want to hear anything about conversion, God, Jesus, or anything else of a religious nature. With the negative taste still in our mouths, we became not so strident. The flame began to die down and lose some of its heat. Yet the embers did not go out completely. They smolder, and the heat continues to burn at the core of our lives, still shines in our memories, glimmers in our hope, and invites us to be one with God again.

Shame gives us a little nudge from our true selves. We look for this so-called true self. It's there, we know, hiding somewhere inside us, like a forgotten ghost that haunts us with the memories of the self we used to be. How do those embers of our true self get its message to us? There are several ways. Some of us receive it directly from our conscience. Some of us receive it from the lives, witness, and stories that surround the saints who have gone before us—*Since we are surrounded by so many examples of faith* (Heb 12:1). Some of us learn from what wise and profound minds have taught us. All of us have the opportunity to obtain the message because the divine hasn't given up on us yet. The Spirit prods, pushes, nudges, and shoves us with the intimations of the better self we have been created to be when we are in a right relationship with God. God holds the standard high before us and there is no compromise.

> **PRAYER:** Father in heaven, we need your help to discover, perhaps for the first time, our true selves. Let the wind of the Spirit begin to blow against the glowing embers of our souls, until there is a tiny flame leaping up with other glowing embers building that

once-smoldering pile of wood into an inferno that cleanses like the refiner's fire. We are unable to reach your standards alone, but with the help of you Son and the Spirit, we are able to not only reach the bar but clear it. In the name of the one who makes it possible, Jesus Christ, our Lord. Amen.

⫷◇⫸

Day 94
Facing the Facts

Jesus started to indicate to his disciples that he must go to Jerusalem and suffer greatly there (Matthew 16:21).

ODAY, ALL IT TAKES IS one look in someone's medicine cabinet to see how far we would go to keep from having any pain. The slightest discomfort and we make a beeline Íto the medicine cabinet to get whatever we need to take the edge off our discomfort. Most of us don't have a high pain threshold—most of us really don't know what our pain threshold is thanks to the pharmaceutical companies who provide their products to lessen our reason for having to know. These pharmaceutical companies expend huge amounts of money to convince us we don't have to live with pain. We as a people will do just about anything to ward off any type of suffering. Some folk believe that becoming a believer and trusting God with one's life will make one immune to any suffering. But that is not the message Jesus left with us. In fact, Jesus tells us that a believer's life is the opposite. He says that we are more likely to experience suffering and pain when we become believers than not.

Once Jesus set his face to go Jerusalem, there was no turning back for him. Jesus faces his suffering and death directly, and he asks his disciples to face theirs the same way. Usually, we think of only the twelve hearing Jesus's encouragement, but I have not really explored that possible train of thought. If it is to be so, then we too should be included in the number. After all, if there were not others listening to Jesus, then why was a Roman cohort plus all he religious leaders of the Sanhedrin sent to arrest one simple carpenter who had shone no leanings toward fighting or violence?

Jesus, knowing what was about to take place, told his disciples how they should react to the coming of their suffering and death and to follow his example. Jesus never predicted an easy road for his disciples or himself. Jesus went against the human inclination to avoid suffering and death, but his followers realized it was better to face up to the truth.

Suffering and death were partners along the narrow road of Jesus. Jesus does not glorify them or call them beautiful, good, or something to be desired. Jesus does not call for heroism or suicidal self-sacrifice. No. Jesus invites us to look at the reality of our existence and reveals this harsh reality as the way to new life. The core message of Jesus is that joy and peace can never be reached by bypassing suffering and death, but only by passing right through them.

We can deny the reality of life or we can face it. We face it with the eyes of Jesus. We discover that where we least expect it, something is hidden that holds a promise stronger than death itself. Jesus lived his life in the trust that God's love is stronger than death and that death therefore does not have the last word.

PRAYER: Father, your way is not going to be easy, but with the help of your Spirit we will emerge victorious. Amen.

Day 95
Hearts in Conflict

My eyes have seen your salvation. . . . He is a light that will reveal salvation to the nations and bring glory to your people Israel (Luke 2:32).

*W*HAT DOES IT TAKE TO BE really ready to die? When his parents brought Jesus to the Temple, Simeon took him in his arms and blessed him. What a beautiful scene we have: Simeon standing there in the middle of the hustle and bustle of people carrying on whatever business they had at the Temple. He took the child in his arms, and whereas the crowds were totally oblivious to the holy moment that was taking place in their midst, Simeon offered his prayer of blessing for the baby of the world. There was the quietness of the blessing while all the others in the Temple carried on their business. Some things never change, do they? Following the blessing, Simeon told God that he was now ready to die, for his eyes had seen the Messiah. Now he was ready to die because he had seen that power in the face of the Christ child and because he had seen total peace and love in the face of that baby. He was holding God's salvation in his arms.

God's salvation: not the false salvation of power and connivance born out of fear, which is not salvation at all, but God's salvation, the salvation of love.

It's a difficult theme to teach. It puts our hearts in conflict. We've got to arm ourselves against all the forces of the world that are pitted against us. That is the darkness of this world. But Simeon's readiness shows us the light shining *through* the darkness, even though the world's darkness will always be here. We can love each other through that darkness, for we, too, have seen the Christ child, both in his cradle and on his cross.

And do you know where I see that light shining? I see it when I look into your eyes. That's where it is: when we look into each other's eyes. If it does not shine there, where else will it shine?

PRAYER: O God, this little light of mine, I'm going to let it shine. Everyday, I'll let my little light shine. Thank you. Amen.

Day 96
Prayers Like Lead Balloons

Never stop praying. Whatever happens, give thanks (1 Thessalonians 5:17).

HERE ARE TIMES DURING OUR spiritual journey that our prayers seem to take on some serious weight. You know the times I am talking about: those times when the words we utter do not seem to reach beyond the ceiling of the room in which we are. And if they can't travel that short distance, there is no way that they will reach "up" to God. Soon, if we aren't careful, we lose patience, and the only motivation we have to go into our closet is to hang up some of our clothes. Why does this happen? Have we done something we should not have or not done something we should have done? Is this a stumbling block to our listenability to hear God's response? What would keep our prayers from soaring into the heavens for God to hear and respond?

Purity of heart, a concept advocated by the Danish philosopher, Søren Kierkegaard, is one way to combat our low-hovering prayers. It is a profoundly interior experience. It is the bliss that attends when we hoist the weight of our worries from our shoulders and commune in blessed simplicity with a God whose only concern is that we have none, who lifts our kite and lets it soar unencumbered by the tug of baser impulses. The only way we can experience this purity of heart—we can do nothing to earn it—is to receive God's gift of mercy. Mercy is nothing if not finding our own pain mirrored in the pain of a fallen world.

Another way to achieve this high soaring prayer is to ask God to grant us peace but really, in our heart of hearts, trying to dictate its terms.

Yet another way to reach this goal is to mature in our prayer life. To understand this better, let's hear the advice of Harry Emerson Fosdick, who penned these words: "If we stop asking God to 'give us . . .' and instead ask God to 'change us,' then our prayers will take on a different look."

The next morning, I promise to do better, to be at peace with anyone I encounter that day, but I quickly renege when I see the guy with twelve items at the supermarket's "ten only" checkout line. Then I feel ashamed, petty, and not a little embarrassed at my petulance over something so small and stupid.

Whether bridled by a reluctant conscience, a fear to change, or simply the childish impulses to satisfy my own desires at the expense of others. I find that making peace is truly one of the most daunting tasks.

Which isn't to say that it's impossible; it's just not reflective. We must, as a child in the meadow, anticipate, prepare, and assume a disposition that allows for peace.

> **PRAYER:** O God, may we learn from the saints of old as well as the contemporary saints the importance of coming before you with purity of heart. We are guilty of having too many distractions when our prayers seem to hang in the air and generate nothing to help our situation. Help us to follow Paul's admonishment not to stop praying no matter what, as well as Kierkegaard's advice of this one thing I do. If we are persistent, our prayers will become lighter than light and go straight to God. Amen.

———— ◇ ————

Day 97
The One in Last Place Wins!

I can guarantee this truth: whatever you failed to do for one of my brothers or sisters, no matter how unimportant they seemed, you failed to do for me (Matthew 25:45).

ALKING DOWN CENTRAL PARK WEST IN New York City late one evening, I could see each of the benches being transformed into sleeping quarters for the homeless of the city. They lie on the bench, arm or coat as a pillow, exposed to the thousands who are oblivious as they pass by to go to their comfortable homes. They surround themselves with everything they own. Much like the covered wagons of the pioneer days, a grocery cart, an abandoned wagon, large garbage bags, and broken, discarded suitcases act as repositories in which they store their precious finds. Like the pioneers of old, they carry with them everything they posses in this world. I could not help but be saddened by it.

I was pondering this last night after being awakened, as one little girl in Greenwich said was God clearing his voice, by a loud thunderstorm. Have you lain in your bed in the dark during a thunderstorm? The sudden burst of light from a lightning flash catches the family pictures on the dresser. One can feel the wall shake with each clap of thunder. Yet one is surrounded by the reassurance of those things that are familiar. When we have bad weather, we have a shelter. When, like an old dog, we need a place where we can lick our wounds after bad things happen, we have it to go or retire to. All of this we have, whereas thousands of people—a lot of whom are children—sleep on park benches, traverse the dark streets of our cities, and search for some nook or cranny to enter in order to ride out the storm.

Here's an interesting turn: Perhaps we need to expand our definition of homelessness. Surprisingly enough, these people might not be the only ones who are homeless. So consider this: Could it not be said of us that we are homeless when we have homes but are really not at home in them? The only way we can have real homes is for peace to abide. Yet that peace cannot be experienced until there is some feeling of real peace for all of us. When we turn an insensitive eye from the deep needs of others, whether they live on the streets or under our own roofs, and when we close our eyes to our own deep need to reach out to them, we can never be fully at home anywhere.

PRAYER: God, help us never to turn an insensitive eye and heart to anyone. We are all fellow travelers, passing through this world to our home that awaits us, built by none other than Jesus himself. Amen.

Day 98
Highly Unlikely

But the Lord told Samuel, "Don't look at his appearance or how tall he is, because I have rejected him. God does not see as humans see. Humans look at the outward appearances, but the Lord looks into the heart" (1 Samuel 16:7).

HUMOR IS AN IMPORTANT NECESSITY that helps us cope with life. Much to the shock of some of my conservative and fundamentalist friends, Jesus had a sense of humor. If you want to question God's sense of humor, sit down in a park or go to the mall and observe the people as they walk by. And if that is not enough to convince you, go look in a mirror. It is not a negative reflection on God's holiness and majesty. God has an immense sense of humor, which is recognition of the amazing way God works in human affairs. Simply put, God is seldom impressed with our definitions of what is important.

God chooses not to recognize how we categorize people or the way(s) in which we believe God should respond to certain situations. This is borne out in some choices God made early in history, some of which were very humorous. God chose Amos, a mere shepherd, to be a spokesperson; God used the pagan King Cyrus to execute justice; God called a teenage girl to give us the Christ; and God used uneducated fishermen to establish the church. It is penned that the most unlikely people are chosen by God in order to make us see.

It is sad but true that more times than not we miss the message because we have a problem with the unlikely mouthpieces of God or because we are reminded of our shortcomings or such folk are unacceptable and therefore not credible and worthy of our attention. Yet from someone young in the faith, we can hear wisdom from the secular prophets, we can hear legitimate criticisms of the church from the poor, we hear God's cry for justice, and from those who have suffered much we can frequently hear words of graciousness and forgiveness.

Yes, we do have the tendency to pass judgment on how one looks on the outside rather than where a person is on the inside. Folk with Parkinson's can certainly adhere to that wholeheartedly. People watch as we drop food from our utensils, have difficulty swallowing, or have a very visible tremor.

One can easily see how important these voices are, including those of God's unlikely spokespersons, if we wish to hear all that God might want to say to us. The difficulty is usually not a lack of voices, but rather a lack of discernment in listening to what we most urgently need to hear.

> **PRAYER:** Father, help us not to take ourselves but your message extremely seriously. Give us the freedom to laugh at our own short-comings, and may the redeemed of the Lord look and act redeemed. Amen.

────◄○►────

Day 99
Highly Unlikely

As Christ was brought back from death to life by the glorious power of the Father, so we, too, should live a new kind of life. If we've become united with him in a death like his, certainly we will also be united with him in a resurrection like his (Romans 6:4–5).

THIS TEXT FROM ROMANS SPEAKS TO that strange and mysterious mixture of glory and pain, of life and death. Perhaps we used to think that we knew that some things were right and some things were wrong. Now, the things that we used to think were right are either not quite right and even a little bit wrong, whereas the things that we used to thing were wrong are either not quite so wrong and are even a little bit right.

What has happened? We have failed to recall that we have to be willing to sacrifice something before we can get anywhere. We've got to be willing to start losing before we can begin to win. We've got to be willing to die before we can really live. Those that heard Jesus speak this way thought that he was crazy, and Jesus said he would prove it. That was the day he set his face like flint toward Jerusalem.

In order for us to remember what Jesus was telling his followers means that we have to make his words real, present, potent, demanding, here and now. We are to remember, and by our remembering, Jesus is real and alive in and through us.

Two principles we might live by are self-interest and self-giving. Which principle is it going to be? Either way, it's going to mean sacrifice. I don't know about you, but I know that for me there is a bit of me that is hypocritical, greedy, resentful, and bitter. I have to throw all that away and bury it for the love of Christ. Yes, it is going to mean sacrifice: sacrifice of privilege; and beyond all of my fear, I have a love and a longing for a quality life both personal and sacred.

When we live that kind of life, however inadequate, when we die to the painful death of self-interest, the life we come to experience is beyond words. It is a glimpse of heaven. To live that quality of life, we must be like a grain of wheat, buried and dying in order to give for there to be a rich harvest. As we share in Christ's sacrifice, we share in his death, and we shall we share in his life.

PRAYER: Father, grant to us the courage to join with your Son on the cross. He bore the cross for our sins that we could have life everlasting. Help us to be willing to make that commitment—not with empty words, but with words aflame with commitment. Amen.

Day 100
Down for the Count?

God can guard you that you don't fall and so that you can be full of joy (Jude 24).

ONE OF THE MOST COMMON problems people with Parkinson's have is inability to maintain balance, which can cause us to fall, sometimes causing injury. I have fallen quite a few times, as I am certain that others of you have. I have fallen down stairs, fallen while getting in and out of my car, fallen while trying to move something alone, fallen while trying to carry too much, and the list could go on. The falls might have been avoided if I had been more careful. Other falls, however, cannot be avoided at all with all the care I can muster. They just occur with out any warning at all. I suddenly lose balance, and down I go. Someone's attempt to be humorous encouraged folk with Parkinson's to make friends with the floor because we will be on it enough. Suggestion: While you are on the floor, take a few moments to do a quick inventory of what is down there, especially under a bed or couch. You might be surprised by what is found.

Once the dust has settled from a fall, I stay and mentally go through my checklist of what moves and works and what doesn't, as well as where I am. I remain there until I finish my checklist to inspect for any possible injuries. Once I am satisfied, I rise and take care of any cleanup, if necessary. I am usually sore from the fall for about two to four days afterward.

All of my falls have really been minor, except for one. I went on my morning walk/jog and had not gone very far before I realized I would not be getting any help from my legs that morning. When it started to rain I headed back to the house. Before reaching the house I had fallen five times on the highway— thank God it was very early, and folk around there had not left for work. The doctor told me the excruciating pain coming from my left wrist was caused by shattered bones there. I had surgery in which the doctor said it was like putting together a jigsaw puzzle to repair it. I left the hospital the proud owner of a six inch scar starting at my wrist, a titanium plate, four screws, and two anchors. It would have been an extremely horrible experience that day if the medical staff at the hospital had not been so great. I have full use of that wrist and hand. Now, I listen to my body more.

Yes, there are things you can do to help reduce the number of falls, thus preventing the major injuries. Wouldn't it be great not to fall at all? We must trust the promise. In the book of Jude we find it to be a comfort to know that God is guarding us to keep us from a fall. I don't about you but I can see where this would bring extreme peace, comfort, and joy, preventing any major injury.

PRAYER: Father, thank you for your love for us, for watching over us and for the comfort that that brings. Amen.

[Ask your doctor for some possibilities of how you can "fall-proof" your home.]

—◁◇▷—

Day 101
Do It All for Love

The person who doesn't love doesn't know God because God is love (1 John 4:3).

LIFE WAS A BURDEN FOR Vincent Van Gogh, the Impressionist painter. We gather this from reading the letters he wrote to his brother, Theo. The massive amount of letters is intimate, as he and his brother shared their hearts with one another. From these letters we have a portrait of Vincent slowly coming into focus. He had health problems, depression, epilepsy, and seizures. These letters reveal a very troubled man, who was lonely and starved for companionship and love.

He did not think very highly of the clergy of his day and thought they were as dead as a doornail. That doesn't make him an atheist, except with the clergy that saw him as such. All that Vincent wanted was to love and be loved. He penned these words, "A great fire burns within me, but no one stops to warm themselves at it, and passers-by only see a wisp of smoke."* This caused me to ask myself, "Do I pass by someone in need of my attention or go by the great fire and warm myself?" Do you?

Vincent was a man of great passion, a passion that he believed could only be obtained by loving many things, people especially. He writes,

> [There] is nothing more truly artistic than to love people. I think that everything that is really good and beautiful, the inner, moral, spiritual, and sublime beauty in men and their works, comes from God.**

The opposite, he holds, doesn't come from God, and for good measure, he adds that God doesn't approve of that.

Two years later in another letter to his brother, Theo, Vincent advises, "What is done in love is done well. . . . This is my ambition, which is in spite of everything founded less on anger and more on love."† Should this not be our ambition, too?

> **PRAYER:** Father, help us to grasp the importance of love in every aspect of our life. Give us courage to even love the unlovely as you have loved us. Amen.

* Letter from Vincent van Gogh to Theo van Gogh, Cuesmes, July 1880.
** Ibid.
† Letter from Vincent van Gogh to Theo van Gogh, The Hague, 21 July 1882.

Day 102
When the Way Becomes Dark

God didn't spare his own Son but handed him over to death for all of us. So God will also give us every thing with him (Romans 8:32).

WHEN IT BECOMES DARK ALL around us, and it will, one thing we can do is to hold on to what we know. Life can, at times be very difficult. Even in the most trying times, men and women can put down what they know. We may be surprised at how much we know. God might give us a job to do, a goal to reach. In looking for our destination, we might not be able to see it, but we must realize that before we can reach our goal or do our job, our first step is waiting to be done. We can't always take the first step.

When the dark is darker still, we can remember what we know, and that will make all the difference in the world. We know that life can be very bewildering at times, and it can be very wounding at times. Sometimes it is difficult to even see a sense in doing it. There are many things that seem to have no explanation, and some of those very things must remain wrapped in the cloak of mystery.

As Jesus hung on the cross, he was in excruciating pain from the beatings and his mistreatment. Stumbling most of the way up the hill outside the city's gate to be hung on a cross between two thieves, two things Jesus knew. Jesus knew he must accept God's will, and he knew that the name of the God, whose will he must accept, was Father. Sometimes, it will be like that for us. We know the darkness of our lives and that there are times when the end is out of sight even though the next step is there. One step is enough for me.

PRAYER: O God, our Father, as the darkness creeps in, help us to hold on to what we know: that you are the creator God who loves us unconditionally. Help us to remember that you have already won the battle. Amen.

Day 103
Are You Happy?

And Jesus began to teach them (Matthew 5:2).

ARE YOU HAPPY? I'M NOT talking about a happiness that the world considers happiness. I am talking about a happiness that transcends anything this world offers or will ever be able to offer. I am talking about the type of happiness in which everything that is falling down around your feet, when the word of the day is "chaos," and on the inside your soul is at peace and is smiling, whether or not you are smiling on the outside. I'm afraid the world can't understand the smiling of the soul and the peace that comes with it. So the world goes back to the drawing table, back to itself to explore the options it has. Where does the world go to search out these answers? Does it go back to search its own offerings for meaningful living? Or does it try and come up with some new product to convince folk it will bring them true happiness, anything that we give it the heads-up for what is needed to be content?

The "gospel" for today's market-driven world announces that happiness is pencil-thin models showing off expensive designer clothes. Happiness is a fast car. Happiness is popularity gained by the use of several plastic surgeries, lotions to keep the skin young-looking, dyes to keep the hair looking "natural," breath mints, toothpaste, and deodorants. The marketing folk know the weaknesses of the world today and that is what they drive home. Some claim the world says that happiness is in whatever you can buy and that we are to immediately get it!

Jesus had a different slant on this, which is strange in the eyes of the world. He says that blessedness, or happiness, is in humility, gentleness, giving, forgiving, justice, peacemaking, and righteousness. It sounds rather tame and mild. It is certainly not like dancing on the table because you have the most popular diet cola in the country.

No one enjoys being pushed around by arrogant people, or having to step into the middle of a fight to make peace, or seeing another take credit for his or her achievements. Jesus tells of happiness transcending the outward appearances of life. It is the inner condition of spirit by which we know true values such as serenity, love, faith, and good relationships. To live by such values gives us the most exhilarating experiences life has to offer.

Let me ask you: *Are you truly happy?*

> **PRAYER:** O God of Love, whose way is truth, we give you thanks for every experience by which we might witness to your grace and peace. In the name of Jesus Christ our Lord, we pray. Amen.

----◄◦►----

Day 104
The First Mile

And if any one forces you to go one mile, go with him two miles (Matthew 5:41).

ONE SYMPTOM OF PARKINSON'S DISEASE IS that of a person "freezing," usually in a doorway. Such a one remains there immobile until what ever force was holding him or her there is broken and he or she can take a step. Other sufferers of PD have to be so deliberate that they catch themselves sliding or shuffling their feet rather than taking steps. Taking the first step can be difficult for someone who doesn't have PD, as well. Moving one's feet might seem to be a minor thing for most. Allow me to suggest that it is a major thing for everyone.

You can read a great deal in religious literature about going the second mile. With the words first spoken by our Lord they are words that demand attention, and we should heed their bidding. The lesson that we all can glean from our Lord's words is that all of our actions should bear witness to the goodness within us and should be without limit. In pondering this statement, something strikes me about which I can't find a great deal of extra reading and discussion, and that is the importance of going the *first* mile. Going the first mile is extremely important. Without it there would be no hope for a second mile in order to demonstrate goodness. Our morality, however heroic, begins with honesty, truthfulness, kindness, and being a good neighbor.

If we were to go the first mile wherever we find ourselves living, the lives in those cities, towns, and communities would be transformed immediately. Life would be safer and more pleasant, and everybody would be more prosperous. Because if you were to make a comparison study you would find that going the first mile is rather staggering. We can never go the second mile without taking the first one.

PRAYER: Heavenly Father, you have called us to go the second mile, which is difficult because many times we go the first mile reluctantly. Give us the courage to be willing to go an extra mile with a cheerful heart. Amen.

Day 105
When All Else Fails

Be joyful in hope, patient in affliction, and faithful in prayer (Romans 12:12).

EVERY DAY CALLS FOR US TO make a decision. There are some people who have made the decision not to decide anything at all. They have long since relinquished the opportunity, relieving themselves of any of the fallout either positive or negative that they might incur from having made the initial decision. And there are some who knowingly make decisions every day. Some are made unconsciously, and some are not made until a great deal of time, thought, and due process has been given to the details of that decision. Depending upon the decision that is made, resolutions color our existence, even the living out of our days. Along our spiritual journey, one major decision we all are faced with is whether we will live in hope or in despair.

In your walk of life, there are many people—you might know some—who live with little or no hope. A lot of people with Parkinson's disease fall into this category. Those who have no hope and live in despair usually can be detected in their demeanor, the way they carry themselves, their posture, even the expressions on their faces. They appear to be frightened, not exactly sure of themselves, like a deer caught in the headlights of a car. A hesitancy encompasses even the blinking—or lack of blinking—of their eyes. They are scared and look at life with a sadness that taints everything.

On the other side of the coin, those with hope live better than people who inhabit despair. They are so much happier. They respond more effectively to crises. They are stricken but not crushed by tragedy. When everything good about life shakes them at the foundations and they cannot be sure of what will happen next, they turn their eyes to the possibility that something good can still come of it—a friend would comment on this by reminding us that we can turn every negative into a positive—and then they act on the possibilities of rescuing some good out of it all. These folk don't stop with themselves; they often do the hoping for their families, their children, and their friends, and pull the others through the tough times by the infectious force of their hope.

People with Parkinson's are an especially good example. They can go through their day looking on the bright side of life, and with their positive attitude touch the lives of those they meet, even those folk who do not have Parkinson's.

May God's grace help make us to become infected with this hope.

> PRAYER: God of those who have hope, we ask that you empower us to live our lives so that those in despair can be delivered to lives of hope and joy. Amen.

Day 106
God's Permanent "Senior Moment"

Because I will forgive their wickedness and I will no longer hold there against them (Jeremiah 31:34).

He is the one who forgives all your sins, heals all your diseases, the one who rescues your life from the pit. As far as the east is from the west, that is how far he has removed our rebellious acts from himself (Psalm 103:12).

THERE ARE VERY FEW DAYS that go by when we don't hear someone say, or you think to yourself, "Wait, I'm having a senior moment." What folk are saying is that their memory is not what it used to be. There are times that a great deal more effort and concentration is needed to recall some particular memory.

As we age, we do begin to lose some brainpower and become forgetful. Therefore, if we experience any lapse in memory or thought, it is attributed to growing older and not being as sharp as we once were. If we are honest with ourselves, we must admit that it is true a line can be drawn from one to the other. It is clear that the trail from the brain to the mouth sometimes becomes congested, and verbal traffic is thus slower. We don't like it, but it is a truth about aging. The older we get, the more likely our memory will fade.

But there is a time when a senior moment is welcome and that is in our relationship with God. We all have sinned and fallen short of the glory of God. God doesn't stop there. Whereas we might make light of someone having a senior moment, we don't do so when it comes to the spiritual part of our life. God doesn't make light of our shortcomings. Instead, we confess our sins and shortcomings. Scripture says God throws it as far as the East is to the West, never to remember them again, which means that if we sincerely ask God to forgive us for a sin that we have committed, God will not only forgive us but will also throw it away and will not bring it back up at a later date. God remembers them no more.

The one responsible for this is Jesus Christ. He left his home in glory and came to earth as one of us, lived, died, was resurrected, and ascended into heaven where he sits at the right hand of the Father, making intercession for us. The text tells us that while we were sinners Christ died for us.

The next time that you have a senior moment and your mind clears, thank God for God's love and mercy as well as for your deliverance.

PRAYER: Faithful Father, not only did you provide a way for our sins to be forgiven. You gave us the reason and the way to accomplish this. Thank you, God; thank you, Jesus; thank you, Holy Spirit. Amen.

⟨◇⟩

Day 107
Our Hearts' Desire

Sir, we would like to meet Jesus (John 12:22).

A GREAT MANY OF US have put ourselves in situations in which we agreed to do something and, although we thought nothing of it at the time, as it got closer to the actual day; we began questioning our mental stability. We couldn't help but feel a little anxious. What on God's earth possessed us to agree to such a task? We were quickly coming to understand what someone meant when they said they have "butterflies." It felt as though all the Monarch butterflies paused on their migration to South America in the pit of your stomach. As the time drew closer we each found ourselves asking, "What was I thinking to ever agree to do this?"

Little did I realize that I would find myself in a situation such as this. As I hung up the telephone from speaking with Dr. Gardner C. Taylor and accepting his invitation to preach at the Concord Baptist Church of Christ in Brooklyn, New York, it hit me like a ton of bricks: I would be preaching in Dr. Taylor's church, and he would be there. Talking about questioning one's decision. It was going to be my thirtieth birthday. The big day arrived, and I was treated in such high fashion. Worship began and the butterflies reminded of their presence. As the sanctuary choir was singing "Leaning on the Everlasting Arms," Dr. Taylor leaned over and said, "When you are ready, stand up and they will stop. I stood up with every nerve ending in my body pulsating. I walked to the pulpit and my heart leapt to my throat, for in the floor of that pulpit were the words written in Luke: "Sir we would like to see Jesus." I was speechless.

For those of you who unfamiliar with Dr. Taylor, here is a very brief biography: Dr. Taylor was pastor of the same church, the 17,000-member Concord Baptist Church of Christ for forty-two years. He is a much sought-after preacher who received numerous honorary doctorates from some of the most prestigious institutions in the world. He was called by Time magazine the "Dean of Black Ministers." Now, perhaps, you can understand my anxiety. From that time since, our friendship has grown; I preached three more times In Concord Church—perhaps they wanted to see if I ever got it right. We prayed together weekly until recently, when his good and bad days determine for us the length of our conversation.

That is what it is all about it, isn't it? People who are in search of the words of life want and need to see Jesus. We never know when someone comes to us and asks the same question. And yes, we should be ready to give an account. After all, our heart's desire is to "see Jesus" and to show people to him.

PRAYER: Father, keep us ready to answer the request the Gentiles asked of the apostles, showing in both word and deed that we know where Jesus is, realizing all the while that they, like us, are simply "one beggar showing another beggar where the bread is." Amen.

Day 108
Uniquely You

These things have I spoken to you, that my joy may be in you, and that your joy may be full (John 15:11).

As I was watching a suspense movie, I thought it quite interesting to see that the writer of this movie had gone to great lengths to include special gadgets that would let those in power know you were who you said you were. He had included a retina scan, hand scanner, and another scanner in which one stood much like those used at our airports. The remaining parts of one's body were checked out, including the earlobe. If any features failed to match what was in the computer, the person was interrogated. All of that security just to prove one was who one professed to be.

Now here is an assignment: Go look in the mirror, and as you look closely you will realize that there is no other person in the world just like you. There has never been and will never be anyone like you, even if you are one part of identical twins. *You are uniquely you.*

Even if you could have the exact DNA make-up, it still wouldn't work because of the effect of the environment in which you are raised and the family you have. The experiences you share will influence you differently. You don't have the same lusts, loves, hates, fears, and anxieties as someone else. You are you, and no one else is just like you. You are yourself, and there never has been, never can be, someone who is just like you. Neither is there anyone else on earth that can fill your place in the world.

If our physical makeup is unique, then what about our personal and spiritual makeup? God has shown a desire for a personal relationship with us, as God and we are unique. Thus it follows that our personal relationship with God will be uniquely ours. There are things, people, places, and events that can only be made good and positive with our participation. As one elderly man told me once, "Your life is the only key that will open the lock of someone else's heart."

There are people who will respond to your uniqueness in a healing, holistic way. This way of life, even our prayers, is something unique about ourselves.

That being said, when this world is no longer and we go before the judgment seat by ourselves, the question will not be asked, "Why weren't you like Billy Graham, or Norman Vincent Peale, or Paul or Peter?" We will be asked, "Why were you not yourself?" You might have had good and bad influences that have steered you down their path of life, but in the end you are responsible for yourself, for you are you and no one can take your place.

> **PRAYER:** Dear God, we say we want a relationship with you and then question whether or not we deserve it. We say we want to help the poor and others in need, and then we decide the sacrifice is too great. You provide all we need to be in relationship with you. We are made acceptable through the life, death, and resurrection of your Son, Jesus, in whose name we pray. Amen.

Day 109
Who Needs Forgiveness?

God used his power to give Jesus the highest position as leader and savior. He did this to lead the people of Israel to him, to change the way they think and act, and to forgive their sins (Acts 5:31).

WOULD YOU WANT GOD'S JOB? Isn't it a relief not to be God? Just think of all the millions of prayers and requests, both legitimate and frivolous, offered up to God by billions of people. By a frivolous prayer, I mean something like, "O Lord, if you help me to win the lottery I'll give you your share." On the other side of the coin, a legitimate prayer would be, "O God, please guide the medical staff as they perform surgery on my friend's cancer." The difference comes from where we believe that we stand in relationship to God. Are we a changed people, or are we the same as we were fifteen or twenty years ago?

An obvious statement issued to believers is that most of us are our own worse critics whereas others are not critical enough. It is not until we truly admit our shortcomings that there can be transformation in our lives. Not until we experience this transformation will we be able to take a new walk, a walk that includes our ability to move in and with the Spirit. To experience this feeling of peace, we must celebrate with an observance that is worthy of the faithful. This transformation causes a noticeable change in our walk that will see harshness softened, wrath calmed, and every one of us will be called upon to forgive the faults of others while we seek forgiveness and reconciliation without demanding vengeance. By forgiving others of their failings, we can obtain the forgiveness of our own sins—*If you forgive others their failings, your Father who is in heaven will forgive you yours* (Matthew 6:4). We can be assured that God is merciful and just, as God not only hears our prayers but answers them out of that same mercy and justice. We will not accept all people as brothers and sisters until we ourselves are really humble; and we are not really humble until we measure ourselves by the revelation of the living God.

A natural flow of these answered prayers will be generosity. This generosity makes us part of God's divine work. When the hungry are fed, the naked clothed, those in jail are helped, and the sick cared for, everyone who helped advance God's plan are gifts of God for those aided, from the hands of the minister to the servant and all those in between. Although God has no need of help in applying mercy, God so regulates the divine power that God supports the sufferings of human beings through other human beings.

Who needs forgiveness? You can find the answer in John 3:16.

> **PRAYER:** Father, thank you for your patience as we become babes in Christ. Help us to grow in our trust and commitment in your Son and help us to experience time with your Spirit who is our constant companion. Thank you for your part in our transformation into carriers of your love. Amen.

Day 110
Holy Waste

Jesus said, "Leave her alone! Why are you bothering her? She has done a beautiful thing for me" (Mark 14:6).

I N THIS STORY, JESUS CAME TO A spirited defense during a remarkable incident in the home of Simon the leper. Here was a clash between the market mind and the spirit. Jesus knew that there are people in life who know the cost of everything and the value of nothing. He saw in it the clash between the abundant heart and the calculating eyes of the world.

Why all this waste? I asked that question when I was told I had Parkinson's disease, and it became apparent that my having it would force me to leave something I loved and felt called to do. Not that I was great or anything, but I too wanted to know why all this waste. Those men of old recognized that in a few moments the aroma of the perfume would have dissipated, and they wanted to know why the waste. But the fact is that those persons who look upon a forest as so many feet of lumber, fields as so many bales of hay, or life as so much money in the bank, those persons who look at life through such eyes must confess already that they are operating life at a loss.

This is one of the highest tributes Jesus paid anyone in the New Testament: "She has done a beautiful thing for me." Here, love is lifted to a fine art. The woman forgot all about arithmetic in the service of love. Isn't it rather strange that our television sets have progressed from black and white to color, whereas our lives have regressed from color to black and white? Far too many of us are sitting down in despair and defeat because we have to live out our days with an unwanted guest. We cannot become what we need to be by remaining as we are, but the lesson learned in the house of Simon the leper is: our lives are precious perfume, and it is an unspeakable tragedy to carry them through our span of days in an unbroken jar. Break it, spend it, and use it, and you will be rewarded by the discovery of why you are alive.

PRAYER: O God, give us eyes to see your truth rather than what the world professes is the truth. And may our energies be channeled into helping your kingdom come on earth as it is in heaven. Amen.

◦

Day 111
Asking, Getting!

Peter said to him, "I don't have any money, but I'll give you what I do have. . . ." Springing to his feet, he stood up and started to walk. The man was walking, jumping, and praising God (Acts 3:5–8).

HOW MANY TIMES HAVE WE prayed fervently about a particular matter, be it a person or certain circumstances that surround us? We reach up to God out of our despair and hopelessness. We are avid readers of the Old Testament book of Psalms because it is as if it the psalmist could read our hearts. I think parts of the book of Psalms could very well have been written by folk with PD, or at least was a caregiver to one who was afflicted with this dreaded disease, although people back then probably didn't know what it was. The book is filled with example after example of the cries of God's people being answered beyond their dreams and expectations. God was able to change the feelings of emotions like fear, pain, loneliness, despair, hopeless, helplessness into positive words such as joy, celebrate, freedom, hope, restoration, and praise.

We all have heard the old adage, "Be careful what your pray for, because you might just get it." I am going to take some literary liberties with these words so it reads, "You had better be careful what you ask, because you may get it plus more!" This could be more than your hearts can believe.

Peter and John could not help the man monetarily with gold. They had something much more precious than that. The man was restored. He was healed. His legs, crippled since birth, were now healthy legs that enabled him to walk and jump. He asked for money and he got healthy legs.

You can continue reading and see that the lame man directed his appreciation of being healed not to Peter and John but to God The passage goes on to say that he was walking, jumping, and praising God. Now isn't that the attitude we should have for the way God answers our prayers. I believe it to be a grand example to follow.

PRAYER: O God, you hear and answer our prayers no matter what the circumstance, and for that we are truly grateful. Many times you go beyond our request to the real need in our lives, and you heal and restore us once again. May it be said of us that like Peter and John we speak the word and speak it boldly. In the name of the Christ, we pray. Amen.

—◇—

Day 112
Creative Suffering

I give my life for my sheep (John 10:15).

I WAS LOOKING THROUGH SOME OLD books that a vendor was trying to sell in New York City at the Columbus Circle entrance to Central Park. While looking, I happened upon an autobiography of someone I had never heard of before. The book piqued my interest for several reasons: It's one of my favorite literary genres; its condition was good; it was about someone I knew nothing about; and best of all it only cost three dollars. I asked the bookseller if he knew anything about the book and its author. He did and was most happy to tell me all I could possibly want to know and then some.

He proceeded to tell the story of the Russian Christian, Julia de Beausobre, who was arrested and tortured in Russia in the early 1930s. She later wrote about it in the book I was holding, *Creative Suffering*. The title itself grabs your attention the moment you read it. In this book, she made the point that those who suffer, are tortured, or experience other deliberate mistreatment and abuse can, only by the dignity of their response, participate in the possible redemption of those administering the pain. How incredible! Have you ever given that any thought? I think not. We are too busy coming up with ways to get revenge. But Julia says that that is the wrong way to deal with those who mistreat you. The way to treat them is like my granny would say, "You just kill with kindness. It will do it every time." Our response to that, or any other kind of suffering can make a difference. We can light a candle for all those others who are administering the suffering and grope in the darkness of suffering.

Why should this be surprising? Didn't the suffering of Christ play a vital part in our redemption? From the depths of his suffering, there has come to us forgiveness and new life. How could we even begin to equate Christ's suffering with our sufferings? Ours fade away in comparison.

Suffering is usually a stumbling block for us. We see it only as hurtful, as limiting our activity, as totally evil. Yet it can also be a key to God's kingdom, opening the door of hope for us and for others as we face it in the transforming presence of the crucified Christ. When the dice have been thrown, we will take any possible hope that we can possibly receive.

PRAYER: Lord Jesus, who suffered for us, we pray that you will take the cup of our suffering from us, if that is your will. Until then give us the courage to live boldly in spite of the pain, and hurt. Amen.

Day 113
Where's Your Closet?

Peter said to him, "I don't have any money, but I'll give you what I do have.
. . ." Springing to his feet, he stood up and started to walk. The man was
walking, jumping, and praising God (Acts 3:5–8).

THIS MORNING, I WANT TO SHARE with you something that I have
been pondering of late. Have you noticed how life moves as such a
fast clip today? Everything is traveling at the speed of sound: Palm
Pilots and BlackBerries organizing, cell phones text messaging, and instant
messaging makes us available 24/7. Some folk get up in the morning, and as
their feet hit the floor they have turned on the computer to check their email.
Then there's the busyness of the day's activities before returning home, as well
as talking on the cell phone again on the return commute, arriving just in time
to change clothes before going to the soccer field or music lessons. As soon as
we return home, we check our email before going to bed. A fretful night's sleep
ends with us starting another day like the day before. With such a hectic pace
of life and all the schedules, how can we find time to ponder, let alone think?
We don't! And the daily layers of neglect soon render us strangers to the people with whom we interact, as well as in our relationship to God. We seem to
have turned into a generation of programmable robots!

Where do you go to think, solve the problems of the world, ponder the in-
tricacies of life, the decisions you have to make? Some of my best pondering
comes in the early morning. As a matter of fact, the source of these thoughts
was formulated while I was taking an early morning walk through Central
Park.

Someone once complained that the trouble with life is that it is so daily.
This is what he meant: we get out of bed every morning, shave or put on our
face, travel to work, put in the hours, and come home in the evening, weary
and empty, to catch our breath before doing the same thing the next day, and
the next, and the next. We do this daily without taking the time to explore
the caverns of our hearts. But before we allow this thought to depress us, we
should remember the things we love to do every morning. We see the morning
light and the faces of loved ones. There might be orange juice, coffee, and

breakfast. I'm glad life is so daily; it's like the love of God, which is "new every morning and faithful every night." Chesterton was right when he said, "The sun doesn't rise by natural law; it rises because every morning God says to it, 'get up and do it again.'"

Every new morning is a gift of love. Make it a point this week to thank God for this daily gift.

PRAYER: As the quiet overwhelms us, O God, let our spirits be in your hands for safekeeping. Amen.

⸺◅◇▻⸺

Day 114
Wall Street Wisdom?

My house will be called a house of prayer for all the nations. But you have turned it into a gathering place for thieves (Mark 11:17).

IT IS EASY TO BECOME cynical about Wall Street when we read stories about greed and fraud there. Even though they have received millions of dollars in bailout money, some still continue in the ridiculous bonuses and lifestyles. We are tempted to think that the financial world consists of thieves and charlatans. One thing we must remember is that not all of those people working in the financial world are selfish, greedy so-and-sos. That industry is comprised, by and large, by caring, dedicated, and concerned people who are concerned about what is happening there.

Another thing we must remember, of course, is that the whole system is built upon trust and that every day shares, bonds, and currencies change hands because men and women who buy and sell them give their word and may be trusted to stand behind it whatever the cost. Signatures come later. We might say that Wall Street exists at all because the integrity of these men and women holds up well against the value of the dollar.

Giving of one's word: How crucial that is! Have you noticed when reading the Jewish or Christian scriptures that you read about a God who doesn't do much? It is enough for God to speak, and it is done. God's word alone accomplishes intention: "And God said, let there be light and there was light." To think of the power of God's word is to be reminded of the value of our own. Broker or not, words are not idle, lifeless things. God is in God's word, for it—the word—expresses the mind, reveals the heart, and fulfills the purpose of God. And you are in your word. When you give your word, you put yourself behind it. To break it is to crack your character. To lose your word is to lose yourself.

PRAYER: Father in Heaven, you are the only entity that can truly be trusted. We have our moments, but we need more such moments so we can be the trusted keeper of the word. Help us to realize the power of the word and enable us to be the trusted sharer of that word, in the name of the one who is the true Word, Jesus Christ, our Lord. Amen.

Day 115
Everything in Order?

Everything has its own time, and there is a specific time for every activity under heaven (Ecclesiastes 1:1).

ANOTHER YEAR IS NEARLY A THIRD OVER. It started out as a year of hope, of expectation, of return to the things about which life should be. Rather, I am afraid it is on the verge of being a year of "giving up": giving up steady legs, strong voice, clear thoughts, understanding, and being understood. It's time to stop burning daylight and get on with it. No more waiting. I say "waiting," but actually I am not sure for or on what I am waiting. Is it a waiting for a return to the rightness we should be faced with each day? Well it's time. Is everything in order?

Many of us have the feeling that we can accomplish all of this on our own without help. In setting my life in order, I have to do so in order without desperation and without compromise. Along the way, a succession of wasted opportunities to be about a serious spiritual discipline beckons. Going on my own, not being held within the limits of accepted practice, is everything in order?

Concerning world affairs, in order for me to address the affairs of this world It is abundantly clear that my obligation is to explore the "interior space" of my life.

When we face the vanity of our best efforts, their triviality, their involvement in illusion, we become desperate. And when we are tempted to do *anything* as long as it seems to be good, we might abandon a better good with which we have become disillusioned and embrace a lesser good with a frenzy that prevents us from the greater illusion. So through efforts that might seem to be wasted, we must patiently go toward a good that is to be given to the patient and the disillusioned.

> **PRAYER:** Father, we often become frustrated and disillusioned when we have to give up something else. Frankly, we get a bit resentful when we are asked to give up something else. We would like to get something back. Help us to find other things that can replace those we have lost. Unto you, and only you we give our praise for your power and glory. Amen.

Day 116
Do You Remember?

It is the Lord (John 21:7)!

I WAS ONCE TOLD THAT resurrection stories are stories of recognition, that is, of re-knowing, knowing for the second time. It is through the words of Jesus that the first knowing occurs. Each day, day in and day out, those who followed Jesus listened to his words. Although it took a lot of time and patience, the disciples began catching on to what he was saying and started assimilating his words into their lives. Gradually, what he said took hold of them and something new was born in them. Yet the full depth and power of his words remained hidden. They had already come to know him with a knowledge of the heart. This was the knowledge that made them recognize him. Because there were times that knowledge was forgotten, Jesus had to re-awaken it by calling them by name or explaining the scripture to them.

It is important for us to be prepared to recognize Jesus in anything and anywhere. Now, there are those who have never heard his words, and not having eyes to see, they cannot be expected to see him when he appears to them. They can see because seeing Jesus is a seeing with eyes formed by the word. Only eyes that have already seen him can see him again. Only hearts that know him already can know him again.

What will finally give me full joy and complete peace is to be with the risen Lord. But before that can take place, I have to keep feeding myself his word so that a first knowing—a still imperfect knowing—can develop in me. This puts me in a state of waiting. But the waiting is not an empty waiting. It is a waiting with a heart prepared to recognize when he comes again and calls me by name.

> **PRAYER:** Help us to see, our Heavenly Father, so we can believe what we are seeing. As the scales fall from our eyes and we no longer have to look through a window all clouded up, help us to follow you as you send us to the outermost parts of the world. In the name of the one who paid the price for us, Jesus, our Lord. Amen.

Day 116
Restless or Restful Spirits?

Come to me, all who are tired from carrying heavy loads, and I will give you rest (Matthew 11:28).

ASK ANY BELIEVER TRAVELING ALONG life's journey, and that person will attest to the fact that there is a difference between a restless spirit and a restful spirit. Sad to say, but most of us find ourselves counted amongst those with a restless spirit, and one soon discovers a life lived with a restless spirit is a life that is lived free of hope or victory.

If we are brave and wish to have a restful spirit, there is work to be done that involves a type of movement that attempts to bring us to the place where we might find a new center. Just as this movement is not an escape from ourselves, it is also not an attempt to simply escape the pressures of the world. These escapes are just illusions. This movement is the bringing of our entire selves, with all of our brokenness, fears, pains, and anxieties to find a new center of inner peace.

An important spiritual goal that we need is one in which we teach ourselves and come to acknowledge the inner pain and frustrations that we have often covered up over the years. Even more so is the importance and need to recognize our powerlessness in attempts to achieve the good and control our own existence. Yes, we are to act decisively and be responsible for our own choices, and in the same breath we need to be reminded that we are not the masters of our own fate.

These insights should not drive us to despair but make us ready to accept our creatureliness and our need to come to a new center: a relationship with God. That relationship, that new center, is where our strivings are transformed into a new sense of trust. The trust is in the one who not only created us in love but who also loved us all the way to the cross and beyond.

When we make it to that new center and meet God, we soon discover that God does not necessarily promise to relieve us of our burdens or answer all our concerns. Yet God is the one who embraces us so our burdens are filled with the presence of God and we might become light for our journey ahead.

And God is sufficient.

PRAYER: Heavenly Father, your graciousness, love, and patience are exactly what we need to calm our restless spirits. Help us to keep our eyes on you as we pass through the broken shards that lie around our feet and call to us to live lives that are restless. Help us to realize just as long as we escape the grasp of all that we experience with a restless spirit, we can experience the transformation of our restless spirits into spirits that are restful in you. In the name of Jesus, we pray. Amen.

———◁◯▷———

Day 117
Locked in a Room with Open Doors

That Sunday evening, the disciples were together behind locked doors (John 20:19).

THE WORDS IN THIS TITLE conjure up a powerful image, causing one's palms to become moist and creating a strange feeling of uneasiness, suggesting that inner weaknesses as well as outer obstacles can immobilize a person. The enemies are not all "out there." Some are on the inside. It is so easy to fall into the habit of blaming our unrealized selves on outside forces. It is possible to change forces with the help of God.

Some people are locked in a room with open doors by hatred. These people are prisoners of the spirit of vengeance. Hate is a cruel master. It hurts the hater as much as the one who is the object of the hatred. We need to hear the words of Jesus in which he said, "Love your enemies and pray for those who despitefully use you" (Matthew 5:44). As believers, we are to deal with others as God has dealt with them.

Other folk are locked in by worry. The people who have and want great possessions fall into this category. Their acquisitions and possessions can liberate. But it is not long before these same acquisitions and possessions tend to clog and jam their lives. Jesus assures us not to worry about anything and proceeds to commend us to the faithfulness of God

There are others who are locked in because of being afraid of the new—new places, new experiences, new people, and the most oppressive reason, the fear of new ideas. It is a threat to the equilibrium that we have established for the management of our lives. We are guilty of striving to be justified by consistency rather than by faith.

This needs to change. As a matter of fact, we are not only encouraged to change, but change is demanded of us. There is good news for those of us who are locked in a room with open doors. We don't have to stay in there. Besides the inner misery that makes us want to get out, there is the call of God. It starts where each individual stands. We don't have to spend our time looking for the starting place, because it starts right where we are. Christ is the way. He will meet us and lead us out as we are and what we are.

PRAYER: Heavenly Father, you are the author of liberty. Forgive us the constricted and fear-filled existences that we settle for when we might have life. Help our spirits realize that we are the ones who have locked the doors and are the only ones that can unlock the same doors with the help of your Spirit. Amen.

Day 118
Less Than Average

So that you may approve what is excellent (Philippians 1:10a). . . .

I JUST CAN'T QUITE UNDERSTAND what makes a believer willing to settle for less than the best, to accept less than what God wants and promises for our lives. Rather than living life on the higher plain that is God's desire for us, some choose to live out their lives settling for second (and sometimes even third) best, plodding along as if this is all there is to life, totally oblivious to that living of a life of excellence that God has in store for us.

By no means am I saying that this way of life is free of trial and tribulation. There will be some instances in which we find ourselves in the wilderness. In those moments, we will be tempted to go back to familiar territory. When such a feeling begins to overwhelm us, we need to hear Paul's words echoing in our hearts, "Press on, press on."

Some people think that the Irish writer, Frank O'Conner, wrote some of the best short stories in the world. I am not here to argue the point either way, but I want to bring to your attention a comforting sentence in his autobiography. He tells us that there can be no appeal to the mediocre. No appeal can be made mediocrity because no appeal will be understood by it. I no longer praise Mozart's music to those who treat it condescendingly. I say nothing of Walt Whitman to those who think all poetry irrelevant. I do not tell those who are indifferent to all literature that Flannery O'Connor is worth their attention. If they don't see these things for themselves, it's hard to show or tell them. As Confucius says, "With those who follow a different way, it is useless to take counsel." The Scots put it even better when they tell us that we should save our breath to cool our porridge.

PRAYER: Heavenly Father, we are your children and are made in your image. Grant to us the insight to know when we are following after the things of this world rather than the things that are holy. Help us not to settle for mediocrity but rather for what is excellent, because we have the mind of Jesus, the Christ, in whose name we pray. Amen.

Day 119
God is Watching Us from a Distance

Let us continue to go and pray before the Lord and seek the Lord of hosts
(Zechariah 8:21).

THERE ARE MANY TIMES IN which we hear ourselves say to someone going through a trial or a time of uncertainty, "I will pray for you." I wonder how many Christians say that, because it's the phrase that they are expected to say. Could you imagine facing life-threatening surgery or some other trauma and asking someone to pray for you, and they respond with a firm and indifferent "NO?" How many of us look to pray for someone or something as a privilege? Do we really take into consideration what is being asked of us?

On the outside, the offer sounds very pious and very Christian. After all, didn't Jesus instruct us to pray even for those who despitefully use us? And don't forget about Paul; he admonishes us to pray without ceasing. We need to come to the realization of why we're praying and for what. Are we just being polite with no intention of praying for the person in need? If so, what will they pray for? How will they pray? When praying for others, what if we mispray? What if we pray at cross-purposes?

Do you have moments in which you feel as though your prayers don't get past the comforter on the bed? And what about the times that the only response we receive is silence? What do we do at those times?

There are many ways of describing what it is we do when we pray. For example, someone remarked, "I do not say that I will pray for you, but I will think of you and God together." But, of course, I can't think of God and you together without praying for you. And then there are the lovely words of St. Teresa: "Granting that we are always in the presence of God, yet it seems to me that those who pray are in his presence in a very different sense, for they, as it were, see that he is looking upon them." So one way of looking at prayer is to understand that God is watching us. Prayer is the awareness that God is looking upon us.

PRAYER: Heavenly Father, come to us and assure us that you are not so far away that you can't hear our cries. Let us be certain of your eagerness to answer them. You are the only one with the power to answer our prayers. We praise you for your touch of assurance. In the name of Jesus, we pray. Amen.

—◁○▷—

Day 120
One, Two, . . . 100—Still Counting

Blessings are on the heads of the righteous (Proverbs 10:6). . . .

IN THIS WORLD, THERE ARE TWO kinds of people: There are the people who are constantly surprised that life has been so good to them—and they are by no means always the people who have the most money. Then there are the people who are always bitter and resentful because life has, as they see it, withheld so much from them. It is easy at times to feel that way when you have Parkinson's disease or any other kind of terminal illness. Sure, there are times when we might find ourselves on the bitter side even for a short time. But then we come to ourselves. When we find ourselves visiting the negative and bitter side of life, one thing that assists in making our stay ever so short is stopping and begin counting our blessings. There are a great many things of which we may not have thought, so it is well to begin to count. I heard the lyrics of a song not long ago: "When I can't sleep, I count my blessings instead of sheep." That's good advice.

Blessings color life, and life is always a mixture. Life is never one color. Neither is life always in black and white. Life, like a dome of many pieces of colored glass, "Stains the white radiance of eternity," as a poet had it. Or for us a much more homely simile would be that life is like a patchwork quilt.

Yet the strange thing is that the colors in a stained-glass window and the colors in a patchwork quilt for all their diversity can make for harmony. Life can be like that for those who have learned to accept life with its hardships and blessings and make the best of it as it is.

Life has its prizes, and life has its blots. It has the things we can do and the things we cannot do, the pleasures we can have and the pleasures we cannot have, the things we get and the things we do not obtain.

But for those who love God, it can still be harmony, for God always works things together for good to them that love God (Romans 8:28). Try counting blessings next time the waters get rough. The number of them might surprise you!

PRAYER: Gracious Father in heaven and on earth, outside of us and in our hearts, help us to receive your blessings in order that you may be blessed in return. Amen.

⸺⟨◇⟩⸺

Day 121
Trusting in God's Word

You prepare a table before me in the presence of my enemies, you anoint my head with oil; my cup overflows (Psalm 23:5).

I AM NOT SURE, BUT I imagine that many of us have often repeated the words and knew they were true, whereas others say the same words with a skeptical tone in their voice. You know the words:

The Lord is my shepherd; there is nothing I shall want;
Fresh and green are the pastures where he gives me repose.
Near restful waters he leads me to revive my drooping spirit....

The words can be prayed first thing in the morning as we try to sit quietly, if only to keep our mind focused on what was being prayed. You might pray them as you run your errands, going here and there. You might even pray them during moments of your daily routine of the day.

There are countless numbers of people who can attest to the comfort and solace that these words have brought to them during good times as well as faith-testing times. When we pray we are not alone. Countless men and women surround us: those who are close by and far away, those who are presently living, and those who have died recently or long ago. And we know that long after we have left this world, these same words will continue to be prayed until the end of time.

Sometimes in the life of a person with Parkinson's disease, one is faced so many times with the feeling that one is alone, battling this disease by one's self, fighting a lost cause. At times, we have a spirit so agitated that we feel overwhelmed and are ready to throw in the towel. Then these words echo through the chambers of our hearts minds, and they become an anchor of hope onto which we can hold.

Soon we realize that as we allow these words to go deeper into the center of our being, the more we become God's people, and the better we understand what it means to be in the world without being in it.

> **PRAYER:** Dear Shepherd, you make it so easy to trust you enough to get to know you better. Your constant provision and love add to the ease of following these words and allowing them to take us even deeper into our being and your heart of love. We unite with all the saints—the living, the dead, and those yet to be made—to be able to find comfort, peace, and solace in our new resting place, your heart. In the name of Jesus, we pray. Amen.

Day 122
Courage for a Difficult Life

When Jesus saw their faith, he said to the man, "Cheer up, friend! Your sins are forgiven" (Matthew 9:2).

I STOPPED FOR A TRAFFIC light. Crossing the road just in front of me was a most attractive young couple. The woman was tall, blonde, and slender, maybe 25 or 30 years old. Her hair was neatly braided. She wore a beige blouse and slacks. They could have come from a discount store, but she wore them as though they had come from a fashion boutique.

The man with her was suntanned, dark-haired, and handsome. By the look on the girl's face you could sense a real bond of affection between these two. I couldn't tell how tall the man was, because he was in a wheelchair. She was pushing him across the street toward the low-rent apartments.

Why was he in a wheelchair? A degenerative disease? Parkinson's disease? A sports injury? Perhaps a car accident? I sensed from the way the were talking and looking at each other, however, that they had come to terms with their tough times and that they would not accept defeat. They had found their victory in spite of what life was giving them.

Courage! Courage! Courage! Definitely a trait one with Parkinson's needs for the daily battle that is fought to force the body to respond to your commands, the deliberation one must develop to even live, and the frustration one feels when things just don't work. And we cannot forget the most valuable person(s) we depend on every day: our caregivers. Why do they need courage, you ask? They need courage to deal with us and make sure our medical and physical needs are met: courage to help us when we fall, courage to be patient with us, and courage to help us not to quit and not give up. The life of a PD person is huge, but we follow a God who is bigger.

PRAYER: Gracious God, we thank you for people of all ages who, refusing to be defeated by hardship or tragedy, live in faith and hope. May we too have the courage to learn from their stories through Jesus Christ to triumph over difficult circumstances. Amen.

Day 123
Little Black Book

His mother treasured all these things in her heart (Luke 2:51).

I HAVE HAD THE PRIVILEGE OF studying with some of the most effective preachers of our generation, two of whom were Dr. Ernest Campbell and Dr. John Killinger. I mention these two because their sermons reflect a freshness and creativity that is lacking in today's preaching. They encouraged their students and seminar participants to keep a small notebook with them to jot down anything that they saw in their day-to-day living, for example, billboards, bumper stickers, any posted advertisements, observations of people around them, etc. These notations would serve as prompters for sermons and provide illustrative material at a later time. This is one of the contributing factors that helped to keep their sermons pertinent and not dated.

At first, I did not keep a notebook; but as the slips of paper grew so did the need for these ideas and illustrations to be better organized. I had an assortment of notes written on napkins, envelopes, paper towels, and folders. I enjoyed re-reading them and experiencing the closeness of God's presence.

Reinhold Niebuhr had a summer home in Massachusetts and at times preached at the local church there. One Sunday on his way to worship, he wrote a prayer on the back of an envelope and offered it during the worship service. When the service was over, a neighbor of his, a man named Robbins, asked for a copy of the prayer. Niebuhr gave it to him. Here is the prayer:

> God, grant us the grace
> to accept with serenity
> the things that cannot be changed,
> courage to change the things
> that should be changed,
> and the wisdom to distinguish
> the one from the other.

I cannot imagine that the back of an envelope has been put to better use!

PRAYER: Father, we thank you for the serenity that is here for the asking and how it helps us to see through kingdom eyes so you can teach us to have a saving heart. Amen.

-----◄◊►-----

Day 124
What Are You Afraid Of?

Jesus said, "It is I. Fear not" (John 6:20).

THESE TWO SIMPLE WORDS—*fear not*—have been the prelude to many a grand and holy occurrence in scripture. Their importance is attested to by being enjoined in scripture over forty times. The message is carried and delivered to the recipient by a messenger of God. After a sense of fright, the recipient was in need of some word that would calm the spirit. In order not to let fear have a place in our lives, however, we must face our fear. We might even discover ways to combat this feeling of which we had not thought and come from the strangest places.

What are some fears you have? There are so many. Jesus had told his disciples to get in a boat and cross to the other side of the lake where he would meet them. They were doing what he told them to do when a storm erupted. They battled the wind and the waves in fear for their very lives. Things seemed bleak and hopeless, but Jesus walks into the picture, telling them, "Fear not." We were to meet there; but you were in need, and here I am.

The outcome, more often than not, does not turn out the way we planned. We like things to remain the same, to be in order and in their place. God, on the other hand, enters the picture, turning things upside down, and life becomes uncomfortable. Like the bewildered disciples in the boat, we also are fearful. What do we do now?

It is written: "There is no fear, but perfect love casts out fear" (1 John 4:18). Now we know what it takes to be free of fear: *love*. That love comes from God in abundance. How easy that sounds. God is love, love casts out all fear, and we realize how life is so easy when Christ is beside us. We know that we still harbor fears that prevent us from reaching perfect love. I know the things that prevent me from reaching perfect love. I can practice injustice with the best of them. I know how to be cruel, and so do you, preventing us from basking in God's love. Once again, I know God is not done with me yet, for each day has enough troubles of its own. As I face each of these fears, I am reminded of my need to refocus my intent, to start a new beginning. It is through these new beginnings God intervenes with no end. This means that no matter how dark it might become, God in Christ will come walking toward us on the water and change the courses of our lives. If we can hold on and walk through these fears, the experience of spiritual growth in perfect love awaits us on the other side.

> **PRAYER**: Father, The miracles of perfect love lie on the opposite shore. Help us to learn to let go and allow the changing mystery of life to move through us without our fearing, without holding or grasping. Whatever fear is before us, help us to be ready to experience the miracles that will most certainly occur through Jesus Christ, our Lord, in whose name we pray. Amen.

Day 126
I've Got Rhythm; Who Could Ask for Anything More?

Do not abandon your friend, or your father's friend. Do not go to a relative's home when you are in trouble (Proverbs 27:13).

MANY PEOPLE SEARCH FOR THE peace of the inner life, that movement from where we are with our fears, needs, and busy-ness to the place of quietness, no burdens, and renewal. It is here that transformation can occur.

How does one obtain this rhythm? Through our own spiritual development. It is a highly personal development that is our responsibility to keep in rhythm. In this rhythm, others can assist in the journey. We are not to expect to be the lone traveler on this trip. We need, we must have someone to be a partner to share the adventure of companionship as we travel our spiritual journey. We need a companion who is close to us: God's Son, Jesus Christ, who will help us to a continued faithfulness.

Even though your friend is there to help, such a friend cannot do the journeying for us. That task is ours and ours alone; but neither does that task have ready-managed answers. Such a friend cannot take away the struggle.

It is a fact that we all have a journey we must travel, decisions we must make, actions we must perform, pain that we must bear, transformation that we must experience, and peace that we must imbibe. But a friend who journeys with us can encourage and challenge us to faithfulness and authenticity. Such a friend can assist to keep us honest. Such a friend can encourage us to continue to make the hard decisions. The challenge such a friend offers is the challenge to continue to choose life.

PRAYER: We choose "life," heavenly Father. That life that gathers other like-minded pilgrims who are also journeying. Enable us to encourage one another to live according to the leadership of your Spirit. Help us be able to stay the course. In the precious name of Jesus, we pray. Amen.

Day 127
Comfort Needed

The Lord shall prevent me (Psalm 59:10).

*W*E SHOULD NEVER BE SURPRISED AT where or when we catch a glimpse of God. We might catch a glimpse of God in music, in a sunset, in a book, in another person's life, or in a song. The key to catching this glimpse of God is to be as if we are prepared and waiting for the Almighty.

I was going through a difficult time in my personal and spiritual life at one particular juncture in my journey. I needed a break. I needed comfort. There were a few folk who knew what I was experiencing. I was visiting with an elderly man from my church. Knowing of the events that were unfolding in my life, he offered these words of comfort:

> Dr. Greene, when I go through a difficult time in my life I find enormous help in the words of the Psalmist, which were given to me by a friend of mine. The text, which is in the King James Version of the scriptures, reads: "The God of my mercy shall prevent me." After several stories we prayed together.

Returning to my study, I was eager to do some additional reading that dealt with this passage in the book of Psalms. I made an interesting discovery that elevated the passage and offered words of solace to my troubled heart. The word prevent is a word whose meaning has changed. It used to mean, "to go before." The text really affirms, "The God of my mercy shall go before me." In the margin of the commentary I was reading, someone had written, "My God, in his loving kindness, shall meet me at every corner." That's great isn't it?

I don't know what corners each of you will be turning now or in the near future, but I know that corners are always a bit menacing because we never know what demands will be made of us, what wisdom, courage, or sensitivity, when we turn them. But I believe that the writing in the margin is correct: "My God, in His loving kindness shall meet me at every corner." We dwell in love. We move in mercy. It is kindness and grace that wait for us.

PRAYER: Gracious God, we are a sin-sick people in need of your abundant mercy, totally unconditional, and we are truly grateful. Amen.

⟨○⟩

Day 128
Saved for What Purpose?

A blind beggar named Bartimaeus was sitting by the road. He began to shout, "Jesus, son of David, have mercy on me. . . ." Jesus said, "Your faith has made you well" (Mark 10:46–47, 52).

THIS IS A SUBJECT THAT most denominations discuss: the need to be made whole. Being "saved" does not mean that from here on out we follow any way different from that of Jesus, as if to continue in the old way of life. By being "saved," we relinquish independence, leaving in its path extraordinary spiritual energy and vitality because we are then connected to the source of divine power.

I cannot imagine what this blind man felt in being healed and able to see. In order to receive Christ's blessing, he must have been filled with humility, frankness, boldness, enthusiasm, and energy, and, most of all, have trusted in the Lord. Perhaps we would see greater blessings in our own lives if we allowed Jesus to ravage our hearts as he did that of blind Bartimaeus.

A friend in Connecticut sent the following quotation to me. It reads:

> Let us pray that our own miseries and blindnesses, all the apparent dead ends of our lives, once exposed patiently and thoroughly to God's mercy in Jesus may become occasions of loving surrender and may, therefore, yield such fruits as these in our lives. But remember that this requires an ability to pray continuously with great concentration and energy, and we will be too weak and scattered to pray as we ought if we habitually squander our spiritual energy in other directions. We may say that wise practice of "energy conservation" is essential to a vibrant spiritual life, so that our

169

whole soul may be spent in Bartimaeus' cry: "Jesus, Son of David, have mercy on me!"

PRAYER: Father, it took only one word from you for the man to be healed. May you grant us the same miracle for healing of our sin-sick souls. Amen.

Day 129
The Final Heresy

I am not saying this because I'm in any need. I've learned to be content in whatever situation I am in (Philippians 4:11).

THERE IS AN INTRIGUING SERMON title that reads, "No Man Need Stay the Way He Is." The excuses come flying. Often a person will defend himself by saying, "I can't help it. I'm made that way," or, "That's my nature, I can't change myself." Leaving God out of the picture of the changing process is shameful. This is the final heresy.

Whereas it s true that a man cannot change himself, the same cannot be said of Jesus. If we accept that Jesus cannot change us, then the whole claim of Christianity is a lie.

If the church is to change the world and to change men and women, however, it must be changed itself. If we look closely at the church, we can sense an attitude of defeat. Diminishing and aging congregations are abandoning their belief that with God nothing is impossible. They simply accept these beliefs as things about which there is nothing to be done, and that attitude cannot do anything but cause the church to begin its acceptance of the situation as a death sentence.

If Christianity means anything, that is exactly what it does mean: It is Jesus's power that he can enable us to get further along the road to holiness, if only we will ask for and take the help that he continually offers us.

Of course, nothing will change without commitment, along with blood, sweat, toil, and tears. God did not give us the defeatism that accepts things as they are. Rather, the divine discontent, which is the life and the strength of Jesus Christ, will battle to change them.

Paul writes, "I press toward the mark" (Phil 3:14). It is not enough for a Christian to accept life that is stuck in one place. Life for the Christian should be this road to holiness, an upward and onward way.

PRAYER: Father God, you encourage us to move forward. If any changes need to be made in our lives, may your Spirit direct us so that we live in truth. In the name of the Christ, we pray. Amen.

Day 130
Grateful—for What?

He quickly bowed at Jesus' feet and thanked him. Jesus asked, "Weren't ten men made clean? Where are the other nine" (Luke 17:16–17)?

GRATITUDE. *WEBSTER'S DICTIONARY* DEFINES *gratitude* as "the state of being grateful, appreciative of benefits received."

"Either I did something right, or you have too much free time on your hands," said an elderly man in my church, referring to a note I had written him, thanking him for taking water and snacks to the migrant workers that were in the area until the sweet potato crop had been harvested. The elderly man continued. "At no time, in all the years I've been a churchgoer have I ever received a handwritten thank you note from my pastor for something I did for the church. I'm thinking about having it framed," he said with a chuckle.

I am a firm believer in the ministry of letter writing even now, and there is no topic or job too small or insignificant as not to take five minutes and write a note of appreciation for what was done. You will be surprised what happens after you do that. A neat hand written note, however, is not possible now because Parkinson's has taken the fluidity away. So now I type notes.

There is nothing so ugly and so hurting as ingratitude, or as Shakespeare's King Lear said, "It is sharper than a serpent's tooth to have a thankless child." Someone said that today's kids think they are "entitled." Perhaps they haven't seen gratitude as a part of the lives of those around them beyond the Thanksgiving holiday.

We spend too much time waiting to see which direction the world's winds will blow so we can follow. God calls us to be different because it is easy to go with the crowd and a difficult thing to be different.

With such indifference and ingratitude, there is in the church a need for those people who are different and brave. No doubt there is in each generation a desperate need for women and men who are brave. Not only we ourselves, but God also is in need of them. God equips them for the carrying out of those gifts. What we need is to heed the advice given by Robert Louis Stevenson to a young man: "Stop saying 'Amen,' to what the world says and keep your soul alive." And that is achieved in part through gratitude—gratitude for the church and its faithful, or for those who have been called to be the brave ones. Done with gratitude, this lifestyle keeps us fresh, alive, and filled with Spirit, rather than choosing to number us among the scandal of ordinariness of the lives of so many who claim to be Christian.

PRAYER: Dear Father, thank you, *merci, danke, takk, köszi, grazias*! Amen.

Day 131
A Refreshed Spirit

They have made up for your absence. They have comforted me, and they comforted you. Therefore, show people like these your appreciation (1 Corinthians 16:17–18).

YOU CAN TELL A LOT about people by what they recognize and appreciate. Recognition is an echo of our values. Think about your job, club, or church. Who gets recognized? Those whose work is exceptional in service or accomplishment? Probably.

Paul never undervalued exceptional service, but, he also appreciated other deeds that were less than spectacular. This is the reason for these lines of appreciation for three friends who brought him news about the Corinthian church. Hearing good news has a way of lifting the burden we might be carrying, some stress we might be under, some uncertainty, some anxiety we could be experiencing. That good word provides us renewed hope, a lighter load, a refreshed spirit. It did for Paul.

We need to be careful not to limit the possibilities for a refreshed spirit to only the big and miraculous events that occur on a daily basis. We must not imply that our spirits can be refreshed if they meet certain criteria.

Opportunities abound to lift the spirits of those who are discouraged or weary. But how often do we recognize the gentle care of those who lighten dark days? Not very often. How often do we fail to say a word or make a small gesture of concern or gratitude because it seems trivial or unnecessary? Too often. God doesn't call many of us to exceptional service, but we're all involved in the sometimes unappreciated ministry of refreshing the spirits of others. We can be sure it is recognized in one another; remember, Jesus said, "As you did it to one of these least . . ." (Matt 25:40).

PRAYER: Lord, show us opportunities to refresh our lagging spirits. May we not count the cost. Also, open our hearts to appreciate the refreshing existence others give us. In Christ's name, we pray. Amen.

Day 132
Real Christian

The disciples were called Christians for the first time in the city of Antioch (Acts 11:26).

SOME SEVENTY-FIVE PERCENT OF THE people with Parkinson's disease develop *micrography*, which means "small writing." The person with micrography finds it hard to write because it is difficult to start and sustain motion with a writing utensil. The result of this is that one's writing becomes small and cramped.

This is what happens with Parkinson's patients who have micrography: Their writing starts out being readable, but soon deteriorates from there. A problem with this is that once something has been written and has become "cold," it is more difficult to piece whatever ideas one had back together. That is what happened to today's devotion. I have attempted to put it together and hope you are as blessed by the following truths as I was. It shares the same title of today's devotion, and I believe that A. W. Tozer wrote it:

A Real Christian

Real Christian is an odd number . . .
He feels supreme love for One whom he has never seen,
Talks familiarly every day to someone he cannot see,
Expects to go to heaven on the virtue of another,
Empties himself in order to be full,
Admits he is wrong, so he can be declared right,
Goes down in order to get up,
Is strongest when he is weakest.
Is the richest when he is poorest, and happiest when he feels the worst,
Dies so he can live,
Forsakes in order to have,
Gives away so he can keep,
Sees the invisible, hears the inaudible, and knows that peace which
  passes knowledge."

PRAYER: Father, as we ponder these thoughts, we are reminded of just how little we have given and done, compared to how much you have given and done in order that we can do and have. Help those with smallness of writing be able to write in bold, readable letters of their lives your promise to watch over your children and to give to them your love for all of us. Amen.

⋯◁○▷⋯

Day 133
What Do We Do Now That We've Forgiven Each Other?

Put up with each other; forgive each other, if anyone has a complaint. Forgive as the lord forgave you (Colossians 3:13).

HAVE YOU EVER GIVEN ANY thought to having someone write your biography? What would it say about you? Would they say that you were happy, compassionate, angelic, had a sweet spirit, always thought of others? Or would the picture they paint resemble a list straight from the gates of hell: unhappy, mean, nasty, bitter, and angry at the world, a snake in the grass? I wonder if we would be shocked to see what we thought of initially compared with what we saw as the truth?

A good little exercise that follows this confession is to come to an understanding of how we got to that spot. What did we experience or not experience that led us to this place? I am sure the possibilities would be called Legion.

One possibility that would be on both lists would be the willingness to forgive; both groups are in need of it, but few bask in the warm happiness of a forgiving heart. What exactly is forgiveness? I am not advocating that forgiveness is a manner of exonerating people who have treated you badly, have betrayed, hurt you, and used you. They might not deserve exoneration. Forgiveness means cleansing your soul of the bitterness of "what might have been," "what should have been," and "what didn't have to happen." Someone has defined forgiveness as "giving up all hope of having had a better past." The past is past and there is little to be gained by dwelling on it. Do you know of any sadder people than those who have a grievance against the world because of something that happened years ago and have allowed the memory to sour their view of life ever since? Life is the culprit. It has disappointed them, and they spend the remaining years of life being miserable and complaining about it.

If that sounds familiar to you, we need to gather around us those things that serve as reminders that it was not always like this. A warning needs to be expressed here. The purpose of this exercise is not to relive the pain that comes with disappointment or to tear open a scar that covered an emotional wound so that it would never heal. The purpose is to serve as a reminder that there was a time when we dreamed a beautiful dream that shaped and defined us, even after we realized that it was not going to come to fruition the way we had hoped.

It is then that we can feel more ready to accept our real, though imperfect, world. This is a good starting point for overcoming life and people disappointing us, and before you know it you are actively involved in forgiveness: forgiving others, forgiving yourself, forgiving the world, and maybe even forgiving God.

> **PRAYER:** Father, the scriptures say that all of our sins are forgiven by you and you want our relationship with you restored. We do, too, even when our actions and reactions do not show it. Help us to get our footing on a solid foundation that we can build upon the love and forgiveness of Christ our Lord. Amen.

Day 134
Caring Love

He who does not love does not know God, for God is love (1 John 4:8).

THERE WAS A MAN IN MY last church named George Moore. George was one of those saints who was short in stature but extremely tall in heart. He loved to laugh and have a good time. I would be hard pressed to find another man that has compassion as deep as George's. Our friendship began when I went to Triangle Baptist Church in Raleigh, North Carolina and it has been steadily growing ever since. He is quite learned in many fields but particularly in the area of computers. He has been to my house at some of the craziest times whenever we had problems working and helping everybody without accepting anything in return. He says he just loves to do it, and he does. If a member of the church stopped or called George with a computer problem, he was more than happy to look at it. You never heard him complain or talk badly about anyone. Even when his family was going though a difficult period, he was as steady as a rock. Always ready to pitch in in whatever project was being done. He and I learned how to fly a glider, and we have made a bucket list for future "wants," too.

He never told me "no" when I asked him to do something for the church or for me. He always showed up with a smile in his voice, sharing God's love. He took a day off work and traveled close to three hours on the day I had the deep brain stimulation surgery at Duke. Not only did he come for a visit, he also spent the entire day with my family while I was in surgery. He returned the next day with his wife, Melody. I was not their pastor at the time, which makes it even more special. *That's caring love.*

The way in which George is able to share God's love to others is due largely to his lovely wife, Melody. She has that same sweet spirit as George, but she is much quieter. She directed the music at my church. She gives of her talent and gifts freely, and everyone around her is blessed by her unselfish giving to the kingdom of God. She also is the choral director of the magnet school in Raleigh. She and George are quite compatible, complement each other, and they attest daily to the world that God is love.

Through this bold picture of the Moores and in our own lives, our sins and shortcomings did not wipe out God's caring love. God sought all of us and offered to forgive and receive us.

PRAYER: Dear Father, may your love fill the deepest parts our beings. Enable us to have a strong witness of your love as is shown to us in the lives of George and Melody Moore. Thank you for such witnesses. Amen.

—◇—

Day 135
Don't Be Left Out

Five were wise, and five were foolish (Matthew 25:2).

HAVE YOU EVER RISEN FROM THE table, gotten ready to go, started toward the door, keys in hand, only to be stopped dead in your tracks because you couldn't remember where you were going or what you were going for? How about misplacing your cell phone, purse, or wallet? Or two of my personal favorites: "Where are my keys?" and "Why did I come to the store?" when I need either one of them. They are not where I put them. They are *not* to be found. I re-trace my steps for the twenty-first and last time. When I finish I pick up the pile of bills and advertisements, and guess what: the keys fell out and hit my foot. Who put them there? I did not put them there. Somebody else must have done it. Ah, a conspiracy.

Jesus told a story with some of the same themes running through it but without the modern-day illustrations. All we are told or know is that there were ten virgins. Five were wise, and five were foolish. They gathered around at the gate waiting for the arrival of the bridegroom. May be he misplaced his money purse or couldn't find his camel's reins. Whatever the reason, he tarried. Some time passed before the shout went out that the bridegroom was about to arrive. Everyone was feverishly readied for his arrival and the celebration to begin. The five foolish virgins had forgotten to expect the unexpected and had not brought enough oil, whereas the wise brought just enough oil for their lamps. After looking and looking through their blankets, the foolish virgins realized they had forgotten to bring more oil for their lamps. They went to borrow some from the wise ones only to be turned away because the wise ones wanted to be sure that their lamps had plenty of oil. It was suggested that they hurry and go into town and buy oil there.

While the foolish virgins were gone, the bridegroom arrived at midnight. There was much celebration, but the terrible sound of the gates clanking shut caused the arrival of the oil-purchasing virgins to plead their case only to have it rejected. Once the gate was shut, if you did not have an invitation you could not enter the celebration. So the being fastened shut brought a horrible feeling for those not already inside. They even recited their excuse for being late; but to no avail. Jesus was trying to say in this text is that it doesn't matter when he returns, but the call is for all virgins and non-virgins alike to be ready for the bridegroom's coming and not be left out. For Jesus, it doesn't matter if you have trouble keeping up with your car keys, cell phone, wallet, or remote control. What matters is that we are looking and finding the correct things of this life to be lifted to an even greater life for the years ahead.

With Parkinson's disease, one can have a problem with mild cases of dementia. It can become difficult to process concepts and numbers. The call for us is to keep the mundane in its place and continue in strength and love. Even for those of us who are dealing with Parkinson's, in whatever state we find ourselves in, the call is to be ready, so we don't find ourselves left behind.

PRAYER: Father, thank you for providing a way out for us and helping us to be sure and ready so as not to be left behind. In the name of Jesus, we pray. Amen.

Day 136
I Can't Take Any More!

How long must I be with you? How long must I put up with you (Mark 9:19)?

ON MORE THAN ONE occasion, Jesus tolerated the thick-headedness of his disciples. Even he allowed his frustration, disappointment, and exasperation to show. After following him three years and listening to his teaching, they still didn't get it. But before we are too quick to cast the first stone, let's take a look at our own lives. How many of us have had it? We are just as bad if not worse, for how much longer have we had to judge the evidence; and we are still blaming others as we hear Jesus say, "How many times do I need to tell you?"

The excuses abound: "I've had it! I can't do anymore!" "My plate is full." "I am only one person." "I can't put anymore on my plate." "I'm spread too thin." "I pass myself coming and going." "I'm all booked up." "If I hear anyone call my name again, I'll scream." "I'm going to take my marbles and go home."

There are times that one or more of these thoughts has entered our minds and might have even come out of our mouths. And even if what we say is true, there is an unwritten law that we are not supposed to feel this way, so we heap loads of guilt on everyone's already weary shoulders, especially our own.

Facing such uncertainty, telling patients that they can't do the things they were able to do once upon a time, stress, fatigue, lack of sleep, pressing financial problems, problems of other family members who might not agree with your treatment plan . . . the list could continue. All of these could affect the patient and the caregiver's relationship. Rather than a combative situation, it becomes an ongoing, loving non-combative stage, where no one feels any hurt if those involved have learned to forgive. I wonder how many times Jesus would have had to repeat the same frustrated words to us that he said to his disciples? Probably more than we think.

PRAYER: Father, increase our love for one another and may the certainty of our compassion grow with each passing day. Amen.

Day 137
The Same Sweet Truth

God loved the world this way: He gave his only Son so that everyone who believes in him will not will not die but will have eternal life (John 3:16).

IF YOU ARE A STUDENT OF church hymns, you are aware that with every new or revised hymn book, the committee compiling the hymns is given the opportunity to make whatever changes they deem necessary to modernize them so as not to offend groups of folk. So the committee tries to stay true to their job by eliminating any hymn that could be taken as sexist, racist, or has questionable theology. Therefore many hymnbooks today have been whittled down so much that they are almost unrecognizable. It is a shame that some of the great hymns of our faith have slowly either been changed or have disappeared altogether. I know they attempt not to say too much on one side or the other as to be biased; but I am afraid that in order not so say too much, we are guilty of saying too little.

For example, the hymn "At the Cross" has in its first stanza the words, "for sinners such as I." But when I was growing up the same stanza read "for such a worm as I." It's good to know that we have evolved from the lowly state of worminess to the state of sinner. I am not going to enter a debate on the positives that have come with either side. As with the changing of the hymns, our lives could stand an occasional revision and evaluation and be brought up-to-date. As our hymns have changed over time, so do our lives. It's called conversion, or being born again.

What we are talking about here is a changed behavior about *being*. And once we grasp this concept, we come to realize that the part of us that we haven't given to God creates a longing that demands a response. Someone wrote that when there is a willingness to see the truth of things and one conforms one's conduct to it then one has the conversion experience. Without that conversion in the drama of life we not only fail to perceive the meaning of life, but to also live a life without a meaning. So once again we find mercy. Where we discover mercy, we find God as the source, and our hope is renewed.

You might remember that in William Shakespeare's play, *As You Like It*, two of the characters are brothers. The evil one, Oliver, conspired to kill his helpless brother, Orlando. But before Oliver carries out his plot, he has a tremendous conversion, in which he confesses, "I do not shame / To tell you what I was, since my conversion / so sweetly tastes, being the thing I am." May our lives move from "I was" to "I am."

PRAYER: Gracious and patient Father, thank you for making it possible for us to change. What a blessing to know we don't have to live as despised sinners with no hope to make things right and be able start all over again. Thank you for your unconditional love. Amen.

Day 138
Our Constant Companion

Be strong and courageous. Don't tremble! Don't be afraid of them! The Lord your God is the one going with you. He won't abandon you or leave you (Deuteronomy 31:6).

DAG HAMMARSKJÖLD, WHO SERVED AS secretary general to the United Nations for eight years, was the only person to receive the Nobel Peace Prize posthumously. He is also the only secretary general to die while in office. He died in a plane crash as he was going on a cease-fire mission. President John F. Kennedy called Hammarskjöld "the greatest statesman of our century."

It was not until his death that the discovery of his private journal, *Markings*, was made. It doesn't take long in reading his journal before one realizes Hammarskjöld was a man of deep faith. *Markings* also puts before us a man of compassion who realized his role in helping the people of Third World countries and the myriad of people all over the world. He had been given opportunity to serve and he did.

In reading his journal, one will see that what sets Hammarskjöld apart from others was his dependence on a higher power to accomplish his service: God. Who was this man, and how was he able to make such an impact in the lives of so many people? Hammarskjöld tells us that once he discovered who he was, courage ceased to have any meaning for him. It was hardly any longer to be regarded as courage. It was simply the expression of who he was, what he believed, and the truth to which he had committed himself.

You can see this sort of courage in those who pride themselves on being professionals. Professional singers, fighters, or players, however they act off the stage, out of the ring, or stadium know that in their professionalism they have an expectation of themselves that they must not disappoint. They must not give up or give in; they must bring their best to what they do or they know themselves seriously diminished: They find their courage in the sense of self that comes of pride when they say, "I'm a pro!"

But we all have that sense of self and the courage that goes with it. We all have a self to lose and an expectation, which to violate is a kind of death. Martin Luther put this into words that not only gave him his courage, but have brought courage to others ever since: "It is neither safe nor right to go against conscience. Here I stand! I can do no other, God help me."

That is courage eloquently expressed. There are certain things we cannot and must not do because of who we are, what we believe, and the truth to which we are committed.

PRAYER: Father God, giver of everything good and holy, grant to us this day courage to face what life throws our way, for we all need help when courage is called for. Amen.

Day 139
No More Regrets

Because you have rejected the word of the Lord, he rejects you (1 Samuel 15:23).

The Lord said, "Go ahead and anoint him." The Lord's spirit came over David and stayed with him from that day on (1 Samuel 16:14).

O YOU DO THINGS, knowing that they are wrong but do them anyway? Do you have regrets? What are they? Are they physical or spiritual in nature? And where does God fit into all of the reasons and excuses for doing them? The first book of Samuel gives examples of both lifestyles. There was impatient Saul, doing things that he knew were not quite right, but he resolves to go ahead and do them anyway. It was part of the prophet's job description to offer up a sacrifice and bless the troops before going into battle. Saul was a bit eager to get on with it, so he tried to be prophet and do the prophet's job. He had regrets.

When Saul tried to pull one over on God and Samuel by not killing the defeated king, Agag of Amalek, God rejected Saul as Israel's king. Saul knew that he was not being obedient to God on both occasions, but something got in the way of his making the correct decision. If we ourselves follow Saul's path of disobedience, we end up having regrets. Saul certainly had them. God rejected him as Israel's king.

David on, the other hand, as the writer wrote was a "man after God's own heart." Following God's instruction, Samuel went to the home of Jesse, met all of his sons, and sent for David. David, the youngest son of Jesse, was keeping watch over the sheep. He was also a singer of songs to God. Jesse was instructed to bring David to Samuel. Jesse brought David to Samuel, who then anointed David as the new king. David ruled Israel through most of its golden years. Even with his incident with Bathsheba and Uriah, David knew what he needed to do.

In our own time, our world moves at such a click it is hard to keep up with it. As long as everything is going well, all is well; but let the first thing go wrong and we are history. We have given in to letting computers and the Internet replace our communication with information—we have regrets; 13,000 children a day die of hunger—we have regret. Some have more personal regrets: job offers, education opportunities to better themselves, relationships with family, colleagues, and God.

We know where we need to go with all our regrets. We take them to God, as did David (read Psalm 51 to get a hint on the regret David felt). We need to follow his example with our regrets, and who knows what God can and will do.

> **PRAYER:** Dear Father we regret not taking time with you as we should and could have. Forgive us and forgive us for those of your children we have failed to feed, clothe, give a cup of cold water, visited while in prison, and not sharing our faith. Give us the courage to face our regrets with the hope and promise of a better tomorrow. Amen.

—◁ ○ ▷—

Day 140
No Radio

A time to weep and a time to laugh (Ecclesiasted 3:4), . . .

ONE DAY, WHEN I LIVED IN New York City, I was walking past Columbus Circle as a homeless man came out of Central Park pushing an old grocery cart filled with all of his worldly possessions. As we passed one another, I nodded my head at his direction but our eyes never met. I started thinking about the man. Who was he? Where was he from? What events in his life led him to this sort of existence? Did he have family? Did he feel alone?

What I saw next made my spirit chuckle. There he was, a disheveled homeless man, wheeling all his worldly possessions in a supermarket cart, and on the front of the cart hung a notice that announced, "**NO RADIO**." Now, we all know that neither homelessness nor the theft of radios from cars is in any way amusing. Yet when one homeless man retains a sense of humor to laugh at such conditions, it is a triumph of the human spirit. I knew this man probably had more insight into how to live and how life really was than I did.

One night following a revival service, all of the people who had attended were invited to the fellowship hall for refreshments. I had just made light of a situation, after which I was rebuked by an eavesdropping older woman who said, "There is no room in a preacher's ministry for a sense of humor. How do you expect people to take you seriously if you are always joking around?" To which the revival speaker responded like a flash of lightning, "You are wrong. He can't have an effective ministry with out a sense of humor. Besides, a sense of humor takes the sting out of the bites of life and people like you whom we have to confront. It is like flashes of lightning along the horizon."

As someone has said, every joke is a revolution. We may need to be reminded that laughter is the mark of the nonconforming woman and man, a declaration of one's sacred independence. The notice might have said "NO RADIO," but what it announced was the greatness of the human spirit.

PRAYER: Heavenly Father, there is no doubt that you have a sense of humor that can be seen every time we look into the mirror of our minds and hearts. We are not speaking of physical features, which in some case are humorous in their own right. But we come asking that you help us not to take ourselves too seriously but take our message extremely serious. And may we do it with a bit of humor. In the name of Jesus, we pray. Amen.

Day 141
Do I Have to Go?

We should not stop gathering together with other believers, as some of you are doing. Instead, we must continue to encourage each other even more as we see the day of the Lord's coming (Hebrews 10:25).

I WANT TO SHARE A story with you that you might have already heard: A woman entered the bedroom, opened the blinds, and said, "Time to get up and get ready for church." The man turned over in bed and said, "They don't like me down there. I'm going to stay home this Sunday. I'll go back next week." Her demeanor changed, the lilt in her voice became stone cold, and her cheerful disposition had but all disappeared. She spoke, "You *are* going to church, and I am not going to repeat myself. Get up and get ready for church."

"But they don't like me at the church," he whimpered pulling the comforter over his head. "I am not going"

"Don't be silly honey. You have to go! You're the pastor! Get up and get ready."

Funny, but this is often the sad case, and what we glean from this point plays on what we feel the church as well as ourselves are suppose to be and is doing. It was this "called out" group of individuals who were willing to receive the spirit and allow Jesus to continue to do through them what he had done earlier.

Let's say that Jesus decided to come back to earth in human form. He took up residence in our part of the world. Ask yourself, "If Christ came to my part of the world, what kinds of things would begin to happen? What would Christ do?" Our task is to discern the mind of Christ and do what is right. As we think on these things it becomes very clear that people are what mattered to Christ.

Jesus was concerned about people's needs, whatever was wounding, troubling, or burdening them. It mattered not to Jesus how they had come to be in such straits. The simple fact was that a need existed, and a ministry was justified. Jesus saw our ministry to be more than a hospital for sick souls and bodies. He was also concerned about people's gifts and power and was anxious to make them aware of the potential they possessed to make a difference for good in the world.

All God wants is for us to be the church and to be a place where people are taken seriously. Are you and your church doing that in your part of the world? Is it known as place where people are taken seriously and one is so challenged to become a creative problem-solver? Christ's church is where it is acceptable to have needs and to ask for help, but it is also a place where our powers are linked up with a world that needs them.

Years ago a young man left a farm and went to the city. He heard D. L. Moody preach on the other side of the city. The young man took a streetcar every Sunday to be a part of that congregation. His landlady asked him once why he went so far to church. He simply answered: "Because they love a fellow over there. So should we!"

PRAYER: Father, give us the desire to join you in being such a reality! Amen.

<hr>

Day 142
Hurry up and Wait

Surrender yourself to the Lord, and wait patiently for him. Do not be preoccupied with an evildoer who succeeds in his way when he carries out his schemes (Psalm 37:7).

I waited patiently for the Lord (Psalm 40:1).

I RECALL VERY CLEARLY MY mother's ritual of gathering a wet sponge, a couple of paper towels, and two shoeboxes. One box contained little green and white books wrapped with rubber bands, and the other box was filled with a lot of loose stamps. My brother and my job was to glue whatever value was on the stamp to its corresponding value found on each page of

THE MUSINGS OF A WHOLLY MAN

the green and white books. One was the smallest; the stamps increased in size and value until they reached the maximum per page of fifty, the largest stamp in size and value. You received these stamps when you shopped at certain stores, and for every dollar you spent, the store would give you a certain amount of stamps to show their appreciation for shopping with them. Ours came mostly from where we shopped for groceries. These stamps could be redeemed at any S&H Green Stamp store for items like appliances, jewelry—I remember getting my first pair of cuff links there; they were black onyx—sporting goods, even a boat. People paid the sales tax and it was theirs.

Before any of this took place, upon entering the store one had to go to a machine and get a number and wait until the number was called. No number, no service. Once a worker was through with a customer, he or she would call out the next number and change the number on two monitors at the front of the store. The excitement would build the closer they came to our number. My mother had to pull in reins sometimes to try and calm my brother and me—today it is called "delayed gratification"—even for just a few moments. We would become fidgety as we waited for what seemed like hours. "How much longer do we have to wait?" I would ask each time a number was called that was not ours. Our excitement would begin to wane, and then it would happen: our number, finally our number would be called. "Hey, that's our number," my brother said as he jumped in front of me, heading for the counter. I handed the lady behind the counter the crumpled up number on which I had had a death grip since being in the store. She smiled. I smiled back. We obtained our purchases and headed home.

Each one of us has experienced at some point in our lives a need to wait patiently for God. We probably get fidgety holding our breath waiting to hear the medical report or reading the letter that our job is being phased out . . . waiting . . . services have been terminated. No matter how long we are called to wait—it might be long or it might be short—but we are sometimes called to wait. It does not matter how tragic or painful the wait, but we do not have to go it alone. As a matter of fact, scripture promises us in more than an isolated passage that God hears our cries for help, sets our feet upon a rock, and makes our steps secure. What comfort!

PRAYER: We are encouraged to wait patiently for you, and you will give our heart's desire. We go in your promise, strength, and love. Come now, O holy God, and deliver us from the evil one and from ourselves. Amen.

Day 143
The Problems of Prayer?

At the same time, the Spirit also helps us in our weakness, because we don't know how to pray for what we need (Romans 8:26).

WE HAVE HEARD THE ADAGE when trying to talk someone into trying something they have never done before, "It's so easy, a child could do it," knowing all along that there wasn't anything simple and easy about it, yet not wanting that "little" technicality to prevent them from missing out.

I want to apply this same line of thinking to prayer. There is nothing simple and easy about praying. Grant that a child can do it, cry out to God. That does not make anything simple or easy about it.

The fact of the matter is, prayer is surrounded by difficulties. The most obvious is the lack of prayer, followed closely behind by knowing how to pray for particular situations. For example, should I pray that God would heal that person seriously hurt in an accident or for God to be merciful and end their suffering?

The difficulties sometimes are compounded when the situations and circumstances that touch the event are so clouded with complexity and ambiguity that we are not clear on how to pray. We are literally confused. Do we pray that the one who has abused and killed children be caught and punished, or do we pray for their conversion and extend forgiveness?

Prayer is hard. How do you pray? I believe it was Mother Teresa who said,

"If you find it hard to pray, you can say, 'Come Holy Spirit.'" Those words combined with Paul's words assure us that we can receive wisdom from the Holy Spirit to instruct us in *how* to pray.

We might find that we are led to pray in very general terms: *Do as you see best in this situation, O God.* Other times we find ourselves praying that God would fill the situation with God's presence and assurance. Yet, at other times our prayers are running over with boldness and full of faith: *We thank you ahead of time for your merciful and gracious hand on our family member.*

PRAYER: Father, thank you for your gift of love: the Holy Spirit who guides us in how to pray. As we open up to you we open up to all that God may do. That's where we want to be. Amen.

Day 144
It's for You, Too

Behold, I stand at the door and knock; if any hear my voice and open the door, I will come in to him, and will sup with him, and him with me (Revelation 3:20).

GOD IS CONTINUALLY CALLING US IN order to awaken us to the wonderful feeling of loving and being loved. God wants fellowship with us throughout the days of our lives. Sure, we have failed and fallen short of the glory of God. But God never gives up on us. We are never an embarrassment to God. With Parkinson's, our clumsiness, the shuffling of our feet, our falling, our drooling, our slurred speech can all cause a caregiver to have stranded patience. But not so with God. God calls us into relationship with the divine at all times.

God desires more than our works, our sacrifices, or our constant busyness on God's behalf. What God wants is the deep and secret space in our hearts where we abide in the Lord and God with us, the God of the universe, the Almighty One who created the world, created us, and who wants to live with us. It is hard to believe that God wants to have communion with me.

The word sup is quite a curious word. It symbolizes the ultimate communion and fellowship with God that can characterize our days. Every ordinary moment carries the possibility of awareness and encounter so deep and close that it is like sitting down to share an intimate meal with God.

God knocks, wanting not just our salvation and our good works, but also to awaken us to a journey further and deeper into the spiritual, into the depths of God's presence.

There's the knock. . .

PRAYER: It boggles our minds and our spirits stretched to know that you, the creator God, want to come to where we are and to sup with us. You honor us. Now make us faithful and true. Amen.

Day 145
God Chose to Reveal Divine Love

For Jews demand signs, and Greeks desire wisdom, but we proclaim Christ crucified, a stumbling block to the Jews and foolishness to the Gentiles (1 Corinthians 1:22–23).

THE POWERLESSNESS OF THE MANGER became the powerlessness of the cross. People jeered at him, laughed at him, spat in his face, and shouted, "He saved others; he cannot save himself. He is the King of Israel; let him come down from the cross now, and we will believe in him" (Matt 27:42). He hung there, his flesh torn apart by pieces of metal, and broken glass embedded in a cat-o'-nine-tails, his heart broken by the abandonment and rejection of his friends and abuse from his enemies, his mind tortured by anguish, his spirit shrouded from his enemies. By this time in his life and ministry, Jesus knew what was to befall him. It was a different story with the rest of his followers. Even at the time he started toward Jerusalem the last week of his earthly life, they were still voicing their support to him: "No, we will die with you. I will not forsake you. We will die with you." Where were those devoted, brave men and women who were going to die with him just a few hours earlier? That's how God chose to reveal to us the divine love, bringing us back into an embrace of compassion, and convincing us that anger has been melted away in endless mercy.

The question that arises is what amount of that divine love will we use for our enemies and those that persecute and have persecuted us?

> PRAYER: Oh, how God loves you and me. Oh how God loves you and me. He gave his life so we may all live. Oh, how God loves you. Oh, how God loves you. Oh, how God loves you and me. Thank you Father, dear Father, for sharing your incredible love with all who accept it. Amen.

Day 146
Dead or Alive

You are like whitewashed graves that look beautiful on the outside but inside are full of dead people's bones and every kind of impurity (Matthew 24:27).

AN ELDERLY AND WISE PROFESSOR made the dramatic claim that he had the ability to walk into the library of one of his former students and tell them the year that they died. What he referred to was the year that they stopped buying books, lost their edge, surrendered their interest in things, and stopped reading.

There is example after example of those who never do. Gardner C. Taylor is 96 and still reserves part of his day for study, prayer, and reflection. John Killinger is in his 80s and still actively writes books and speaks. There is Anneal Ledbetter in her late 90s, and she still visits the jails every Wednesday to meet the unique needs that each of the inmates has. And there is Anne Pace, who took early retirement in her 50s to look after her mother in her final years of suffering and her death; now she goes around quietly ministering to and praying for the needs of many others, including her brother.

All these folk are examples of what still can be done so as not to be among the living dead. What are some things we do to help keep our edge and not grow old and stale, not contributing anything to this old world's idea of what is realistic and what is not. What about you and me? When did we die? When did we give up? When did we lose interest and become satisfied with praise, veneration, and our reputation, like those ministers who live off of their reputations of days gone by, when we might have had greater insight, heightened sensitivity, and deeper wisdom? We have sold our souls to mediocrity and the shallows of the ocean of life rather than launching out into the deep for the adventure or catch of our lives.

Throwing in the towel, so to speak, folk hear a sentence of constant deterioration. They give up and quit rather than stand up to PD, seek support from family and friends, and tap into the medical side of the disease, causing some to contribute their life in ways they haven't done before.

It is written of the Irish writer, Brendan Behan, that he died of "alcohol and adulation." Have you died? Do you know the year you died? Are you alive and living, or are you are dying or dead? Do you know when are we staying alive all of our life? Paul encourages us to press on toward the mark of the high calling of God. That's living.

PRAYER: Father, thank you for letting us know that it's never too late to live. Amen.

⸺◦⸺

Day 147
Disappointments

Without counsel, purposes are disappointed (Proverbs 15:22, KJV).

IF YOU HAVE BEEN BRAVE enough to love, sometimes you won and sometimes you lost. If you have cared enough to try, sometimes it worked and
sometimes it didn't. If you have been bold enough to dream and found
yourself with some dreams that came true and a lot of them didn't and the
earth shattered, then you can look back from the mountaintop you now find
yourself standing upon, like Moses contemplating the tablets that would guide
human behavior for a millennia, resting in the ark alongside the broken fragments of an earlier dream. And you, like Moses can realize how full your life
has been and how richly you are blessed.

Ask too little of life, and you risk coming to the end of your days never having tasted many of the pleasures put on earth for you.

Mariana Caplan asks in her book, *The Way of Failure*, "Are we going to use
our remaining time to finally love well, cherish others, to forgive them and to
forgive ourselves?" Our stories are not stories of uninterrupted happiness, but
we choose to give them a happy ending. Though it is not in our power to dictate the end of the story, it remains in our power to choose how we will respond to the final decree. We can articulate pride rather than regret, gratitude
rather than bitterness, praise rather than envy.

"Life can be painful if you do it right." To wish to forget the hope because
it wasn't realized, to try to cleanse your mind of the beautiful dream because
it didn't come true is to miss out on life altogether, because life is designed to
be lived in an alternation of hours of sunlight and hours of darkness. My life
needs a reasonable amount of light and darkness. Does yours?

To be brave enough to dream even as you realize that many of our dreams
won't come true, to dream is to imagine a world and a life better than the one
we know now. Perhaps failures and disappointments can teach us that we
might fail at one thing or that we might fail at several things, but that does
not mean that we are failures. The worth of a person's soul is not measured by
the size of his or her bank account or the volume of applause a person evokes,
but by one's humanity, by one's compassion, even by the courage to keep on

dreaming amid the broken pieces of one's earlier dreams. True success consists not in becoming the person you dreamed of being when you were young, but in becoming the person you were meant to be, the person you are capable of being when you are at your best.

PRAYER: Father, help us to face our disappointments as did Christ. Strengthen our witness. Amen.

Day 148
Words That Heal

Peace I leave with you, my peace I give to you (John 14:27).

MOST OF US AT ONE TIME OR another have felt as did the writer of the book of Proverbs when he writes, "I'm weary, O God. I'm weary and worn out, O Lord" (Prov 30:1). The one place we could find solace, hope, and peace is no longer the safe haven that it once was. Now in the past year, great conflicts within the church have been fought. Many good-hearted people have been wounded so deeply that there is hardly a conflict-free zone left in their hearts. Even words like prayer, contemplation, adoration, and worship have been drawn into the conflict, and they are no longer just words to indicate ways of being with God. They are often perceived as words used by conservatives to keep people in line and remind them of the good old days when piety still flourished.

Is there a way out? Maybe we have to train ourselves to speak more from the experience of grace than from a wounded, frustrated, and disillusioned place within. We feel rejected, misunderstood, neglected, or displaced whether we find ourselves on the left or the right in the church political spectrum. As long as these feelings dominate our discussion, little building of a community of faith can take place. But if we try to speak from the place where we have experienced God's forgiveness, God's healing touch, God's new life, God's abundant grace, a new language might be found: a language of gratitude, yes a Eucharistic language.

PRAYER: Our Gracious Father, help us not to be side-tracked by words that have been twisted in order for them to fit our particular agenda to get our way with things. Plant in our hearts the gift of your Spirit so it can aid us in daily battle. Amen.

━━━━◀◇▶━━━━

Day 149
Dying to Live

I can guarantee this truth: a single grain of wheat doesn't produce anything unless it is planted in the ground and dies. If it dies, it will produce a lot of grain (John 12:24).

JESUS COULD WORK A CROWD BUT would always leave them with food for thought. We don't know what the makeup of the crowd was on any particular day. Could he be talking to a group of FFI (Future Farmers of Israel) or a group consulting the *Farmer's Almanac*? Maybe the majority of the crowd present were farmers, and Jesus wanted to leave them with his message in terms that they could understand. He could have been talking about himself and the type of life he was trying to usher in through his life, death, and resurrection. I can imagine heads were bobbing in agreement as he told them the seed must be planted and die before living and producing the crop. They knew that; that's obvious.

But what life was this Jesus was ushering in? It was a life on this planet in which human life would be changed irreversibly and forever. But something went wrong. We can sit where we are with our feet propped on our spiritual foot stools wondering what is the secret? It is the same secret that it was over 2,000 years ago. You've got to be willing to sacrifice something before you can go anywhere. You've got to be willing to start losing before you can begin to win. You've got to be willing to die before you can really live.

There are two principles by which we can live our lives: self-interest or self-giving. Which is it for you? Don't answer this one too quickly or easily. This can be scary stuff. It's going to cost; it's going to mean sacrifice. What does that mean for you? I guess for most of us it means that there is a bit of us that is selfish and proud and hypocritical and greedy and resentful and bitter, and we have to throw it away and bury it for love of Christ if we are ever really going to live. And if we live that kind of life, however inadequately, when we die, the painful death to self-interest alone makes that new kind of life possible. The life we will experience is beautiful beyond words. It is a glimpse of heaven, a new dimension of living, in which heaven breaks into this world of ours.

If we share in Christ's sacrifice, we share in his harvest. As we share in Christ's death, so we shall share in his life.

> **PRAYER:** Lord, give us courage to face what we know to be true: no sacrifice, no harvest. Show us what is inside of our living that must die if we truly wish to live; then give us the courage and patience to see the seed grow into the eternal joy of your harvest. Amen.

---<o>---

Day 150
The Wonder of It All

Make the most of your opportunities (Ephesians 5:16).

I AM QUITE CONFIDENT THAT A great many prayers have been raised concerning Parkinson's, prayers for individuals who have the dreaded disease, their caretakers, the doctors that deal with patients on a daily basis, the researchers, and those who willingly participate in the actual experiments. And although there is no cure, great strides have been made in helping folk with this disease. Since being diagnosis with the disease, I have been pleasantly taken aback at the progress that has been made. My mother also had

Parkinson's, and when we were together or talked on the telephone, we would compare and see who had to give up what. We would do our own experiments and research. Sometimes we were wrong, but most of the time we were correct.

It broke my heart to see her body losing control more and more each time I would visit and knowing that 2.5 million others, including me, would awaken hoping and praying that today would be good day. If some part of my body didn't want to work, then I would find another that did, and usually I was successful more times than not.

For example, here are some things that I do to help me through the day. I have some elderly friends and family that I talk with each week to check on them. If my speech is clear that day, I'll make some telephone calls. If my speech is all garbled, I will send an email. If my fingers and hands are not working too smoothly, I use Nuance-Dragon Speaking software that prints on the computer what I am saying.

If there is not a problem with my gait, I will walk short distances or ride my bike—I use extreme caution doing this one, for I have fallen (just walking) and shattering my bones in my lower wrists. There are always stretching and flexibility exercises to do. If you have a total body shutdown, then it's okay on days such as these to lounge around and give your body the time it needs to refuel.

What I am attempting to say is: find something to do, stay active, and remember, you have PD—PD does not have you. Even Paul gets in on the circumstances when he encourages and admonishes those at the church in Ephesus to make the most of their—and *your*—opportunities!

> **PRAYER:** Father, open our hearts and minds to the opportunities that are all around us. Keep us aware of the kingdom work that surrounds us. Amen.

Day 151
Have You Been Drinking?

They grope in the dark with no light, and he makes them stumble like drunks (Job 12:25).

*I*T HAPPENED WHILE WALKING ON THE beach. I was experiencing an unusually long off-time, and it was not very good to be walking anywhere, much less on a sandy shoreline. In my effort to stay vertical, I was stumbling and weaving and really struggling to stay upright. I only had a short way to get to my destination. I paused long enough to let my lungs catch up with the rest of my body, and then continued clumsily along. I passed a group of ladies that were casting a critical, suspicious eye my way. My wife was several steps behind me, watching our daughter, who was playing in the ocean. Once I was out of earshot, one of them said, "That man has had one too many drinks." "He should be made to get off the beach." "Our children do not need to be exposed to that." All the other ladies continued bobbing their heads in agreement.

Finally, my wife had caught up with me, had overheard their comments, and had enough. She interrupted their little gossip session by saying, "That man you have been critical of is my husband. He has not had too many drinks because he doesn't drink. Besides if he were to mix alcohol with his medications he would suffer from extreme side-effects. He walks clumsily because he has Parkinson's disease. And for those of you who don't know, PD is a progressive neurological disease. There is no cure for it, and it affects his motor skills and the fluid motion that you and I have and take for granted. I just hope and pray that none of you or your families will have to experience such a debilitating disease. Hopefully, you will be a little more sensitive before passing judgment," and with that she walked back to where I was, away from the ladies with their apologies hanging in the ocean breeze.

Parkinson's is certainly not a disease that you can disguise or cover up for very long. It is what it is, and it affects people differently. For me, my balance and walking are certainly areas that are affected by Parkinson's. But in whatever circumstance I find myself, I will trust that God will reassure me that all this suffering is not wasted.

PRAYER: Father, sometimes, as with Job's friends, things are not always as we may think. We know that only you can reveal true wisdom. When we try to cope apart from you we fail. You know all things as well as the things in our lives before they happen. We are an ignorant people because we do not listen to your wisdom, a wisdom that would direct us to a higher way of living, in which there is peace that passes all understanding. Make us receivers of your wisdom. Amen.

<hr />

Day 152
Unexpected Loveliness

You will always have the poor with you, but you will not always have me with you (John 12:8).

A NOVEL WAS WRITTEN SOME years back in which its British author attempted to describe a second marriage. It was not just the man and woman in this relationship. The woman had a teenaged daughter from a previous marriage. The husband tried hard to build a relationship with the teenager. The girl was always walking around sullenly, with an unloving character and without any quality that would cause her to stick out.

Time passed, and the girl's mother became very sick. Suddenly, the girl opened up like a rosebud, and she went about her tasks like another Florence Nightingale. Her demeanor and even her looks changed. There was a radiance that emanated from her. There was nothing that was a bother to her. She served with a servant's spirit. She was transformed.

Now, if the man had made a judgment about her based on her first appearances, if he had made a decision about her based on his first impression, he would have been mistaken. He was kept away from making a hasty decision wrongly based on their initial encounter.

A man in my church who is a rock hound tells me of a rock that when you take it in your hand looks rather dull and lusterless. The more you turn it over and over, however, and handle it and if you hold it just right so the light rays hit it a certain way, it will begin to shine and sparkle like a diamond. The sparkle was there in the rock all along and has been there, if you are willing to look for it.

People are like this. Everybody has a gift, and everybody does something well and has a redeeming feature. For the teenaged girl it was her mother getting sick and her being called upon to help care for her.

What kind of difference do you think our world would experience if we were to stop looking for faults and rather spent that time looking for gifts? If we were to do that, there is no doubt that we would certainly have some surprises—pleasant surprises—because we would often find loveliness where we never expected loveliness to be found.

> **PRAYER:** God of our hearts, keep us in your loving embrace as you share with us how you wish to use us and our talents. Then give us the courage to faithfully share the loveliness within us. Amen.

Day 153
Don't Turn Back!

When the young man heard this, he became very sad, because he was very rich (Luke 18:23).

TURNING BACK TOO SOON. It is such a good description for the reason that there is a great deal of failure in life. It explains why the faith of so many people fails in the hour of trial because it is not theirs. It is something that they have accepted because someone else said it, not because they discovered it. I know a man who would agree with the Greeks of Plato's time that the lie in the soul was the worst of lies. He insists on telling the truth, yet he has less passion for seeing the truth. He is quite good at self-deception. He loves a dim religious light, cultivates a fog, and calls it reverence.

This is the way with goodness, and a perfect example is the Bible story of the rich young ruler. What was he truly seeking? He wanted goodness, and he came to Jesus and asked for guidance. After Jesus quoted the Ten Commandments, the young man replied that he had kept them all. To which Jesus told him one more thing that he had to do. He told him to go and sell all he had and give it the poor. This time he responded to Jesus by walking away sorrowfully. Scripture says he did so because he was very rich. If he had put this thoughts into words, he might have said, "I want goodness, but I don't want it that badly." He turned back too soon. Without giving it a try he turned back too soon.

In generosity to others, we so often turn back too soon. In forgiving others we so often turn back too soon. In trying to understand the other person, especially if they are hard to like, much less to love, we so often turn back too soon. Think of all the richness of life we could experience if did not have this habit of turning back too soon.

With that said, it is clear that what Jesus wants is full women, men, and children who will go all the way with him. The tragedy is that we meet lots of people every day who turn back too soon. Hopefully, their turning back is not because they see us live, for theirs is a lack of being able to see things to completion.

PRAYER: Father God, we ask of you a clear mind and a grander sense of direction, so as to know where we are. We want to join you and your other followers in your grand march to the kingdom so we will not turn back too soon. Forgive us for the times we have failed. Restore to us the joy of our salvation. Amen.

Day 154
Do You Belong?

Through him we have received God's kindness and the privilege of being apostles who bring people from every nation to the obedience associated with faith. This is for the honor of his name. You are among those who have been called to belong to Jesus Christ (Romans 1:5–6).

DO YOU BELONG TO ANY CLUBS? If you do, how many do you belong to, and what kind of clubs are they? Whatever the club, you can rest assured that they have a Mission Statement. In that Mission Statement, the group attempts to put into words their purpose for being and maybe even some of their goals they hope to accomplish. The club members are expected to know this statement. At the opening of every meeting the members may include reading or reciting the Mission Statement along with the Pledge of Allegiance. In addition to the recitation at the opening of the meeting, a roll call is taken to see who is present and who is not. You can be sure that the members know the requirements for becoming a member, staying a member, and for belonging to the club or lodge. To belong means we own a membership. With that membership comes certain relationships and activities. Paying dues is mandatory. And once one has obtained a membership, he or she can use it as often and responsibility as desired. But we never belong!

The word *belong* has another meaning when it is used among people. If I were a slave who belonged to a family, I would not use them; they would use me.

Paul says that we are called to "belong" to Jesus. We are to become his possession. He is to own us and use us according to his purpose. Jesus's ownership of us, of course, is not mandatory. We are free; the only way Jesus can possess us is if we give ourselves to him. I know you believe in Jesus. Have you given yourself to him? Only when we give ourselves to him is he able to use us freely.

Paul's vocation was to bring about obedience of faith in those who belong to Jesus. Faith here does not mean assent to statements about Jesus. It means "trusting" him. The obedience that comes from trusting is the measure of belonging to him.

PRAYER: Lord, may you so possess us that all we do or say may be an expression of your love and will for us and for your people. Amen.

⸺◇⸺

Day 155
I Am So Afraid

Jesus told them, "It's me. Don't Be Afraid" (John 6:20)!

But perfect love casts out fear (1 John 4:18).

I BELIEVE THAT OUR PRIMARY purpose in life is to grow spiritually. This means that even in the midst of the most excruciating pain and loss where we confront our fears most readily, as well as in times of great joy celebration, we can ask, "How did I get working?" and "What spiritual lesson or lessons should I analyze and learn?" Such lessons come to us in more surprising moments. We never know when we will be stopped in our tracks, or, figuratively speaking, when God will come toward us on the water and change the course of our lives. Fear will be our first response, and we tend to hold onto our comfortable fears. But if we can walk through the veneer of fear, the spiritual growth of primary love awaits us on the other side.

The play, *Harvey*, by Mary Chase, is about Elwood P. Dowd, an eccentric man who drank quite a bit. His closest friend is an enormous white rabbit called Harvey, who is unseen for the most part by anyone but Elwood. His family hired Dr. Chumley, a psychiatrist, to cure Elwood and relieve the family of Harvey's embarrassing presence. But being a good psychiatrist and therefore willing to move beyond the boundaries of fear, Dr. Chumley has a spectacular conversion. Finally, in one scene, he blurts out, "Flyspecks! I have been living my life among flyspecks while miracles have been leaning on lampposts." One of Harvey's natural habitats was a lamppost outside Elwood's favorite drinking establishment.

So how would you respond to a six-foot tall rabbit leaning against a lamp-post? Run away? Walk hurriedly past it? Would you stop, search within yourself for an explanation, and trust that there is a spiritual lesson to be learned? The miracles of perfect love lie on the other side of the boundaries of fear we have set in our lives. Breaking familiar and spiritually deadening patterns, with God's help, fear not, is to move beyond the flyspecks in which we have existed. "Sooner or later," writes Jack Kornfield, "we have to learn to let go and allow the changing mystery of life to move through us without our fearing it, without holding or grasping." What ever boundary of fear we break, be it fear of death, fear of life, fear of the unknown, fear of men in sandals and flowing attire walking on water toward us, we will find ourselves hanging around lamp-posts a lot more, ready to experience the miracles that will most certainly occur. *Surprise . . . and . . . fear not*!

> **PRAYER:** Father, open our eyes that we may see the abundance of Harveys in this world. Remind us that the fear this world uses to immobilize and consume us has already been defeated, freeing us to live generously. Grant more of us the willingness to launch into the deep without any fear because you are on that side as well. Amen.

Day 156
Be Careful What You Pray For

I will do anything you ask the Father in my name (John14:15).

I ONCE WAS TOLD A about how a man's prayer for patience was answered. During his devotion time one morning before going to work, he had been challenged to a deeper commitment to God. His daughters were late getting off to school, which made him late. But he wasn't going to let anything ruin this feeling. So kissing his children goodbye, he uttered an off the shoulder prayer that God would grant him more patience. The man was flying high after being refreshed by his time with God.

Grabbing his case, he was off to the train station, humming a hymn as he went. He stopped at the top of the hill, suddenly realizing that the train pulling out of the station was *his*. His day was scheduled to the hilt with very little time for anything else. He had prayed that God would give him patience, and in less than an hour he missed the train that would have taken him into New York City where he worked. He had to wait for the next train. Upon its arrival he discovered it was a local train, which meant that it stopped at every train station on its trek into NYC; the next train that was not a local would not be there until much later. Needless to say, he spent a lot of his time fretfully calling colleagues and rearranging his schedule until it dawned on him that God had answered his morning prayer for patience. This gave him the time and the opportunity to exercise it. He had not only missed his train but had nearly missed the opportunity to exercise patience.

If you pray for patience so that you will be a more effective and stronger believer, you had better get ready for a rocky ride. You will be tested time and time again. But you also need to hear Jesus' words, "I will never leave you or forsake you." Such circumstances are usually not happy moments and could be filled with great distress. We covet by having experiences we don't welcome. Courage is never easy. Fortitude is demanding. Patience is difficult. Hope is exercised when it is easier to despair. It was the harsh north wind that made the rugged Vikings.

> **PRAYER:** Our dear benevolent Father, once again we approach your throne with our list of wants. You are patient and listen, but you do more than just listen; you answer. Open our eyes that we may see your working and your answers to our prayers. So many times we are guilty of holding a preconceived notion of how they should be answered. Though the way might be difficult, you are there to smooth out the roughness so we come out on the other side of the situation better and stronger. In the name of Jesus, we pray. Amen.

Day 157
Words Spoken?

In quietness and trust shall be your strength (Isaiah 30:15).

THE CHILDREN'S RHYME, "STICKS AND stones may break my bones, but words will never hurt me," must have come from someone who was a deaf mute. I take issue with this chirpy statement because I occasionally have felt the sting of ugly and hateful words.

Words have two opportunities for dwelling places. There are those words that emerge out of silence and return to it. It is in this first category that we find silence being fearful and hostile. When that silence is fearful and hostile, words can hurt and destroy. But when that silence is a silence of love and peace, words can heal and recreate God's silence. And that silence would be the place from which God speaks. It is a silence free from fear, anger, suspicious hatred, or violence. And in that silence, there in God's silence, there is only love. When God speaks out of silence there is only love. When God speaks out of the silence, that Word creates new life. In Jesus that Word becomes flesh and dwells among us to reveal to us the love-filled silence of God and to lead us always closer to that silence.

What a difference words spoken out of a love-filled silence are. The silence spoken here is between a fearful and love-filled silence, and between words spoken in fear and words spoken in love! May our fearful silences become more and more love-filled, so that our words can become increasingly creative. Prayer is the way to let this happen. In prayer we gradually enter into the love-filled silence of God, and we find there words to speak in the name of God to each other.

PRAYER: Dear Father in heaven and on earth, we pray for our brothers and sisters who do not know you as the loving God that you are, those who have not basked in your glory and benefited from your words of love and forgiveness. Empower us to share our experiences with them so that they may join the community of true believers. May our own vocabulary become more love-filled.

In the name of the one in whom we find our being, Jesus Christ, our living Lord. Amen.

Day 158
Growing Resentment

From Mount Hor they set out by the way to the Red Sea, to go around the land of Edom; but the people became impatient on the way. The people spoke against God and against Moses (Numbers 21:4–5).

MANY TIMES IN OUR WALK OF life, we find ourselves on a downward spiral because we have allowed some hurt spirit go unresolved. We are slow in dealing with it such that it continues spiraling downward. Unless it is resolved, it will fester into resentful spirit. Then it becomes a free-for-all. We begin resenting everything that is being attempted and does not cater to our way of thinking or doing. PD folk and their caregivers have to work particularly hard at this point. It is so easy to fall back into feelings of jealousy and resentment because we cannot do what we once did and even if we can, the speed in which we work is much slower.

An excellent example of this growing resentment can be found in Jesus's story that has become known as the parable of the prodigal son. The resentment falls squarely on the shoulders of the elder brother. The first thing the elder brother has to do is to be willing to try and bridge what has been created by resentment. That will be the beginning of becoming an equal and returning to intimacy. Remember the resentful words of the elder brother? "All these years I've worked hard like a slave for you; I've never once disobeyed one of your commands." Do you remember the resentment? He could have said, "I'm so glad that I was always obedient and listened to you," but instead he lashed out at his father, saying, "Never once have I disobeyed." In angry virtue the elder son continues, "You've never given me so much as a little goat for a celebration with my friends."

There are times the elder son rises up in us. We experience emotions of jealousy and anger because the elder son in us believes we have earned our father's friendship. "I've done this, I've done that. I've done such, I've done so-and-so, and you have not given me anything in return." The elder son in us sees the relationship to our father as that of boss over slave worker. He couldn't celebrate the younger son's return because his heart was full of anger, jealousy, and resentment rather than grace, forgiveness, and love, which are the only emotions that can heal the elder son in all of us.

> **PRAYER:** Our gracious heavenly Father, all too often we have hearts like the elder son. Instead of joining in the celebration we sit outside and let the negative emotions win out. When our spirits get so bitter that it is difficult for us to find space for your love, melt our resentment down with your love and restore our relationship with you and all of the elder and younger brothers. In the precious name of Jesus, we pray. Amen.

Day 159
The Silence of the Books

You have already received whatever you prayed for, and it will be yours. Whenever you pray, forgive anything you have against anyone. Then your Father in heaven will forgive your failures (Mark 11:25).

WHEN LIFE BECOMES TOPSY-TURVY, I find escape, oddly enough, in my study. The air is thick with the solitude and peace that I find both nurturing, even healing, here. Sitting amongst my silent companions, the great cloud of witnesses that surrounds me, I begin to mend. My troubled mind, my fractured spirit, my diluted self-esteem are waiting, ready for some form some degree, some rightness.

There I confront my demons, trying to make sense of the whys and the hows. There I receive help with the fight against evil as well as myself. Are they two separate entities or are they one and the same? I seek answers to my questions, and in seeking the answers I am met with the undeniable assurance that I am not alone as much as I thought. I haven't been thrown out or discarded. My study is transformed into a holy place, a place where the high business of the soul is transacted. I bow my soul before God's presence. What am I looking for?

The call word is forgiveness. Forgiveness as the truest form of love means being accepted by God and our fellowman without bitterness, even with the flaws, and imperfections. This unconditional love and forgiveness needs to be given to another person, and I pray that they accept my flaws as well. If that person doesn't do that, if one has done all he or she can do to restore a broken relationship and is still refused or given conditions to the parceling of forgiveness and love, then rest in the knowledge that you have done your part. What matters most is that one is restored to God, whose mercy is not conditional!

To be whole before God means to stand before the Almighty with all our faults, as well as all of our virtues, and then hear the message of our acceptability.

But at the end, if we are brave enough to love, if we are strong enough to forgive, if we are generous enough to rejoice in another's happiness, and we are wise enough to know that there is enough love to go around for us all, then we can achieve a fulfillment that no other living creature will ever know. We can re-enter Paradise.

PRAYER: Gracious Father, you who provide for any and every sin if we but come to you in prayer and give it to you: You give us the gift of forgiveness and allow us to rejoin all the saints, both living and dead, in praising you for your gift. Amen.

Day 160
Being Converted

I'm convinced that God, who began a good work in you, will carry it through to completion on the day of Christ Jesus (Philippians 1:6).

IF YOU HAVE ATTENDED A Protestant church for any amount of time, you have heard Sunday school teachers, preachers, and traveling evangelists speak fervently about being born again, or converted. I am afraid to admit it, but many in my Baptist tradition place more importance on the initial stage and remain there, falling short in saying that conversion is more than a one time happening, that if you have been born again, you have to go through baptism and the like because the first doesn't count, since it didn't take. They tell us that our lives will be different, and they will. But we must understand that we all start at the same place: the center of our lives. The center is not so much a state of being as a point of beginning. What needs to be stressed is that to be converted is to enter into a process of change and growth. To embrace this new birth, we must understand that conversion is a process with God as the center. And the center is not simply an inner place where we are in touch with God's presence. We respond to the world from our center. We love as we are loved. We forgive as we have been forgiven. We show our compassion as compassion has been shown to us.

Being converted is when God taps on our heart's door and invites us to join God on a spiritual journey. It is when we realize that God loves us and has nothing to do with who we are, what we do, or what we have done. Perfection is not required. It's more than going to sleep one night and waking up the next morning completely new and whole. No. It is a birthing process, and, as in a normal birthing, we are dependent upon others to make sure that we receive the things we need to go and grow the right way. In matters concerning the spiritual birthing all we need is the Holy Trinity. But we must not impede the process. Come, let us grow into Christ.

PRAYER: Here we are Lord, waiting to be more like your Son but questioning whether or not we really want to change from the life we are living. Help us to be like Paul, who changed from being a hindrance to being a blessing to you and your church. Grant us that power and the desire to change and to grow where we are planted. In the name of the one who made it possible, Jesus Christ, our Lord. Amen.

◄○►

Day 161
That's Enough

Stop doubting and believe (John 20:27).

HAVE YOU SEEN THE COMMERCIAL IN which the little boy is following a man around and asking, "But why?" The little boy follows the man everywhere he goes, posing the same question each time: "But why?" The man answers each "but why," only to hear the little boy follow up with yet another, "But Why?" Then comes the last straw: The man has had enough, and his frustrated response shows he is close to edge of ringing the little boy's neck. The little boy's next "but why" is followed by, "Why don't you go and ask your father?"

How many of you, who are nodding your heads and chuckling, have been in the same predicament? Most of us, at some point, have been there and done that. There seems to be a flow in the steady stream of questions, until we are so inundated with their unquenchable curiosity that we might blurt out in thunderous frustration, "*Because!*" We just want them to believe us because we said so. As a child growing up in North Carolina, when we heard the word "because," our comeback was, "Because is not an answer." Sometimes that would settle the matter, or there might have been an explosion. In those moments, who knows if we are right in our response? Kids want to know why things are the way they are, what makes things and people tick, why they can't be different, and why they have to be a certain way when it doesn't seem right or fair.

As adults, when we are faced with a crisis or tragedy, our heads erupt with questions and, especially, the question, "Why?" Loss has a tendency to shake us up. It makes us question who we are and what we believe. In many ways, we lose our sense of direction, our vision. Everything becomes confused and out of focus, and we are uncertain as to which way to turn. The thought of venturing forth into the unknown looms as a threat to our very well-being. When this happens, we, like the disciples, retreat into our safe hiding places and lock the doors behind us.

John uses Thomas as an illustration of what many of the disciples were thinking. Their hopes and dreams had been destroyed on the cross. They needed Jesus for his direction and vision and missed his physical presence among them. Some doubted what kind of future they might have without him to lead them and give meaning to their lives. That's why I like Thomas so much, because he was able to voice what others were afraid to say.

Thomas doubted the resurrection. He wanted proof, tangible truth, something he could grasp with all his senses. When Jesus appeared the second time, he offered to alleviate Thomas's doubt by letting him put his finger in his hand and to place his hand in his side that he might be moved from unbelief to belief. That was all Thomas needed. He responded to Jesus's invitation with the words, "My Lord and my God." Can that be our response, too? Will we let our hearts be changed from self-centeredness and hate to faith in God to work in people's lives? We are being called to love. By faith, we can reach out to those who may seek to destroy us. We need to be willing to see the faces of persons and respond to human need.

Now, are we allowing the Spirit to change us? How are we recognizing the dignity of people around us? How are we moving from an insistence on knowledge to a belief by faith in the power of God to work miracles not only in our lives but also in the lives of people everywhere. Can we, like Thomas, proclaim, "My Lord and my God?" Do my actions witness to Christ's love and forgiveness for all?

> **PRAYER:** Father, help us to trust you to bring about change in our lives to do what is needed that we can join with Thomas as he moves from knowledge to faith, saying, "My Lord and my—our—God." Amen.

Day 162
Yonder Shining Light

Your eye is the lamp of your body . . . it will be as bright as a lamp shining on you (Luke 11:34, 36).

ERNEST HEMINGWAY ONCE WORKED FOR A Toronto newspaper but gave that up to write stories. Some people thought him crazy to give up a steady paying job for one that was filled with so much uncertainty. It was a terrifying decision, for he surrendered security by making it. He would have to write novels the rest of his life, and at that time he didn't have a single novel to his name. As a matter of fact, he didn't even have one good chapter to his name—not even one good paragraph. But he decided that he could write one true sentence, and he did. The rest is known to anyone who can read.

What do you believe would have happened had Hemingway waited until everything was in place before he wrote his one perfect sentence? Our world would be bereft of many of the classics in literature, such as *The Old Man and the Sea*, *A Farewell to Arms*, and many others. Hear the message, here: we don't have to do it within a day, a week, a month, or a year. When we attempt to meet goals or instincts on our timetable rather than God's, we find ourselves coming up short. We had rather have everything in place and ready for it to happen with little or no help from us. But Hemingway showed us a different side, a side of faith. What courage to launch out into the deep, as Jesus instructed his disciples. Don't wade in the water that only comes to your ankles out where it is twenty fathoms over your head. If God is leading us, then we have to do it no matter the cost. All that is needed is to follow the warning of John Bunyan's Evangelist, who said, pointing with his finger over a very wide field,

> "Do you see yonder wicket gate?" Christian said, "No." Then the other, "Do you see yonder shining light?" He said, "I think I do." Then encouraged the Evangelist, "Keep that light in your eye and go."

Can we write one true sentence? Take one step? Don't heap up your responsibilities until they are overwhelming you. Just take the first step. Write one true sentence, but be sure the light stays in your eye.

PRAYER: Father, help us keep our eyes on your light that we might know the path to follow. Amen.

Day 163
An "Aha" Moment

I love you, O Lord, my strength. The Lord is my rock, and my fortress, and my savior. . . . I called upon the Lord, who is worthy to be praised (Psalm 18:1, 3).

ISN'T IT JUST LIKE GOD TO answer prayers in ways we least expect? God neither waits for the gathering, cheering populace nor waits for herald trumpets to begin blaring to alert the people of God's coming. There are no pre-healing announcements, no upcoming media releases, no waiting for the press corps to arrive to give a bulletin release for the forthcoming event. God's actions are not dependent on what the political and spiritual pundits have to say about whether a miracle should or should not be performed. Neither does it matter what the polls say. The only motivational force behind God performing miracles is love. Nothing else can move the event to happen. I cannot find the words to express what we are feeling except "aha!"

More often than not, we are unaware that God performs a miracle until it already happens. Those who experience it firsthand are not given any advanced notice; neither are they consulted about the best place and time. There are no invitations mailed out. If we are fortunate enough to be at the right place at the right time and somebody has a little faith, then we will all be blessed indeed. Even with hundreds of eyes watching, most folk are unaware of the high and holy business of the body and soul being transacted between individuals and God. When God acts, a miracle happens and someone's prayer is answered.

Although folk are given no advanced notice and might be unaware of it even happening, once the miracle is done, it cannot be kept quiet. After all, it would be difficult to see a man walking and talking to you who was still in his burial clothes.

The stories of Jesus' miracle working are very abundant. A legion of the demons was cast into a herd of swine and the swine destroyed, freeing a man who ran around naked (Mark 5). When the townspeople came to see Jesus, there stood the previously demon-possessed man, totally clothed in his right mind. There was blind Bartimaeus (Mark 10:46ff.), and there was another blind man in Bethsaida whose friends brought him to Jesus to be healed (Mark 8.22ff.). Jesus led the blind man out of the city where he spat on the ground and made mud that he applied to the man's eyes. Jesus asked him if he saw anything. The man replied, "I see men but they look like trees walking." So Jesus did it a second time, and the man's eyes were healed. Another miracle; another answer to prayer: an "aha" moment.

I was even blessed to be a part of a miracle when I had the deep brain stimulation surgery. It can only be described as an "aha" moment. I was not totally healed, but I now am able to function better than before. We all need to be on the lookout for our "aha" moments lest we miss them.

PRAYER: Thank you Lord. Just thank you. Amen.

Day 164
Fondness or Kindness

Be kind to one another, tenderhearted, forgiving one another, as God in Christ forgave you (Ephesians 4:32).

I WAS WATCHING TELEVISION ONE night when an actress said to one of the actors, who was madly in love with her, "Dennis, this isn't going to work. I am fond of you but I am not in love with you." Of course the man was crestfallen, but he carried on. That started me thinking about relationships and emotions, and I recalled the dialog between the two characters on the television program. I remember Jesus's words to love one's enemies and pray for those that persecute us. If someone hits you on the cheek offer the other one. Then a quotation came to mind. I believe it was Dr. Samuel Johnson, the English poet, essayist, and lexicographer, who wrote, "Kindness is within our power, fondness is not." That could be a liberating sentence for some of us who often mistakenly interpret Jesus's words to mean that we are to love others, and if we can't get them to return our efforts and like us, we have failed. Taking Jesus's words to heart, we think that we have the duty to like everybody, and when we can't manage it, we become discouraged and feel guilty.

It's sad to say, but there are some people that make it difficult for anyone to like them, much less love them. Efforts made have failed and all parties involved soon quit trying. That is why these words are such a comfort: Fondness is not within our powers, but kindness is.

We know that we can be kind, even to people we don't like. And then comes the surprise! What begins as kindness often leads to fondness. When we treat people correctly, we begin to feel right about them. Don't worry about liking or not liking. Be kind, and see where it takes you. Remember Jesus' words to Peter, who asked how many times should he forgive: seven times seventy, or until it becomes a way of life.

PRAYER: Our heavenly Father, here we are standing in the need of your help to start showing more kindness to all we meet. But we can't do it without your help. Bring to our minds the words of Jesus, who as they were nailing him to the cross, prayed, "Father forgive them, for they don't know what they are doing." In his name, we pray. Amen.

Day 165
Are You for Real?

Are you the one who is coming, or should we look for someone else (Matthew 11:3)?

HAVE THE CIRCUMSTANCES OF YOUR life ever caused you to doubt? Doubt your faith, doubt your call, doubt if God can help you when your life is in shambles? Do you ever doubt who you are, or whose you are?

I believe that this is what John the Baptizer was feeling. John's doubts were growing because of all that was happening to him. He had been thrown in Herod's dark dungeon and could hear the executor sharpening his axe. He wondered if his cousin, Jesus, was actually who he had told people he was. "Look! There is the Lamb of God who takes away the sins of the world." John was concerned. If Jesus was not the one, then who was the deliverer, and where was he? If Jesus was the one John had preached about, he was ready and eager to hand over the cloak of his preaching. John was not only eager, but he had to know; so he sent an emissary to Jesus to ask if he was the one.

Someone wrote about what could have been one of Jesus' responses. Jesus said, "You go and tell John what you've seen around here. Tell him there are people who have sold their seeing-eye dogs and taken up bird-watching. Tell him there are people who have traded in their aluminum walkers for hiking boots. Tell him the down-and-out have turned into the up-and-coming, and lot of deadbeats are living it up for the first time in their lives." Three cheers for the man or woman who can swallow all of this without choking.

We have no record of John's response once he heard what Jesus told John's disciples. I wonder what John did or said at that moment. Maybe he jumped up and down, dancing and whooped and hollered until the guards came to his cell.

I believe that once John heard from his disciples, his once burdened, drooping shoulders became erect and thrown back as if someone had put an iron rod in his spine. I believe his heart grew a couple of sizes with a good kind of pride that lets you know you have been faithful which God honors. John's soul must have smiled, knowing he had a part in the coming of God's kingdom. John met all his adversities with renewed hope, courage, assurance, and the firm conviction that Jesus *was* the Lamb of God, the one who ushered in the kingdom of God and was sent to take away the sins of those who asked to be a part of that kingdom. Those who witnessed John's death probably asked themselves how John could go to his death without ranting and raving, instead meeting it in peace and calmness of spirit. Although Herod thought he had defeated the Baptizer, his actions only served to strengthen his followers' resolve to continue preaching his message because in the end it was not Herod's victory. It was the Lamb's.

PRAYER: Father, we need the inquisitive mind of the Baptist to be sure that our actions are manifesting your kingdom on earth and in the lives of those whom we are among. Thank you for such heroes of the faith. Amen.

Day 166
Passing It On

Gladden the soul of your servant, for to you, O Lord, I lift up my soul (Psalm 86:4).

OFTENTIMES DURING OUR ALONE TIME, our time of solitude, we can slowly unmask the illusion of our possessiveness. It is then that we discover in the center of our own selves that we are not what we can conquer. In solitude we can listen to the voice of the one who spoke the world into existence and who spoke to us before we could speak a word, who healed us before we could make any gesture for help, who set us free long before we could free others, and who loved us long before we could give love to anyone. It is in this solitude that we discover that being is more important than having, and we discover that our soul is not a possession to be defended, but a gift to be shared. It's there that we recognize the healing words we speak are not just our own, but are given to us; that the love we can express is part of a greater love; and that a new life we bring forth is not a property to cling to, but a gift to be received.

PRAYER: Dear Father, we are a loveless people on a loveless world, and still you sent your Son to love to us. Your love—Jesus—came to show us the transforming power of unconditional love. Please unleash your love so that all who see and hear it might experience its power and then pass that beautiful message to all we meet that they, too, can experience such love. Amen.

⸺◖◗⸺

Day 167
That's All I Can Do

She did what she could (Mark 14:7).

IT WAS SAID OF Albert Schweitzer, who died at his mission post in Africa, that the greatest tragedy in all the world is what dies inside a person while he lives: The death of faith, hope, feeling, awareness, and response.

The writer continued. He said that Schweitzer had proven to the world that even though we have no control over the fact of our existence, we do hold supreme command over the meaning of what that existence is for us. Our greatest tragedy is that we shall die and never know our greatest power: the power of love to give itself for others. Surely that is the supreme tragedy of life. The question I put to each one of us today is: What is dying inside us while we live? For ultimately, death does not come simply with the cessation of physical life. It comes when we no longer care. When those forces that make for righteousness, beauty, truth, and goodness die in the human heart, we truly are dead

It is sometimes difficult for folks with Parkinson's and their caregivers not to walk around their arena of life feeling as though life is over. Perhaps our uninvited guest has helped to exile our hope of being a concert cellist or pianist. Or, maybe we put on the shelf our dreams of teaching or using our skills as a surgeon. Or, it could be that our non-expressive face lends folks we meet cause to think that we have given up. But we can't give up. Whatever our gift or talent might be, with God's help we still can make a difference in our world, no matter how small some may believe those gifts are.

We think of some of the great minds of history: an Einstein, a Michelangelo, a Bach, or a Shakespeare, and we say, "If I belong to that company, what I would do?" But then I realize I have to live irreconcilably with my "stunted powers." So along comes that dull prosaic business of saying after all that, where do I come into the picture as part of the useful host of mediocrity?

God is not calling us to be one of the great company but to be ourselves with our own unique gifts and talents, which God can use to make a unique difference in the world.

> **PRAYER:** Our loving Father, we might have neither the calling of those great heroes of the faith nor great influence and power, but we still have the blessings you have given us; and you expect us to live our lives with the same commitment and devotion as the heroes of our faith. We need your help to accomplish blessings. Amen.

Day 168
Sleeping Like a Baby

Eutychus was gradually falling asleep. Overcome, he fell from the third story and was dead. Paul took him in his arms and said, "Don't worry! He's alive" (Acts 20:9–10)!

THERE WAS A PHYSICIAN IN one of my churches who would sit in his pew, and when it came time for the sermon he would politely cross his arms and close his eyes, not to open them again until time for the invitation. Although he slept, he had the uncanny ability of being able to discuss the sermon. He was not alone, for he shared this ability with some other notables from history's pages, including Thomas Edison and Leonardo da Vinci. Napoleon napped, as did Stonewall Jackson and Winston Churchill. What about Brahms, who was said to have fallen asleep at the piano while he composed his familiar lullaby? The scriptures tell us that even God rested on day seven of creation. Remember the story of Jesus falling asleep near the stern of a fishing boat that was getting battered about by the waves on the Sea of Galilee?

Even Hemingway had a special place in his heart for sleep. It is said that he wrote, "I love sleep. My life has the tendency to fall apart when I'm awake, you know."

Paul had an encounter with a sleepyhead in Troas. Paul was on a roll and had preached well past midnight and dealt with the interruption when he took the time to revive the fallen sleeper. They then returned upstairs, had the Lord's Supper, and Paul went back to preaching. He preached until dawn.

Sleep is important for our health and well-being. It is through thousands of people taking part in sleep studies and identifying the sleep disorder called sleep apnea that people are being helped to have a good night's sleep, maybe for the first time. By learning all that we can about this disorder, we can make it more manageable. Our bodies and brain need that sleep time to process the day's events. This allows them to rest and heal themselves.

We need to heed the advice from Elijah, who also needed sleep and was running from Queen Jezebel. Notice that it was not until after the third time of sleeping that Elijah was ready to converse with God. He encourages us to "rest in the Lord."

> **PRAYER:** Father, we need your guidance in helping us to achieve
> the right balance between being awake and being asleep. Help keep
> us ready and rest to be able to do what you would have us do.
> Amen.

———◈———

Day 169
Laughing Until It Hurts

*God said to Abraham, "I will also give you a son by her. . . ." Immediately,
Abraham bowed with his face touching the ground. He laughed* (Genesis
17:15–7).

ONE OF THE HOTTEST BREAKTRHOUGHS IN pharmacological history is the development of Viagra. The little blue pill has made millions and millions of dollars for the pharmaceutical company Pfizer.
Viagra is a medication for older men with erectile dysfunction. This medication has helped millions of men who experience this problem.

We've no idea if this was the problem with Abram and Sarai, but the message given to Abraham that ninety-year-old Sarai would bear him a son did
bring a lot of laughter from Abraham's tent meeting. I can see Abram laughing
as he slapped the messenger on the shoulder and said something like, "I think
God may have made a mistake with this one. There must be a mix up." Even
Sarai, who was eavesdropping, also laughed. After all Sarai was ninety, and
Abram, according to Hebrews 11:12, was as good as dead. One can understand the laughter that filled the night air. They even named the promised
child, "Son of Laughter," and all this talk about a son must have made them
laugh until their sides hurt.

Abraham must have thought that this was some kind of divine joke, but to have a son would be tremendous joy. There was, however, something in that laughter other than unbelief. They were wrestling with the question that God had asked Sarai earlier when she laughed after hearing the angel's message earlier: "Is anything too hard for God" (Isa 18:1)?

This is one of the first accounts of people laughing that we have in the Bible, although I believe that if we take into the account the situation in life, we would see there is more humor in the Bible than we think. It would also show that God has a sense of humor as well; after all, God created us.

Here we are, created in God's image and receiving the abundant life that Jesus came to give us. That abundant life includes the element of joy that finds its universal expression in laughter, an expression that knows no barriers.

PRAYER: Father, help us not to ignore all the serious and sad events in life. Plant within us a joy-filled faith that nothing is too hard for you. Amen.

⸺◁◇▷⸺

Day 170
Is This Your Peace?

The light came into the world. Yet, people loved the dark rather than the light because their actions were evil (John 3:19).

HAVE YOU EVER PONDERED—really pondered—the words of our Lord Jesus recorded in Matthew 5:16, which reads, "Let your light shine before others so that they may see your good works and give glory to your Father in heaven?" Are these words grounds for a religious arrogance to be lorded over others? Absolutely not. Are these words unattainable for us believers? Is the task too big? After all, there is only so much one light can let shine. Yet, with the addition of the light of other believers, what was a single light piercing the darkness has grown into a blazing inferno.

Is there more to it than that? Does letting our light shine encompass life? I believe it does. It starts with our being at peace with God, for when we are at peace we are at service to God, a service that is a reflection of the divine peace. God does not let us use this peace for a time and then pull it away. No. God not only gives us this peace but also leaves it with us in the hope that we will use it in our part of the world as a message of love from God, like the lightning bug in the dead of night. The light does not blind the world because its light is not that strong. But to our surprise it breaks though the darkness to remind everyone who sees its little glow that God is watching over us and fear has no place in the believer's life.

Here is an additional stanza of the children's song, "This Little Light of Mine":

> Hide it under a bushel? No. } 3x
> I'm gonna let it shine.
>
> Let it shine. Let it shine. Let it shine.

PRAYER: Father, we ask you to join us with other like-minded believers that our lights might become so aflame that all darkness is forever gone. Amen.

Day 171
Christians Aflame?

He will baptize you with the Holy Spirit and with fire (Luke 3:16).

READING THIS CANNOT BUT conjure images of people in protest who deliberately draw attention to themselves by setting themselves on fire. Their motivation certainly does not agree with the text today.

In one of the most challenging of his sayings, Jesus said, "I came to cast fire upon the earth, and would that it were already kindled! I have a baptism to be baptized with, and how I am constrained until it is accomplished" (Luke 3:16). This saying of Jesus gives us pause to enter into Jesus' inner thoughts about his ultimate mission.

Some think Jesus meant the fire of judgment. He did talk about the fires of hell, but only here in this hard saying does he talk about sending fire on the earth. We grasp what he meant when we remember John the Baptizer's prophecy that the Messiah would baptize "with fire." After the suffering on the cross and the victory of the resurrection, Christ returned to live in his disciples. He set them on fire with love, power, and a passion to serve.

Christ himself living in us is the fire we are promised today. When he takes up residence in us we are set on fire. He is our intellectual fire as he thinks his thoughts through us; he is our emotional fire as he loves through us; he is our volitional fire as he gives us courage to do what servanthood demands. It's the only alternative to burnout!

> PRAYER: Father, our own resources often are burned out. Set us aflame with the fire of your Spirit and make us radiant with your love today. Amen.

Day 172
Random Acts of Kindness

Then the three warriors broke through the camp of the Philistines, drew water from the well of Bethlehem that was by the gate, and brought it to David. But he would not drink it; he poured it out to the Lord, for he said, "The Lord forbids that I do this. Should I drink the blood of the men who were at risk of their lives" (2 Samuel 23:16–17)?

Mary took a pound of costly perfume made of pure nard, anointed Jesus's feet, and wiped them with her hair. The house was filled with the fragrance of the perfume (John 12:3).

I F I WERE TO SPEAK OF random acts, chances are you would think of random acts of violence, or criminal behavior that is careless of human life and limb. It was both a surprise and a pleasure to be told of a bumper sticker that I later saw for myself. The sticker said, *Practice Random Acts of Kindness and Senseless Beauty.* Don't you love it? Go on; live dangerously! Practice random acts of kindness. Behave recklessly. Be prodigal with acts of senseless beauty. As David was with water from the well of Bethlehem, as Mary was when she poured perfume on the feet of the One she loved, such acts of senseless beauty make divine sense.

PRAYER: Gracious God, whose random acts are more than kind and beautiful, may we be courageous to practice similar acts to bring senseless beauty and kindness into the lives of others around us, for Christ's sake, we pray. Amen.

Day 173
What Is That That You Are Wearing?

The fragrance of your clothing is like the fragrance of Lebanon (Song of Songs 4:11*b*).

AROMATHERAPY, INCENSE, AND OTHER UNIQUE mixtures of oils have given rise to national chain-stores that sell these products. These stores advocate that the use of their products can help soothe stress, headaches, and tension, as well as increasing one's romantic interests and one's energy levels. All of this has given way to companies that concentrate on nothing else but the production of different fragrances. We have helped turn these fragrances into a multi-billion dollar industry. Fragrances and the belief in their power is not something new. They have been around for a long time. The scriptures are replete with God instructing the Jewish people to offer up a fragrant offering that is a soothing, fragrant offering to the Almighty that is acceptable.

Let's look at the scripture. Lebanon was a great and high mountain range crowned with mighty cedars. It is refer to in the Old Testament sixty-eight times. As the trees were cut down they filled the air with such a pleasant odor. Cutters came down with their garments saturated with a lasting fragrance, much like the lingering aroma of holiness that surrounds those who have been on the mountaintop with the "lover of their souls." When we have been with God, the difference is quite noticeable: life is different when we have been with God.

As the physician, Luke, writes in the book of Acts, "Now when they saw the boldness of Peter and John and perceived that they were uneducated, common people, they wondered; and they recognized that they had been with Jesus," do your clothes tell others where you have been?

PRAYER: Almighty God, may people who meet us know where we have been: that we have been with Jesus May the living of our lives be a witness to the truth that we have the mind of Christ, for it is in his name we pray. Amen.

Day 174
You Too?

Mary remained with Elizabeth about three months and then returned home (Luke 1:56).

OULD YOU NOT LIKE TO have been a fly on that wall and been able to overhear the conversations between Elizabeth and Mary? The only things we are privy to from Mary's three-month stay are the words Elizabeth spoke upon Mary's arrival, "Mary, you are the most blessed of all women, and blessed is the child that you will have" (1:42). There also was also a confirmation to that statement when upon hearing Mary's greeting, Elizabeth's baby kicked in her womb.

Maybe they talked about how the angel of the Lord appeared to them to tell the good news, shared with them the sacred and secret identities of the babies inside of them, and told them of their mission in life. Maybe Mary talked to Elizabeth about Joseph's reaction and what happened when she told him she was with child and it was not his. I wonder if Elizabeth and Mary both knew and understood what was in store for their babies down the road?

It is nothing short of awesome how God made his plan known to these two special women. In her pregnancy, God offered Mary an intimate friend with whom she could share what seems incommunicable, because Elizabeth, like Mary, had experienced divine intervention and had been called to a response of faith. She could be with Mary in a way no one else possibility could. Amid an unbelieving, doubting, pragmatic, and cynical world, two women met each other and confirmed in each other the promises given to them. For three months, Mary and Elizabeth were connected and encouraged each other to truly accept the motherhood given to them. Neither one had to wait in isolation. They could wait together and so deepen in each other their faith in God.

This surely is the rationale for Christian friendship and community. How can I ever let God's grace fully work in my life unless I live with people who can affirm it, deepen it, and strengthen it? We cannot live this new life of faith alone. God does not want to isolate us when grace comes. Instead, God wants us to be connected, to be in new friendships and new communities, holy places where grace can grow to fullness and bear fruit.

PRAYER: Gracious Father, help us to understand where we are and where we stand, for we are on holy ground, and you might be working another miracle. Give us eyes to see. Amen.

<○>

Day 175
Is There a God?

Then Moses said to God, "Indeed, when I come to the children of Israel and say to them, 'The God of your fathers sent me to you,' and they say to me, 'What is his name?' What shall I tell them" (Exodus 3:13)?

I HAVE HEARD PEOPLE CLAIM that they do not believe in the church but believe in God, that when they contemplate the beauty and intricacy in and of the world, they have to believe that God exists. I feel sure that God is appreciative of their vote of confidence. When I hear this, I am reminded that for the religious mind and soul the issue has never been the existence of God but rather the importance of God, the difference that God makes in the way we live. To believe that God exists the way they believe that the South Pole exists, though they have never see either one, to believe in the reality of God the way you believe in the Pythagorean theorem as an accurate attempt that does not really affect your daily life, is not a religious stance.

As Moses was still trying to find an excuse good enough to get him off the hook with what God was asking him to do, God wanted him to go and be his instrument to free the Hebrew people and lead them to the Promised Land. Moses said that if he did this, the people—not to mention Pharaoh—would want to know who gave him the authority to make such demands. A name. They needed a name. What was the difference between the gods of Egypt and the God of Moses?

A God who exists but does not matter, who does not make a difference in the way you live, might as well not exist. Belief in God this way reduces the

Almighty to a prominent figurehead who is paraded in public only for ceremonial occasions and beloved by everyone because this sort of "God" never does anything. The issue is not what God is like. The issue is what kind of people we become when we attach ourselves to God.

> **PRAYER:** God of all things good and holy, forgive us for living as though you do not exist. We are guilty of letting our actions and re-actions bear no evidence of your influence. Forgive us, O God, and deliver us first from ourselves and the people around us that we may be better attached to you. Amen.

———◇———

Day 176
From Where Does Your Strength Come?

He didn't realize that the Lord had left him. Then Samson called out to the Lord, "Almighty Lord please remember me! God, give me strength just one more time" (Judges 16:20, 28)!

THE STORY OF SAMSON HAS always been one of the sad stories of the Old Testament to me. So much wasted potential and promise: here we have a "before" and an "after" of what life is like when God is with us and when God is not. It has the makings of a Hollywood movie. There is fighting, blood, gore, and death. There is betrayal, greed, revenge, mystery, sex, intrigue, and even a little humor. All of this history packed into a period of twenty years, or fifty-one verses.

Most of us are aware of the stories surrounding this last of twelve judges who ruled the Jews for many years. I see a few similarities between Samson and a person with Parkinson's disease. It is not my purpose to say that these two are equal—only to point out some things that they have in common.

First, a person with Parkinson's can experience moments in which they suddenly lose all energy. It comes without warning and will last different periods of time, depending on the patient. Things that factor into this happening also vary. Perhaps it is because one has been exerting a lot of energy and are just tired; it can come from the scheduling of the taking one's medicine(s); or it could be that the medication(s) have become totally ineffective. Whatever the reason, persons with PD lose their energy and strength but regain it after resting a while. Again the length of that time of quietness depends on the person with PD.

Second, Samson knew whom he needed to call on for help. We can see this clearly in the last verse, where Samson says to God, "God, give me strength just one more time." Although our motivation for making a request to God is not for the same reason as Samson's, we ask God numerous times during the day to give us strength. The fact is that God hears our prayers, answers them, and gives us the needed strength to accomplish whatever we are attempting.

> PRAYER: Generous God, it is so beyond us as to how you can forgive and forget our shortcomings time and time again. We are so human we want immediate retaliation, but that is not your way. Your way is to help us quickly to find our way back to you. Help us, even though we see through blinded eyes; here we are, O Lord, in need of redemption. Amen.

Day 177
Don't Be Childish

When I was a child, I spoke like a child, thought like a child, and reasoned like a child. But when I became a man, I no longer used childish ways (1 Corinthians 13:11).

HAVE YOU EVER HAD THE good fortune to be able to spend time with small children? Or maybe sit in a park and observe children at play? Usually they are cute and loving, but the story doesn't stop there. Each child has a strong sense of possession. Most of them want to be number one: first in getting the adult's attention, and first in being in the spotlight. "No, don't want to," is a comment that one hears quite often. Then it is remembered that children are normally self-centered. It is not easy to give in and share.

But children don't have the market-share of self-centeredness. It is hard for us grown-ups to be finished with childish things! We who are supposed to be mature can certainly put on a display of childishness. Our actions and responses can be very childish. We are childish with those in our family circle, in arguments, with our neighbors. And let's not forget about the Church, which is not immune to such attitudes. It has given us some painful lessons learned from being childish. Certainly this is true in relationships among the other nations. All seek wealth. All want power. All must have their own way. Wars have been started by one nation wanting power over another nation.

Compare such childish behavior with Paul's classic description of the way of love:

> Love is patient. Love is kind. Love isn't jealous. It doesn't sing its own praises. It isn't arrogant. It isn't rude. It doesn't think about itself. It isn't irritable. It doesn't keep track of wrongs. It isn't happy when injustice is done, but it is happy with the truth (1 Cor 13:4–6).

PRAYER: Lord, make me an instrument of your peace. Where there is hatred, may my response be to love. Help me to learn that in giving I may receive. Help us, O Lord, to outgrow our childish

ways in order to be more like your children for your kingdom.
Amen.

⸺◦⸺

Day 178
What Future?

You don't know what will happen tomorrow (James 4:8).

*T*HAT SUCKS, MAN," SAID AN acquaintance who had just learned that
I had Parkinson's disease. "You don't have much of a future. It's
gloomy every day, I bet. What a bummer."

His words started me to thinking about my future. He was right, it is rather
gloomy, and looking in from the outside there doesn't seem to be too many
good things to which to look forward. It looks to be a life of the brain and
body not being on the same page, causing the body not to function as it
should. The future doesn't look to be anything worth celebrating. Having this
knowledge only intensifies the uncertainty of the future and leaves a great
many things to worry about—if one lets it. Is there a positive alternative? Yes,
but a lot of it depends on one's understanding of God.

If in your understanding God belongs to the hoary past, a past filled with
mystery and superstition, you probably believe that in this modern and sophisticated world we live in God has become outdated and is, consequently,
irrelevant.

God is the God of the present, even as God was the God of a long gone
past. The same Bible reminds us of a God who is with us, a very present help
in times of sorrow. But we must not stop here, for if we stop here, we will miss
out on many of the blessings God promises us.

If God is the God of the past and of the present, then it would naturally
follow that God is also the God of the future. God is ahead of us. As believers,
with or without Parkinson's, we have no reason to be obsessed with the future,

for God is there.

What does it mean to say that God is the God of the future? Yes it speaks to God's omniscience and sovereignty, and that statement does, in fact, bring those of us living in transition and uncertainty some assurance. But there is more. Now hold onto your hats: It means that God is ahead of us, preparing the way and calling us forward. God beat us there.

Doesn't that give rest to your worried spirit? Doesn't it show the folly of being concerned about, even obsessed with the future? To say that God is the God of the future also means that there is nowhere and no time that God is not.

With that said, remember that God is the faithful one of the past, the blessed one of the present, and the hoped for and expected one of the future. If there is nowhere and no time in which God is not, then all of humanity, all of my family, and all of my life are safe in God's gentle but powerful hands. "I am the Alpha and the Omega," says the Lord God, "who is and was and is to come, the Almighty" (Rev 1:8).

> **PRAYER:** Heavenly Father, your faithfulness to us is immeasurable by any standard. May we rest, live, move, and have our being within your gentle, powerful grasp. In Christ's name, we pray. Amen.

Day 179
Finding the Lighter Side of Life

How long will you try to have it both ways (1 Kings 18:20)?

THE WRITER OF THE BOOK OF First Kings poses a silly question when he asks if we want "it" both ways. Of course, it would be appealing in some situations if you had it both ways. It would be great to have it both ways, such as choosing between butter pecan and rocky road ice cream, but not so appealing to have to choose which side effect that comes with Parkinson's, for example, whether to have vivid nightmares or severe leg cramps.

There was a movie starring Goldie Hawn and Steve Allen as Professor Know-It-All. Goldie was very interested in learning, and she asked the professor to impart his knowledge to her. She asked Professor Know-It-All, "Tell me, Professor, is there anything definite in the world?" Professor Know-It-All thought for a minute and replied, "Well, yes and no."

I know someone who used to think that he was indecisive, but now he is not sure. And I heard of another person who didn't know whether he cared about apathy. Now, I don't know what most you think of jokes of this sort, but I think they're childish.

Some friends know that I have changed and outgrown them. Not really. For I enjoy a good joke, and if it's funny I laugh.

Some people who enjoy jokes don't have to have much of a sense of humor. My neighbor collects funny stories. He files them and keeps them in great order like a miser does money, but he might as well collect stamps because he lacks the humor that sees and hears the laughter in everything.

Robert Frost put it a better way when he wrote, "Forgive, O Lord, my little jokes on Thee, and I'll forgive the great big one on me." Cathedrals have a perfect sense of humor, for they have spires to honor our aspiration and gargoyles to mock pretension. I think all true humor begins in an all-embracing "Come off it!" And that is expressed not only in a chuckle but a wink as well.

PRAYER: Father, we are certainly a sense of humor: just look at us humans. Forgive us for seeing the lighter side of life but not responding to and for not seeing it because we think ourselves too busy with the heavier side of life. Amen.

Day 180
You Are Forgiven

Her many sins are forgiven because of her great love (Luke 7:47).

THE PHARISEES AND SADDUCEES WERE IN A dither every time they heard that Jesus was in town, particularly when Jesus did miracles and forgave individuals their sins. They were first upset because God was the only one who was supposed to be able to do that. They knew that because of all the people in Israel, the Pharisees and Sadducees were the only ones who had the inside track to God. God had chosen them to be the protectors of the law. God had entrusted them to fence the law so that they would be able to keep people, like this carpenter, from violating the law that God had entrusted to them. They had blinders on and could not see that the one whom they were calling a blasphemer was the one who came to fulfill the very law they thought they were protecting. We modern folk don't wear blinders. We know Jesus the Messiah is the Son of God and that he came to forgive us of our sins.

The real struggle is to allow Jesus to forgive us, to allow his forgiveness to touch the deepest places in our hearts that are broken and filled with doubt, pain, shame, and guilt. These feelings are often so great that we cannot truly believe that God indeed wants to forgive us completely. To believe is to trust fully in God's endless mercy and return again always to that mercy. But often we hold on to our sins, our guilt, and our shame, and act as if we were too bad, too ugly, or too dirty to be forgiven. Some folk with Parkinson's believe that they have done or not done something, and this is their punishment. That's the reason they have poor balance, that is why their speech or lack thereof prevents them from being understood, and that is why they isolate themselves from the rest of this world and stop being contributing members of society. The greatest act of faith—that is, of trust—is to let God be for us a God without hatred, revenge, anger, or resentment, a God who is love, mercy, compassion, and forgiveness. That's the kind of God I want in control and in charge. Don't you?

The woman who washed Jesus' feet had truly accepted the forgiveness Jesus came to offer, and that forgiveness set her free to show her love to Jesus without fear. She no longer worried about what others thought of her. How stingy and self-conscious we often can be. Because we are!

PRAYER: Dear merciful God, your love, mercy, and forgiveness go way beyond any of our pettiness, and you forgive us our sin and restore in us the joy of our salvation. Help us to accept fully your forgiveness. Amen.

Day 181
Eating the Elephant One Bite at a Time

I run straight to the goal to win the prize that God's heavenly call offers in Christ Jesus (Philippians 3:14).

A FAMOUS MAN WAS ASKED what he thought was the most characteristic feature of modern people, and he answered, "Tired eyes." We are a tired people. We pride ourselves on how many things we can do at the same time. But psychologists warn us of the downside of multi-tasking. It affects our immune systems, our health, our sleep (sleep deprivation is a growing concern), and our response times. It can affect our concentration and emotional outlook and even our mental states, they say. A great many people you pass by everyday can't do any tasking well, much less multi-tasking. So be on the alert.

Some of us who have Parkinson's disease, can attest to the validity of this. You could be moving along, having a good day, and suddenly, without warning, what was a good day can turn into a day in which your body rebels like a spoiled child refusing to do what you want it to do. We are robbed of all our energy and strength. It becomes a struggle to get on our feet, much less to being able to put one foot in front of the other. But after a time, strength and energy return and we can go back to the activity we were doing—until the next time. These down times are unpredictable, and they can grow in length.

Parkinson's for me has progressed to where I am unable to multi-task effectively as I once did. I am slower in what I am doing. It now requires more effort to get through the day without a rest period or in some extreme times, a short nap. Without proper rest, my body doesn't function as it should for the condition in which I find myself. But I push myself and fight as hard as I can, and most of it passes. Sometimes I do doze off while reading, watching TV, or working on the computer. I kid my friends and family by saying, "I get some of my best sleep while I'm driving." I don't understand why they look at me so funny. I am not like Eutychus, who, while Paul was preaching, fell asleep, out the window, and to his death (Acts 20:9–12). I must confess that I've been close but never have.

You can see why Paul's statement in his letter to the church at Philippi—this one thing I do (Phil 3:13)—is so crucial. Notice the emphasis on the *one* thing. Perhaps we can take his words to heart and realize that it is better to do one thing exceptionally well rather than many things half-way. Let's see how God is going to work. Paul knew the energy that has to be expended to do one thing.

> **PRAYER:** We need to be more single-minded, O God. It is only with your assistance that we will be able to be preservers. Also, grant us the courage to face what is needed for us to have the patience that is called for to be about this one thing. In Jesus' name, we pray. Amen.

Day 182
Renovation in Progress

I will give them a single purpose and put a new spirit in them. I will remove their stubborn hearts and give them obedient hearts (Ezekiel 11:19).

MY FAMILY AND I ARE IN THE middle of renovating my parents' house. My dad was a very heavy smoker for the forty-plus years they lived there. You could walk into their house, and it would look like they were smoking hams. No amount of asking, pleading, or begging him to quit was successful. Upon leaving, even your clothes would smell of smoke for hours to come. It is not too hard to guess that when my father died that it was from breathing problems.

In the renovation, we have been shocked at how much everything in the house had a coating of yellow nicotine on them: the light fixtures, blinds, ceiling, and even the walls once sprayed with a cleaner would cause yellow rivulets of nicotine to run down the walls or whatever we were cleaning at the time. We removed everything, including the carpets, trying to rid our house of the cigarette smell. Some of the residue had stubbornly affixed itself to whatever was available and stayed there.

I am in no way putting equal value on what meager things we are doing to the house to God's work on us. But they do share some things in common. Comparing these two examples, one can come to the conclusion they are the same. But when compared with each other, they share only *some* commonality. Just as we had to deal with the old before applying the new and fresh, God had to deal with all the disgusting and detestable things we were doing before renovating our lives. There must be a singleness of purpose so that our stubborn hearts are replaced with obedient hearts.

We need to hear God say that to become God's people we need to follow God. If we follow after other gods and idols, they will certainly come up wanting.

PRAYER: Gracious God, help us to have ears to hear your voice and the courage to follow against all odds. Amen.

Day 183
I Can Do *All* Things

I can do all things through Christ who strengthens me (Philippians 4:13).

NOTHING CAN HAMPER OUR ATTEMPTS TO live a whole and holy life more quickly than trying to cover the treacherous landscape of life complete with its challenges and crises. Even at the conclusion of our lives, of really trying to live a holy life, we still need the touch of the divine artist. With this touch, God will bring to completion within us God's eternal plan for our lives. But while we await that time of wholeness, we continue on our journey along life's pathway, accompanied by Jesus telling us we will always be blessed. These blessings may not always be enjoyable, but they will certainly nudge us forward in our efforts to love as God loves.

A rabbi was once asked, "What is a blessing?" He prefaced his answer with a riddle involving the creation account from chapter one of Genesis. The riddle went this way: *After finishing his work each of the first five days,* the Bible states, *God saw everything that he had made and that it was very good.* But God is not reported to have commended on the goodness of what he created on the sixth day when the human person was fashioned.

"What conclusion can you draw from that?" asked the rabbi.

Several answers came from members of the class, but the rabbi sat quietly, listening to each of their responses. Then someone volunteered, "We can conclude that the human person is not good."

"Possibly," the rabbi nodded, "but that's not a likely explanation." He then went on to explain that the Hebrew word translated as "good" in Genesis is the word, *tov,* which is better translated "complete." "That is why," the rabbi contended, "God did not declare the human person to be tov. Human beings are created incomplete."

It is our life's vocation to collaborate with our creator in searching, discovering, and fulfilling the Christ-potential In each of us. Yes, we can do all things.

PRAYER: Our gracious Father, what a comfort it is to know that there is nothing we can't do because Christ is with us in all that we encounter. We are also grateful that you did not make us complete, but that through your love and presence you have chosen to allow us the blessing of working along side of you for the completion of your kingdom. In the name of the one who strengthens us for and accompanies us on the journey, Jesus Christ, our Lord. Amen.

⋅⋅⋅⋅⋅⋅⋅⋅⋅⋅⋅⋅⋅⋅⋅⋅⋅◄◯►⋅⋅⋅⋅⋅⋅⋅⋅⋅⋅⋅⋅⋅⋅⋅⋅⋅

Day 184
Gaining the Prize

I run straight toward the goal to win the prize (Philippians 4:14).

It's far more than that! I consider everything else worthless because I'm much better off knowing Christ Jesus my Lord. It is because of him that I think of everything as worthless. I threw it all away in order to gain Christ and to have a relationship with him (Philippians 3:8).

BELIEVERS AND NON-BELIEVERS DOWN through the centuries have read the writings of St. Thomas à Kempis. They contain words of challenge, inspiration, and encouragement as how to live a life with God. Some time ago, a friend of mine put me onto one of à Kempis' sentences that we both agreed is a great sentence: "The humble in spirit dwell in a multitude of peace."

What do you think? This humbleness of spirit is in sharp contrast with the inordinately competitive spirit that is so prevalent in today's world. A world where the budgets for the arts programs are being radically cut and in some instances completely shut down, whereas budgets for sports increase by leaps and bounds, a world that advocates competition not only in the arena of sports but also in the workplace, in neighborhoods, even in schools. Don't get me wrong; I am not advocating a demise of competition. First, there is no way you could stop it or even control it, for that matter. Second, competition in moderation can be a positive motivational tool that can be healthy.

There can be no peace for those who are unduly competitive, for the single reason that for them it's never enough to have enough. They always have to have more than anybody else, and they never can. It is akin to the cartoon that has a big fish eating a smaller fish only to be eaten by larger one that is eaten by a larger . . . and on it goes. No matter how big you think you are or what you possess, there's always someone who is bigger and whose quantity of possessions is greater. Play the game of owning the biggest toy and there's no end it and no contentment in it. If you have enough, be content with what you have and dwell in a multitude of peace.

PRAYER: Father, make me an instrument of your peace. Where there is hatred let me sow love. Amen.

Day 185
Forgetting Hurts

Jephthah judged Israel for six years. Jephthah of Gilead died and was buried in one of the cities of Gilead (Judges 12:7).

I AM SURE THAT IF YOU have been to the ocean, you have seen huge ships and tankers whose hulls are covered with thousands of barnacles. They attach themselves and grow on the hulls of the ships—even on whales—until they are removed. It was said that at one time the waters of New York Harbor were so polluted that a ship's captain would deliberately take his ships through those waters in order to kill the barnacles.

There are a many of us who collect reactions, defeats, hurts, and setbacks and hold onto them, letting them fester and build until there are deep wounds and scars. Jephthah was an illegitimate child, the son of a harlot. As he grew older, his brother mistreated him, much like Joseph's brothers did to him. They were so relentless that Jephthah had to leave home. Some of you can understand what Jephthah went through because you have experienced the same cruel rejection from older siblings. Others of us cannot even understand such behavior. Today, if we knew of a case like this, we would immediately put that child into therapy.

It is clear that this unhappy past did not prevent Jephthah from making a new start. He moved to the land of Tob, where he made a name for himself. There he established himself as a man of conscience who feared God and also as an able military leader.

When under attack of the Ammonites, Jephthah the outlaw was called back to lead his people, although the victory cost him the life of his only daughter due a rash promise he had made (Judg 11:1–12:7). He led Israel for six more years, which was during the period that Israel was ruled by the judges. When this outlaw died, he was taken home to be buried in his homeland from which he had been expelled.

PRAYER: Father, you are a healing God. Help us to grow above our hurts and mistreatment. Amen.

⟨○⟩

Day 186
By the Way of the Desert

Then the Spirit led Jesus into the desert to be tempted by the devil (Matthew 4:1).

IF YOU ARE INTERESTED IN delving deeper into your spiritual life, you need to know that part of the way of your journey will entail passing through the desert. Will it be easy? No. We are shown and told that the journey tells us there is hope for this world and that we can make something of it and of ourselves, but it will not be easy. Seekers of spiritual formation know that the desert has to be passed through. Yes, *through*. I know people, as do you, who have chosen for some reason to give up, having lost hope. To remain in the desert is to perish. Yet many choose to stay in a desert of guilt, grief, addiction, inferiority, destructive relationships, cynicism, or grievance, when they should have passed through this desert long ago.

Sometimes our best hope of passing through is to seek the help of others: a wise physician, a skilled therapist, a spiritual counselor, or trusted friends banded together for mutual encouragement. Sometimes, we are perfectly capable of emerging on our own, allowing a new insight to create a new attitude, but it's not easy.

We know people who don't merely have complaints but have become the complaints. They have so dwelt in their petulance that their disgruntled nature has taken them over. They would lose their identity if they were to surrender their sense of grievance and their right to be miserable. Others wouldn't know who they were if they didn't see themselves as victims. They find it easier to blame others for their difficulties than to accept responsibility for their foolish and thoughtless actions.

We all know people whose grief, anger, inferiority, or inordinate touchiness is not their problem but their solution. It defines them. It has become the dominant characteristic of their personality, what their friends have come to expect of them. Even when they catch a glimpse of what they are really like, they find it easier to remain where they are than move.

The poet was right: We would sooner die than change and because we will not change, the most heroic, loving, and generous part of us withers in the desert because we refuse to leave. We all need to hear, "If you don't change anything, nothing will change."

All the time, God offers us the strength of the divine presence. God's promise is not that God will save us from the desert experiences, but that God will bring us through them. If God denies us peace, it is to give us glory. If God stirs us up, it is to bring us home. The Lord will give us a light to bring us to everlasting life.

> **PRAYER:** Father God, your promise to never leave us or forsake us is new and real every morning. Thank you for your love, your mercy, and the power of your presence. Amen.

Day 187
Do We Have to Suffer?

In the world you'll have trouble. But cheer up! I have overcome the world
(John 16:33).

ONE THING WE CAN BE SURE OF IS that coming into the presence of
God carrying our suffering still intact does not remove the underlying
causes of the suffering. It does not cure cancer; it does not reunite us
with loved ones who have died; and you will come up short if you spend time
looking for the answer to the deep question, why God allows suffering. To
bring it closer to home, we ask why God allows us to suffer. The message of
the cross is not that God will not shield us from suffering, but that we can encounter God in our suffering, even as God has encountered us in human suffering.

You can rest assured that the Lord knows our suffering. Remember the story
of the rich young man who came to ask Jesus what he needed to do in order
to have eternal life? The scripture says that Jesus loved him. When his friend
Lazarus died, he wept. And on his entrances into Jerusalem, Jesus cried because
the city knew not his coming.

I am sure through that during the ordeal of his torture, he, if not outwardly,
inwardly was moved by the pain he was having to bear for his kingdom to
come. And I am equally certain that the Lord, being the loving Father that
God is, was beside God's self to see what the Son was bearing for the redemption of God's sinful creation. When as sufferers we come into God's presence,
we can learn who we are, both in our suffering and beyond our suffering, and
we can learn whom God is. God is the Christ who suffers and the Spirit who
both transcends and transforms our suffering.

Though we do not seek suffering, we become, as our faith deepens, increasingly sensitive to its presence in our world.

PRAYER: Father of the living and the dead, we come to you seeking your assurance of your presence with us during our suffering.
With your help, not only will our faith increase, but so will our
sensitivity and love. Amen.

Day 188
Be Gentle with Me

In returning and rest you shall be saved: in quietness and in trust shall be your strength (Isaiah 30:15a).

I AM MY OWN WORST CRITIC," we hear people say. There is a lot of truth in that statement. Whereas we can be too soft on ourselves and make excuses for our shortcomings, we can expect too much as well, especially regarding our spiritual growth and development. People in the church expect to be able to measure that growth like they do their company's projections for profit or loss margins. We make meager attempts to find ways to measure our growth, such as in the number of courses we have taken and projects and work assignments we might have completed. In the corporate world, such developments can clearly be seen that track and record results in promotions and remuneration. From this information, personnel are given as rewards.

It is difficult, however, to use this same sort of scale to grade victories in one's spiritual life. The rules are so very different from the way we experience things at work. Much of the spiritual life remains a mystery hidden deep within us, so we deal with the spiritual life and our secular life on two different planes.

When making these considerations, we run into the backward reasoning of the kingdom. This is needed for our spiritual existence. In this type of spiritual reasoning, progress sometimes means going back; being first, for instance, will require us to be last and maturity involves becoming childlike. Having means letting go. To be great, we must become servants. We can safely say that the spiritual life operates on a different wisdom, and all the pushing and shoving that so characterizes our workaday world will hardly serve us in our spiritual growth. We can't push our spiritual growth and make it happen with gimmicks or quick-fix methods.

Rather, what is needed is for us to begin to make gentle moves that are born of a wisdom from above. In discovering that wisdom, we can learn that we do not have to move faster than we can. Our spiritual development won't result from human behavior. It will only come from careful listening, quiet surrender, and active and purposeful engagement. It will come from what we do, if it is done in harmony with God's wisdom. Most of all, it will come from what was given, not what was expected.

PRAYER: Father in heaven, unstop our ears so that we will be able to hear your holy whispers to us as to what we need to be concerned about. Help us to know the backward reasoning of your kingdom, which is so vital to our eternal salvation. Come, now, O Father. In the name of Jesus, we pray. Amen.

Day 189
Staying at It

It's not that I have already met or have already completed the course. But I run to win that which Jesus Christ has already won for me. . . . Whoever has a mature faith should think this way. And if you think differently, God will show you how to think (Philippians 3:12, 15).

THERE ARE SOME EXCELLENT translations out there. The final product does not show all the hard work, time, and research that went into its preparation. As for me, in my sermon preparation I would study the text in at least three different translations. I chose from the New English Bible, the New Revised Standard Version, the Jerusalem Bible, and the God's Word translation. Looking at these would allow me to see the different facets of their work and provide the words that would enhance the scripture, much like holding a diamond up to the light.

If you read only the King James Version, you will not find the word "mature." Instead the translators used the original Greek, which is "perfect." It is truer to the actual Greek, however, and to Paul's whole outlook on life to think in terms of *growth*. No matter how completely the apostle was dedicated to Christ, he never thought that he had arrived. He was always pressing on toward the goal.

Could it be that maturing as a believer is a never-ending *process*? Forget what you have attained, whether in the life of spiritual contemplation or in the service to others. The prize of God's call in Christ Jesus is always beyond one's grasp. No matter how many hills one has climbed, there is always another peak to scale. Even a saint like Francis of Assisi was humble to the end.

We can also see that Paul was not content to seek the high goal for himself. He aimed to present everyone mature in Christ (Col 1:28). God forbid that I should ever be satisfied with things as they are, for myself, for my community, and my world. If I should ever feel too good about keeping the Word, I read again the Beatitudes and become "poor in spirit."

PRAYER: Deliver us, O God, from all forms of self-righteousness. Free us from pride, especially the pride of being humble. Remind us of the unfinished tasks of your kingdom. Amen.

⋯⋯◦⋯⋯

Day 190
Have You Found the Treasure, Yet?

Though outwardly we are wearing out, inwardly we are renewed day by day (2 Corinthians 4:16).

As A CHILD, DID YOU ever play cowboys and Indians? Or how about pirates? I did. Props were important and we worked feverishly to make every thing just right. We would go to Austin's store and buy some little bags of gold (it was really bubble gum) and anything else that a pirate would use. One or two of us would transform pieces of discarded wood and nail them together into fashion swords and knives. A curved small tree branch made a great pistol. The patch that covered the injured eye would actually hide a large cat's eye marble. We would add anything else we would find: a bird feather, clear quartz to serve as diamonds, bottle caps for gold coins; pieces of coal would be the made into the most precious bit of the treasure: "black coral." It came from the deepest parts of the ocean and was quite a find. Last but not least, a map was drawn to direct the others to where the treasure was buried. We had to fight several other pirates along the way, their ship a log we boarded and took the special cargo meant to go to the New World. Those who did not obey were made to walk the plank. When we found the treasure, you would think we had found the real thing. Make-believe is sure fun isn't it?

Now these words of Paul remind us of yet another treasure that is still being overlooked by many and reminds us of our Christian existence. Paul is certain about what this treasure is. It is the light of the revelation of the glory of God in the face of Jesus Christ. It is the good news that God loves sinners. It is the proclamation that God acts to bring people into the Lord's loving purpose through the life, death, and resurrection of Jesus Christ. This is the treasure we each can have. It is not so much that we have this treasure but that it has us! This treasure is the gospel, and the gospel is God at work in Jesus Christ. The treasure is the Word of God at work in us. It is the glorious treasure of redemption. This precious prize transforms our human existence into a Christian existence. Paul goes on to say that our having this treasure does not preserve us from the hard realities of human existence. God does not write into any confession of faith a favored person's clause that exempts the faithful from the tribulations of this life.

You remember the story of Theresa of Avila, when after embracing the nun's vocation she was staggered at the successive blows that rained down upon her. "Why?" she cried like most of us would. "My friends are not excused," was the purported divine reply. "Ah, Lord," she sighed, "No wonder you have so few of them!"

Now clearly in this context, God means to emphasize to us the resources that we have in this life; nevertheless, God makes it clear that there is the darkness as well as brightness in the Christian life. The darkness comes to the Christian as well to the non-Christian in the world. Life has its way of reminding us that we Christians, too, are earthen vessels. *We* are scarred; *we* are marred; *we* are shattered; *we* are broken—just like other people. Our salvation does not lie in our indestructibility, but in the power of God who makes all things new. That is the precious treasure Paul was talking about.

God loves us! God is for us, not against us. God is radically and totally for human beings. And what does this "God-for-us" want from us? Just one thing: that we become like God and begin to love what the Lord loves and join God in helping those God wants to help, our neighbors, our brothers and sisters, our fellow human beings. The helping of needy people was precisely where God was most active and where God wants us to be as we can.

Well, what are you going to do with your treasure?

> **PRAYER:** Father help us, once we have found our treasure, to join you shoulder to shoulder in addressing the needs of "the least of these." Thank you for changing our hearts and lives. Amen.

◄◇►

Day 191
Love of God Means Love of Others

Then the King shall say to those at his right hand, "Come, you that are blessed by my Father, to inherit the kingdom prepared for you from the foundation of the world; for I was hungry and you gave me food" (Matthew 25:34–35).

HAVE YOU EVER THOUGHT IT strange that a nonbeliever can speak to the Christian virtue of compassion without missing a beat? The nonbeliever says things like, "I know of no other person who was as compassionate as she was." His or her actions spoke volumes to their practicing before us the virtue of compassion. This poses a question: What does it mean to live in the world with a truly compassionate heart, a heart that remains one to all people at all times? It is very important to realize that compassion is more than sympathy or empathy. When we are asked to listen to the pains of people and empathize with their suffering, we soon reach our emotional limits. We can listen only for a short time and only to a few people. In our society we are bombarded to sit through so much "news" that our hearts easily get numbed simply because of overload.

But God's compassionate heart does not have limits. God's heart is greater, infinitely greater than the human heart. It is that divine heart that God wants to give us so that we can love all people without burning out or becoming numb.

It is for this compassionate heart that we pray when we say: "Create a clean heart in me, O God, and renew a faithful spirit within me. Do not force me away from your presence, and do not take your Holy Spirit from me" (Ps 51:10–11). Wouldn't it be sad that the only acts of compassion we saw or experienced were those of nonbelievers?

The Holy Spirit of God is given to us so that we can become participants in God's compassion and so reach out to all God's people at all times with God's heart.

> PRAYER: Father, grant us our request that we find echoed in David's psalm of repentance. We ask for your help because we are all in need of you producing a new work within us. We know how weak we are in trying to do something without you. Come now, Lord Jesus. Amen.

⊶◦⊷

Day 192
Do We Have to Suffer?

The thing that has been is that which shall be; and that which is done is that which shall be done; and there is no new thing under the sun (Ecclesiastes 1:9).

THAT THERE IS NOTHING NEW under the sun is a view widely held by many in our world. They believe that people basically don't change very much. But the church says that this is not so.

Jesus came into the world to establish a new kingdom into which he introduces *new* men and women who are *new* creatures that enter the kingdom by a *new* and living way. And one day he will create a *new* heaven and *new* earth as he sits upon his glorious throne and says, "Behold, I make all things new."

Jesus makes all things new. If we are not *in* Christ, then we are not *new* creatures, no matter how many times we might have rearranged the furniture. He doesn't merely change our outward behavior; he changes our nature. Christ gives us new desires and new affections. He sets our affections on things above, not on things here below.

If we become new creatures in Christ, we have new purposes for our lives. They now center on the kingdom of God and God's purposes.

If we become new creatures in Christ we have a new goal. It is our great desire to glorify God. We have a new citizenship, for we are citizens of the kingdom of God. We have a new birth: we become a different person.

New. So what now? Are you growing in Christ? If not, what is your excuse? What progress have you made in your Christian life in the last year? How is your devotional life? How is your stewardship to God? How is your witness for Jesus Christ? How much of God's Word did you hide in your heart? How much did you determine and resolve to become a better Christian, to become more like Jesus Christ: more loving, more gracious, more forgiving, and more faithful?

Ah, my friends, Christ can make us more and more new. But if we have been born into that glorious kingdom, we have the responsibility and the privilege to cooperate with his grace. I ask you to resolve to do something new, to do something to cooperate in the making new of your life that which has never experienced such a transformation. If you have not become a new creature in Christ at all, then I urge you right now to receive him as savior and Lord, I encourage you to put your trust in him. If any person is in Christ, if they trust with all their hearts, then join me in sharing our faith, our hope, our forgiveness, and our love.

PRAYER: Gracious God, come into our lives this day and make us new creations for your heavenly kingdom. In the name of our Lord, Jesus Christ, we pray. Amen.

Day 193
Hello, Stranger

I am a stranger on earth (Psalm 119:19).

*W*HEN I WAS STILL PREACHING, I would sometimes imagine a balloon cloud above the heads of some of our church members and say a prayer specifically for their need. This is an amazing paradox. On the one hand, there are believers who lament that our world is filled with everything but God; on the other hand, some people have not even noticed God's absence. We must first come to the argument that God is a stranger on earth, then explore the "how to" of reintroducing God into our world and into our lives.

We resolve God's being a stranger in our world by doing things that give room in our lives so that we are able to deal with God's absence in our world. To resolve this vacancy of God, we have to begin with ourselves. Then and only then will we be better equipped to introduce God to the world. When the Lord is no longer a stranger in our lives, then God will not be a stranger to our world.

> **PRAYER:** Father, there are many times when our actions do not show the presence of God but rather your absence. We pray for better vision, direction, courage, and commitment to no longer make you a stranger but a welcome member our loving family. Amen.

Day 194
Jesus' Invitation

Look, I'm standing at the door knocking. If anyone listens to my voice and opens the door, I'll come in and we'll eat together (Revelation 3:20).

HAVE YOU EVER NOTICED HOW many of Jesus' interactions with people occurred at meals. Sometimes the meal was shared with one person, such as Zacchaeus, and sometimes with a large group, like when he fed the five thousand and at another time when he fed four thousand. In each account, we catch a glimpse of the Jesus who was both divine and human, the Jesus who could use such everyday mundane happenings as eating, to teach the astonishing love and mercy for each one of us. These were special opportunities Jesus that he shared with his followers. Remember when he met those two disciples on the road to Emmaus? They talked and talked about the things that had just occurred in Jerusalem concerning Jesus' death on the cross, but it wasn't until they shared in the breaking of the bread that they recognized whom he was.

Oftentimes, it would have been nice to be a part of one of those meals. I would have liked to have been there myself to hear the tone of Jesus' voice and catch the inflections and mannerisms that become lost in the printed word. Obviously, going back physically is an impossibility for me or any of us, for that matter. But that doesn't stop us from thinking about going back over two thousand years ago in our thoughts and spirit. It is possible for me to believe that the risen Lord is bound no longer by time and space. He is present with us, and the message he spoke to his first disciples is the message he speaks to us. He is here in the breaking of the bread and the sharing of the cup.

> **PRAYER:** Our ever-present Lord, we know you invite us to seek, to knock, and to ask. When we seek you, we find that you were already seeking us. Nourish our spirits, for we grow weary and famished; nourish our minds with your holy word; and nourish our bodies with your daily bread. Amen.

Day 195
What Will It Cost Me?

I must buy it from you at a fair price. I won't offer the Lord my God burnt offerings that cost me nothing (2 Samuel 24:24).

IT'S AMAZING HOW MANY THINGS you find while looking for something else! I do not know how long ago it was that a pastor friend of mine gave me a copy of the introduction to a little book entitled, *The Power of Commitment*. It was not what I initially was looking for, but I am glad that I found it.

Keep all options open. Never make a commitment to anything unless absolutely forced into it. People today value their options: their fathers had obligations, they have freedom; when new options become emptiness, company workers rarely demonstrate loyalty and commitment. Couples postpone having children to retain their personal freedom and options. Children find themselves in the backwash of mothers and fathers pursuing their personal freedom.

With selfishness being the root, someone suggested that it be called the "do-your-own-thing syndrome." Among Christians, non-commitment takes on subtle forms. Many factors produce this lack of commitment. It is easy to be a Christian in our society today. It is wholly acceptable, even commendable. It takes so little in the way of commitment to be totally accepted in the world and in the church.

There is more to a lack of commitment than ease of living. It is a creeping worldliness, a desire to be a Christian but to live like a non-Christian—not so much in the blatantly immoral areas—but in lifestyle.

There is another side. Many people make strong commitments to the wrong things: career, success, leisure, a lovely home, a summer cottage, an extensive wardrobe, a time-consuming hobby. Their intensity of commitment leaves no room for more significant commitments to God. They are believers who consciously opt for lesser commitments.

But why would anyone make such an absurdly incompatible choice? For many it is simply that the cost of true Christian commitment is too high, if not too hard. Every commitment involves a cost. Every day a clatter of choices clamors for our attention: buy this, go here, and eat there. All commitments cost something: money, time, and energy, and some cost one's very life.

The author goes on to say, "Most Christians want to commit themselves to God. They don't want to waste their lives." I agree. But the time comes for us to be sure about where our commitments are. We do not want to reach the age of 60 or 70 and look back and realize that we have wasted so much of life because of commitments to the wrong things. It's not too late to choose to make a stronger commitment to God.

PRAYER: Father, give us the courage and the determination to be more committed to the one that truly matters: you. For Christ paid the supreme sacrifice for us, and it is in his name that we pray. Amen.

Day 196
Wondering about Wandering

The Lord said to Abram, "Leave your land, your relatives, and your father's home. Go to the land that I will show you (Genesis 12:1).

HETHER IT IS PARKED IN front of someone's house or out on the Interstate, whenever I see a moving van I am reminded of the parade of biblical characters real and legendary who were commanded by God to pull up stakes and go to strange lands about which they knew nothing at all. Adam and Eve were summarily dismissed from their idyllic Eden. Abraham left Haran for unnamed territory. Moses headed for the desert and back to Egypt, only to return to the desert wilderness with a stubborn and stiff-necked people. Jonah went to Nineveh. Jesus wandered throughout Galilee and back and forth into Gentile country. St. Paul had a trio of "Club Med" journeys. Moving wasn't easy, at least for people like Abraham, who had to do more packing without Allied Van Lines or the Mayflower

Moving Company to help out. Jesus had it a little better: just the clothes on his back—anything else could be carried by his disciples.

Moving, however, does involve a bit of fear. When Moses moved the people of Israel from the fleshpots and minute luxuries of Egypt, God wanted them to be a people on the move. When they ran out of foodstuffs, God graciously provided the manna in the wilderness with certain conditions: not more than an omer, or 6.4 pounds, per person per day. Don't keep any leftovers. They discovered that when they tried to store it in ancient Tupperware jars, the manna became rancid and bred maggots. God wanted to keep them moving. Even though we don't have to worry much about spoilt manna, bands of thieves, or marauding tribesmen, we worry about not being over the maximum weight limit. We worry if the moving company's insurance policy will cover all the damages to breakables. And we worry whether everything will get where it's supposed to go without incident. And so it goes. Such is the terror of moving.

But there is something healthy about moving in that the act of moving makes us alive and keeps us going. Life is given a bit of freshness. Discoveries are made: "Where did we get this?" "I forgot that such-and-such was packed away." "I've been looking for this thing for ages, and here it is!" We are moved to encounter newness, to celebrate life, and to grow acclimated to being like that wandering Aramean, Father Abraham. And eventually, God willing, we can put down some roots and enjoy a sense of permanence of place. But through it all, wherever we go, there is God, and for this we are truly thankful. We leave, knowing not only that God will point out our way, but also full of the knowledge that God will be with each of us along the way, too.

PRAYER: Bless our lives, heavenly Father, with your continued presence that we may know you are always with each and every one of us wherever we happen to be. This we pray in our Lord's blessed name. Amen.

Day 197
Be Yourself

*Even when I am old and gray, do not abandon me, O God. Let me live to
tell the people of this age what your strength has accomplished to tell about
your power to all who will come* (Psalm 71:18).

HAVE YOU STOOD IN A room as someone walked in such that it was
as if the appearance of the entire room changed and did so without
realizing it was even happening?

People with PD feel the opposite at times. Instead of helping make the fes-
tivities alive, they sometimes can be found looking for a way out, standing in
a corner or some out-of-the-way place, choosing rather to be one of the silent
minority. Why do people with PD act this way? The reasons for being this
way could range from fear of spilling or breaking something to fear that no
one will be able to understand him or her because one's speech has been affected, or worse one becomes choked and the attention in the room is then
turned onto one. In short, folk with PD don't want to call attention to themselves or be an embarrassment to anyone.

Even though Parkinson's disease is still primarily a disease of the elderly,
younger people are having to learn new coping skills as the disease gains a
strong foothold among them.

Someone once said that whereas the first half of life belongs to the extro-
vert, the second half belongs to the introvert. I believe there is something to
that, but it is not so clear-cut, is it? Young people are often shy and unsure of
themselves. Loudness and aggressiveness seem to win the day over sensitivity,
tenderness, and insight. Energy fades, but wisdom increases. Brashness sustains
nothing, but stillness runs deep. The thoughtful, perceptive one gathers
enough to sustain oneself or a lifetime. So don't be discouraged. Be patient
with yourself. Your time will come.

> **PRAYER:** Father, we pray for steadiness of foot: give us the assur-
> ance that no matter where we go or what we find ourselves doing
> you are there. With you as our companion there is nothing that
> we can do to embarrass you because we are your children. Amen.

Day 198
Out of the Darkness

"I've had enough now, Lord," he said, "take my life" (1 Kings 19:4)!

EPRESSION. DESPAIR. WE KNOW THIS SET OF twins quite well don't we? They are no respecters of persons and not biased in anyway. Many of us are well acquainted with these "robbers of light and life." They are quite talented in sending negative information and presenting negative feelings about ourselves, that we begin to question our own self-worth. They are good at convincing us that we are unlovable. The feelings of depression and despair can be so pronounced that they sometimes reach a point at which they can cause us to become suicidal. How can anyone love somebody like me? When depression and despair are in control, we hear how good we *are not* so often that we begin to believe all the bad press they funnel our way. We feel, at these times, that we are no good at or for anything, and what is even sadder is that those twins don't want us to, either.

When thinking about depression and despair, two people stand out: Vincent van Gogh, the Impressionist painter, and the prophet Elijah. Elijah had just finished a long-distance run to escape the clutches of Jezebel, only to find himself alone in a cave with nothing else but a pity party. God asked him, "What are you doing here?" To which Elijah replied that he was the only prophet left and he was on Jezebel's "most wanted list." God left food and water for him and offered Elijah a chance to sleep. It was not until after the third reception of the food, water, and sleep that God dealt with Elijah, assuring him that he was not the only one left. After God dealt with Elijah's issues, God gave him a job to do. Elijah was to find and name his successor, Elisha.

Vincent van Gogh, following one of his bouts of depression, wrote,

> In the depths of my misery I felt my energy revive, and I said to myself, in spite of everything I shall rise again. I will take up my pencil, which I have forsaken in my great discouragement, and I will go on with my drawing. From that moment everything has been transformed for me, and I will go on.

Here he is: it is his turn. And here we are, for it is our turn, as well.

PRAYER: Father, we thank you for your provision of help in times of sadness, depression, and despair. We join our voices with the millions of people who cry out to you for deliverance. Thanks for helping us walk through the dark places of life, for feeding us, and granting us rest so that we, too, can say, "Here I am. It is my turn." In Christ's name, we pray. Amen.

⸺◇⸺

Day 199
Thar She Blows!

You will not be angry forever, because you had rather show mercy (Micah 7:18).

TAKEN FROM HERMAN MELVILLE'S BOOK, *Moby Dick*, the phrase, "Thar she blows!" refers to the sighting of a whale's spray from its spout. We have, however been given an added definition. The additional definition carries the connotation of someone who is mad or angry. Who are you mad at these days? We might be mad at a relative, a teacher, an employer, another colleague, or ourselves. What are you mad at? Who is mad at you?

How would you illustrate anger? A teakettle letting off steam? Smoke coming out of a cartoon figure's ears, along with a train whistle blowing? Throwing dishes? Becoming silent and not speaking? Or have you possibly taken it to the spiritual level?

The Lord was angry at the Israelites on more than one occasion to the point of wishing God had never created them. Jonah was mad at God for saving the Ninevites and their livestock. King Saul was another with whom God became angry by taking his spirit away from him for disobeying the law and giving leadership to David. There are more episodes in the biblical story that we can safely say the topic of anger is a major player.

If you really want to be bold you can add words, phrases, or actions to show your anger. For example, I know two ladies who, when they drive, talk to the other drivers as though they can hear them and respond: "The speed limit is fifty-five! The slow traffic is supposed to be in the right lane!" How about these phrases: "I am so mad, I could eat nails," or, "I was so mad I couldn't see straight." Psychologists and therapists offer anger management classes to help folk with their outrage. There is even a very popular video game entitled "Angry Birds." People are just plain mad at the world, and you can tell the ones that are the most critical and are potential candidates for cardiac arrest by the look of their faces. We are grasping at any straw to help us cope with the anger that builds inside us until we "blow our tops" or "lose our cool," whereas the Bible gives us the simple answer to our problem.

Anger affects our health and can affect our relationships with our family and friends, especially our spouse(s) who have the inside track on our lives. It is not said to be a sin to become angry, but we should deal with anger before the day is up. How? It depends on the people and the circumstances. The Bible just says to deal with anger before you go to bed. Perhaps that advice was given that way because it was understood what could happen if we don't lay the anger to rest.

PRAYER: O God, thank you for loving us and offering that love in abundance to resolve any anger we might have in our lives. Thank you for having forgiven us for anything we may do to make you angry with us. Amen.

Day 200
Bread of Life

Jesus told them, "I have food to eat that you do not know about. . . . My food is to do what the one who sent me wants me to do" (John 4:32, 34).

As I DROVE, I TURNED THE radio to NPR. I tuned in during the middle of an interview but listened to it anyway. An author, whose name I did not get, had just completed a book that was attempting to explain the reasons for the decline in most all denominations in the West. He went through the usual lists of villains: secularism, relativism, and scientism. As he responded to listeners' questions, he was adamant that these were the root causes for the decline.

At the conclusion of the interview, I was struck by the fact of how easy it is to point the finger at someone or something else and reposition the blame on the other's shoulders. There is no denying that these factors might well have played a part, but the church is not innocent. The church itself has to take some of the responsibility, and it is because the church has not been a good portrayer of the gospel. It has failed to live the gospel of Jesus's upside-down kingdom.

The gospel is such good news. Everyone should hear it. This is not the gospel of an angry and demanding God but of a welcoming God, all of which is shown clearly in the hospitality that God offers. God welcomes us with this precious invitation each time we share the Lord's holy meal. This hospitality not only sets a bounteous table but offers us the gift of God's nourishing life in Christ. "I am the bread of life," Jesus declares.

Someone wrote that God comes to us as a gift. The same person continued by writing that in each of our lives, Jesus comes as the bread of life. Although this is a more familiar explanation, it is not the only one. This gift involves another dimension that is more often than not neglected. We must not forget that Jesus also comes as the "hungry one."

What is a clearer definition of Jesus being the *bread of life*? That he spiritually sustains us by his love and presence. That he is the 'hungry one' reflects the mystery of the gospel in that what we do to the poorest and least is a service to Christ himself.

This dimension of understanding and living the gospel means that the true worship and following of Christ involves service to the poor. And this has basic implications. It means that the work of care, mercy, and justice is not for the strange few who promote such causes. It is central to the life of every Christian.

Just as all need Christ, whose body was given for us, so all are called to be the servants of Christ and to bless Christ in "being there" for others.

PRAYER: Father, may we be as one with you as Jesus is. Amen.

Day 201
Passion or Action?

God did not spare his own Son, but handed him over (Romans 8:32).

WHEN DID JESUS' PASSION BEGIN? Was it when he was born to the young girl, Mary in that Bethlehem stall? Was it when he was baptized? When he went into the wilderness and was tempted by Satan for forty days? Was it when he started his preaching and teaching ministry amidst the constant sparring with the Pharisees, Sadducees, and scribes? Was it when he healed and restored people's lives? Or was it when he was betrayed, handed over to his death, his resurrection, and his ascension?

It will probably be discussed for years to come, but for certain a turning point in Jesus's life and ministry was the moment when he was handed over to those who did with him what they wanted as well as to his ministry. It is a turning from action to passion. After three years of teaching, preaching, healing, and moving to wherever he wanted to go, Jesus was handed over to the unfounded fears, desires, and reasoning of his enemies. He chose not to stop them and received what they planned and played out against him. He was beaten, and on his head they placed a crown of thorns. He was spat upon, laughed at, stripped, and nailed naked to a cross. He was a passive victim, subjected to other people's actions. From the moment Jesus is handed over, his passion begins, and through this passion he fulfills his vocation.

Jesus' mission is fulfilled not by what he does but by what is done to him. Most of life is determined by what is done to you and me, and in this is our "passion." And because most of our life is passion, a being-done-to-us, only small parts of our lives are determined by what we think, say, or do. Now if we had our druthers, we would be inclined to protest against this and want all "action" to be originated by ourselves. But our passion is a much greater part of our life than our action. We, too, have to let ourselves be handed over, as it were.

PRAYER: Our heavenly Father, it is difficult for us to be handed over, to be no longer in control, or have any power to do, only to be done unto, and that makes us quite uncomfortable. It would be easier for us to live our lives according to what we think are the things with which to busy ourselves. Help us to see that only in being handed over can we fulfill the purpose(s) we were placed here to accomplish. As we proceed, help us to see you walking by our side, shoulder to shoulder, for your greater glory. In the name of Jesus, we pray. Amen.

Day 202
Goodbye, Anxiety! Hello, Wholeness!

This is what the Almighty LORD says: My people, I will open your graves and take you out of them. I will bring you to Israel. Then, my people, you will know that I am the LORD, because I will open your graves and bring you out of your graves. I will put my Spirit in you, and you will live. I will place you in your own land. Then you will know that I, the LORD, have spoken, and I have done it, declares the LORD (Ezekiel 37:13–14).

No one patches an old coat with a new piece of cloth that will shrink. Otherwise, the new patch will shrink and rip away some of the old cloth, and the tear will become worse. People don't pour new wine into old wineskins. If they do, the wine will make the skins burst, and both the wine and the skins will be ruined. Rather, new wine is poured into fresh skins (Mark 2:21–22).

JESUS TAUGHT US THAT CHANGE IN THE human spirit is insignificant unless we change the world around us. That's the message behind saying about new patches on old coats and new wine for old wineskins. Even Ezekiel experienced this in the vision of the Valley of Dry Bones.

Change is all around us. At the Mental Research Institute in Palo Alto, California, the types of changes people make have been studied. They have found that we generally make two kinds of changes throughout our lives, which, for want of better terminology, are called first order changes and second order changes.

We make first order changes all the time. They're the kind of changes we make to adjust to our current life situations. It's like using a thermostat. Set it on "hear" or "air" and then adjust the temperature to suit you. It's still heating or air conditioning, but you've adjusted the output to your situation. In first order changes, we basically learn to function better—to adapt, make the best of it—but the situation itself doesn't change.

Second order changes, however, are not so frequent. What occurs in these sorts of changes is that one's whole system of beliefs, attitudes, and actions change because of a new viewpoint on reality. We see this sort of change in people who've had life-changing experiences and are so deeply moved that they are inspired and compelled to share their transformation with us. It happens over and over in the scriptures: Moses, David, Isaiah, Ezekiel, Job, Mary, Jesus—it's the stuff of the entire Bible!

You had a second order change when you fell in love. People you know have experienced second order changes when they've been diagnosed with a serious illness, such as cancer, Parkinson's, and Alzheimer's. The whole outlook on life is turned around, inside out, and upside down. Sometimes chaos enters in, but usually—if we are watchful—it is most often God who enters the picture when a second order change occurs.

When Jesus spoke of new wine, he was talking about life lived in a fresh way. New wine skins are simply the new context in which life is to be lived. What is the new context? The kingdom of God, which is here and now. This new context, this kingdom, is inhabited by anyone who seeks to do the will of God.

Ezekiel's vision of the dry bones is a lot like a picture of a dried-up garden that needs attention. The English mystic, Julian of Norwich, wrote a little meditation called "Be a Gardener." In it, she wrote:

> Be a gardener.
> Dig a ditch
> toil and sweat,
> and turn the earth upside down
> and seek the deepness
> and water the plants in time.

Continue this labor
and make sweet floods to run
and noble and abundant fruits to spring.
Take this food and drink
and carry it to God
as your true worship.

PRAYER: Heavenly Father, we about to partake of the transformation of life around us whenever we come into your presence and turn a corner in our lives. Let us be changed in the highest order that we may be filled with your new life as we enter into your kingdom. This we pray in the name of your beloved Son, who gives us new wine and the skins to hold them. Amen.

------◄ ◊ ►------

Day 203
Bad Beginnings, Good Endings

You are extremely happy about these things, even though you have to suffer different kinds of trouble for a while now (1 Peter 1:6).

I WAS FORTUNATE TO HAVE A partner in a charity golf match who was considered to be one of the top three players for this particular golf course. Whereas I am only a duffer, I could tell my lousy game was affecting his. He had sliced his tee shot, spent an extra shot getting to the green, and then he three-putted. Bad day for golf. A great day for philosophy.

"Well Parson, you know how to tell a really good golfer?" he asked. "The really good golfer is one who can recover from a bad lie. He hits his ball into the bunker twenty feet away from the green. He doesn't throw down his club or mentally give up the game. He just hunkers down, concentrates, and hits it out of there, right to the pin."

There's a lot of good theology in that advice.

In our lives, we all have made some lousy shouts. We drive the ball right of the fairway into the rough or hit it in the bunker. Every businessperson has an off day; every politician exercises bad judgment on occasion; every chef has some flops in the kitchen. Every preacher can preach sermons that need immediate CPR.

The important thing, when you know you've made a made a bad beginning, is not to panic but to hunker down, concentrate, and hit the ball out in the right direction. Folks with Parkinson's understand this. We get so worried about falling or not feeling comfortable in being in a crowded room. We start out breathing the prayer, "Lord, help me not to panic." That is a good prayer for any of us when things don't look so good. But for those times it gets a bit rougher, a prayer we might think of adding is, "Help me not to despair." Don't panic and don't despair. Just hunker down, concentrate, and hit the ball out of the bunker toward the green. Who knows? Perhaps the shot on the next hole will be a hole-in-one.

PRAYER: Our heavenly Father, thank you for being our constant companion through the good and easy times and, more importantly, through the bad and difficult times. Help us to keep in mind that when we make a bad shot, that does not mean we are through, all washed up, and should retire to the rocking chair on the front porch because of the bad shot. Rather, show us the way to recover and play afterward. These things we pray in the name of Jesus. Amen.

Day 204
Hidden Treasure

The kingdom of heaven is like a treasure buried in a field. When a man discovered it, he buried it again. He was so delighted with it that he went away, sold everything he had, and bought it (Matthew 13:44).

ONE AFTERNOON, WHILE CHANNEL SURFING, I caught a few moments of *Oprah*. The show was dedicated to the things people buy at auctions and flea markets. One woman had attended the Sotheby's auction of Jacqueline Kennedy-Onassis' jewelry and other personal effects. She and her husband were on their honeymoon, and they bought two pairs of Jackie O's earrings. There was someone else who had sold all he owned to possess several pieces of Hollywood memorabilia. Then, Oprah went into the audience to talk to a man and his wife who frequent flea markets. He had bought an old iron strongbox for $2.00. When he opened it at home, he discovered it had a false bottom, and in the box's hidden compartment was a collection of gold bars and old gold coins worth a great fortune!

On the Internet, you can access holdings of fine museum collections throughout the world. The British Museum, for instance, houses a wonderful collection called the Hoxne Hoard. When the Romans abandoned their claim to Britain in the early fifth century, someone buried a treasure of nearly 15,000 coins along with 200 gold and silver objects. The hoard was discovered a few years ago when a young man was out with his metal detector in some tall grass, trying to locate a hammer his best friend had lost while on a construction job in Hoxne. Talk about treasure hidden in a field!

It's fun finding old things in the attic or basement. In fact, one may have something of value there. The folks at Sotheby's say that history lives in the attics and basements of people's houses, and there are untold treasures there: letters, newspapers, toys, musty military outfits, old grammaphones Grandpa had to crank by hand, hat pins and straight razors, tools, mason jars (the blue ones with the tin screw lids) filled with pennies and china sets—if it's been there for a good long while and is in reasonable to excellent condition, you can be sure it has some value.

Wouldn't be interesting to think how much of a treasure we are to God when the Lord finds us?

PRAYER: Father, let us discover with great joy that the real thing for us to know is that you seek us. Come now, Lord Jesus, and discover us anew. Amen.

⎯⎯⎯◦⎯⎯⎯

Day 205
New?

The thing that has been is that which shall be; and that which is done is that which shall be done; and there is no new thing under the sun (Ecclesiastes 1:9).

THAT THERE IS NOTHING NEW under the sun is a view widely held by many in our world. They believe that people basically don't change very much. But the church says that this is not so.

Jesus came into the world to establish a new kingdom into which he introduces *new* men and women who are *new* creatures; who enter the kingdom by a *new* and living way. And one day he will create a *new* heaven and *new* earth as he sits upon his glorious throne and says, "Behold, I make all things new."

Jesus makes all things new. If we are not *in* Christ, then we are not *new* creatures, no matter how many times we might have rearranged the furniture. He doesn't merely change our outward behavior; he changes our nature. Christ gives us new desires and new affections. He sets our affections on things above, not on things here below.

If we become new creatures in Christ, we have new purposes for our lives. They now center on the kingdom of God and God's purposes.

If we become new creatures in Christ we have a new goal. It is our great desire to glorify God. We have a new citizenship, for we are citizens of the kingdom of God. We have a new birth: we become a different person.

New. So what now? Are you growing in Christ? If not, what is your excuse? What progress have you made in your Christian life in the last year? How is your devotional life? How is your stewardship to God? How is your witness for Jesus Christ? How much of God's Word did you hide in your heart? How much did you determine and resolve to become a better Christian, to become more like Jesus Christ: more loving, more gracious, more forgiving, and more faithful?

Ah, my friends, Christ can make us more and more new. But if we have been born into that glorious kingdom, we have the responsibility and the privilege to cooperate with his grace. I ask you to resolve to do something new, to do something to cooperate in the making new of your life that which has never experienced such a transformation. If you have not become a new creature in Christ at all, then I urge you right now to receive him as savior and Lord, I encourage you to put your trust in him. If any person is in Christ, if they trust with all their hearts, then join me in sharing our faith, our hope, our forgiveness, and our love.

PRAYER: Gracious God, come into our lives this day and make us new creations for your heavenly kingdom. In the name of our Lord, Jesus Christ, we pray. Amen.

Day 206
Hello, Stranger

I am a stranger on earth (Psalm 119:19).

WHEN I WAS STILL PREACHING, I would sometimes imagine a balloon cloud above the head of some of our church members and say a prayer specifically for their need. This is an amazing paradox. On the one hand, there are believers who lament that our world is filled with everything but God; on the other hand, some people have not even noticed God's absence. We must first come to the argument that God is a stranger on earth, then explore the "how to" of reintroducing God into our world and into our lives.

We resolve God's being a stranger in our world by doing things that give room in our lives so that we are able to deal with God's absence in our world. To resolve this vacancy of God, we have to begin with ourselves. Then and only then will we be better equipped to introduce God to the world. When the Lord is no longer a stranger in our lives, then God will not be a stranger to our world.

PRAYER: Father, there are many times when our actions do not show the presence of God but rather your absence. We pray for better vision, direction, courage, and commitment to no longer make you a stranger but a welcome member our loving family. Amen.

Day 207
The Wrong Way

Don't be surprised when I tell you that all of you must be born again (John 3:7).

ONE MUST BE AWARE OF QUITE A lot of road signs when driving. One particular sign that always makes me take a quick second look is the one about moving to the center lane to turn left. That lane allows you to either cross the road or make a "U" turn to the left. The sign you see is the one that says "Wrong Way." You obey the sign or cause an accident.

It is so easy for Parkinson's patients to spend their waking days searching for the answer to the question, "Why?" Why this disease? Why now, when I'm in my prime? Why, when I have put aside chasing after the world's ideals and taken on ideals of he kingdom? Why now, after holding down a job and career for forty years, do I have to deal with this disease? Why?

When we are truthful with ourselves we know that we cannot partake deeply of the life of God unless we change profoundly. With that said, we come to realize that it is essential for us to go to God in order that the Lord should transform and change us, and that is why, to begin with, we should ask for conversion.

Conversion in Latin means a turn, a change of direction of things. The Greek word *metanoia* means a change of mind. Conversion means that instead of spending our lives looking in all directions, we should follow one direction only. It is turning away from a great many things that we value solely because they were pleasant to or expedient for us. The first impact of conversion is to modify our sense of values. God being at the center of all, everything acquires a new position and a new depth. All that is God's is positive and real. Everything that is outside God has no value or meaning. But it is not a change of mind alone that we call conversion. We can change our minds and go no further; what must follow is an act of will, and unless our will comes into motion and is redirected Godward, there is no conversion; at most, there is only an incipient, still dormant and inactive change in us.

PRAYER: Dear heavenly Father, as we adhere to the signs on our highways that say, "Wrong Way" and do not drive there, help us to adhere to your signs when we are going in the wrong direction and refuse to drive there as well. Some of us have already started down the wrong direction. Forgive us. Grant us the courage and fortitude to turn around and change our direction in order that your holy love will be active in us. In the name of Christ, we pray. Amen.

❧⟨○⟩❧

Day 208
In the Midst of Us

The whole group of believers lived in harmony. No one called any possessions his own. Instead, they shared everything. With great power the apostles continued to testify that the Lord Jesus had come back to life. God's abundant good will was with all of them (Acts 4:32–33).

*T*HE PEOPLE OF THE CHRISTIAN church need to remind themselves that we have hope, not because of something that we have decided, or found, or created, but rather hope based on the stunning act of God who hears, who cares, and who moves in among us.

If there is to be a hope for us as humanity, it must be from some power; some force that manages to be both with us, for us, yet not arising out of us.

We believe that hope is in the resurrection of Jesus. The significance of the resurrection is a fact upon which our faith is built. We believe, not on the basis of our wishes, our emotions, or our insight, but on the basis of the act of God in the resurrection of Jesus.

This is important. We live in an age in which human actions tend to be the only actions, in which it is up to us to be helped.

First Church Jerusalem was made up of people who had nothing in common, but here they are, together, sharing their goods with one another. How can this be?

You know how serious our differences are, the walls between us. How can the differences, all the barriers be overcome? What on earth could make people even share their property with one another?

Is there any basis for hope beyond human wishful thinking? With all the problems facing humanity, is there any hope other than humanity?

The only hope worth having would be that hope which arises from some event outside us, some hope not utterly dependent upon us, and at the same time a hope reaching toward us..

When we speak about the origin, we are not talking about a new program for human betterment, or a noble idea. We are talking about the very basis of our faith: faith not in ourselves, but faith that there is hope beyond ourselves. Faith, however, is not the result of our human aspirations, a projection of our longing. Faith is the result of being met by the living Christ. Here is hope that is greater than us or our means of dealing with the world, hope based not upon what we can do, or us but based upon God and what God has done in resurrecting Jesus.

PRAYER: Thank you, God, for providing us with the hope that we need. Amen.

------◀◦▶------

Day 209
Letting God Renew Your Life

God has rescued us from the power of darkness and has brought us into the kingdom of his Son, whom he loves (Colossians 1:13).

I WANT TO SHARE A COUPLE OF words that are at the forefront of our daily living, and are basically the same word in the Bible. These words are very important to us both physically and spiritually. They are especially important to people with PD, or any other illness: the words "health" and "salvation." The Biblical meaning for salvation is "wholeness of the personality before God." It is a process of recovering the relationship of man and woman to themselves, their neighbors, and to God. One viewpoint is that it is an idealistic concept that man strives after. The other viewpoint is that it is a mental concept in which the hope is to receive God's gift. If we were to search the history of the word "salvation," we would find that through Latin, Greek, and Hebrew there are two fundamental roots: to release a prisoner, and to rescue a victim.

From this perspective, salvation is basically a personal experience. The Bible teaches that the gift of wholeness comes from God and is received in a personal way and is responded to by human persons.

Ask anyone with PD, and he or she will tell you how easy it is to fall into despair and hopelessness. Yet unity commences in the midst of personal desolation. Hope clears a path through desperation. The lost soul becomes a found person in the same locale where once that person had wished the earth would swallow him or her up. The Almighty, who seemed afar, draws near. This vital experience of personal renewal comes close to what the Bible means by salvation.

All of the figures of speech used in the Bible to describe salvation lead one to see the full variety of the healing experience. It involves rescue, release, renewal, and rededication of the central focus of life. We need to realize that salvation is not simply a forgiveness of sin but a restoration of wholeness to one's being and the reversal to the kingdom of God's rule.

> PRAYER: Father, oftentimes we make promises and move from the outer realms of life to the inner realm where you stand with arms wide open, ready to receive us back into your family. Accept, we pray, our wish to renew our relationship with you and our fellow sinners so we may live in the fullness of life. Amen.

Day 210
Keeping One's Balance

You are extremely happy about these things, even though you have to suffer different kinds of trouble for a while now (1 Peter 1:6).

WHEN WE MAKE A TERRIBLE mistake, there are two ways to respond in order for healing to begin. Two examples—the lives of Simon Peter and Judas Iscariot—can help us see this well. Peter did not fully understand the difference between words and actions. "No, lord," he said, when Jesus told his disciples that he had to suffer and die. "No way," he said, "They all might run and deny you, but not me. I won't." Yet later, when a woman points at Peter and accuses him of being one of Jesus' followers, he responds by cursing, saying he never knew the man.

It's one misstep after another, but it is said that Peter went out and wept bitterly. Peter didn't panic or despair. He kept going. And later, when the risen Jesus asked him three times, "Peter, do you love me?" Peter responded, "Lord, you know I do." In spite of all his missteps, Jesus still gave Peter a job to do.

Not Judas. Judas made an awful misstep. When he realized how bad it was, he completely gave up believing that there was any chance of making it right. He panicked, fell into despair, and went out and hanged himself. Would he have hanged himself had he stepped solidly and not lost his balance? Could he make the needed steps toward Jesus? Probably not, but I imagine that there are some people who are so mentally ill that they feel the only alternative is to do as Judas did. When PD folk allow depression to regress into despair they can succumb to the temptation to remove themselves from the suffering.

So the question is asked of each of us, "Is Jesus what we are aiming for?" We want meaning and purpose in our existence. We want to feel that our lives are counting for something beyond our own happiness. We want to know that when we come to the end of our journey, we feel good about our lives and believe that we have not wasted our opportunities to do something worthwhile with them.

PRAYER: Our beloved Father, it is so easy to make a rash decision or a hurried choice because of a misstep. These decisions usually lead to more negative repercussions and our feeling less useful. These feelings seem to be more vivid in the lives of those who have Parkinson's. Because of the added difficulty of day-to-day living, it is so easy to get tired and give up. Help us all not to give up when we make a misstep. May we follow the example that Jesus lived, hunker down, and walk confidently in his way. In Jesus' name, we pray. Amen.

⸺◈⸺

Day 211
Encouragement from Whom?

"But now, Zerubbabel, be strong," declares the Lord. "Chief Priest Joshua, son of Jehozadak, be strong. Everyone in the land, be strong," declares the Lord. "Work because I am with you," declares the Lord of the armies (Haggai 2:4).

I WONDER HOW MANY OF YOU have had projects in your life that you have given up on because you were burned out with it all? Dreams you let fall the through the crack out of frustration, the dark clouds of despair gathering and becoming darker. You are on the verge of giving up totally, that is, until you hear an encouraging word. Encouraging words are unique. They, like other words, have power of their own. Encouraging words are filled with hope, power, and promise. That is why words, particularly these words—because they came from God—were helpful in restoring the purpose of doing and being of Judah. Encouraging words have a way of helping hold us up until our legs gain strength, our backs straighten up, and we are ready to resume what God instructs us to be doing.

That is what happened in the in the rebuilding of the Temple of Zerubbabel. When Judah became serious about the work of rebuilding God's temple, the prophet Haggai brought God's encouraging words to them, which were that God was still with them and would bless them again if they remained obedient.

People today, as in the times of Judah, turn from God and do not obey the Lord. All of us are God's creation, and we have experienced the emptiness that only God can fill. Unfortunately, we learn this following agonizing years trying in vain to fill the void in our lives with things like material possessions, drugs, sex, or alcohol. Then we turn our backs on God. Even when we turn our backs on God, the Lord still seeks us out. One need only to look at the Bible stories of people turning away and God's drawing them back. This back and forth continues throughout our lives.

Only when we dedicate our lives to Christ can we experience the fulfillment, joy, and peace of the Lord, knowing that God is truly with us.

PRAYER: Father, draw us into an ever closer relationship within you. Help us see and to obey your will for our lives. Amen.

Day 212
God in Three Persons?

After he had said this, he breathed on the disciples and said, "Receive the Holy Spirit" (John 20:22).

HAS YOUR SPIRIT EVER BEEN SO full emotionally or spiritually that you felt you needed to say or do something but couldn't figure out what? How could you ever truly express yourself when all you could do was just sigh, frustrated that you were unable to find the words to adequately express what you were feeling? Here is where the Spirit is. After all, all of our experiences of God are experiences of the Spirit. The presence of the Holy Spirit is the power of our seeing.

I challenge you to find three qualities of the Holy Spirit in three words.

Even though Parkinson's has its talons buried deep in you and tires you quicker than it use to, the truth of the matter is that because of Parkinson's, there is nothing that we can do that we could not do quicker and better than before. We get a bit frustrated when we are working on a project, and by early afternoon the body is pleading for a break, the energy level wanes. But if we stop, we know we are done for the day. We try to fight it all the way and not give in; our minds say, "stop," but we manage to flounder alone, slower but still doing. Our "off" times seem to last longer. But if we can, we must keep on keeping. It is difficult to explain how we are feeling or what we are experiencing to someone who does not have PD. That is why some folk depend more at this time on the Holy Spirit.

The presence of the Holy Spirit is the power of our seeing. It moves its energy to every cell of our bodies, bringing life and vitality with it. Sometimes there are longings so deep, hauntings so tenuous, emotions so profound, that we cannot understand them ourselves, let alone explain them to anyone else. As human beings, we are a confusion, even to ourselves. Paul said a grand thing when he wrote that the Spirit knows us at the depth of our groaning breath as a sigh, too deep for words, or even tears; at that depth, says Paul, we are understood by the Spirit.

Have you ever heard someone groan? In that sound is all the sorrow of one's soul, and all the longings of one's heart. Paul says that when we groan like that, the Spirit interprets the groaning because it knows what that means. The Spirit interprets us to ourselves, deepening and refining our understanding, sharpening our insights, and honing our our sensitivity, drawing us into greater depths of self-knowledge and self-acceptance. Our best prayers are those in which the Spirit intercedes.

When we have very close friends, we call them "kindred spirits." Those folk who see life with their eyes and feel with their sympathy, know what they think they do. We know them from within; we catch their spirit, and they share ours. God wants to make us fellow kindred spirits. Not merely by God's commandments but also by the Lord's heart. What if we can so know and love God that we begin to see others as the Almighty sees them, and to love them as God loves them?

This Spirit cannot be contained by anyone. For example, look at the lives of Nicodemus, Ruth, Rahab the harlot, or Jonah, and see how the Spirit used them to further God's cause. The Spirit is moving where it wills, not where we will it to move. And we cannot possess the Spirit, though we might be possessed by it. The Spirit is too great to become our possession.

What if we were sailboats, not generating our own power, but able to find the wind and lift a sail? What if all the breezes of heaven are blowing, and all we needed to do was catch and allow them to bear us to our destination. Can't you feel the wind on your cheek, and moving in your hair? Are you not now dreaming of where it might carry you, and of the sense of adventure of the journey? You just might have caught the Spirit in this moment.

PRAYER: God, we thank you for the gift of your Spirit in this and in every moment. Grant that we may feel its presence in our lives now and forevermore, even as your beloved Son comes into our lives, freely, and groan once in a while with sighs too deep to know, save that your Spirit knows and understands our love for you and everyone. Amen.

Day 213
You've Got Mail!

The person who is saying those things should take note of this fact: When we are with you we will do the things that we wrote about in our letters when we weren't with you (2 Corinthians 10:11).

EVERYONE LIKES RECEIVING MAIL, especially personal mail. Our mailboxes get filled with a lot of junk mail, too, all those advertisements for all that stuff we don't really need and all those flyers about things that we're not terribly interested in. But the personal mail is something altogether different. There's something special about it. You might have won a sweepstakes prize. Or maybe you're getting some special news from someone you love, or a note from a friend you care about. Maybe it's a new novel from the

Book-of-the-Month Club, or a Social Security check. Could it be an invitation to write an article for a magazine or a refund check from the IRS? You see, it's the anticipation that gets you, isn't it? That's all part of the fun of receiving mail.

Do you ever watch the old *M*A*S*H* reruns on TV? A lot of the shows had to do with getting mail from home. Sending mail to the men and women at the front during wartime has been of special importance for centuries. Receiving mail during wartime has also been significant. Until the advent of junk mail, seeing the postman coming up the walk with letters in his hand signaled something important was stepping into your life.

Someone recently said how much she enjoys going to the post office to get her mail. By the time the mail has been put up in the boxes, she says, she has seen just about everybody she knows in town in a few minutes. And it's true! If you have a post office box or have to drop off something at the clerks' counter, you will probably see two or three people you know while you're there. The mail is that important.

Think about the church and other institutions from centuries past. The apostle Paul found it necessary to convey his message of hope and good news to the people he couldn't always be with by means of letters. His letters answered questions they had, solved dilemmas they found themselves in, soothed their fears, eased their burdens, and helped them to understand the world in which they lived. They were so important that they were shared throughout the various regions he had traveled through, and then they ended up in the Bible. There was some really good mail being delivered then!

How many of you listen to *A Prairie Home Companion* on the radio, with its weekly installment of the news from Lake Woebegone? Garrison Keillor, who started the whole thing, took out a two-page ad in weekly news magazines, like *Time* and *Newsweek*, getting people interested in writing letters again. To continue his campaign, he signs off another of his daily broadcasts, *The Writer's Almanac*, "Be well. Do good work. And keep in touch."

> **PRAYER:** May the God of hope fill you with all joy and peace in believing, in that you may abound in hope by the power of the Holy Spirit. Thank you, O Lord, for this day, for the mail we receive, for the love we share. And may we continue to be well, to

do good work, and to keep in touch with you and with one another, in Jesus' name. Amen.

———◇———

Day 214
Life in the Neutral Zone

*At once the Spirit brought him into the desert, where he was tempted by
Satan for 40 days. He was there with the wild animals, and the angels took
care of him* (Mark 1:12–13).

WHEN WE THINK ABOUT IT, Jesus gives us a good model for how
to deal with certain aspects of change. Driven into the wilderness, or desert place, that place out in the middle of nowhere,
he shows us another aspect of transition: he enters, for want of a better term,
a neutral zone.

William Bridges, who conducts seminars on transitions and how to cope
with them, has said of the neutral zone experience:

> You might feel this is heavy stuff—and it is. You only wanted a little help
> getting out of this strange crack between life's floorboards you unexpect-
> edly fell into. Well, first you've got to understand what you're doing there,
> and then you've got to see why it's important to stay there for a while—
> and then we can talk about what to do (William Bridges, *Transitions :
> Making Sense of Life's Changes* [Reading, MA: Addison-Wesley, 1980],
> 121).

Learning to appreciate the neutral zone experience is an important task.
One morning, an acquaintance of mine was pouring his first cup of coffee.
He just happened to look up and out the window over the kitchen sink. There,
in the front yard, in magnificent splendor were five deer. It was a grace-filled
moment, and the entire day seemed more whole and holy because of that brief
bit of "hind-sight."

In his neutral zone experience, Jesus' own ability to see and understand was greatly enhanced. One account of Jesus' time out "there" tells us that upon his return, he proclaimed that the kingdom of God was within our grasp, so clearly did he see it. The neutral zone gives us an access to a particular way of seeing life we cat get nowhere else.

Even though there are things that we could do in the neutral zone, such as take a rite of passage journey or vision quest over the course of several days, we can all think of what would be unlived in our lives if life should end today. Like Jimmy Stewart in *It's a Wonderful Life*, we might try asking ourselves, what would life be like if I wasn't here living it? Say a tree fell on you right now. There. It's all over. Whatever you've done is the you that goes in the record books, and everything you might have done fades away. At the time of death, you were . . . were what? Considering a fresh start? Stuck? Miles from home with the darkness falling? Watching deer cross your front yard? A friend sent a story via email sometime ago:

> A store owner tacked a sign above his door that read, "Puppies for Sale." Signs like that have a way of attracting small children, and sure enough a little boy appeared under the store owner's sign. "How much are you going to sell the puppies for?" he asked.
>
> The store owner replied, "Anywhere from $30 to $50."
>
> The little boy reached into his pocket and pulled out some change. "I have $2.37," he said. "Can I please look at them?"
>
> The store owner smiled and whistled. Out of the kennel came Lady, who ran down the aisle of the store, followed by five teeny, tiny balls of fur. One puppy was lagging considerably behind. Immediately, the little boy singled out that lagging, limping puppy and said, "What's wrong with that little dog?"
>
> The store owner explained that the veterinarian had examined the little puppy and had discovered that it didn't have a hip socket. It would always limp. It would always be lame. The little boy became excited. "That is the little puppy that I want to buy."
>
> The store owner said, "No, you don't want to buy that little dog. If you really want him, I'll just give him to you."
>
> The little boy became quite upset. He looked straight into the store owner's eyes, pointing his finger, and said, "I don't want you to give him to me. That little dog is worth every bit as much as all the other dogs, and I'll pay full price. In fact, I'll give you $2.37 now and 50 cents a month

until I have him paid for."

The store owner countered, "You really don't want to buy this little dog. He is never going to be able to run and jump and play with you like the other puppies."

To this, the little boy reached down and rolled up his pant leg to reveal a badly twisted, crippled left leg, supported by a big metal brace. He looked up at the store owner and softly replied, "Well, I don't run so well myself, and the little puppy will need someone who understands."

The next phase of life should be taking place as you ponder how you answer the question, "At this time of life, you are? . . . For Jesus, the next phase was announcing the coming and the presence of the kingdom of God. It is a time for us to do something that expresses ourselves in a significant way. It's our chance to begin a new chapter and *really* have life in the neutral zone.

> **PRAYER:** God, sometimes we just want to get out of the neutral zone because it seems so empty. Let us find you there at its center that our lives might remain focused on your kingdom and we may life whole and holy lives as your children, for the sake of our Lord, Jesus Christ, in whose name we pray. Amen.

Day 215
All Alone

There are people who are all alone. They have no children or other family member; even this is a pointless and terrible tragedy (Ecclesiastes 4:8–9).

ONE DAY WHEN I WAS living in Connecticut, I made a trip to North Carolina to visit my mother and dad. While I was there, I also visited my granny at her home. During my visit, I kidded her about wanting to watch certain soap operas on television. She knew all the characters by name, their backgrounds, which ones she thought were good and sweet—she left no question as to whom the bad guys were. When she named them, she would make a face as if she had just bitten into a green persimmon. We could really get her riled if we said something nice and good about the ones whom she thought were bad. Then during the laughter, she made a shocking statement that silenced all of us. She said, "Well, they are all I have to talk to for very long times. Matter of fact, there are sometimes I can go for a day or two not having contact with any other human being." I'll admit that was a kicker, but I can understand; one of her daughters had Parkinson's disease and getting around was becoming more difficult for her. The other two had demanding jobs that required them often to work long hours. They all made extra efforts to stay in contact with her, but there would be times that she would find herself alone. Home alone is something to be concerned about because it is reaching epidemic proportions with the growing number of elderly.

But we need to careful and not think that this is limited to just the elderly. Feeling alone can be found in all age groups, professions, and walks of life. There are times when I have felt alone, even when in large groups of people. I find myself wanting to withdraw and be alone. When I feel this way, I take heart in knowing that Jesus himself felt the ultimate aloneness. The night of his arrest, he went to the garden to pray with his followers. Instead of their support and keeping watch, they all fell to sleep and in the end ran away from the arresting group, leaving our Lord all alone. He knows the pain, the hurt, the heartbreak, the sadness, and the feeling of betrayal that come from being alone. His promise to us is that he will never leave us or forsake us. Now that's a promise you can count on.

PRAYER: Father, although we know that when everyone else is gone, you are still there with us. Bring someone into the lives of the elderly that will cheer them up and help them to look forward to getting up in the mornings. Remind them of your promise and your presence. Amen.

Day 216
The Haunted

The wind blows wherever it pleases. You hear its sound, but you do not know where the wind comes from or where it's going. That's the way it is with everyone born of the Spirit (John 3:8).

ONCE, A WELL-KNOWN PREACHER came to town to lead a conference that a group of us young preachers attended. The conference center where we met was packed, and there were people lining the walls as well as watching and listening in rooms that were made available for the overflow crowds. His message was quite stirring and thought provoking.

During a break that followed the speaker's presentation, someone asked the question, "Why can't we draw crowds like this, these days? Here we are, a group of women and men who have come together for a common reason: to garner some tidbit of information from one another that would help us be more effective in our particular ministries." The question was also asked for insight as to what made this meeting so successful and helpful.

I believe we were given a partial answer through the words of an elderly retired minister who had joined our group. Just a short conversation told one that he was gifted in his own right. He responded by saying, "First, you don't see your role as preacher to be a craft to be studied and practiced. Second, because you have never had your life threatened or your heart broken." Here we were, a group of young preachers, well-educated and some gifted in preaching, but none of us could hold a sparkler to the effectiveness and depth of the sermon we had just heard. We had all we needed, except God speaking to us through the Spirit. There is a kinship between preaching and art.

Art is a house that tries to be haunted. Those words express the mystery of the creative spirit. All serious artists build a house. They do it by mastering their craft, whether it's notes, words, or paint. They do it through their gifts, their discipline, their learning all the tricks of their trade. But even their best efforts cannot ensure success. Greatness is theirs only when the Spirit comes to dwell in the house they have labored to build, inspiring them beyond the capacity of their craft.

PRAYER: Father, make our lives fertile ground for the planting of those of us who desire to touch many lives by telling your good news. Help us to work on our craft of preaching so we can be as effective as we can be. Amen.

◄ ◊ ►

Day 217
A Little Bit Closer, Now

Draw near to God, and God will draw near to you (James 4:8).

SUCH A BEAUTIFUL PROMISE James gives to us, isn't it? I picture this promise as God sitting in a room with someone I love—or even with me—holding us, comforting us, soothing our pain, and making right whatever is not. James tells us that God, the creator of the universe in whose image human beings are made, will meet us—not just meet us, but draw close to us. We can feel God's divine breath on our necks. What a comfort these words are to those who feel alone and hopeless because of the ravages of Parkinson's disease. But what do we do once we have drawn close?

By drawing near to God, we afford the Lord the opportunity to come near us. Every part of our being, our hearts, and our minds all focus on God, who then takes that moment and fills it with presence. One interesting thing to me is that God *wants* to be near us, in spite of the spiritual, mental, or physical condition in which we happen to find ourselves. God is not embarrassed if we shake or drool or if we walk like someone who has had too much to drink. When our hearts are fixed on God, the Lord draws near and fills the moment with God's self.

But wait! This is not an automatic event, for not everyone wishes to draw near to God. That choice is left up to every individual. God is not going to force anyone into a particular decision, even though it might the right decision. If a person wishes to go it alone with his or her half-hearted gestures of commitment, God will not honor such a lifestyle. Although God is available 24/7, we are not prone to utilize that promise. This does not mean that we are to go to God with every whim or change in the weather. Such a way of thinking makes God into a glorified, cosmic, bellhop waiting for our beck and call, instead of being the Creator of everything bright and beautiful that God is. This is not part of what the scriptures promise. Maybe that is because we are afraid of what we might find. It is obvious that God wishes to show us a willingness to draw near to everyone, particularly those loved ones that need God's healing presence.

PRAYER: Hello, God... it's me again. For your willingness to draw near to us even though we are masters at creating and finding ways not to draw near to you, take away all fear, doubt, and trepidation that prevent us from getting a little bit closer. In the name of the one who desires a close relationship with us, even Jesus, our Lord. Amen.

─────────◄○►─────────

Day 218
Where Did You Put Your God?

My plan will stand, and I'll do everything I intended to do.... I have spoken, and I will bring it about. I have planned it, and I will do it (Isaiah 46:10–11).

THOMAS CARLYLE WAS A highly controversial Scottish historian, essayist, and critic. His writings were very influential during the Victorian age. Carlyle became seriously ill in his latter years. One day, a friend dropped by to visit him. The subject of religion came up, and the friend said, "I can only believe in a God that does something." It was reported that Carlyle winced as if in pain and said with a deep sigh, "But that's the problem. He does nothing, nothing at all." If you have read any of Carlyle's writings, however, you will know that this statement was in no way an accurate rendering of his faith. It did reflect at that moment the gathering clouds of depression that totally engulfed him. This causes me to wonder if any of you have ever felt, as I have, that it seems that God did absolutely nothing when God was, to use H. G. Wells' bitter phrase, "an ever absent help in time of trouble?"

All one needs to do is to compare our God alongside of the gods of the world and see how much taller and active our God is. Just look at history. We forget, from the very beginning, that God has been an active presence in the goings-on of creation. The God of the Bible is pictured in such a vibrant image because this is a God who does something. The Lord carries us, we do not carry the Lord. Because God does not fit into the little box we have created, we too often join in from the depths of despair with Carlyle's words, "He does nothing, nothing at all." We fail to discern God's working in our midst when in fact the Lord is very active. One tremendous way God did something and acted in a way that has forever changed our relationship can be found in the Christmas story. There God became like one of us in our human struggle. The Almighty dared to enter the world the way everybody else does: from the cradle to the grave. There you have it, the sign that our God does something. Here, God is found as a babe wrapped in swaddling clothes, lying in a manger. Now God has a new name, Emmanuel, meaning "God with us." The Lord has become as we are so we could see God as God is and know the love that has always been there for us. There is no experience or problem common to humans that the Lord did not face, which means we can now be assured that God understands our dilemmas no matter what they might be.

God does not come alongside us and say, "I understand your problem." God actually does things about those problems that make all the difference in the world. But here we need to be reminded to be cautious. God does not always act in the same way or solve our problems in the same fashion, as we might desire. God does not always work in just one way.

Thomas Carlyle was mistaken that day. The God of the Bible does do something! This God is everywhere and always at work for good. This God will bear us up unceasingly, without fail, but not in perpetual infancy, that we may increase in wisdom, in stature, and in favor with God and man—that is this God's agenda and toward this goal God works unstintingly. Therefore, if you believe that the Lord "does nothing, nothing at all," could it be that the problem is with you and not with God at all, that you are expecting the wrong thing and therefore missing altogether the right thing that is happening?

PRAYER: Father, thank you for being a God that does things. Help us to be so alert to your working in our lives that we do not miss your presence in our world. Help us to see, take, and live life with your unconditional love. Amen.

―――――――――◀◯▶――――――――

Day 219
Jesus' Friends

He called you friends (John 15:15).

WHEN I WAS GROWING UP, there was a popular television show called "I've Got a Secret." The game show centered around three individuals, two of which were imposters, with the remaining person being the one who was telling the truth about his or her work, achievements, and so forth. They were questioned by four panelists, who asked the players questions that might or might not help them discern who was telling the truth. At the conclusion of the questioning, the panelists would vote, and the real person of the three would stand up. I found it interesting to hear the panelists' reasoning as to why they chose a particular person. They guessed, and many times their guessing was correct.

We never have to guess when it comes to God, because Jesus tells us that God's friendship is so deep that Jesus has made known to us all he has learned from the Father. He pulls no punches, holds nothing back. There are no secrets. We know what he knows because there is nothing to hide. All he knows, he lets us know. Jesus wants total participation between him and us, a friendship that is close and not at a distance. Friendship with Jesus is total participation between him and us and he does not want us to keep any distance from him. All he has, he wants us to have; all he knows, he wants us to know; and all he does, he wants us to do. Perhaps our prayer life remains so often superficial because we do not dare to take seriously the truth that we are given the same knowledge as Jesus. That is really hard to believe, isn't it?

If we believe that the first commandment is to love God with our whole heart, mind, and soul, then we should at least spend more time during the day with no one else but God. Whether it is helpful, useful, practical or fruitful is completely irrelevant, because the only response to love is love itself. Everything else is secondary. Although this hour might not even seem like prayer because of inner confusion and many distractions, sitting in the presence of God for one hour daily might cause ridiculous changes.

PRAYER: Our heavenly Father, the longer we live, the more we realize the truth in the words of St. Augustine that our souls cannot find their rest until they rest in you. We thank your for Jesus, your son, who has made you known to us. We no longer have to search for a friend because you are our friend, and there is none other like you. As we walk together shoulder to shoulder down life's road, may our friendship grow deeper and more loving to you and all we meet. In the name of Jesus, we pray. Amen.

Day 220
He's Everywhere, He's Everywhere!

For in him we live and move and have our being (Acts 17:28).

ET'S BE TRUTHFUL, GOD IS the only one that can satisfy our longing. It is good to know that God is everywhere. We should be grateful, because God's presence calls for you and me to search for the Lord. As we journey along in our search, it doesn't take very long before we realize that the world's answers fall short in trying to describe the realities of the spiritual side of our lives. Then we find ourselves on a search for God. In that search, we hear Jesus encouraging promises. We must seek if we are to find, knock, if it is to be opened to us. Yet here's the oddity in all of this: As we search for God, we discover that our search ends in the discovery that God is and has been with us all the time, that God is not far off but is as near to us as the breath of our nostrils and the air we breathe. This is a sheer gift. We can do nothing to earn it. Rather, it is a free gift to all. In all of our talk about God, we will become tied up in all sorts of inconsistent metaphors. But that doesn't matter; what godly people try to tell us makes sense in spite of the apparent contradictions.

We discover God is everywhere. We see that according to the psalmist God is about our path, about our bed, and familiar with all our ways. And to quote Paul, we live, move, and have our being in God. God is around us and within us and refuses to be an alien in our being. Rather, the Lord chooses us to be in our truest selves, destroying our autonomy and forcing us into God's own mold so that we can kiss our own identity goodbye and be copies of the Almighty's.

God is not like any human being, for God is our creator, and not until we choose God and let the Lord dwell within us are our true selves established and given personal identity. God lessens who God is in order to find the divine in us. God limits God's self so that instead of overwhelming us, God gradually and gently calls forth into being the tender, vulnerable, and fragile part of our true self, fragile—which when made perfect—is the Lord's presence. Thomas Merton wrote somewhere, "God begins to live in me not only as my creator but as my other and true self—other and true because I spend much of my time lying by presenting a false self instead of allowing God to create me."

PRAYER: Dear heavenly Father, give us eyes to see you everywhere and in everything. You are the only God, creator of everything good. And because you are everywhere observing what we are and are not doing. May this promise give us strength and courage to face what we have to face. In the name of Jesus, we pray. Amen.

⸺⟨○⟩⸺

Day 221
A Loneliness Not to Be Overcome

Out of the depths I cry to you, O Lord (Psalm 130:1).

I WOULD LIKE TO ASK YOU A question for you to ponder throughout the day that deals with loneliness: Have you ever thought that there are different kinds of loneliness? Through reading and meditating, as well as talking to others along the journey, I have come to the conclusion that there are two distinct types.

The first loneliness is the emotional loneliness in which people are needed. A person with Parkinson's would fall in this category, although oftentimes we withdraw from people, making our situation worse. What is needed is the opposite: We need to go to people to meet that loneliness, we need our family, we need friends, and we need home. We can be content here until we have had all of those needs met. All the while we see that there is still another loneliness, one which our world cannot complete.

The second loneliness requires something more than what any characters of the first loneliness can provide. The second loneliness is on a much deeper level than the first. It is our answer to God calling us to a deep and personal intimacy. It should be pointed out that this intimacy is quite demanding. The loneliness calls for us to let go of things that are]very satisfying to us as anything emotional or intellectual. We must grow to realize and to trust that this deeper loneliness is not to be overcome, but lived. You must live with trust,

295

must learn to try to say, "Yes, I am lonely, but this particular loneliness sets me on the road to intimacy with God. It does not pull me away from God or my deepest self but brings me closer to the source of love in the depths of my being."

It is very important for us to welcome the fullness of this level of loneliness. This second loneliness can be traced all the way back to the oldest mystical traditions about spiritual life and prayer. The "dark night of the soul" is another expression of the second loneliness. In a way, this loneliness pushes us to know personally the true God. When we touch the darkness, we know that God cannot be owned; neither can God be grasped in the affections of the human heart, because God is greater than our hearts and God is greater than our minds.

PRAYER: Heavenly Father, we thank you that you fill our loneliness with your presence, so our loneliness doesn't paralyze and prevent us from coming to know you more intimately. In the name of Jesus, we pray. Amen.

Day 222
Forgiveness, Or Something Else?

I am writing to you, dear children, because your sins are forgiven through Christ (1 John 2:12).

OH, HOW OUR SOULS' SALVATION IS dependent on this powerful and inclusive word, forgiveness. Actually, it is needed by all human beings who wish to become a part of that "great cloud of witnesses" spoken of in the book of Hebrews. How do we come to receive this most precious gift? By our reception of forgiveness given so freely. It begins with the confession of our sin(s), which are taken as they are uttered and are forgiven, never to be remembered.

Have you ever given consideration to the possibility that when we are asking for forgiveness, we are actually asking to be excused? In comparing these words, we picture forgiveness as saying, "I know you have done wrong; but you have apologized, and I accept your apology and promise to take that wrong and throw it as far as the East is to the West, never to bring it up again. In forgiveness, your wrongs are no longer allowed to live, and everything between us will return to as it was before." Whereas we picture excuses as, "Don't worry, I see that you couldn't help the wrong you have done. You didn't mean it, and you really aren't to blame." If we are excused, then what is there to forgive? Thus we see that these two are almost opposite in nature.

We can see in any relationship we have with God or with other people, that there is an odd mix of the two: forgiveness and excuse. What started out as sin turns into finding no one at fault and is therefore excused. If there be any remnants, they are forgiven. The trouble comes when we "ask" God for forgiveness, for we are often asking God to accept our excuses. It reminds me of a Bible study published several years ago entitled, *Yes God, I Have Sinned, But I Have a Good Excuse*. We feel that with every wrong that there are some "extenuating circumstances," and we certainly are experts in pointing those out to God. We are so eager to point them out that the really important thing is left out: the remnant that excuses don't cover, the remnant that is inexcusable but not, thank God, unforgivable. And if by chance this slips our mind, we shall go away imagining that we have repented and been forgiven. Even though all that really has happened is that we are content in ourselves and our own excuses, which are usually very bad excuses, we are guilty of being all too easily satisfied with ourselves.

PRAYER: Father, awaken within us the need to truly be forgiven. Help us to lay aside all the excuse-making that we do and let you take our confessed sins and cleanse them in all righteousness. Amen.

Day 223
Different Kinds of Tears

*He will lead them to springs filled with the water of life, and God will wipe
very tear from their eyes* (Revelation 7:17).

EARS. MOST PEOPLE HAVE SHED them at one time or another in
their lives. Physically, we know what tears are, their source, their
makeup, as well as their purpose: that's universal. But the reasons we
cry vary with each person.

You know people, as I do, who can cry at the drop of a handkerchief. By
the time they watch a movie or come to the end of a song, a story about the
mistreatment of animals or children at the South Pole freezing, they have emptied an entire box of tissues. And yet, there are those who can't be moved. They
can watch or hear identical stories and sit without even a tear coming to their
eyes. They sit there, stone-faced, unmoved by the scene. These folk didn't even
shed a tear when Ol' Yeller died.

There are tears that show personal bitterness. Folk with Parkinson's disease
can fall into this group. PD patients shed tears for what could have been, for
dreams unrealized, for a normalcy that never will be theirs, and those folk have
no way of knowing when the tears are going to come. It may be out of the clear
blue, but tears come at the times when they can break through all the rubbish
that PD brings with it. But our tears come, nonetheless, and not just for ourselves, but also for others who are suffering. Unfortunately, there are folk who
don't understand the tears and are—or can be—guilty of turning their eyes
away from someone with PD, embarrassed, not knowing how to respond.
These are the folk with the hope that they will be restored to a more tolerable
way of being in the life to come.

PD patients also shed a different kind of tears. All we know is that they
come, and when they, come, it is from the depth of our hearts. They have no
name or cause. Why weep? I am not sure. Perhaps it is the utter gratuitousness
of life, of being. These are the moments we are certain we are loved truly,
deeply, for ourselves. A gift like this is so beautiful and grand, and these tears
are tears of gratitude, of wonder, of love.

PRAYER: Father, help us to keep the east window of our souls open for your gift of a beautiful sunrise that is new every morning. At times, they move me to tears, both outwardly and inwardly. Thank you for reminding us that you still have a work for us and that all of our tears are not wasted. Amen.

Day 224
And Great Is Its Fall

Pride precedes a disaster, and an arrogant attitude precedes a fall (Proverbs 16:18).

I WANT TO WARN YOU OF something that can cause you to take your eye off the goal, causing you great distraction. It can destroy friendships, careers, jobs (both present and future). It can destroy relationships in families.

What I am talking about is one of the seven deadly sins. It is pride. Pride favors folk who are highly visible, gifted, and talented. It mingles in the shadows, ready to spring at anyone at any given moment. It might follow a rave review on your first Broadway show. It might follow the announcement that you are the new CEO of a Fortune 500 company. It might occur after your record goes platinum or that your first art show was a huge success. Pride likes all these good and positive vibes floating around. They are for the people who have been blessed with these precious gifts. Along with these gifts, however, comes added responsibility to develop, maintain, and nurture their growth. You are the caretakers of these precious gifts.

And when reaching and climbing the latter of success, happiness, and even notoriety, it strikes. Pride leaps out at you. How far it goes with you is up to you. It might be a passing guest, or it might take up permanent residence in your body—that's when the destruction begins. You begin believing your own press.

What is pride? To put it very simply, pride is the lack of true humility. The story is told of several friends gathering together one evening. They gave themselves the task of trying to think of a genuinely humble man among the great and famous. They couldn't think of one among the present leaders of the world. One member of the group looked up a passage from a speech by Abraham Lincoln. This passage seemed to these friends to be an expression of true humility. Lincoln wrote:

I have been selected to fill an important office for a brief period, and am now, in our eye, invested with an influence which will soon pass away; but should my administration prove to be a very wicked one, or what is more probable, a very foolish one, if you, the people are true to yourselves and the Constitution, there is but little harm I can do, thank God.

Thank God, indeed.

PRAYER: Father, we need your help to rid our lives of the pride that is destructive and replace it with your love. Amen.

Day 225
How to Live

Simon Peter answered Jesus, "Lord, to what person could we go? Your words give us eternal life" (Luke 7:68).

HOW MANY TIMES DO YOU catch yourself wondering how you are going to make it? There always seems to be more month at the end of the money. And when thinking like this dominates our minds and controls our thoughts, life feels very uncertain and coarse.

Scripture frequently tells us that this is not the way to live. Accordingly, our only concern for the present is to allow God to reign in our hearts by and through God's grace and opening our hearts to God's ever-present love.

PRAYER: Lord, in these times when economics seem to be the rule of law and we think we cannot keep ahead or even up, we open our hearts to you to welcome your gracious love. May we trust in you to lead us where you most want us, where we may live and move and have our being in the name of your Son, Jesus Christ, through your Holy Spirit we pray. Amen.

Day 226
The Power of Words

For the word of God is living and active, sharper than any two-edged sword, piercing to the division of the soul and spirit (Hebrews 4:12).

WHOEVER CAME UP WITH THE rhyme, "Sticks and stones may break my bones, but words will never hurt me," is, in my opinion, delusional. Words do hurt, and they can cause great negativism, depression, and even despair. In Hebrew, the term *dabar* means both "word" and "deed." Thus, to say something is to move (it) to action. "I love you." "I hate you." "I forgive you." "I am afraid." Words can have a positive or negative effect on us, depending on how they are used, but we do know the pain, hurt, and emptiness because we have experienced them ourselves. Unfortunately, words once spoken can never be undone. Something that lies hidden in the heart is irrevocably released through speech into me, is given substance, and is tossed like a stone into the pool of history, where the concentric rings radiate endlessly.

Words are power, essentially the power of creation. It was by the spoken word that the God made everything that was made. And it is by the spoken word that everything is given power to move on its own, adding or taking away from life. It is by my words that I elicit a word from you. Through our conversation, we create or destroy one another. It is apparent that we need to be careful and to watch our tongues so no one is brought to despair because of what we might say.

God never seems to weary of trying to get God's self across. It is so important to the Lord to communicate with us that God would try something; and when that didn't work God looked again. God first tried by creating. God created the sun, moon, stars, and all of it, but creation itself didn't seem to grasp the concept. God moved to the patriarchs, then to Moses and the law; then God moved to the judges and the prophets. Word after word, God tried to search for the right word but was unsuccessful. In the search for the right word God found a word that could be understood. The Lord tried flesh and blood, sending his only begotten son into the world in an effort to get it right, and it worked. Jesus provided the only way that God and the creation can communicate with each other.

> **PRAYER:** Gracious God, creator and sustainer: Help us to be careful in our selection of words because of the action and power that each one harbors. Thank you that you did not give up on us but continued to search for the right word until that Word became flesh and came to earth to live and die in order that the word would become the message of love for the ages. Amen.

⟨◇⟩

Day 227
Anger

The Lord says, "I will love them freely, I will no longer be angry with them" (Hosea 14:4).

ONE WOULD THINK THAT living in a society that is so characterized by self-interest that it would be easy to start with taking a good long hard look at ourselves. But this is certainly not the case. It is hard, particularly, when it comes to re-evaluation and problem-solving.

We are very good at passing the buck and more than ready to point our finger at someone or something else other than ourselves. It is always the other person who is in need of help with the problems of which they are a part. The answers loom in the shadows until they are retrieved. This is such a deformed way of looking at the situation. To look at it from this point of view renders God as one with all of the answers and the devil as the one with the problems.

This approach totally bypasses our responsibility and participation. Wrongdoing always involves our participation, even when we are looking for answers. Answers can only be found in our seeking, searching, and questioning, as well as our digesting, embracing, and acting. So we both create the difficulties, and in finding the solution, we play a part. Our participation has a lot to do with the persons we are becoming. It is not strictly outside forces that cause our difficulties in life and shape our lives. We also create the tone and tenor of our lives. We do so by facing life realistically, by making good choices, and by seeking to live with integrity.

In the shaping of our lives, it is important to learn to deal with the issues at hand. Take, for example, our present anger: should it be addressed now, particularly because we are able to look at its beginning, shape, and outworking?

The flip side to this is for us to put addressing it off and blaming others. Or perhaps we hope that someone will work some magic, then the wrong anger will become a shadowy reality that will etch an unfortunate pattern into the fabric of our beings. When anger settles into a bitter resentment, it slowly paralyzes a generous heart. This signals for us a gradual but significant degeneration.

Therefore, we need to learn to come sooner rather than later to the scene of our own actions in order to put things right. Delay only reinforces our lack of responsibility. Learning to face the issues at hand particularly our own issues, will free us for creative problem-solving in which we may play a part but in which we can also experience the grace, healing, and forgiveness of God, who always calls us to the light.

PRAYER: Father, we are aware of the damage unrequested anger can do. Empower us to follow your teaching in handling anger before it grows into an unmanageable inferno. Amen.

Day 228

Keeping Score

The spokesman said, "This is what I found: I added one thing to another in order to find a reason for things (Ecclesiastes 7:27).

I REMEMBER THAT WHEN I WAS growing up that one of my favorite books was a picture book of farm animals. One horse standing tall; two ducks swimming on the pond; three puppies playing in the grass; four baby calves jumping and kicking up their heels; five chickens pecking at their feed; and on it went. By the time my sons arrived on the scene, there were no longer any cute farm animals. Ugly dinosaurs replaced them: triceratops, brontosaurus, and T-Rex. But as with my counting book, each page had enough animals to correspond with the number being taught.

Do you remember learning to count with the help of picture books like the one I

had? Or perhaps you used wooden blocks, fingers, and toes? We've been counting ever since: our money, our children, our years.

Yet sometimes, the happiest thing we can learn is not to count. Peter asked, "How often should I forgive my brother?" Three times was the standard requirement, but Peter generously suggested seven times. Jesus replied, "Not seven times, Peter, but seventy times seven." And he did not mean by that four hundred ninety. What Jesus implied was that we are to continue to forgive, because when we forgive someone of a wrongdoing, something happens to us. We are to forgive until it becomes automatic, a way of life. Jesus meant that there is a time to stop counting. You see, if we count offenses, we are waiting to get even, and that is a denial of the forgiving spirit. Paul put it perfectly when he wrote, "Love keeps no score of wrongs." In divine arithmetic, seventy times seven is an infinite number.

PRAYER: Forgiving Father, teach us to make the act of forgiving others a way of life and that we will not keep score. Amen.

Day 229
Automatic Responses

This also is a painful tragedy: They leave exactly as they came. What advantage do they gain from working so hard for the wind? They spend their entire lives in darkness, in constant frustration, sickness, and resentment (Ecclesiastes 5:16–17).

*E*VENTUALLY, WE NEED TO COME TO grips with who we are and why we act as we do. Are most of our responses automatic and repetitious? Have we settled forever our stand on certain issues or people? Are we locked into an automatically repetition of our heritage's mistakes?

Much of the futility of life comes from making habitual responses: habit-thinking and habit-living. Life then indeed becomes a treadmill of expressing distaste for the daily headlines, bemoaning the misspent lives of our near neighbors, and getting up and getting through the day in the easiest possible way.

The psalmist wrote in Psalm 31:10, "My life is spent with sorrow, and my years with sighing." Yes, our automatic responses produce countless sighs. Not so for those of us with PD. We would welcome some of the automatic responses to return. We would welcome a reprieve from having to be so deliberate in all we do. One of the major problems for us is the loss of automatic reactions and responses. Where as a person without PD can button a shirt, is not clumsy, can take a step without falling, pick up a fork and use any motor skills without any thought, we must be deliberate. It is as though our bodies don't use the brain that it came with but instead has a separate mind of its own. We are forced to have to decide on an action, and then make our bodies obey. That is one reason why many PD folk live day-to-day in apathy and despair.

Our habitual responses can make prisoners out of us. Paul's word, *bondage* (Gal 4:8), is an apt description. Christ's Spirit frees us. What a beautiful relief to experience the growth of a spirit-filled life: our own.

PRAYER: Father, you are our eternal joy. You have led us out of bondage. You have made us new and free. You have saved us from foolish escapades that dim our vision and drug our being. In Jesus name, we give you thanks and praise. Amen.

⸺◇⸺

Day 230
Dare to Care

Bless the Lord, O my soul, and all is within me, bless his holy name (Psalm 103:1).

PEOPLE WITH PARKINSON'S OFTENTIMES ARE mistaken for people who do not care about a particular issue or situation. Nothing could be further from the truth. Just because the blank expression on our faces might be fixed, or we do not become all giddy or excited doesn't mean that we do not care. Oftentimes, we have a real passion for a particular issue, but PD robs us of the ability to show it convincingly. Many of us yearn for the day when we can show our emotions. Make no mistake about it, folk with Parkinson's do care.

When we really get down to it, it is tough to care whether or not one has Parkinson's. Because to care means that we let others come close to us only after we have emptied our own cup, which to that point has kept us separated from others, preventing us from entering into communion with them. When we dare to care, then we discover that nothing human is foreign to us, that all the hatred and love, cruelty, compassion, fear, and joy can be found in our own hearts. Daring to care also means we have to confess when others kill, we could have killed too. When others torture, we could have done the same thing. When others were instruments of healing, we could have healed, too. And when others give life, we could have done the same. We then experience that we can be present with all who are involved in all of life. To the soldier who fights, to the young man who plays as if life has no end, and to the old man who stopped playing out of fear of death, we have a kinship.

By the honest recognition and confession of our human sameness we can participate in the care of God, who came not to the powerful but to the powerless, not to be different but the same, not to take our pain away but to share it. Through this participation, we can open our hearts to each other and form a new community.

> PRAYER: Father, place our souls in front of the mirror of your Holy Spirit in order to show us the true picture: that we are capable of the same bad and evil things that occur around us. Strengthen us to be bold in the living out of our faith so there can be no mistake whom we serve. In the name of Jesus, we pray. Amen.

⸺◇⸺

Day 231
Play upon Your Instruments

O God, I will sing a new song to you. I will sing a psalm to you upon a ten-stringed harp (Psalm 144:9).

IT HAPPENED AT A MIDWEEK prayer service. An elderly gentleman, when asked to pray, offered this prayer: "O Lord, we will praise you. We will praise you with an instrument of ten strings!" People wondered what he meant, but as he continued, it became clearer. He continued, "We will praise you with our two eyes by looking only to you. We will exalt you with our two ears by listening to only your voice. We will extol you with our two hands by working in your service. We will honor you with our own two feet by walking in the ways of your statutes. We will magnify you with our tongue by bearing testimony to your loving kindness. We will worship you with our heart by loving only you. We thank you for this instrument, Lord. Keep it in tune. Play upon it as you will and ring out the melodies of your grace. May its harmonies always express your glory."

When Frances Ridley Havergal penned the familiar words, "Take my life and let it be consecrated, Lord to Thee," she was expressing the need of making every member of our physical bodies responsive to the Lord's will. Paul underscores the same truth when he exclaims, "Offer yourselves to God as people who have come from death and are now alive. Offer all parts of your body to God. Use them to do everything that God approves of" (Romans 6:13).

When the apostle wrote to the church in Rome, "Brothers and sisters, because of God's compassion toward us, I encourage you to offer your bodies as living sacrifices, dedicated to God and pleasing to him. This kind of worship is appropriate for you" (Rom 12:1), he was encouraging every believer to praise God on his and her "instrument of ten strings."

We all are instruments of ten strings. The question is whether or not we will play upon them the beautiful harmonies that can only come when played by the master. I encourage you to both play upon your instrument and allow God to keep you in tune.

PRAYER: What beautiful melodies we can make when you are directing us, O God. We ask that you keep us in tune when we break strings because of too much tension. May the world know your marvelous grace because we are in unity, in tune, and in harmony with the other ten-stringed instruments being played by all the saints. Amen.

Day 232
Go Ahead and Ask

Anything you ask in my name, I will do (John 14:14).

I REMEMBER IT CLEARLY. The setting was the funeral home, and we were greeting people who were offering us their condolences on the death of our twelve-year-old son, Thomas. I kept watching down the line of people seeing how many more were entering. Then I saw him, an elderly man, Raymond Waddell, who shared the same birthday as Thomas and was also his godfather. Every year he would ask to come to see Thomas, and he would give him a present in celebration of their shared birthday. They were quite fond of one another. He came to me, with tears streaming down his cheeks and the wrinkles of time etched across his forehead. Weeping as he embraced me, he asked if there was anything he could do. I gave my pat answer: "Pray for us," to which he replied, "How do you want me to pray?" I was in shock; no one had ever asked me that before. I was speechless. I could not be so bold as to ask for the return of my son. His casket spoke to that impossibility. After regaining my composure, I responded, "For peace."

This chance meeting caused me to think about how we pray, what we pray for, and how we lose our prayers. Asking in Jesus's name: that is the great challenge. I ask for so much in my own name or in the name of my friends. Then I ask for what I want or for what I think my friends want. My own little world then shapes my prayer, and God becomes my helper in doing my own thing.

Asking in Jesus' name is something else! It means asking for God's will to be done, for God's glory to be established, and for God's love to be celebrated. The name of Jesus is a place where we ask. It is a house, a tent, a dwelling place. The more I live there, the more is revealed to me God's needs, God's desires, God's expectations, and there I gradually, with all my heart and mind and soul, come to know for what to ask. The act of asking in the name of Jesus allows one to come to know true prayer.

I now see also how important it is to say with the disciples in asking, "Lord, teach us to pray." Help me to ask what leads to your greater glory and honor. I know that if I really pray this way, my prayer will be heard.

PRAYER: Our dear Father, we come boldly before you, asking your help in our praying and lack thereof. We know that whenever we do not pray, our souls become as arid as the desert, but when we do pray in the name of Jesus, you restore our souls. We sometimes are rather silly being afraid to ask you for things. You are not going to bring any harm to those who go to you in prayer. Thank you for your patience. In his name, we pray. Amen.

⸺◁◯▷⸺

Day 233
Hope?

Then you will have deeper insight. You will know the confidence that he calls you to have and the glorious wealth that God's people will inherit (Ephesians 1:18).

HERE DO WE FIND REASON TO hope, believers and non-believers alike? Hijackers use anything they can get their hands on to add to the threat and fear of those around them. Terrorism cheapens life. The motivation for such actions are from someone else. They try to put the blame on Allah or God. The transference of the blame and their failure to take responsibility from God is insane. We have far too often done things we know are dumb and stupid and said, "God told me to do it." It doesn't matter that our actions go in direct opposition of what all the rest of scripture instructs us to do, be, and act. Looking at all of scripture, to hear terrorists blame God just does not hold water.

Nothing in the writing of the New Testament tells us that things have changed. Roman soldiers could still commandeer a Jewish person to carry his backpack for a mile. There was fighting between all religious groups, and citizens were put to death on trumped-up charges. There was violence, and that group of people, who were the tax gatherers for the Romans, were guilty of getting as much money as they could prevailed.

There have not been many changes, have there? There have been some times in my life that I feel totally hopeless. It is hard for me to see a lot of positives coming out of my having Parkinson's disease. As I go through each day, the slightest twitch, jerk, difficulty getting out of a chair, fatigue, or tightness causes my mind to go through a checklist so I can decide if what I am experiencing is a progression of the disease, or, as Scrooge claims, an undigested piece of beef. Where can hope be found?

All we need is to look no further than God's calling us to hope. Paul saw things that were going on but saw something else on an earthly level. When his heart's windows were opened, Paul saw through deeper eyes the significance of God's presence and actions of the day-to-day events of which we all are a part. Paul sees and so can we, if we know where to look, God calling us to hope. Can you imagine a more dependable caller to hope?

PRAYER: Father, help us to see through eyes of hope that you give to all who ask. Amen.

Day 234
Home Sweet Home

God is our refuge and strength, a present help in trouble (Psalm 46:1).

I REMEMBER MY FIRST TRIP back home after leaving to go to college. Several times I caught myself speeding, and the excitement and expectation grew the closer I got there. My heart was racing, and I was almost giddy when I turned into my parent's driveway. I hurriedly threw the car in park, got out, and then I remembered I was in college and I had to be cool. I went to open the back of my car to get my bag, and as I turned I was met with a multitude of hugs and kisses and pats on my back from my beloved parents and my dear, dear twelve-year-old sister. I was home, and there were not words to describe that feeling. No matter where you go, how long you stay, there's just something about being home, sleeping in your own bed, eating your mother's meals, conversation while watching a ball game, and just being among your things.

My family can be considered a loving, normal family with no major dysfunction. And yet, at times, we can't help but feel lost and alienated even amongst that love of family members regardless of the midst of the goings and comings of life. We can be in the middle of a room full of people and think that we are the only ones present. We can even believe that God is nowhere to be found. This sense, this feeling, is prevalent among those with Parkinson's disease. Whether it is because the person with PD is hard to understand or that our self-confidence is shaken for any reason, we will want to get out of where we are and back to our home, sweet home, where it is safe.

What is needed when this feeling overwhelms us is to be reminded that our heavenly Father loves us as if there is no one else in the world to love, and God loves each of us the same. Because of that the Lord has a place for us. We have only to hear the call to come home to the Father's house. Home is a place where we have a sense of belonging; home is a place where we find shelter, protection, and refuge.

This haven can be found in the midst of the ongoing busyness of today's society. This haven is the place of prayer. There, in that place of fellowship with the Father of all grace and consolation, we hear him inviting us to join the Lord. When we accept, we go to the place that is really home. It is from that home that we seek to build families of openness and joy, churches of reconciliation, workplaces of productivity, and partnerships and friendships that are not stifling, but are marked with servanthood and reciprocity.

PRAYER: Dear God, thank you for helping us feel right at home. You provide that haven of peace and love that reminds us how much you do for us. Thanks! Amen.

Day 235
A Needed Breath of Fresh Air

How can I talk to you, sire? I have no strength left, and the wind has been knocked out of me (Daniel 10:17).

HAVE YOU EVER HAD your breath restricted in some way? Whether chocking on food because of some breathing disease, or at the hands of someone, not to be able to get one's breath is quite frightening. In some severe cases, CPR has to be administered to assist the person to breathe again on his or her own.

About four years ago, because of another one of my uninvited guest-hostile take-over-victories, I have developed a swallowing problem that occurs from time to time without any warning. When it happens, it scares the bee-gee-bees out of the people around us, but we have learned a few tricks to counter the episode. The fear, however, is still present. It is certainly wonderful when you are able to take a diaphragm/chest-expanding breath of air, and it is even better when it is fresh and not polluted air.

We can we find, in one of my favorite passages of scripture, that the challenge of the gospel lies precisely in the invitation. The invitation is for anyone to accept the gift for which we can give nothing in return. That gift is the gift of God. The Spirit, who is poured out on us through Jesus Christ is the breath of life that frees us from fear and gives us new room to live. Anyone who prayerfully goes about life is constantly ready to receive the breathe of God and to let one's life be renewed and expanded. The person who never prays, on the contrary, is like a child with asthma: because he is short of breath, the whole world shrivels up before him. Such a child creeps in a corner, gasping for air and is virtually in agony. But the person who prays opens oneself to God and can freely breathe again. That one stands upright, stretches out one's hands, and comes out of the corner, free to boldly stride through the world because such a one can move about without fear.

A person who prays is one who can once more breathe freely, who has the freedom because he or she can move as desired with no fears to haunt him or her.

PRAYER: Thank you, O gracious Father, for the ability to breathe; and not only to breathe, but also to inhale the pure air of your Spirit. For it is breathing that air that we are able to nurture our spirits and let them grow. In Jesus' name, we pray. Amen.

Day 236
Ten Down to Two

"Which is the greatest in Moses' teaching?" Jesus answered him, "Love the Lord your God with all your heart, with all your soul, and with all your mind. This is the greatest and most important commandment. A second is like it: Love your neighbor as yourself" (Matthew 22:35–39).

WE KNOW THAT GOD GAVE THE Israelites, camped around the holy mountain of Sinai, two sets of Ten Commandments, or words by which to live. The first set of the tablets were broken when Moses came down from the mountain to a people who were caught up in a frenzy as they danced around a golden calf that Aaron, the brother of Moses, had fashioned with a tool. They were partying big time. Moses in his anger threw the tablets down and broke them. After passing judgment, Moses went back up Mt. Sinai and received the second set of tablets and this second set, along with the fragments of the first, were placed in the Ark of the Covenant. Later, the Israelites were defeated by the Babylonians and sent into exile. They believed that God had allowed this to happen to them because they had not been true to the Law.

It is during this time that we see a group known as the Pharisees, who became strong advocates of fencing the law in their interpretation of it. When they had finished recording their interpretation of the Law, the original ten commandments had grown to over 600! So it is easy to see how important Jesus's answer was to the Pharisees' question. Under Jesus' teaching, the 600 plus regulations were reduced to two. With the reduction from ten to two, Jesus placed these two goals of believers as the center of our faith and the standard by which we should test everything we do. By doing this, it does it make me more loving within and without? The question arises: Are we enhancing the love of God for other people?

> **PRAYER:** Dear God, you were very patient with your children, the Israelites. They seemed always to be doing something to show their disobedience and refusal to let you be God. Before we become too judgmental, grant us the courage to look at our own lives, both personally and corporately, through your eyes to see what kind of witness we are showing the world of you, who loves everyone and us. Amen.

Day 237

Special Places

After sending the people away, he went up a mountain to pray by himself. When evening came, he was there alone (Matthew 14:23).

WE ALL HAVE SPECIAL PLACES to go to where renewal can occur. Maybe it's the particular place where you sit in church or in this room here at the Senior Center. Perhaps you have a favorite spot in the garden or back yard, with a hammock or lawn chair where you can get away from it all and return to the world refreshed and ready to go again. How about a hike in the woods or a stroll in the park? A minister I know goes back to the churches where he's been throughout his life to be renewed. Some folk go fishing. Some climb mountains. Others go to the gym, perhaps to play basketball with a group of friends.

Jesus had favorite places to go when he needed to escape the crowds and be rejuvenated. Most times, he'd get up into the hill country to be by himself. Sometimes he'd take several disciples with him to pray or keep passersby from disturbing him. Sometimes he'd go to Martha and Mary's house. He once said that even a closet was a great place to find renewal because that was one of the secret places a person could be with God.

Where is your special place? Go there, and be refreshed. Find peace and rest, and soon you'll be ready to meet the world with renewed vigor.

> **PRAYER:** Heavenly Father, you have given us a wonderful world. Be with us as we go to our special place to be with you. May we find peace and joy in our fellowship with you and with one another. Cleanse and renew us each day through your Son, Jesus Christ, and the power of your Holy Spirit. Amen.

⸺◈⸺

Day 238
All Mixed Up

"My thoughts are not your thoughts; neither are your ways my ways," said the Lord (Isaiah 55:8).

MANY PEOPLE HAVE FOUND IT TO BE A good idea to keep track of their spiritual life. One has only to look at some of the more renowned characters throughout the history of the church: St. Teresa of Avila, both John and Charles Wesley, William Law, Terese of Lisieux, Bonaventure, and Hildegaard of Bingen, to name a handful. Perhaps you don't think you are important enough to write about yourself and the experiences you have. But aren't you important to you? You certainly are to God! Jesus once reminded his listeners that we are more important than the sparrow that God loves and provides for, and Jesus himself died and was raised from the dead for you. Isn't that a good enough reason to keep track of your life experience(s) as you are affected by this gracious act of God's love? What have been your joys today? Your hopes? Your disappointments? Your dreams? How have you responded to God's invitation to life in Christ?

A woman had been given a journal that was full of questions. When the questions were answered, the book would create a record of what life was like for her mother and father. So for about an hour each day, she would down with her mother asking the questions contained in this journal. One of the questions was, "What is your name?"

"Beulah Esther," wrote the woman.

"Why were you named 'Beulah Esther?'" the next question inquired.

"Well, in our family, it was customary to name the children after biblical names." She was named after Beulah, which in Hebrew is the name of a place meaning "be married," and Esther, who through a kind of Cinderella story became one of the great queens of Israel.

As you write down the things that have been significant to you throughout the day or week, you are developing food for prayer. You find that you have needs that you desire to make known to God; that you have friends and even people you don't even know that you'd like to pray for; and you discover you have things for which you are thankful and therefore you need to offer praise to God. And in keeping a journal, you learn more about yourself and the world around you. Even though our journals might not become best-selling books like Annie Dillard's *Pilgrim at Tinker Creek* or Kathleen Norris' *The Cloister Walk*, we might just find ourselves led to being more responsible and intentional about our faith.

PRAYER: Gracious God, we thank you for the opportunities we have to sit and reflect upon your living and loving presence in our lives. Encourage us to keep track of our journey along your way. May we be inspired to keep a record of that journey to see where we have been, to enjoy where we are, and to look forward to meeting and being with you in the glory of your heavenly kingdom, through your beloved Son, Jesus Christ, in whose name we pray. Amen.

Day 239
The Mysterious with Us

The Lord will come from heaven with a command, with the voice of the archangel, and with the trumpet call of God (1 Thessalonians 4:16).

A HISPANIC FRIEND PUT INTO perspective for me what God did in order that the people on earth could be delivered from the evil one. It is obvious to us that this is made possible not just through serene expectancy of a resolution that will be peaceful. Looking at the scriptures, we see the reality of this. Only a short time after the birth of Jesus, all the baby boys of Bethlehem two years old and under were slaughtered.

He had me. I listened intently and couldn't wait to get to a computer. What I read jolted me, and I remembered traveling to Monterrey, Mexico, a few years back and seeing this but was in too much of a hurry to inquire about it. The information I gathered gave a clearer picture of what this longstanding tradition was. There was a picture of an old Spanish crèche, and in it a carved, wooden Satan, standing nonchalantly among the sheep, shepherds, camels, and wise men. They had placed him near the back, but he was unmistakably there, compete with horns, tail, and saturnine leer! The article quoted a docent, who explained that this was not unusual. More often than not, that the figure of Satan was placed in the crèche scene was an old Hispanic tradition. The last picture was of an old painting of St. Michael the warrior archangel, dressed in full seventeenth-century armor and carrying an efficient looking pistol in his holster.

Now every time I see a crèche, I am reminded that on that holy night Satan was not off somewhere twiddling his thumbs, but he was right there in the thick of things. Maybe he was amused that God's answer to defeat him was a baby. It certainly caused a chuckle to think that the restoration, the deliverance of this world, would come wrapped in swaddling cloths. How nonthreatening. How much like God it is, as well!

PRAYER: Lord, during this Christmas season, and especially this night of all nights, continue to remind us that your plan for us is as mysterious as it was on the night you sought to restore us through a baby wrapped in swaddling cloths, even Jesus Christ, our Lord, in whose name we pray. Amen.

⊰◦⊱

Day 240
Why Always Pray?

He has done this so that they would look for God, somehow reach for him, and find him, in fact he is never far from any one of us (Acts 17:27).

THIS VERSE CERTAINLY RINGS A note of hope for all of us, doesn't it? Paul is giving us an intimate truth here: that God loves us, and we are quite special to this One who created us. Not only does God have an untiring concern for our well-being, but the Lord takes particular pleasure in our company. Even the hairs on our head attract the loving notice of our God (Matthew 10:30). Who would have thought that the creator God would even want a relationship with us hardheaded people? God's presence is at the same time inescapable and cloaked in mystery. In our search for God, there is an inner magnetism that draws us closer to the Master. Is this the reason Jesus encouraged his followers to pray and not to lose heart?

At best, our attempts usually wind up as groping and uncertain. But Jesus showed us through the currents of this love how important it was to draw away alone and be with God so that one could taste the rejuvenating love God gives to all the people of the world who come before the Lord.

It is amazing, isn't it, that Jesus lived that example all the way to the end and did not lose heart. He was strengthened by this current, which even made him strong enough to bear the whole shattered world in God's compassion. Coming from his time alone with God, there emerged a new resonance, which reminds us that not only do we find a comfort and consolation, we discover a service of consecration in that truth, the truth that God is always with us, or as one of desert mothers said, "There is always some way of turning to God which is within our reach."

When we truly yield and participate in the heart of Christ, we come to know what one believer called the "ecstasy of everyday."

PRAYER: May we begin to savor that ecstasy in all the days that lie before us. Amen.

—◁◦▷—

Day 241
I Know You Told Me

The stupidity of fools is just that: stupidity (Proverbs 14:24)!

HAVE YOU EVER DONE something amid the warnings of others, and the moment you did it you knew that it was a terrible mistake? You did it with the warnings of others still ringing in your ears.

I was ten or eleven when I committed my moment of stupidity. It was baseball season, and my team had had a perfect season and already had clinched a berth in the playoffs. My coach loved Red Man chewing tobacco. To this day I do not know what possessed two of my team members and me to do what we did, but the three of us found one of his tobacco pouches and helped ourselves to it. Some of the others on the team warned us not to do what we were doing, and even told us that we would regret it. We laughed at them as we each put a chew into our mouths.

The tobacco was still burning my mouth as I heard coach say, "Tommy, get ready to relieve. Go to the pitcher's mound." I trotted to the pitcher's mound in total control. A slight dizziness washed over me, but I recouped. I got the first two batters out on strikes. They were at the bottom of their line-up, so I didn't feel as intimated as I would have if they were at the top of the batting order. I threw a fastball, and the batter hit a line drive to me. Before I could catch the ball in my glove, I caught it with my stomach. I guess I reacted to compensate for the air that had been knocked out of me from the hit. You guessed it, I swallowed the entire wad of tobacco I had in my mouth. By the time the umpire and coach got to me, I was already green, and after seeing that I was okay, the coach called out to two of my teammates to help me off the field. I could hardly walk on my own. My legs had turned into Jell-O. Everything was on the move, spinning and spiraling. I was extremely light-headed. My eyesight was also playing tricks on me. I was seeing three of everything, so I reached for whatever was in the middle.

And do you know what those cruel, hateful people did? They started laughing at me. I was certain my dad was leading the chorus of laughter. Even my dear, sweet mother had her hand over her mouth trying not to laugh. All I knew was that I was dying, and they were laughing. I was feeling sick like I had never felt sick before. I made it to the restroom and lost everything in my stomach: tobacco, a heart, a kidney, and even a lung. At least it felt like I did. I was told that I was turning colors that were not present on any color chart. I came to find out that the other two teammates with whom I had shared the tobacco had replaced their tobacco with a mouthful of bubble gum. I never saw that they had thrown theirs away. What a host of friends!

I wonder if God laughed at my stupidity or chalked another check under my name. I glad God has a great sense of humor. All I know is that I am grateful for God's unending, unconditional love. Looking back at that game, I am also very glad that I was able to bring so much happiness and laughter and enjoyment to all those parents and grandparents and friends.

PRAYER: God, thank you for being not so high and mighty that we cannot come to you with our stupid mistakes. Amen.

Day 242
What It Takes

Some of the Pharisees in the crowd said to Jesus, "Teacher, tell your disciples to be quiet." When he came closer and saw the city, he began to cry (Luke 19:39, 41).

COURAGE IS A VIRTUE THAT IS needed by every believer who lives in today's world with all its mixed-up philosophies. Yet, many of the same believers come up short and have little or not enough courage to face life. Our idea about courage is fairly superficial, isn't it?

For one thing, *our* courage is often insensitive. You and I know people who take an action, thinking it brave and heroic in their own eyes, and everyone except them might pay the price for their actions. Their actions cost them nothing, but they brought great pain to their spouses and other members of their families. Whereas they strut in the conceit of courage and moral superiority, they weep and suffer over the consequences of their actions. They appear to have no awareness of how cheap their bravery was.

Have you ever heard people say, "I speak the truth, regardless"? Regardless of what? Regardless of the hurt caused to others? Regardless of the restraint of love, which Paul tells us knows how to be silent. People with attitudes like these who claim fearlessness are distinguished not for their courage but for their coarseness. They are insensitive. The New Testament exhorts us not to speak the truth "regardless," but to speak the truth in love.

We all know some folk whose courage lacks imagination. They do not have enough imagination to be afraid. Jesus's courage was instructed by his kindness of spirit and perceptiveness of mind. He knew the cost and went on anyway. That is true courage. It is aware, it sees things clearly, and it faces them fearlessly. But more times than not, our courage is cheap because it is fashionable, and Jesus knew that the cost of courage is often loneliness. And yet, knowing all of that, Jesus went on. Genuine courage is nearly always lonely.

Can you see this man on his way to Jerusalem with his face set like flint and his heart breaking for love of those men and women who would never be the same again because of his journey?

Where are we to find this courage? It is found in being loved. We sometimes think we are loved because we have worth, but the deeper truth is that we have worth because we are loved.

PRAYER: What a very profound concept that you love us in our sin and that you love us as we are and the way we will be, O God. Thank you. Amen.

------‹◦›------

Day 243
When Is Enough Enough?

I guarantee this truth: This poor widow has given more than all the others. She, in her poverty, has given everything she had to live on (Luke 21:2).

WALKED IN ON THE END OF A television show about mobsters and was struck by the comment made by one of the members of the crime family. The interviewer asked in closing why all the expensive religious relics and plaques acknowledging his benevolence to church and community, to which the interviewee shrugged his shoulders and answered, "I guess he felt he could buy his way into heaven." Talk about how much is enough.

Turning to the scriptures, one thing is perfectly clear: Jesus never wanted to stand between people and their sacrifices. We know there are people in this world who never know the heart's breathless wonder and the soul's adoration. We are part of life that is always saying to us, "Nothing over much." But as far as I can see in the New Testament, Jesus never said to people, "Be careful with your life. You can spend too lavishly. You can give too much. You can invest too richly." It is as though Jesus is saying for us to put our money, our treasure, where our hearts are. This would certainly point us to face the question, are our hearts really committed? What exactly are we doing with our money? The gospel encourages us to find the poor and help them. Paul says that God is looking for "cheerful givers." The Greek here for *cheerful* means "hilarious giver." The picture this presents to us is one of people who are beside themselves to the point of being giddy as they give their offerings. I don't know about you, but I have not witnessed any behavior like this.

We do, however, see this with the instance of the widow giving her two mites—all that she had. There was nothing left. Jesus, as he was watching, remarked that others had given from their surplus, but not this widow: she gave everything. Now, I don't read this story without wanting to put a Hollywood ending to it. I always have wanted Jesus to call her back and say, "You cannot do this. You have nothing left." But whatever he might have done later to help her, in that moment he let her give all she had because he knew that she already had her reward.

PRAYER: Benevolent Father, we come to you with overflowing hearts of gratitude for all that you have blessed us. Help us to understand that you do not expect everyone to give to your work in this world kingdom the same: not equal giving, but equal sacrifice. And through that giving bless them, you, and us. Amen.

---<>---

Day 244
Me and My Shadow

People carried their sick into the streets. They placed them on stretchers and cots so that at least Peter's shadow might fall on the sick people as he went by (Acts 5:15).

IT WOULD BE EASY TO have these folks committed. To think that their sick and infirm would be healed simply by contact with a passing shadow. How absurd! Let's load them up and take them to the funny farm. But wait; aren't they practicing what we preach, that of one of the pillars of faith? *Faith assures us of things we expect and convinces us of the existence of things we cannot see* (Heb 11:1). Can you imagine having that kind of faith? To believe that anyone has healing power in his or her *shadow* and that all one has to do is to position the sick person in a place where they can be certain the holy man's shadow would pass over them, and they would be healed. A shadow has the power to heal? That is either faith, or it is hope that has gone insane. And what about those who were said to have had that power? What did they do to get the reputation to have that kind of power to believe that if only their shadow would pass over their ailing loved one they would be healed? Where did they get that power?

I know, personally, that if there were one or more people who had that kind of power, I would crawl to get to them, if need be. It would not matter where or how far I would go to find that passing shadow and be healed of this unwelcomed guest that is gaining control of my body. My journey would not be an isolated one, for millions of folks with PD would be going too, their caregivers helping to carry them so they could be healed of Parkinson's and no longer suffer.

But what was the source of this power to heal? The scripture said that Peter and John had no education or special training. They were "ignorant men" (RSV). So where did they get this power to heal, the religious leaders wanted to know. Peter and John answered, "Through the power alone of Jesus," as the once lame man, whom they knew had been lame since birth and they passed by every day going into the Temple, was walking and jumping around the room praising God.

Then the religious leaders answered their own question without even knowing it when they said that they realized these men had been with Jesus. Isn't that the source of all our healing? It may not be a complete healing of our illness, but he fills it with his presence, his shadow. Jesus' cross is where the healing waters spring. How large is your shadow?

> **PRAYER:** Our heavenly Father, we now know the source of the power that the disciples had and freely gave away. May you give that power to heal to those today who have been with you, for that is the only way our relationships, our lives, our bodies, our minds, our spirits, and our churches can be healed, restored for the building of your kingdom. In the name of Jesus, we pray. Amen.

Day 245
When Tragedy Strikes

Lord, if you had been here, my brother would not have died (John 11:20).

*I*F YOU HAVE A terminal illness of any kind, you most likely will have asked the question, "Why did this have to happen to me at this time?" Mary and Martha put this question to Jesus. There was sadness in their bitter disappointment. "If you had only been here earlier, he would not be dead now." In this scene, we see mixed emotions in the face of this personal tragedy. There was *belief*—you could have done something—and we also see *reproach*—but you didn't come in time. There was *faith*, but there was also *frustration*. There was *love*, but there was also *puzzlement*. There, sticking its ugly head out again was the unanswered question: "Why?"

Sometimes, faith can be a problem as well as a support when tragedy strikes. But if God is "great and good," as our children pray, then where is God when we need God the most? If the Lord is alive and active, then the question is always raised, "Why did God allow this to happen? Why did this have to happen to me?" This is not a question of doubt. It is rather a faith question; it is the cry of a wounded believer.

We must each of us find our own answer, our own meaning for the many things that happen in our lives. I cannot give an answer for you; but I do know that when you ask that question, there is something that I can tell you. When asked, *Why*, I answer, "I don't know; but this I do know: Christ understands you." Jesus, just like any other being, was moved to tears, filled with grief at Lazarus' death. The tears and emotions of Jesus in the face of this tragedy show us a God who sympathetically cares and understands, and we see in Jesus' humanity a God whose very heart is wrung with the sorrow in the anguish of his people. Here is a God, who in the most literal way is afflicted in our affliction.

Even in death, Lazarus was in the midst of Jesus' love because he loved him. This was no impersonal love. How strengthening to know that he calls us by name. In the face of tragedy, we can depend on Christ's love for us. We can be sure that whatever happens to us takes place in the context of Christ's love for us.

All through this passage there is hope. Christ in the midst of tragedy brings triumph in spite of it. He brings light out of darkness, victory out of defeat, salvation out of suffering, redemption out of crucifixion, and resurrection and life out of death. Not everything that happens is good, but in his strong hands it can be used as a tool to bring good for our lives.

PRAYER: O God, our creator: when tragedy stops our lives in their tracks, enable us to hear your voice directing us to the life you have in store for us. We need your help not to waste all our suffering. Help us to bring our human emotions in line with Jesus' emotions. In his name, we pray. Amen.

◄ ○ ►

Day 246
Only Minutes Left

For everything there is a season, and a time for every matter under the sun (Ecclesiastes 3:1).

WHEN I LIVED IN NEW York City, there was this bakery—I believe it was on Third Street—that warned passers-by that since life is uncertain they should eat dessert first. My sweet tooth likes that way of thinking, eating dessert first. That, my friend, is a bakery after my own heart. I have a confession to make: when I go into a restaurant, I am immediately on the lookout for the dessert cart or the dessert listing on their menu. It always makes the entrée taste better knowing what awaits me. Will it be a New York cheesecake or banana pudding or apple cobbler or their triple chocolate suicide cake or their creamy carrot cake or a red velvet cake or banana nut cake or an Italian cream cake? I told you I had a sweet tooth.

If the owners of the bakery are correct, and we know from experience that they are, when they say life is uncertain, what should we do first as we eat our

327

dessert? What thing or things would move up your list claiming the spotlight? It is so easy to treat life trivially or reduce the importance of a particular event or person in our lives. You know what I'm talking about: those things that we put on our "to do" list that never change position on the list for deeming other things more important. We have been putting them off for a later date.

Someone once said that if we were told that the world was going to end in five minutes and we were given only that amount of time to say all that it had meant to us, every phone booth, every cell phone, every telephone line in the country would be occupied by people desperately trying to reach other people to tell them that they loved them. I would like to think that my family and I, knowing of the impending doom, would gather together, and if there were any need to make amends with one another that that would take place. After expressing our love for one another, we would hold hands as the catastrophic event took place.

Life is uncertain, so don't wait. The words are *relationship* and *love*. If you love someone, tell him or her now, before you eat your dessert.

> **PRAYER:** Our gracious heavenly Father, we acknowledge the truth that life is uncertain. Many of us could recite a plethora of uncertainties that we have experienced. What we need is for you to help us to be courageous enough to go through our list and move things around to their proper position of importance. And help us not to wait until we only have five minutes before we tell the people we love of our love and devotion to them. Help us to do that now. You did, in the name of the One who showed us to love in the moment, Jesus Christ, our Lord. Amen.

Day 247
Conversing with the Heart

But I call upon God; and the Lord will save me. Evening and morning and at noon I utter my complaint and moan, and he will hear my voice (Psalm 55:16–17).

HY ARE WE GUARDED WHEN WE PRAY? Sometimes we actually convince ourselves that if we don't say how we are really feeling that God will never know. That is one reason why we dare not to think of any harsh words that might come from our troubled and angry hearts. If we give avenues of expression for our consoling, peaceful, and calm words, we need also to give an avenue of expression for those words that are not so sweet and peaceful. We should believe that we can say whatever is on our hearts, our true feelings. Why not level at our Creator all of our questions and doubts, our disappointments, and our concerns? A great many people don't, because they think that God might get mad and hold it against them.

Beyond prayer being sweet, polite, or like a friendly chat with a family member, we come to realize that it comes from the dirt of life. Often it is the passion from the depths of our hearts. It is in this type of prayer that we can utter our doubts and hopes. Our fear and faith mingle together when we allow our gut to say what bothers us and what we long for. This speech is not always sweet, quiet, affirming, or nurturing. And, oftentimes, faith and charity are at a minimum.

There are times when I take God to task: "Why Parkinson's?" "Why now?" "Why did you let it happen?" When I pray with my heart, I feel as though I'm in great company—I join the psalmist(s), Job, Jeremiah, and so forth. They were not afraid to take God to task, for this kind of praying calls for answers and looks for relief. Its source is born of hope and not anger. It comes to life by pain and not bitterness. It also speaks of a relationship that is not weak but rather is strong enough to deal with the hard and real issues and does not choose to hide anything out of fear of rejection.

The truth is that not any and every prayer heals. It is the prayer of openness, of the heart, the words spoken to God, that cry out to God, that bring relief, peace, and healing.

PRAYER: Our heavenly Father, whose goodness is overwhelming, we are glad that we can come to you with all of our anger, disappointments, hurt, betrayal, and the answers to the whys in our lives without any fear of repercussion. There are no hidden books, no set orders, or instructions as to how we pray. You are the same no matter our attitude. You listen and respond with the same compassionate, understanding, and love. In the name of Jesus, we pray. Amen.

<hr />

Day 248
Remember Me

Jesus, remember me when you enter your kingdom (Luke 23:41).

I WAS VISITING WITH AN elderly friend who shared with me an insight that he said he had been pondering for a while. He started by saying that he had never thought much of the adage, "You don't appreciate something until you don't have it any longer." He continued, "For a long time, I do not remember the topics of our conversation." He didn't want to forget, but he had no say in the matter, for he had developed Alzheimer's disease. He was in the earlier stages, but he knew what lay down the road. "Hey, we have something in common, doc. We both have an ailment that we will not be able to do anything about. My mind is going to be erased like an eraser on a chalkboard. You have Parkinson's and you will be left with the memory of what was and might have been. There will be things you want to do, but you will be unable to do them. You will get frustrated and find yourself in the grasp of despair. Mine will just prevent me from doing anything because I can't remember from one event to another. But you will be stuck here to remember. That sucks, doc, and in my opinion I think I have the better end of the deal." My friend had a unique grasp of the issue, didn't he? I see some of you shaking your heads in agreement.

Fortunately, I have not gotten to that place yet. Oh, I have my moments, but by and large I do not suffer the extreme prophecy he laid out before me; but I don't ignore the possibilities of them coming to play in some fashion or form. Unfortunately, there are some folk with Parkinson's who are not as lucky as I am and who suffer from this dreaded disease's full wrath.

Whether we have Parkinson's, Alzheimer's, cancer, or any other ailment we have to remember in order not to fall into despair and live without hope. Here are some reminders of the importance of this:

> *Such a person drinks and forgets his poverty and does not remember his trouble any more* (Proverbs 31:7).
> *As my life was slipping away, I remembered the Lord* (Jonah 2:7).
> *We should remember the words that the Lord Jesus said, "Giving gifts is more satisfying than receiving them"* (Acts 20:35).

PRAYER: Help us, O God, to never forget. In Jesus's name, we pray. Amen.

⸺◦⸺

Day 249
Disabilities

Strengthen limp hands. Steady weak knees. . . . The eyes of the blind will be open, and the ears of the deaf will be unplugged. . . . Those who are lame will leap like a deer, and those who cannot speak will shout for joy (Isaiah 35:3–6).

I ONCE READ A STORY ABOUT A young boy who was crippled. His mother was asked his name, and her reply caught the one asking the question off guard. His mother said that they called him, "Teacher of Love." So often, those with disabilities are seen as a burden. The patient can be seen not only as a blessing but as a voice, a spokesperson, a teacher.

What a remarkable declaration! So often, those with little power and influence in worldly terms become God's unlikely voices. And there is reason for this. Their vulnerability embodies the message: the winsome gentleness of God's love.

Even though the mighty God of this universe can and does command, this is often not the Lord's way. God's way is the language of love, which does not force but woos us to openness, repentance, transformation, and obedience.

Too often, we find ourselves disappointed having wasted our time wanting and waiting to see God in the huge miracles, only to be faced with deafening silence that echoes, loud and clear, through the chambers of our hearts.

We need not discount the littleness, the disabled, or the broken, for they have a job to do. They transmit to us the love of God for all humanity. Let's face the challenge before us all, that we spend our time developing a new attentiveness to the way in which God matters, seeking to arrest our attention and to transform us into "teachers of love."

PRAYER: Dear Teacher of Love, we know that in order to become "teachers of love" ourselves that we need to be taught. The best teachers are those who care about their students and provide them not only with the head part but the heart part of teaching as well. We thank you for the provision you have made so that we can study with the best—your Spirit. In Jesus' name, we pray. Amen.

Day 250
The Welcome Guest

I was hungry and you gave me food; was thirsty and you gave me drink; was a stranger and you welcomed me (Matthew 25:35).

WE ARE ENCOURAGED REPEATEDLY TO serve others. As a matter of fact, that is one of the mandates we are admonished to follow if we indeed are true believers. It is, after all, one of the proofs that shows we are part of the vine. But another way we can serve others is to be present with them. This does not mean that we control them but rather provide for them a place of freedom that can be offered by hospitality, which in my opinion is a spiritual gift. One writer says that this type of provision creates a place in which a stranger can become our friend. So this is another way of serving people through the ministry of hospitality.

Now this does not necessarily mean that we do something special for our guest or friend; rather, it means being ourselves and allowing another into the rhythm of ourselves as well as that of our family and community life. It also means that we are willing to share part of what we have experienced on our life's journey. It also means that we are willing to be open to what our guests wishes to share.

Once while waiting for my house to sell in North Carolina so I could work as the head of a new international ministry based in Texas, a professor I knew during seminary offered to let me stay with him and his family. When I tried to compensate him for room he would have nothing of it. I was allowed my freedom to come and go; and if I wanted privacy, I had it. I even fell into their routine of day-to-day living. The entire family was Trekkies, and each evening at 6:00, we would all sit down in the living room and watch *Star Trek*. This family was and is a perfect example of what scripture means about hospitality.

Hospitality is not only a time for sharing; it also provides the guest a place where he or she can be still and at peace. One must not make the mistake thinking that hospitality is simply a time for entertaining or is a time of crowding the guest. It is a time that always shows a rhythm that allows freedom and participation in which the guest can be enriched. Like so many things of our faith, this is no exception. When we provide this ministry, not only are our guests enriched but we too are enriched.

> **PRAYER:** Precious Father in heaven, help us to get our hearts clean and in order for any of our brothers and sisters that might need the spiritual hospitality that we can provide: a place for rest, contemplation, and restoration. In the name of Christ, we pray. Amen.

Day 251
Is Listening a Gift?

Bear one another burdens (Galatians 6:2).

THERE WAS A FELLOW IN ONE OF MY churches who had to have hearing aids to boost his hearing. His wife was one of those brazen women who didn't mind giving you her point of view, whether you asked for it or not. She had one volume, and that was loud. They had been married so long that what she did or said no longer embarrassed him. When she began to go a bit too far, he would put his hand to his ear, and the little beep that followed told everyone that he had turned off his aids (as if we didn't know what he was doing). We playfully picked on him by telling him when it was safe to turn them back on. I thought it was quite humorous and had many laughs picking on them and encouraging the banter between them.

One Sunday morning as I was coming to close of my sermon, I caught some unusual movement out of the corner of my eye: he had nodded off so deeply that he was leaning on the man beside him and actually started snoring. I spoke over the giggles and chuckles and told those sitting around him to let him sleep. He had driven all night to take his wife to the hospital and returned home nonstop. For, you see, their only son, who was worshiped and adored by his mother, had been in a serious accident and was lying in a coma. Their only son, who was a Load Master Sergeant, was in the military, stationed at Fort Dix in New Jersey. His father, who was in his late sixties, not knowing how long his son would be in a coma, had driven all night to be at church, made arrangements to get someone to keep the business open, and packed some things he and his wife needed. He had left his wife with their son. Guess why he could sleep without waking up: Correct! he had turned off his hearing aids. There were more smiles on the people's faces as they left the sanctuary than I had ever seen in the church.

No one that I know of ever said anything negative to him, because everyone involved, by giving him a place to rest, became reflections of God's love, a love that cares even for one's brother's basic need to sleep. Their comforting gesture was a sign of God's peace.

I recall times when others comforted me with a phone call, an e-mail, a visit, and others that simply listened to me. All of the open hearts helped lighten if not remove the weight of a heavy load. It is not easy to be a good listener. Good listening, in a caring relationship means entering into a creative process. We must open our hearts to the full extent of the other's pain. By listening, we help folk unravel the snarled web of feelings. When issues appear complex and words inadequate, powerlessness might be all we can claim. Good listening, then, attends to the silences. We listen for a more profound voice: God's voice of love and compassion. We discover that good listening then attends to the silences and that listening is not only creative but also contemplated. Healing can begin in the mystery of hushed silence.

To bear one another's burdens means offering others a space to come and rest. That acceptance and love might just be what the person needs to discover God's healing and generous grace. Yes, I believe that it is indeed a gift, a precious gift.

> PRAYER: Father, you know our hearts and the gifts that you give to us. You also know our occasional reluctance to take time from our busy schedules to stop and listen forever how long it is needed. Thank you for the opportunity to be used by you in your kingdom. Amen.

Day 252
Lose Something?

But in every situation let God know what you need in prayers and requests while giving thanks. Then God's peace, which goes beyond anything we can imagine, will guard your thoughts and emotions through Christ Jesus (Philippians 4:6–7).

ON THE DAY THAT THE GATE OF Eden swung shut, we humans have been trying to understand the eternal rhythm of life, found in the words of the preacher of the Old Testament: a time to build up, and a time to break down. Because we are in a constant state of dying and emerging, we realize that nothing lasts forever. As Stanley Kunitz put it, "Unless the leaves perish, the tree is not renewed."

We are reminded in daily examples of the permanent impermanence of life around us. And we are left with those times that we wish it were not true, that we could bask in the moment savoring everything we can out of it. But that is not the case. No matter how wonderful it is, no matter how much we wish against reason, the cold unvarnished truth is that we don't. Deaths and losses, the big ones as well as the little ones, come at their own pace and in their own time. They could be celebrated or mourned; they could be wise or foolish; they could take a huge amount of preparation or happen as quickly as the tick of a clock; they could be welcomed as a long lost friend or resisted as a terrorists attacking in the night; one marriage floats on love's wings for sixty graceful years, whereas another does not last a year. Loss is as uncertain as it is unpredictable and is as arbitrary as a tornado striking one house and bypassing the one next to it.

Loss enters all of our lives, and, either for a moment or forever, life is disrupted, and we are frozen in our tracks. It catches us up short and forces us to reckon with it eyeball to eyeball. Whatever course in life we have, no matter how well planned it all is, life is altered by loss.

Our salvation lies not in denying the inevitability of loss but in learning how to fold it into our lives, learning how to mourn and, perhaps more importantly, how to use mourning. When my son died, there were times of lucidity wherein I saw things in perspective, and I could utter words heavenward to our Father's throne. It was a simple one-sentence prayer uttered from the depths of my loss and abandonment. It was: "God, don't let me waste all this suffering."

PRAYER: Father, you yourself know how it is to lose a son. You had to watch his pain and suffering through blood-smeared glasses. You did not waste your suffering. Rather, you used it to provide us with life abundant and the promise of that great homecoming in the sky. Thank you Father. Help us to follow your example when loss enters our lives. Amen.

—◇—

Day 253
Do What?

I am too deeply troubled now to know how to express my feelings (John 12:27).

WHEN COUNT NICHOLAS ZINZENDORF (1700–1760)—a theologian and social reformer, as well as Bishop of the Moravian Church—was a young man, he had an experience in an art gallery that changed his life forever. He was born an aristocrat and had always known wealth and luxury. He was also in the Court at Dresden. It was said of him that he was a child of God. One day, on a trip to Paris, he stopped for a rest in Dusseldorf. During his stay in the city, he visited the art gallery. There he caught sight of Sternberg's painting of the crucified Jesus, entitled *Ecce homo*. The artist had written two short lines in Latin beneath the painting:

Ego pro te haec passus sum
Tu vero quid fecisti pro me?

[This have I suffered for you;
now what will you do for me?]

As the story goes, when Zinzendorf's eyes met the eyes of the thorn-crowned savior, he was filled with a sense of shame. He could not answer the question in a manner that would satisfy his own conscience. He stayed there for hours, looking at the painting of the Christ nailed onto the cross until the light failed. And when the time came for the gallery to close, he was still staring at the face of Christ, trying in vain to find an answer to the question of what he had done for Christ. He left the gallery at nightfall, but a new day was dawning for him. From that day forward he devoted his heart and soul, his life and his wealth—all that he had—to Christ, declaring, "I have but one passion: it is Jesus and Jesus only." The sight of the crucified one, high and lifted up on a tree, made a sudden and permanent change in his life, and the resurrection bore fruit then and there in his heart and soul.

PRAYER: Blessed Father, help us to be able to answer the question asked by Sternberg in his painting. If we cannot render a positive answer to the question, may your Holy Spirit deal with us as it did with Zinzendorf. Amen.

Day 254
Speaking in Love

I might speak in the languages of humans and of angels. But if I don't have love, I am a loud gong or a crashing cymbal (1 Corinthians 13:1).

EVERY MINISTER COVETS THE ability to speak articulately and compellingly. In so doing, he or she helps the individual worshiper to have a life-changing encounter with God. One definition of preaching is "to afflict the comfortable and comfort the afflicted." As a matter of fact, a portion of our training provides us with a basis in homiletics, the art of preaching. At the same time, we each function within the limits of our own native abilities.

One of my favorite artists is the Impressionist, Vincent van Gogh. Vincent came out from what he called his "molting time," a time in which his former fanaticism had disappeared and was replaced by a burning wrath against the organized Church; but, in rejecting the Church's establishment, Vincent only drew closer to the heart of Christianity. He came down on the side of love and love's being his way of knowing God:

> The best way to know God is to love many things. Love a friend, a wife— something, whatever you like—and you will be on the way to knowing more about Him: that is what I say to myself. But one must love with a lofty and serious intimate sympathy, with strength, and with intelligence.

A lot of preachers shudder at being compared with former homiletic masters or even with numerous contemporaries, but the responsibility to speak *with love* comes to us all. Whether in the study, behind the lectern, or in the pulpit, being guided by the love of God is instrumental for all who speak in the name of Christ.

What is more, the same principle holds for our conversations between spouses, parents, and children, as well as brothers and sisters in Christ. Our homes and churches ought to be overflowing with loving words. Unless we learn to speak the truth in love, our discourse turns into little more than gossip with idle words.

The greatest orators and the plainest of speakers stand or fall to the degree that they are consumed by love when they speak. Love is something so positive, so strong, so real, that it is impossible for one who loves to take back that feeling, as it is to take his own life. Without love, we only make noise.

PRAYER: Dear Father, help us to build up one another, both friend and foe, in love. Help the motivational force behind all our actions, both in word as well as in deed to be love. Our Father, thank you for your love. You have not only made it known to us through your spoken word but you have shown us that love in your Son, Jesus Christ, our Lord. Amen.

Day 255
Seeking, Finding, Living

Don't ever worry. . . . So don't ever worry about tomorrow. After all, tomorrow will worry about itself. Each day has enough troubles of its own (Matthew 6:31, 34).

THE BIBLE KNOWS THE HUMAN heart well, doesn't it? Burdens. Cares. Anxieties. Everyone has them. Some people try to quell their anxieties by overeating, whereas others compensate by drinking or taking drugs. There are those folk who deal with their anxieties by shopping and buy, buy, buy. Fears and anxieties make our lives miserable, don't they? Psychologists say that most of us will do anything to get rid of anxieties. It's not the future that demands full attention of our anxieties. For the most part we only know how miserable we are, and we want instant relief!

Someone has said that when fear is your faith, the worst will happen. It took me a long time as a minister to admit that I have anxieties about many things. Ministers are thought to be people of good faith, not bad faith. We are paragons of virtue. Paragons of virtue nothing; we are often paragons of weakness! We worry about whether we are reaching the people, we worry about how we are being heard, we worry about moving, we worry about people working together, and we even worry about meeting budgets.

I read a poster once on which was printed, "Not everything that is faced can be changed, but nothing can change until it is faced." One's whole existence can be choked and distorted by terrible anxieties. That Is what they do to us, isn't it. They sit on us and prevent us from doing our best. Not only do they bind us and prevent us from doing our best, they also distort our thinking, confuse our communication, and bedevil our relationships.

Jesus said, "Stop being anxious. Look at what it's doing to you. Don't you know that God takes care of those who trust him? Seek first the kingdom of God and his righteousness." Put this ahead of every concern you have, and you'll come out all right in these other matters. This is the real answer to our anxieties, isn't it? *Seek first the kingdom of God.* Transfer the center of your concern from yourself to the kingdom of God, to the vision of wholeness God has for the creation: the sick becoming well, the sinner being forgiven, the runaway child restored to its parents, the hungry being fed, the homeless being sheltered, the poor having enough, all relationships being healed, all nations coming together under Christ, in short, the vision of wholeness for all creation. When we submit our anxieties to that, they don't have much of a chance. When we give them over to God they melt into nothingness.

It will help when we take the advice of the psalmist and cast our burdens on the Lord, who will sustain us. Or as an old black preacher once put it when dealing with this text, "He will get under the load with you."

PRAYER: Our Father, rid us of all unhealthy anxieties and help us to only trust in you. Amen.

———◄◇►———

Day 256
Overcoming Life

We have this confidence as a sure and strong anchor for our lives (Hebrews 6:19).

PEPPERED THROUGHOUT THE BOOK OF Psalms, one can find words of encouragement, such as, "God's promises are new every morning," "The Lord God lightens my darkness," and "God is our companion." Aren't they great? For folk with PD, they certainly blow away clouds that have been covering the sun. With each morning, new hope can be found. That is a promise that we need to remember, because life is more difficult. We have to learn a whole new way to live. The life we have always known will never be again.

We have to be careful and not allow ourselves to step into the "victim mentality," to live life on a sub-level existence. I realize that there are days wen I have been so occupied with my self that I have closed out all the windows of light. I believe one of the greatest tragedies of our modern time is that some of us can live a trivial life and get away with it. A choice is forced upon us, and the choice is neither easy nor obvious. At times, the best I can do is muddle in the trivial. But I want more from life than that. There are only two ways to approach life: as a victim or as a gallant fighter, and one must decide if one wants to act or react. A lot of people forget they have a choice. My choice is to make my days count, rather than to merely count my days. I am able to live on this high level of renewed zeal because of God's steadfast promise that we have God's presence in the midst of going through our trials here on earth.

Believe me, I am aware of how difficult it is to be bright and cheery, patient and tolerant, and happy and understanding while the body seems to be plotting against me. One way I deal with those cloudy days is with humor. Humor has the unshakeable ability to break life up into little pieces and make it livable. Laughter adds richness, texture, and color to otherwise ordinary days. I believe laughter is a sacred sound to God. It is there, reminding us that even if we can't change the circumstances, we can change the way we respond to them.

Perhaps God gives us difficulties in order to give us the opportunity to know who we are and who we really can be. Or as Nietzsche writes, "You must carry the chaos within in order to give birth to the dancing star."

PRAYER: For all who are making their days count, O God, we pray for your presence through Christ our Lord. Amen.

Day 257
Smaller, Smaller Still

Then the Lord gave me the two stone tablets inscribed by God himself. On them were written all the words the Lord spoke to you (Deuteronomy 9:10).

COULD YOU IMAGINE IN YOUR arms two stone tablets that God had written? No wonder Charleston Heston's appearance had changed. That was Hollywood's attempt to show the viewers that when you are with God there is always change; at least that is my interpretation. We can be changed; the situation around us can change.

I like to sit sometimes and ponder on things a lot of folk don't even deem important enough for any of their attention. Here is one of mine. Have you ever wondered just how large God's writing on the tablets was? Was it large enough for the people to read it from a distance? Or was it small enough you had to be right up at it to read it accurately? Who could even read them? Most of the Hebrew people couldn't even read; that was left to the clan of Levi and, later, the scribes. These words, written in whatever size, became the Law the Hebrew people were to live by daily. They were given to instruct the people how to live.

What about your writing? Does it instruct and explain what you are to do and how you are to live? God promised these people that they were to obey his voice. If the Hebrew people were dependent on the handwriting of folk with Parkinson's, they might still be wandering in the wilderness.

The problem with the person who has Parkinson's arises in the fact that many can develop micrographia. This is when the PD patient's handwriting gets smaller and smaller to where it is anywhere from difficult to impossible to read their writing. Others have handwriting that looks like a drunken chicken has walked across the page after having stepped in some ink—totally unreadable. A graphologist might need to be called in to give his opinion, but unfortunately that is a far as it can go unless he or she can read very small letters. But the words, "Thy words have I hidden in my heart that I may not sin against God," can never be lost or taken away from us, no matter how large or small.

> **PRAYER:** Gracious Father, we thank you that you have the eyes to see what comes from our hearts and our pens, no matter the size; but only let it be representative of our large love we give so freely. Amen.

Day 258
Blind Spots

I run straight toward the goal to win the prize that God's heavenly call offers in Christ Jesus (Philippians 3:14).

WE ALL HAVE OUR BLIND SPOTS. For most, this has to do with our cultural biases. And for many this also has to do with the idiosyncrasies of our personality. Possibly one of the places where we are most blinded has to do with our abilities. Whereas for some, their situation senses that they lack skills, gifts, and know-how, others are very confident about what they can do and contribute.

What is fascinating is that we often learn things about ourselves when we are placed in unusual and even unpredictable circumstances. We also learn things about ourselves when we are with others who challenge us in some way. Thus, there are many ways in which light can shine upon us.

Perhaps we are challenged the most when we are with people who are very different. It is in those moments that we learn from them just what we lack. We then need God's presence to help us resolve the blind spots such that they are blind spots no more.

When such a statement is made not from false humility, it can be something radically opposite. In the face of the one who is so different from me, I can see things about myself that normally would escape my notice.

There are many things we can learn from others, especially the poor. One lesson is that we are far too dependent on what we have. Another is that we look down on the poor and thereby exalt ourselves. A further lesson might be that, even though we thought the poor person would be bitter, we instead discover that he or she is full of hope. It would be a blessing for us to learn the valuable lessons the poor can teach us, maybe to turn from our bitterness to hope.

PRAYER: Father, clear from our being the many blind spots the world creates for us. Enable us to clear the blind spots away so we can be found assisting you in your kingdom's work. Help us to see as you would have us see and help those in need. Amen.

Day 259
I Can See Clearly Now

God will wipe every tear from their eyes (Revelation 21:4).

WE PRIDE OURSELVES ON BEING able to hold our emotions in check, whereby nothing disturbs us. Everyone around might be sobbing, but not us, for we are too cool to show our emotions like that. Even when Ol' Yeller died, we don't shed a tear. Now that's being extremely cold-hearted.

With Parkinson's, one is not sure when one's emotions will show themselves. A person with PD could be sitting in a chair watching television, and a commercial comes on; by the end of it one has tears running down one's cheeks. Or it might be that a scene from some movie one watches or a song one hears, and the next thing you know is that you become a basket case and can't stop the emotion. So you can cry me a river. Because it is as though for folk with PD the emotions have minds all of their own. The show of emotions always comes at crazy times. It might occur at times when everyone else is in tears, or you find yourself a lone cryer. PD has its hold on the expression of our emotions as well.

My mother, when asked why she had no show of emotions at my eldest son's funeral, gave the response, "You can't see it because my emotions are all covered up with stuff. Crying? Yes I am. I am weeping on the inside." I know what she means, now. People around me can be sobbing and wondering if I have ice water running through my veins, because my face is not stained with tears. And on another occasion everybody around me can be dry-eyed, and I am wiping tears away.

It will be glorious when our eyes are no longer filled with tears. The old adage, "If you don't use it, you lose it," could be applied here. John tells us there will be no need for tears. Why? Because there will not be anything to cry about; he writes that there will be no crying, no sickness, and no death. What a day that will be.

PRAYER: Dear comforting God, you hold us in the most loving arms the world has ever known, and you comfort us and wipe away our tears. Thank you. Amen.

⋯⋯⋯⋯⋯◄ ◇ ►⋯⋯⋯⋯⋯

Day 260
That's All That Counts

Jesus said this to show by what kind of death Peter would bring glory to God (John 21:19).

SEVERAL YEARS AGO, THERE WAS A woman who served with me on the board of Head Start. Her profession was as aide in the dementia unit of a local hospital. She shared some stories of how difficult yet rewarding it was to help those in such need. She had the job for six years and recently learned that her mother had Alzheimer's disease. Her work with dementia patients reminded her daily of what her mother was going to experience. She was overwhelmed with grief. She believed that she could no longer work. So she decided to find other work in a different hospital.

On the day she intended to submit her resignation, she went into the room of one of her patients to help her dress. The woman, glad to see her, said to the aide, "Honey, what's my name?" The aide gently told her and felt her heart break for the patient, as well as for her own mother. She couldn't wait to be away from this daily painful reminder. Then the woman went on with her conversation. She pointed to the crucifix on the wall of her room and said distinctly and with seeming incomprehension—and with a laugh—"Honey, most of the time I do not even know who I am, but he does, and that's all that counts."

The aide said that in that moment her fears for her mother and for herself began to fade. In their place, she was flooded with peace and a sense of being protected by someone who dearly, dearly loves her. She said she knew that whatever happened, everything was going to be all right. What joy! What joy!

All that said, where are we? Even in this—of who I am and what I can do— I will trust him. Even when I can no longer trust, I will know that in the elsewhere, he is there. But allow me, Father, one more request. In my dimmest moments, please let me witness your loving care. Let me point to your cross and say to all who need to hear, "I don't know who I am, but he does, and that's all that counts!" And let me say it lightly, with a chuckle!

PRAYER: God, grant us the courage and the "how to" to bring glory to you and your kingdom. Teach us the little things that can be a blessing, for I am afraid we are a bit too lazy a people to recognize the large things that bring glory to you. We go in your strength and your guidance. Without you to bless us, we would be lost. Thank you for allowing us to be a blessing. Amen.

Day 261
Woe, Woe Is Me!

I, the Lord, have called you to do what is right (Isaiah 42:6).

DO YOU KNOW WHAT A "Sunday word" is? It is one of those words spoken in such a way that it evokes reverence, awe, power, and you know that we are in the presence of something really big. Yet its life span is restricted to church on Sunday. It never quite makes it into our daily conversations.

The word "righteousness" is such a word. When was the last time you heard it used in a daily conversation? It doesn't roll off the tongue at a staff meeting, at a ball game or in the break room by the water cooler.

When I think of righteousness, the picture that comes to mind is of a person whose very clothing smells of other worldliness; a person who is floating down a river while the rest of us are fighting our way in the opposite direction. The righteous don't worry about the same stuff we do, such as when will the lawn be mowed or if one will make it to the bank before it closes. The trivial isn't part of their make-up, for they're righteous, holy. Compared to them, I miss the mark.

But let the warning bell be rung. Righteousness is not about piety, that monk-like holiness that is far beyond the way we live. It is about being in right relationship with God, about trusting God to move and do in God's time; in short, righteousness is about relationship.

The early Israelites waited on the Lord on more than one occasion to be their arm and their strength in their times of trouble.

And there was Mary Magdalene who learned in the ancient garden while the morning mists faded that her friend—her rabbi, her leader—had conquered death as was witnessed by the empty tomb.

The apostle, Paul, was so confident that God would ultimately be victorious that even in the belly of a Roman prison facing the real chance of his horrible death, he penned the words to the church at Ephesus, "Christ might dwell in your hearts through faith, as you are being rooted and grounded in love. I pray that you may have power to comprehend, with all the saints, what is the breadth and length and height and depth, and to know the love of Christ that surpasses knowledge so that you may be filled with all the fullness of God" (Eph 3:17–19), the brightness of heaven glimpsed from the darkness of hell.

PRAYER: God of mercy, may we have a new and deeper meaning to more Sunday words, enabling us to better understand what you would have us do and be. In his name, we pray. Amen.

Day 262
Dreaming New Dreams

A faithful man will abound with blessings (Proverbs 28:20).

AT TIMES, I FIND MYSELF IN A not too comfortable situation with some of my friends, who hold a much stricter application of the scriptures. But we tolerate one another and continue our friendship, even if the road might be a bit rocky at times. When they get so dogmatic and judgmental that you would think they were God's right-hand cherubim, however, that's when the conversation heats up. They put on their cloak of infallibility and sit as both judge and jury on everyone. The last time our discussion got heated up, a couple of them had an epiphany, one of those bring-you-back-down-to-earth moments.

The discussion concerned the three old fathers, Abraham, Isaac, and Jacob, who were said to have lived with a "full and complete blessing." Yet we also were reminded that their lives had a great many negative occurrences as well. There were quarrels with neighbors, fertility problems, quarrels between husband and wife, as well as between parent and child. So what is this full and complete blessing? We can only understand this phrase to mean the experience of life in its fullness, to accept everything life has to offer, both the bitter and the sweet, the joys and the sadness, the smooth road and the road filled with potholes, a life that strikes both the white and black keys on the piano such that every emotional tone can be sounded.

If you have been brave enough to love, sometimes winning and sometimes losing; if you have cared enough to try, and sometimes it worked and sometimes it didn't; if you have been bold enough to dream and found yourself with some dreams that came true and a lot of broken pieces of dreams that fell to earth and shattered, then you look back from the mountain top you now find yourself standing in the midst of your shattered dreams, shards of those broken dreams lying at your feet. You had great dreams. You were going to make a difference in the world. At least, I thought that I would, until the doctor said those life-altering words, "You have Parkinson's disease." So much of what I hoped for was simply to make a difference in the world, instead of the world making a difference in me. But this was not the case: new dreams needed to be dreamed while realizing how I was like Moses alongside the broken fragments of an earlier dream. You can realize how life has opened and how richly you are blessed.

> **PRAYER:** Father of heaven and earth, we come before you, amid our shattered dreams, hoping against hope that you haven't given up on us and we are not failures simply because some of our dreams might have failed. We pray that you would give to us new visions, new dreams, new energy, and a new determination get it all done for the fulfillment of your kingdom. In the name of Jesus, we pray. Amen.

<hr />

Day 263
With the Close of the Day

Everything has its own time, and there is a specific time for every activity under heaven (Ecclesiastes 3:1).

E ARE A TORN PEOPLE: torn between how we use our time, live our lives, and how we don't. There is a good number of people who live idle lives. For one or more reasons, their lives are marked by boredom and emptiness. This is affirmed mostly in the lives of the elderly and those in our communities who are vulnerable, such as the sick, infirmed, or handicapped in whatever fashion.

Yet for the larger majority of folk, life is full, often too full. This is mostly affirmed in the ridiculous hours some professionals work. I witnessed his particularly when I lived in Greenwich, Connecticut. Some of my friends would catch a 5:00 or 6:00 A.M. train that headed into the city and would drag back in around 8:00 P.M. or later. Those with such a hectic schedule could be readily recognized. They were the fathers who, with cell phone, the *Wall Street Journal* or *New York Times* in hand would relieve the mothers from their weekly duties on Saturday by taking care of the children for at least the morning. For a lot of these professionals, that was the only "quality time" that they had with their children.

For these families, there is the busy round of work, children's schooling, sports, dance, and church activities, further professional development, and recreation. With such a flurry of activities, there is often little time for reflection and prayer. With the passage of time, everything just piles up and we begin to feel overwhelmed. In circumstances such as these, we recognize that we are faced with the challenge to develop a different rhythm of life, a rhythm that allows us to become more meditative and reflective. If you think that that it is easy for a busy professional to develop a new way to live, then you are sadly mistaken.

So, that's the problem. What is the solution? Every day we need to account for our day's activities. The beginning of this practice might be seen in the spirituality of many of the religious orders, but it is a practice that we can all embrace. At the close of the day, we give an account—or, better yet, we can review God's presence—of what has been life-giving and what has been death-dealing. What has been good and what has been bad? What has blessed or brought grief to the heart of God and to the lives of others?

This is neither a time to see how our grades are, nor is it a time to delve into our psyche. It is not a time that we provide for ourselves with an opportunity to bring out the whips and flog ourselves of all wrongdoing. Rather, this review is a simple act of humility and prayer before going to sleep.

PRAYER: Lord, I lay open before you my life and the events of the day. This I pray in the name of Jesus, the Christ. Amen.

Day 264
Unfounded Fear

Terror and amazement had seized them, and they said nothing to anyone.
They went out and fled from the tomb, for they were afraid (Mark 16:8).

AVE YOU EVER BEEN A PART OF A gathering that watched nothing but horror movies? You become so scared that you pull your knees up on the chair and clutch your pillow as if it were a safety shield against anything that goes bump in the night. The palms of your hands become sweaty, your heart starts beating faster, and you wonder if it is going to beat out of your chest. You are so scared that you and everyone else in the room jerk and jump at the phone ringing or when the pizza guy rings the doorbell.

Folks with PD can be overwhelmed with fear, not from watching horror shows but from watching the quality of our life lessening as it becomes more and more limited. With each passing day, something else quits, or it takes us longer to do an everyday task. It takes a greater effort for us to keep our eyes fixed on the one who never leaves us or forsakes us. That is not to say that people with other diseases don't experience similar feelings or that people with PD have the market on fear and uncertainty. We all have our moments, even healthy people. There are times we all are afraid because of different circumstances that might cause us to lose our way, and we do lose our way, for all of us have lost our way at one time or another.

How often we lose our way in life. What's the reason? Have we given in to the little demons that haunt us throughout the day and night? Do we find ourselves busy worrying about the things we cannot change or building bridges we may never have to cross?

We are also fearful simply because we forget that we are children of God. When we come into the family of God and grow familiar with our position and all of its possibilities, then we can start in on the tasks at hand without fear. Yet there are times we find ourselves preoccupied, trying to please others and we lose our sense of self. It is at this time that we find ourselves working hard to avoid rejection, abandonment, or loneliness, and we might cling to people and places more from fear than from freedom. Making compromises, we might please people, but we lose touch with our original blessings, the deep and everlasting love of God.

Jesus announces to us, "Do not be afraid; I have come that you may have life and have It more abundantly." And the abundance the world has to offer does not even compare to the abundance of Christ.

> **PRAYER:** Our heavenly Father, awaken us from the darkness where fear holds us powerless and in bondage and lead us into the light of your love that frees us and gives us hope. Remind us it is only your voice we should be eager to hear. Cause us to be able to hear that we should not fear, for fear is not of you. In the name of Jesus, who takes away all our fear. Amen.

⸺◈⸺

Day 265
In Love?

Jesus looked at him and loved him (Mark 10:21).

BEING A PASTOR OF A church brings on a myriad of problems, dilemmas, and situations with which he or she must handle or refer to one better equipped to deal with whatever the "problem" might be, especially if it entails an extended period of time and expertise.

One example that sticks out in my mind is one that I did not experience first-hand but was shared with me by an old friend. A young lady and her boyfriend came to see my friend because they had a problem in their relationship. They had both taken first-year psychology, and as a result they couldn't decide whether they were in love. Not to worry. My friend had taken second-year psychology.

He asked them what they did when they were together, and they replied that they spent their time trying to decide if they were in love. He told them to stop worrying about whether or not they were in love. He told them to get on with what interested them, their work and play, their music, books, films, friends, and faith. Their question, he assured them, would answer itself. And it did. We don't discover whether or not we are in love by analyzing the nature of affection but by getting to know each other. And faith is like that. It is at its best, not when we are scrutinizing its nature, but when we have found the right place to put it. As Yeats said, "All God asks is our attention."

> **PRAYER:** Father, you are so good to us. Help us to give you our attention so you can lead us along the path you would have us go, knowing all along that we are being led by the most loving hands the world has ever known. Amen.

Day 266
Does Anybody *Really* Know What Time It Is?

Everything has its own time, and there is a specific time for every activity under heaven (Ecclesiastes 3:1).

Therefore, don't judge anything before the appointed time. Wait until the Lord comes. He will also bring to light what is hidden in the dark and reveal people's motives. Then each person will receive praise from God (1 Corinthians 4:5).

WE ARE ABOUT TO CHANGE TO another year in a very young century. The beautiful cadences from Ecclesiastes give us an occasion to ponder more, more specifically the "right time." We have just lived through what should have been one of the happiest times of the year, Christmastide. And we are entering what is, for many, one of the most melancholy times of the year: New Year's.

At Christmas, all things brighten, glow with hope and cheer. Ebeneezer

Scrooge, who had spent his whole life in miserliness, is transformed at Yuletide. Aren't we all?

How different is this time around New Year's? Many find New Year's depressing, a sort of nonevent, dreamed up by restaurants, producers of Champagne, and makers of party favors. Another year has ended; another has begun. We are one year older and one year closer to our ends. Happy New Year.

New Year's Eve parties reveal the sadness of the season. Why do so many celebrate New Year's with inebriation, unless to mask New Year's event depression? Flip a page on the calendar. Whoopie! It's 2015!

The words found in Ecclesiastes are appropriately depressing, but we should read it as instructive poetry. Think of those beautiful words sung in the sixties by the Kinks, "For everything turn, turn, turn." Beautiful words that suddenly reveal themselves as being terribly dark (vv. 4–8).

See? Everything has its time, as the swift seasons roll along. But such is not the conclusion of Ecclesiastes. If the scripture stopped here, all might be well. Time passes, the seasons all roll along, a time for this, then a time for that. Nice. After considering the passage of time, Ecclesiastes asks, "Where does it all lead? What good comes of it" (vv. 9–10)?

Look back on the past year. Car payments were made. The bedroom was painted. The downstairs carpets were shampooed. But what gain had you for your toil? Here is a time to live, yes, time to write checks, a time for Democrats, a time for Republicans, and a time to die. With that, time, like a January wind, blows through this ancient poem steadily moving somewhere to its gracious fulfillment.

We are in this circular, ceaseless, ticking of time, as in the theme song "The Circle of Life" written for Disney's *The Lion King*. We are the rat in the cage, breathlessly running, turning the tread wheel to nowhere. But we don't have to be that way. Our lives mean more than a rat's life; all it takes is to walk in the forgiveness, mercy, love, and hope of God.

PRAYER: Father, only you can make our lives mean something. Thank you for sending Jesus to our world to make it all possible. Amen.

Day 267
Living with Interruptions

Then your light shall break forth like the dawn, and your healing shall spring up quickly; your vindicator shall go before you, the glory of the Lord shall be your rear guard (Isaiah 58:8).

THERE WAS ONCE A lecture series being given at Princeton Theological Seminary in Princeton, New Jersey that I attended. Following one of the lectures, a small group of those attending met at a local restaurant for dessert. We started to discuss the lecture, when in walked the lecturer. We asked him to join us. He did. The conversation was great! Many questions and issues came from around the table, and many of them have long since gone the way of the dodo bird, except for one. When quizzed about his preparation, writing, and lecture schedule, he said with a certain melancholy in his voice, "You know, my whole life I have been complaining that my work was constantly interrupted, until I discovered that my interruptions were my work." That hit me like a ton of bricks!

Don't we often look at the many events of our lives as interruptions? But what if our interruptions are, in fact, challenges to an inner response by which growth takes place? What if the events of our history are molding us as a sculptor molds his clay and if it is only in a careful obedience to these molding hands that we can discover our real vocation and become a blessing to God by becoming more like Jesus Christ?

We must be careful not to disregard all events of our lives as just another interruption but as challenges from God. God changes negative interruptions into positive opportunities. So get ready for the transformation that follows.

PRAYER: Father, here we are as lumps of clay in your creative hands for you to fashion and make into the vessels that would best serve you and your kingdom. Amen.

Day 268
Frail Children of. . . ?

When I came to you, I was weak. I was afraid and nervous (1 Corinthians 2:3).

WHEN I BEGAN MY MINISTRY several decades ago, I was zealous, ready, and poised to take on all the demons of hell, including Satan himself. I could not understand why everyone did not feel as I did.

Things have certainly changed. I am gentler in my listening and my talking. I look back on those early years, and I hear my spirit chuckle. Now I can see the yawning gulf between my ideals and the actual way in which I have lived. I have learned that if I share my weaknesses, hopefully people will be encouraged rather than impressed. When I am honest with myself, I have learned that we are all frail, vulnerable, and wounded people. And we all know that some folk are much better at concealing their vulnerability than others. It's not a matter of the healthy caring for the unhealthy. We must in turn care and be cared for because this is the way life is.

The hardest thing for professional folk to do is admit that we are in need. And when at last we have given in and allowed someone to care for us, perhaps there is a certain inertia that makes us want to cling to the role of patient, and remain reluctant to take up the task of serving once more. It is easy to forget that so much caring, so much serving has been done for us because we want our cares to be strong and invulnerable, and we project onto them qualities that in fact they do not have. But again, perhaps that is the way things are because that is way people are, and we need to learn to lower our guard with those who are able to accept our weaknesses and cherish us.

PRAYER: Father, enlarge our hearts so we might be on as grand a scale as our compassion should be. Amen.

———◦———

Day 269
Love Is the Key

A time to love and a time to hate. . . (Ecclesiastes 3:8).

IT IS CLEAR THAT SATAN IS sly, cunning, and smart. He knows that it is best not to confront goodness head on with signs reading, "There is no God." Rather, he prefers the backdoor method, sneaking in under the guise of things such as baby chicks or rabbits at Easter or cuddly teddy bears and wide-eyed children at Christmas. Since the major theme, the center of Christianity, is love, subverting Christianity is easy. Make "love" a household word for everything: I love this food, or I love my car, for instance.

We crave possessions in order to make us worth keeping, clutch onto someone for fear of being abandoned, collide with others to prove that we are someone, or keep folks at a distance for fear of being rejected. Since one can love only as one has been loved, we are humanly doomed to a skewed love.

There is always someone before whom my humility is challenged, my patience taxed, or my weaknesses stressed into visibility. There are others waiting in line when one finishes. We seek an unconditional love. What we do need is to be amazed by behavior that makes us feel as though we are the lost coin found or the stray sheep sought. No matter what any one of us wants to do, all we ever really want is to be loved.

Christian love is a life-long process. The unforgivable sin is to take things for granted until life becomes a weary repetition. "If you have seen one sunrise (or one sunset) you have seen them all."

Folk die with memories of simple, unpurchaseable moments, which, when recalled, bring forth gentle smiles. One such memory is that each person is God's love song, born of a divine imagination in love with the diversity that surrounds us. Yet such love is inevitably linked with sadness. To love is to get hurt, guaranteed. Why does it have to be this way? Why are love and suffering bonded remains, shrouded in Golgotha's darkness?

PRAYER: Thank you, blessed Lord, for the moment of sheer mercy and love that causes the bells of joy in our hearts to ring out each time we remember. Amen.

Day 270

On Pointing Your Finger

So I told them to take off any gold they were wearing. They gave it to me. I threw it in the fire and out came this calf (Exodus 32:24)!

M Y GOODNESS! AARON WASTED NO time pointing a finger and telling Moses it was the fault of the people for the golden calf. All he did was throw the gold in the fire and out popped the calf. Aaron had a short memory because earlier it was said that he used a tool to make the calf (Exod 32:1–5). Aaron just was not a very strong leader. He could have stopped the partygoers with just his word, but he didn't. He was just as guilty as all the rest in worshiping the calf. We are all quick on the draw when it comes to blaming other people or circumstances, and folk with Parkinson's aren't immune, either. As a matter of fact, we can be some of the biggest blamers. We blame toxins, stress, the environment, or bad genes; and no good session of blaming is complete without including God as being complicit.

You can see the stark difference when you compare Aaron's failure to accept responsibility for his part in "calf-gate" to President Harry Truman's understanding and acceptance of the reminder on his desk, THE BUCK STOPS HERE. He knew that in the end he would be the one who either would be praised or blamed for what was done or not done.

Doesn't it make you wonder sometimes if we truly believe in the forgiveness of sin? If we do believe in the forgiveness of sin, why worry or try to blame others? Could it be that all the worry we expend to make excuses comes from our not believing in it? We have the notion that before God will receive us back "unto himself" we must do something. And that something is whatever we can gather together to make some sort of case that is favorable for us. But that would not constitute forgiveness, would it? For it to be real and true forgiveness, we have to recognize the sin we have committed, what is left over after the excuses, and any allowances we have given to it. Then we must have the courage to see it for what it truly is, see it in all its malice, horror, dirt, and meanness and yet be wholly reconciled to the person who has done it, whether it is another human being or ourselves. That is true forgiveness, which is ever before us from God, if we ask for it.

> PRAYER: Father help us to have the amount of coinage we need
> to accept the blame that is rightly ours and then help us to do what
> is needed to make things right. Amen.

—◇—

Day 271
Help for the Heroic

*God is our refuge and strength, an ever present help in times of trouble. That
is why we are not afraid* (Psalm 46:1–2).

HISTORY IS PEPPERED WITH COMMON people who dared to move against the negative grain of what was normal for their time. They heard the negative words ringing in their ears on more than one occasion, we have never done that before, and confronted the people who said, "You can't."

I marvel at their courage and their uncompromising commitment to the truth. These folk seemed to only strengthen their resolve to be faithful to God and the heavenly kingdom. It helped give heroes the power to continue to be the heralds of light and hope in the world's darkness. They were not deterred when confronting the negative that remained. These heroes of yesterday and today inspire, challenge, and encourage all believers to be a part of their heroic stand for our faith: Christians, such as Mother Teresa, Kagawa, Martin Luther King Jr., Pope John Paul II, each one knowing where to find help, strength, and refuge. Could I, with Mary Magdalene, have boldly followed the condemned Jesus to the foot of the cross, knowing her life could be in danger too? Could we have refused to recant with Martin Luther, standing on trial before the most powerful ruler and pope of the day? I would like to think I would, but these giants of our faith more often than not found themselves standing

360

alone.

Luther, a strong leader of the Reformation, later proclaimed the source of his strength in an imperishable hymn, "A Mighty Fortress Is Our God" (one of my favorites). He wrote it in 1529, during one of the darkest hours in the history of the Protestant movement.

Surrounded on every side by powerful enemies—he was called the devil incarnate—Luther's so called friends and supporters disappeared from the scene, which did not help his situation at all. It added to the deep depression that the trial and all the activity brought with it. His teaching and writings were brought into question, and he had to deal with the demon called depression. He felt abandoned. His one helper was God. So, as was usual in his recurring bouts of depression, the dedicated reformer went to the scriptures, his "one ground of certainty."

Luther took the title and spirit from Psalm 46, and wrote this hymn as a call to battle and an appeal to God, his "very present help." In it, he reaffirmed that spiritual strength will only be ours by personal contact with God through Jesus Christ and through the gifts of the Spirit.

So strongly does Luther's faith sing through his majestic hymn, that its message has given comfort and courage in times crisis for 450 years.

> PRAYER: Father God, we are grateful that courageous Christians have both told us and demonstrated that you are the true source of sustaining strength. Amen.

Day 272
Grace Is Indeed Amazing

Wearing a linen ephod, David danced in the Lord's presence with all his might. He and the entire nation of Israel brought the ark of the Lord with shouts of joy and sounding of rams' horns (2 Samuel 6:14–15).

ANY OF US ARE ENGAGED IN A quest, and that quest begins with who we are: our identity. Jesus' answer to our search in this all-consuming, results-driven world of ours is grace: divine enduring value because of grace and divine kindness. We are defined by the unmerited love of Almighty God. It is there that we are given enduring value, all because of grace.

When we get right down to it, grace is a dance, an inspired dance between us human beings and the divine. We are reminded that we aren't worthy of this dance not because we have some special abilities, gifts, or talents, but despite them; not loved because of *who* we are, but rather we are loved because of *whose* we are. The love is not hoarded and saved for a select group. It is given fully and freely, bringing life to a barren soul like raindrops falling after a long drought.

Even when we miss the mark, God's love remains. We are reminded that it is not from our own merit but by the hand of a loving and passionate God that we continue along life's journey. It is akin to this statement: "God loves you as if there is no other person in the world to love, and God loves all of us the same." When we absorb this thought and when we accept divine grace, then the walls we have constructed to separate us from one another come tumbling down. When we accept our own acceptability and the acceptability of others, then we become sisters and brothers, children God who deserve to love and be. And the paradox of all of this is that it is God who deserves to love and be loved, not you and I. With all of this grace, God calls us to be his children, and God has woven us into the sacred tapestry.

Grace is what we are called to absorb with our hearts and reflect in our lives.

PRAYER: Grace, grace, God's grace that is greater than all my sin: for this amazing grace I give you thanks. Amen.

Day 273
Flawless?

. . . like that of a lamb without blemish or spot (1 Peter 1:19).

THE ETYMOLOGY OF WORDS IS always interesting. I find it fascinating how words come together and are assimilated into our vocabulary today. You can imagine my surprise when I saw that the etymological folklore for the word *sincere* indicates that it comes from two Latin words that mean "without wax," and the first known record of its usage appears in 1533 and supposedly refers to a very popular trick used by sculptors, who would hide their mistakes by filling them in and covering them over with wax.

It was what it appeared to be, with nothing hidden, with no obvious imperfections, because they were all covered up with wax. The *sin cera* work was the genuine article. It was what it appeared to be, with nothing hidden, with no imperfections covered up. Now that, undoubtedly, is a good idea, except that sometimes it can be carried too far. I remember when some of our sister denominations that, because of their faith refused to allow the use make-up of any kind or any sort of fancy hairdo. Someone remarked that they thought they were insincere if they weren't looking their worst.

> PRAYER: Father, your Son went the cross for our sins even though he was flawless and without blame. Forgive us for our shortsightedness. Amen.

Day 274
Daily

Then God said, "Let there be lights in the sky. . . ." the larger light to rule the day (Genesis 1:14–15).

ARE YOU A MORNING PERSON, ready to go wide-open when your feet hit the floor? Or are you one of those people that can stay in bed half the day, so that when you have to get up, you are like the dwarf in Walt Disney's movie, *Snow White and the Seven Dwarfs*, whose name (Grumpy) aptly described this ill-natured little man's personality? Even after you get up, does it take a while to get going with any energy at all like an old Victrola that has to be cranked, until it gets fast enough to put the needle on the disc to hear the scratchy, recorded music on it?

Someone once complained that the trouble with life is that it is so daily. We know what they meant. We get out of bed every morning, shave or put on our face, hop in our car or catch train, subway, or taxi, put in our hours, and come home in the evening, weary and empty, and complete the reports brought home from the office. Finished, we check in on the children, brush our teeth, and kiss our spouses or partners good night. Then we catch our breath before doing the same thing the next day, and the next, and the next.

But before we allow that thought to depress us, we should remember the things that we love to do every morning. We see the morning light and the faces of loved ones. There are the comics, hot coffee, orange juice, fresh fruit, and English muffins. There are bagels or pastries. Maybe we could meet with a colleague and discuss the events of the day before going to the office. I'm glad life is so daily. If it weren't, we might have difficulty remembering one time to the next.

Although, do you think the reason God made everything so daily is that the Lord hopes that through the daily-ness that one of these days we might get "it" right? Like the love of God that is "new every morning, and faithful every night," it might just as well be said, "The sun doesn't rise by natural law. It rises because every morning God says to it, 'Get up and do it again.'" Every new morning is a gift of love.

PRAYER: Dear God, your handiwork is all around us if we only had eyes to see. Help us not to get caught up in life being so daily but let us use our lives to show your wondrous love. Amen.

◀◯▶

Day 275
There's Help at Every Corner

I will never fail you or forsake you (Hebrews 13:5).

EOPLE WHO ARE CAREGIVERS FOR folk with Parkinson's disease know what it means to go through difficult times. It hurts to see people you love digress into a life of "could-have-been."

There was a man who was going through a difficult time. During his time in the wilderness, he found enormous help and felt great comfort in a new translation of Psalm 59:12. If you look it up in the King James Version, you'll find: "The God of my mercy shall prevent me." Unfortunately the word *prevent* is a word whose meaning has been changed by history. It used to mean, "to go before." The text affirms, "The God of my mercy shall go before me."

The man's caretaker looked the text up in the Bible and found that in the margin someone had written, "My God, in his loving kindness shall meet me at every corner." Wow, what comforting words! It is exciting to think that God is at every corner we have to turn, waiting for us to lead us or, even better, walk with us shoulder-to-shoulder along our journey. I don't know what corners you will turn in the next little while, whether you are sick or are taking care of one who is sick, that you are struggling with many different things, such as a job or finances, but I know that corners are always a bit menacing. For one thing, we never know what will be expected of us. What demands will be made on our physical beings or wisdom, courage, or sensitivity when we turn that corner? But I believe that the psalmist is right, "My God, in his loving kindness shall meet me at every corner."

We dwell in love. We move into mercy. It is kindness that waits for us. And God knows how many of his followers need to show more kindness.

> **PRAYER:** God, it is exciting to know that you want to be a part of our journey, corners and all. Give us the courage to stick to it, especially if we have an idea that what lies ahead of us will not be pleasant. Thank you. Amen.

◀◇▶

Day 276
Warts and All

If we confess our sins, he is faithful and just to forgive and will forgive our sins and cleanse us from all unrighteousness (1 John 1:9).

WHAT DO YOU DO WITH your mistakes? Many take their mistakes, failures, and disappointments way too seriously. It is our choice when we decide to hold onto them or do nothing about them. This becomes far more serious when we take our mistakes to be an adequate description of us as a person, and we then believe that we are labeled a victim, a failure, a heretic, or an infidel. It is very easy to take the next step and allow these labels to become self-fulfilling prophecies. We become what we think we are; yet we cannot just give up. Neither can we be perfect, no matter how hard we try. Perfectionism is not the answer, and we, as mere humans, cannot ever achieve that state, anyway.

There is a place to take all our negative baggage, our failures, and our mistakes. We must acknowledge them and leave them at the foot of the cross. That is how we rid ourselves of the burden we carry.

Where does God come into all of this? What does the Lord require? It is surprising that being pure in heart is not at the top of God's list and that the Lord does not require purity in heart before any contact is made. We do not have to be pure in heart before the Lord takes us into his arms. God loves us in spite of our disappointments and failures. We are invited despite our wrong-doing. We can go back even though we have wandered. We can start again even though things have all gone wrong. The message is clear. We do not have to stay where we are.

What, then, is the secret of the spiritual life? Is it to achieve a state of bliss, becoming blind to our mistakes? No. I believe the secret is to recognize that the lover of our soul welcomes us and inspires us with new hope, warts and all.

PRAYER: Dear heavenly Father, once again you do the unexpected. We do not have to get everything in order before you have anything to do with us. We do not have to clear a checklist in order to be included on your guest list. There is no set attire, no special steps that have to be passed off, and no certain influential people to befriend. We come before you in our tattered souls, and you stand at our heart's door with all the heavenly hosts, arms outstretched, bidding welcome to all who come before you warts and all. In the name of Jesus, we pray. Amen.

Day 277
Journey into the Unknown

Go from your country to the land I will show you (Genesis 12:1).

AN YOU IMAGINE BEING IN YOUR late 60s, getting ready to retire, and you are called into the owner's office? You expect the meeting concerns your retirement. You sit in the chair across from him, exchange niceties, then he drops the bomb. You are such good, devoted, and hard worker that he wants you to forego retirement and move your wife and entire staff to an unknown place to which his directions would lead you. He continues that it was a special place to which only those chosen could go. What would you say to him? You and your wife had been looking forward for some time to retirement and spending time with the grandchildren, traveling, taking up new hobbies.

Although not exactly the same scenario, it has some common characteristics with the story of Abraham. He was only seventy-five when Abraham felt the vibrations in his life prodding him to a new beginning. Abraham did without question what God was thinking or planning on doing. He just up and left. It was a bold and scary thing he did.

We folk with Parkinson's can learn a valuable lesson from this story. There will be times when God strums the chord, and if we aren't too busy or distracted, we will feel the vibrations. Most importantly, we will know that God is with us, that we are not alone. Maybe we will be able to sense God's prodding us to a new quest of interior living. We need to be able to leave behind those things that are hindering a closer walk with the Lord. We need to rid ourselves of anything that is hindering our relationship with God. Perhaps our lifestyle needs changing or altering. It is not easy to say yes without asking questions as Abraham did. On the contrary, if God were to tell us what the Lord told Abraham to do, our reaction would be quite different. We would ask question after question until we had the all the details and we thought everything was okay and on "go." When God gives us a place to go, we want to know all the details. Abraham did not question God; he just took God's word at face value and headed in faith to only God knew where. But he did, and look how God blessed him.

> PRAYER: Our heavenly Father, you know where we can best serve you and our fellow human beings. Give us the faith and courage that Abraham seemed to have. Although there were times that he was not on the same page with you, he continued in faith not knowing where you were taking him; and you were leading him to a land of milk and honey. Amen.

Day 278
Hidden Treasure II

Also, the kingdom of heaven is like a merchant who was searching for fine pearls. When he found a valuable pearl, he went away, sold everything he had, and bought it (Matthew 13:45–46).

STORIES OF HIDDEN TREASURE GIVE pleasure when one stumbles across them. An encyclopedia yields its riches when a student seeks information for a school research paper. a farmer's field can turn up arrowheads and musketballs when the stubble from the harvest is turned over for next year's planting. There's an old French tale called "The Farmer and His Sons," that goes something like this:

> A rich farmer, feeling the onset of death, summoned his sons for a talk in private. "Never," he said with his remaining breath, "sell the heritage that is yours by birth and was mine through my father and mother. Somewhere or other a treasure lies hidden in that earth; where, I don't know, but in the end you'll arrive at the right place, given some guts and toil. When you've finished harvesting, turn over the land, break it up, dig it, plough it, don't allow one inch of it to escape your hand." The old man died, and the sons attacked the soil so thoroughly with spade, mattock, and plough that at the year's end every field gave them a bigger yield. They never found that buried hoard; and yet their father was no fool. Before he died he taught the golden rule: Work is the hidden reward.

And that's part of the thrill behind hidden treasure. The search or Quest, the looking, the temporary frustration, and then the finding. The Hindu religious book, *The Upanishads*, tells a story of a father and son. The father tells the son to bring the fruit of a certain tree in their garden. The son does so, and then the father tells him to cut the fruit open to uncover the seeds. The father then bids him to cut open the seeds to discover what is hidden inside. The son is upset to see nothing. We have to go through the process of seeking, finding, looking beyond the form (which is why Jesus often said not only to believe in him but also in the One who sent him), to recognize the treasure in what appears to be emptiness. It is a process of simplification, whether it is selling everything one has to purchase the field or not. It is a process of learning to see with clear eyes, to discover the secrets that are right in front of us.

But here's an aspect to the hidden treasure that goes overlooked, and I confess I didn't see it until recently. It is right here in the story of the pearl of great price. Listen for it:

> Again, the kingdom of the heavens is like a merchant seeking
> fine pearls; and having found one valuable pearl, he went
> and sold all he had and bought it.

Did you hear it? God is the merchant. The one valuable pearl is us! What God sold to by us was his only Beloved Son, who gave his life that we might have life. And if we believe and seek this life, we shall have the life of the world to come (eternal life, if you prefer).

Let me leave you with this thought: A person struggled for half a lifetime to find God before discovering how close the treasure had been all along. *When I looked carefully, I saw that in reality, God was the seeker, and I was the sought.*

PRAYER: Here we are, O God. Let us hear the good news that it is not so much our life's effort to seek you but rather to be prepared for your finding us. In Jesus' name, we pray. Amen.

Day 279
Wasting Time with God

In the morning, long before sunrise, Jesus went to a place where he could be alone to pray (Mark 1:35).

GOD ALREADY KNOWS EVERYTHING. Why should I pray?" asked an Air Force Load Master Sergeant, who was taking my "Introduction to the New Testament" class. The satellite college classes were offered at Seymour Johnson Air Force Base in North Carolina.

I sometimes wonder if most of us do not live as if time spent with God in prayer was wasted energy, an exercise in an already over-exerted schedule. I'm not speaking here so much of our conventional notions of prayer, which waiver between talking to God by casting out a laundry list of concerns and demanding the seemingly elusive justice of God.

Do you ever catch yourself at times, wondering if God is really listening, especially when the "answers" do not come as we would want them to? Or if our wait is too long, perhaps we find ourselves wondering if God isn't altogether absent. If this is our experience of prayer, it is small wonder that many of us have given up the practice. The truth of the matter is that we are more absent from God than God is from us.

Does the God of life require so much of us that we cannot find time to join God in a little divine rest? Someone once remarked, "Prayer is not a substitute for action; prayer is an action for which there is no substitute."

There are as many ways to pray as there are ways to develop a relationship with another person. We might discover and enjoy more of our Creator by contemplating the creation. That is, we learn to see something of the artist's soul through their works of art, and God certainly has produced a number of masterpieces.

The sole purpose of prayer is to enjoy God and so glorify God's love. The Westminster Shorter Catechism asks, "What is the chief end of man?" and expects the answer, "It is to glorify God and enjoy Him forever." If prayer is a waste of time, then I strongly encourage you by everything possible means to waste a little more precious time with God.

PRAYER: And what is man that you are mindful of him, O Lord? How majestic is your name in all the earth! Amen.

Day 280
Without Warning

Jesus' appearance changed in front of them. His face became bright as the sun and his clothes as white as light (Matthew 17:1–2).

I DON'T KNOW ABOUT YOU, but I love my mountains. When I'm driving drive on Highway 321 and I reach the small township of Sawmills, Grandfather Mountain looms before me. As I see it, something inside of me stirs. It is because I can relate to what the psalmist writes, "I look up toward the mountains . . . my help comes from the Lord . . . he will not let me fall" (Ps 12:1–3). I just know that I am moved each time I see all of the mountains that surround Grandfather and Grandfather Mountain itself.

Have you ever noticed all of the important events that take place on mountains in the Bible? One of my favorites is the story of the transfiguration. Jesus takes Peter, James, and John up a high mountain. Moses and Elijah appear and Jesus is transfigured before their eyes, as was Moses when he spent time with God on Mount Sinai. As it happened to Moses long ago, God's light streams on Jesus' face. The disciples don't fully understand what's going on; they just knew something holy was going on, and they were part of this holy moment; and they offered to put up tents. There are some important things that took place there. God's particular closeness was shown then as it is here. We explore the broad expanse of creation and its beauty. We also see Jesus presented as "light from light." As Jesus was transfigured, one cannot help but see the parallels between the stories of Jesus and Moses. They both were on a mountain; Moses was the lawgiver of the Torah; and Jesus was the new lawgiver of the living Torah. Both their faces glowed because they had been with and talked to God.

Like the disciples, we had rather stay on the mountain than return to the hustle and bustle of the daily grind. But that is not to be. There are times when we have a need to stay on the mountain and times for not remaining on the mountains. So many people get hung up on the fact that they are back down don't really want to be. You see, this journey we all find ourselves on is not about bliss on the mountaintop but rather is about being God's servant and partner in ordinary life. A friend shared with me a title of a book she had just purchased, which was, After Ecstasy, the Laundry. The goal is not the glamor of iridescent light but Christ-shaped encounters with others. Rather than thinking the journey is about getting to the top of this world into some more glamorous place, life is about getting deeply into this world as God did in Christ.

God thinks we are a good idea.

PRAYER: God, thank you for reminding us not to forget the mountaintop experiences, those moments that come our way to illuminate the darkness in and around us; neither let us become lost in the day-to-day earthly drudgeries. Amen.

◄◇►

Day 281
Careful, Little Ears Are Listening

These little ones believe in me. It would be best for the person who causes one of them to lose faith to be thrown into the sea with a large stone hung around his neck (Luke 9:42).

I RECEIVED A TELEPHONE CALL FROM Norm Miller. Norm is the head of Interstate Batteries of America, a businessman who has a heart for those in need of God's love. He was led to begin a new international ministry that would offer laypeople hands-on ministry opportunities locally, nationally, and internationally. The ministry would tag-team with existing ministries that had good track records, reputations, and credibility to keep from having to reinvent the wheel. Norm's dream was to afford the wonderful opportunity for people to grow in their Christian faith. I became the first Director of Front-Line Outreach and served in that position for four years before becoming pastor of Greenwich Baptist Church in Greenwich, Connecticut.

One particular organization we wanted to tag-team with was the Jesus Film Project. This ministry was made up of staff workers, who raised their own salaries, and volunteers, who would gather everything they needed to show the film outside in the barrio. One very important piece of equipment they had was a double-sided screen that could accommodate more people to watch the movie by using both sides. Following the movie, the team would begin to follow up with those who responded to their decision to become disciples of Jesus. Many did.

One evening at dinner, I received a call from the head of the "Jesus" film team in Monterrey, Mexico, where we were scheduled to show the film in two weeks. After we hung up, I made a few calls, and when I finished, I found my boys in the game room. The youngest one said to his older brother, "Go ahead and give it to him," to which my older son presented me with an envelope that I recognized immediately. It was the envelope that held the money they made from the sale of scrap copper and brass they were able to gather from the houses that were going up by the hundreds all around us. Inside the envelope was enough money to purchase the screen. My oldest said, "Papa, we want you to buy the screen so the people won't miss hearing that God loves them," to which my youngest added, "It's cool, Papa, we want to do this." I was visibly moved by their gesture.

The "Jesus" film team said their viewings were seen from 100 people upwards to 475 people, and they would show it many times. I was extremely proud of my boys. They knew what I did and wanted to help. I was inspired and blessed by their gift of love. There is no way that we will ever know how many lives were helped or changed by the showing of the "Jesus" film on that special screen given by my boys. They saw, they heard, and they helped. One thing that this teaches me is to be careful, because little ears are listening, and they hear more than you think. Better be careful.

PRAYER: Father, help us to guard what we say so as to help protect the innocence of the children. Thank you also for the unexpected gifts of love from the most unexpected places. May their gifts touch many lives. Amen.

Day 282
The Attractiveness of Jesus

Simon Peter answered Jesus, "Lord, to what person could we go? Your words give eternal life" (John 6:68).

HOW DO YOU SEE JESUS? What draws you to him? Could it be that we are drawn to him because in him is all we see that is true and beautiful? One thing for sure: if he had not lived, we would have been unable to invent him; we could never have thought of him! That is his attractiveness to us. He is inexhaustible. He is unavoidable. What draws me to Jesus is the inexhaustible enchantment of Christ.

Have you ever read a book that someone has written and then you are able to hear that person speak? There is a transformation. The message becomes the shape of the person who is speaking. When the truth of the gospel becomes a message in the shape of a man or woman, then it is doubly compelling. The message and the person just come together and you can't deny them, they are so much of a piece.

Remember Saul of Tarsus? He watched the stoning of the first Christian, Stephen. He even freed the throwing arms of those who were doing the stoning by holding their cloaks. He was there, watching the stones of those thrown and watched Stephen's expression as they stoned him to death. He heard this dying man utter those words to God, "Lord, don't hold this sin against them" (Acts 7:60). He heard Stephen utter similar words that Jesus spoke during his agony on the cross. Later, King Agrippa looked at Saul—now Paul—saw the same glory in his face, and said, "Do you think you can quickly persuade me to become a Christian" (Acts 26:28)? It is not that Paul had a message; rather, he had become the message.

PRAYER: Heavenly Father, reassure us that this is one temptation that we should yield to and often. Help us to not to only have the message but to become the message so our lives can have double the power of our witness to you. In the name of the one to whom we yield, Jesus Christ, we pray. Amen.

Day 283
Lost Paradise?

After he sent the man out, God placed angels and a flaming sword that turned in all directions east of the Garden of Eden (Genesis 3:23).

As MOST OF US ARE AWARE, life can be difficult at times, to say the least. Sometimes, we feel like the early Christians who awaited the hungry lions in the arena. We know that we too will probably have to face a lion or two of our own. Maybe the lions are problems at work, at school, at home, at church, or corporate or personal time, when we are weighed down by the burdens of others as well as our own. Could that be how Adam and Eve felt as they were driven from Eden?

When I am driven from my paradise, when life happens to me, I escape to my office. The air is so thick with solitude and peace that I find nurturing, yes, and even healing. There, sitting amongst my silent companions, the great cloud of witnesses that surround me, I begin to mend. My troubled mind, my fractured spirit, and my diluted self-esteem are waiting, ready for some form, some degree of restoration, some rightness, if there is any to have. It is there in the confrontation of my demons, trying to make sense of the whys and the hows that I am met with the undeniable assurance that I am not alone and no gate has closed behind me. This assurance is there because of forgiveness, and forgiveness is there because of love. Love?

Love, in its truest form, means being accepted by someone, without bitterness, without the flaws and imperfections, and, yes, even our sins. What matters most is that one is restored to God, whose mercy is unconditional. This is clearly seen and experienced out of our desire to be whole before God. That means we stand before God with all our faults as well as all of our virtues, and then hear the message of our acceptance. Having experienced this unconditional love and forgiveness, we need to give it to other persons and pray that they accept our flaws as well. If they don't, and you've done all you can to be restored and are still refused or given conditions to the parceling of their forgiveness and love, then rest in the knowledge that you have done your part.

From our gift of being accepted, we are called upon to exercise the most precious gift anyone of us has to offer: our love. So important is this that Jesus

said all of the other commandments from God and mankind fade in importance to the lavish giving of this love. But at the end, if we are brave enough
to love, if we are strong enough to forgive, if we are generous enough to rejoice
in another's happiness, and if we are wise enough to know that there is enough
love to go around for us all, then we can achieve a fulfillment that no other
living creature will ever know. We can reenter Paradise.

PRAYER: Father, in days of weariness and ill, in pain and helplessness, you heal, comfort, and bless us. May we be found able to reenter the Garden because of our changed lives. Amen.

Day 284
Small Giants

But Zacchaeus was a small man (Luke 19:4).

*If you have the faith the size of a mustard seed, you can say to this mulberry
tree, "Pull yourself up by the roots and plant yourself," and it would obey you
(Luke 17:6).*

IF YOU ARE QUIET AND YOU listen closely enough, you can hear the ever-
building crescendo of the world's voices repeating the mantra, "Bigger is
better... bigger is better." The world in which we live has this infatuation
with big: big is better. Big signifies success. Even many churchgoing people
today think that only big churches are successful. But that is not so. I am not
advocating the idea that big equals success or that you have to be big to have
any worth at all. On the contrary, I personally know small large churches that
are very effective in ministry and are also compassionate, caring, and willing
to be used by God in whatever way God needs to use them. In order for this
to be true for the church, it must also be true of the people that are involved.
They are the small giants that serve God with a quiet, unpretentious, and hum-

ble spirit that God can and will use in leading, teaching, and praying.

Here we have to be extra careful not to be sucked in by the world and catch ourselves humming or, worse yet, living its mantra. There is that contingent of people in the church today who follow that philosophy. In the church today, there is a growing need to convince the world that the issue is not the size but the quality that we are. We have heard time and time again the words of Jesus echoing in the chambers of our hearts, "To be the [biggest] in the kingdom, we must become small, the size of a mustard seed." That's small. Whether big or small, we can be beautiful for God and practice love and care equal to the honor of God.

Let's do a little exercise. Take your Bible and scan its stories that start out small and wind up big. It will become apparent to you that there are both in God's works and those of his people that start out small and end up large (e.g., the babe in Bethlehem).

> **PRAYER:** Father, help us not to miss the small things because we only are looking for you in the big things. Thank you the many small giants that are faithful in showing us the way. Amen.

—◇—

Day 285
Hearing through the Silence

The Lord is in his holy temple. All the earth should be silent in his presence (Habakkuk 2:20).

ℰARLY IN MY MINISTRY, I WAS A pastor in a city where the different community churches shared opportunities to minister and worship together. One special service that we celebrated annually was the observance of Christian unity. On the Sunday set aside for this observance, the participating churches would celebrate their commonality by exchanging pastors and sometimes alter the church's order of worship. It was our hope that through the different denominations, the pastors, and the different worship styles, we could accentuate the things that bind and unite us together rather than those things that split us and made for disunity.

Two services that stand out in my mind include being at the Roman Catholic Church. The Roman Catholic Church received special exemption from parts of their worship—I believe it was called "special dispensation from Mass"—please forgive me if I have that wrong. The priest, Father Robert Lawson, said that this was a rare thing indeed in his tradition.

Another service that I remember was being part of the worship at the Quaker (Friends) House. I was taken with their use of silence in their worship. Their associate was masterful in how he guided the people and in essence aided them in their worship time. It was certainly a time of silent introspection. In observing this tradition, I realized how much silence was lacking in our worship and in our private lives as well. Let me try to prove my point. The next time you are with group of people, ask them to sit for a few moments in silence, then be on the alert as to how short a time it is before someone coughs, a throat is cleared, or a shuffling of feet is heard. The fact of the matter is that we are frightened to death of silence. Silence is so very important to the life of any believer, but it is often quite foreign to most of us.

Keeping silence is a privilege and opportunity, something to be cultivated and cherished. Silence that is chosen is neither void nor impotent. The paradox of silence is that as it gathers and focuses us from distraction, so it provides space for our minds and hearts to wander freely.

Once when on sabbatical, I spent a little more than month visiting the Trappist monastery at Gethsemane, near Bardstown, Kentucky. There I witnessed another side to silence. It was the part of silence that incorporated waiting. Not just any kind of waiting, but a waiting of being hushed before the holy One. I was shown how this is a form of prayer of gently guiding us to what someone has called the "in a clinch moment." It might be savored alone, as someone wrote, "Be alone and feel the trees silently growing. Be alone and see the moonlight, white and busy in silence. The quite alone, notably the cosmos softly rocking." The in-a-clinch moment might be savored with others. When individuals or groups take up this contemplative way of prayer, the question emerges, "Is there enough silence for the word to be heard?"

Most of our talk is flying chaff from which the grain has long been beaten out. Try to curtail speaking; quiet the mind and spirit into a condition of open, active receptivity, in which God has opportunity to speak. I went to Gethsemane from the print-drenched and word-drenched life of a seminarian beginning to lap up the silence to a preacher drenched in silence.

Out of the quietness comes the silence; out of this other thing, the hearing.

PRAYER: Father, help us all to join in singing, "How silently, how silently, the wondrous gift is giv'n." Amen.

------◀◦▶------

Day 286
Do You Have Peace?

I have told you this so that my peace will be with you (John 16:33).

WOULD WE KNOW PEACE IF IT presented itself to us? How many times has it been presented, ready to bestow itself on us, and we were ready to receive it, our troubles and strivings dissipating? It's moments such as these that a sweet sense of calm comes from our knowing that those things still undone are brought to completion with God's help, the Spirit's guidance, and our own efforts.

Here, peace is not limited to a cessation of an armed conflict. Notice I said limited to an armed conflict. We know when the fighting is over, and there is peace from the conflict. It is obvious when the armed conflict ends, but that is not what we are talking about. Here, peace from the type of conflict we are talking about means *serenity*. It is that inner place where we tiptoe to, knowing there is nothing we must change in the present, regret in the past, or be irked by in the future. No, it is not a state of perfection, but it is a perfect place where we accept our life as it is lived in that moment.

It is easy to try and compensate for our feelings of unworthiness: work hard and let our work identify us. I know people who believe that their friends, colleagues, and families could not do without them. They say to themselves, "I am really needed; I am important." That is all the prompting they need to convince themselves of their own worth. A friend of mine always comments that a person who feels this way is the person whom you would want to buy for what they are worth and sell them for what they think they are worth: definitely a money maker. Sounds like they are trying to convince themselves of their own worthiness. But there are no shortcomings for which we need to compensate. Our wants are few and our needs, managed. Each moment radiates with the soft light of quiet gratitude that rises heavenward in thanks to God. How much would you bring?

> **PRAYER:** Our gracious Father, we know deep down in our souls that we never receive real peace apart from you. You are our peace! And because of that truth, we can face every negative, temptation, and trial the world dares to throw our way with boldness, courage, and power; and in the end, with your peace, we can claim the victory. Amen.

◄◇►

Day 287

What Is Due?

I will pay my vow to the Lord (Psalm 116:16).

*I*WAS REMINDED OF THE WORD *vow* not long ago when attending my youngest son's wedding. It was a beautiful ceremony, held outside, and surrounded by the beautiful in the mountains of North Carolina. As part of the ceremony, the minister asked both the bride and groom to express their pledges of commitment to one another, their vows to one another. They

381

pledged the promise of their devotion to each another. It was a happy and joyous time. It started me to thinking.

I thought how sad it is that a great many of us live merely on the level of inclination. But merely to be carried along on the level of inclination is a sounding board to your world. Is it possible that there is never any high moment for us, a time of fine and generous feeling? I am afraid that our living is characterized more by "blah" than by "ah."

Where are the commitments, these vows, made? The solitary view may be important but it is never as meaningful as the public one. Yes, my son could have married with just a minister and two witnesses, but something would be missing. As the bride and groom stood there, side-by-side, there was a peculiar moral energy that came in standing up before God's people and expressing the desire ever to love God and one another as they follow, as we all follow, and saying that they—we—will follow Christ.

We need to drive the stake of vow into the flux of the soul's life. The very virtue of a vow, or pledge, is that it has somewhere at the heart of it the intention to abide by certain things, come what may. Whatever life might give or may deny, we still stand true to some things.

So let us have hope and live as believers should live: to make sure of the commitment he and his wife made, as well as all those present. Maybe this will be the first time to make a pledge for you, or we are renewing them again. For we have come to believe in the words of Jesus Christ that we have the truth of God, the truth about ourselves, the truth about the world. That everything we see in him is true and beautiful. "To whom else shall we go?" said Simon Peter to Jesus, "you alone have the words of eternal life" (John 6:68).

> PRAYER: Father as we begin our quiet time with you each day, remind us of our pledge to you and cause us to stand up for this, our vow to you. Give us the courage to stand up to the world because of the promises we have made to you and those you have made to others and ourselves. Amen.

Day 288
Looking Where? And Why?

I love the Lord, because he has heard my voice and my pleas for mercy. Because he inclined his ear to me; therefore, I will call on him as long as I live (Psalm 116:1–2).

E MIGHT NOT FIND TIME TO pray each day until some sort of emergency arises. When this occurs, there is no shortage of lines being jammed with people offering prayers to God for help and deliverance. The prayer of escape is the same for everyone: "If you get me through this God, I promise I will. . . ." But when normalcy returns, not only do we forget our promise but we fail to evaluate our part in the emergency. When conversing with God in this manner, it turns the Lord into a form of escapism. After all, it can't be our fault. It must be someone else's. The problem is that we have looked upward, hoping that God has heard us, rather than looking inward, where the real problem lies.

Just looking inward is not the solution either. We are guilty of just looking inward and not upward. When we only look upward to find inner peace and inner reserves of nourishment, we find instead confusion and impoverishment. We find ourselves looking inward, being driven to frustration and guilt because it makes us believe that we have failed.

Then the momentum of the Spirit takes over, looking both upward and inward as well. The Spirit's momentum drives us to look upward so that when we dare to look inward, it is prayerfully looking upward. It is being empowered from above so that we can be honest and realistic with ourselves. Then we are drawn with confession and repentance back to God to once again receive forgiveness and renewal.

The result of this rhythm of the inner life, this inward look, is that we become intimately joined with the One who loves.

PRAYER: Our patient heavenly Father, thank you for tolerating our limited way of looking at life. We choose to look upward at one time and inward at another. Grant us the leadership of your

Holy Spirit so we may look both upward and inward to find your love in both places. Amen.

—◈—

Day 289
Looking in the Face of Fear

I love the Lord, because he has heard my voice and my pleas for mercy. Because he inclined his ear to me; therefore, I will call on him as long as I live (Psalm 116:1–2).

FEAR. IT IS AN EMOTION THAT all of us have experienced at some point in our lives, especially those of us who have PD. I experienced fear following a fall (actually, it was five falls between where I started and home) in which I shattered the bones of my left wrist. The doctor had to make four small incisions to piece it back together. He said he thought he was putting a jigsaw puzzle together. The memory of that fall and the repair of the wrist left me with a titanium plate, eight screws and two anchors.

Another fear for me is choking, because PD has weakened the muscles in my throat that help push the food I'm eating. It is easy for me to get choked, which makes me more conscious and careful when I eat. I am not saying that only people with PD are afflicted with fear. Everyone has a fear of something. One might have a fear of spiders, dogs, or heights, for instance.

The readers of John's letters must have been frightened by something for John to respond in the manner in which he did. John was speaking from experience; he had to face his fear. He had gone through so much that he could write in no uncertain terms and with an apparent boldness, "No fear exists where his love is." Was he speaking to the frightened believers in an attempt to reassure them and comfort them?

"But perfect love casts out fear." The Greek words are emphatic here. Perfect love throws fear out, takes it by the scruff of the neck and pitches it into the streets, ejects it bodily. Think about it: Isn't it true that love does throw out all fear?

But what if it is not enough? What if we love, and love, and love, and what if we say over and over, "I love," "I love," "I love," and we find ourselves still afraid? It is not enough. That is the place wherein the gospel comes. We don't have to do the loving. God will do it. We don't have to create and fashion it on our own. God loved the word this way: God gave his only Son. God in love with us: what more can we ask for? Learning what the cross was all about gave reason for all believers to be excited about this love. And because of that we don't have to be afraid any more.

Still there may be some of you that don't believe. But as you ponder these words of promise, recall Paul's words, "If God is for us, who can be against us?" If God loves us, of what do we have to be afraid?

When we are rid of that fear, we can begin to see the whole world as an arena of love, not fear. After we learn to love, everything is different!

PRAYER: Surround us with your love, O God, until all our fears are forgotten and we are joined to all your saints, both the living and the dead, forever and ever. Amen.

⋯⋯⋯◇⋯⋯⋯

Day 290
Where True Knowledge Begins

"Teacher, which is the greatest in Moses' teaching" (Matthew 18:1)?

HAVE YOU EVER NOTICED HOW obsessed our world is about who or what is the greatest? Who is the greatest coach? Who is the greatest athlete? Who is the greatest actor? Who is the greatest writer? This seems to go on forever. A prime example is Muhammad Ali, the world champion heavyweight pugilist who taunted his opponents by shouting out his self-coined mantra, "I am the Greatest." Our generation is not the only guilty one. We can trace this obsession, this desire to know who is the greatest, all the way back to the time of Jesus. The people of Jesus' time were just as concerned for an answer, as are many today, of who is the greatest. Jesus himself was confronted with the question on more than one occasion: "Who, or which, is the greatest?"

One of Jesus' followers inquired as to who is the greatest in his kingdom, and in his unique way of teaching, Jesus gave the disciples and those around them a powerful object lesson. Can't you see him now? His eyes begin scanning the crowd until they fall on a little child. Gathering the child in his arms, he carries him over to a nearby rock and stands the child there. Walking around the rock, Jesus answered the question: "You want to be the greatest, then you must become as this child. Unless you become as a child, you shall not enter the kingdom of heaven." If you come as a child, as a servant, then and only then will you be a part of God's kingdom.

"Greatest" appears again when the Pharisees ask him which was the greatest commandment that Moses had given them. Jesus responded to their question but not as they thought he would. Talk about putting an editor's pencil to the paper, he whittled the original ten that had grown to over 600 (for the Pharisees' job security) to one. The greatest commandment is to love God with every part of your being: mind, heart, and spirit.

Following Jesus' transfiguration, he returns with Peter, James, and John, and is confronted with the question of "greatness" when he finds his remaining disciples arguing as to which of them was the greatest and would sit on his right side in his kingdom. He answered their question simply and directly: "It is not my place to name that person; only God could do that."

As for who I think are the greatest: men and women who get up every morning to battle PD and any other terminal illness. They are the bravest; they are the *greatest*!

> **PRAYER:** Father, help us to accept your definition of "greatest" so that we may be among the "greatest" in your kingdom. Help us to see as you see, not as the world sees. Amen.

Day 291
On Hitting the Mark

When the chief priests and Pharisees heard his parables, they realized that he was speaking about them (Matthew 21:45).

I REMEMBER THAT AS A CHILD, when the Fair came to town, I walked the midway, seeing all the flashing lights, the rides, and the booths. In addition to the booths where they served food, there were booths for games. There, the "carnies" barked their offers of oversized stuffed animals for any fair-goers who felt lucky.

They had one game at which I always tried my hand. It was a shooting game. I knew I could beat it; after all, I could hit a can with my Daisy "Red Rider" BB gun. The object of this game was to shoot at a red star with one of their guns, leaving no part of the red star attached to the target. You know I never won! I would always leave a fragment of the red star waving in the wind. I always felt anxious and frustrated after such an unsuccessful outcome.

I realized, as I got older, that my life was a lot like that shooting game. No matter how many times I shot, there would always be a piece of red star remaining. Playing the game, I realized I was not quite hitting the mark on the target at the Fair, but I wasn't hitting the mark in my life, either. Oh, I would hit the target on occasion, but there was always some of the target remaining. Following the loss came the avalanche of excuses: How could you miss the mark? Why did you miss the mark? How did you miss the mark? No matter the reason, we still are disappointed.

The spiritual lesson here is that even though we haven't been successful in shooting the entire star out, God still loves us and wants to give us mercy, pardon, and forgiveness. Those with Parkinson's can fall into the trap of excuse hunting because of the great stress in their lives. But these negative feelings are not so clear-cut; they are not so grand, not so spectacular, and certainly not overt. These negative and hostile feelings give off such a smoke screen that it is hard to identify the real problem. These negative and hostile feelings are strong because they sit very deep in us, in our hearts, in our bones, and in our flesh, and often we don't even know they are there. We think we are so good. But, in fact, we are lost in a very profound way, the difference being that we can still return to God and be forgiven.

> **PRAYER:** Our heavenly Father, thank you for your tolerance and patience with us, your stiff-necked people. We go about thinking everything is well with our souls. Help us admit the wrongs in our lives so we will be able to show the world how we are forgiven by your infinite, unconditional love. In the name of Jesus, we pray. Amen.

◄ ○ ►

Day 292
Happiness Is . . .

A meal is made for laughter, and wine makes life pleasant (Ecclesiastes 10:19).

Then our mouths were filled with laughter (Psalm 126:2).

ONCE, AS I WAS PASTORING A CHURCH, I wrote a little sarcastic column for our church newsletter that I intended for the members to take tongue-and-cheek. But as always, there was that one person who took it in the opposite way. In this case, however, it was not one person, but two members that missed the spirit in which the column was written. They were a husband and wife team; and from the looks on their faces when they came into my office to talk, you would have thought they had been told by the doctor they only had a few minutes to live.

He started, because he was the head of the house and therefore spokesperson a well. She sat on the couch the entire time, almost in tears. The only comment she made was, "Don't you agree Dr. Greene?" Then came his shocking statement: "We just don't feel it appropriate for our pastor to make light of such serious topics and to set such an example before his members, trying to be humorous, and we hope that you will not repeat this mistake again."

I heard the little bell inside my head announce, "Ding, dong, your time is up."

I wish I'd had in my arsenal of comebacks, something witty. I read a few weeks later, "If it isn't fun, you're not doing it right." I agree with that. If we ask someone, "Wasn't it fun?" others might think that we are being frivolous when we are really expressing the ease, grace, spontaneity, and joy that we found in whatever we were doing.

There are still those who think that to be serious requires one to be solemn, and that to be godly one must be grave. It was this kind of joylessness that moved Paul Tillich to complain of religious folk as, "the redeemed do not look redeemed." I like to remember that the enthusiasm of the early church disciples was such that the first criticism brought against them was that they were drunk. And one of them replied, "We are not drunk. It's only nine o'clock in the morning." Their supposed intoxication was of a different sort. They had caught the Spirit—or the Spirit had caught them—before whatever bars were open, and they were having fun.

> **PRAYER:** Dear God, help us to take our message seriously but not take ourselves so. Give us the courage to laugh on occasion, to have fun, and to enjoy this world you have given into our stewardship. For we know many of the benefits physically, mentally, and spiritually could be handled with more power and effectiveness when we enjoy life and have fun with you. Amen.

Day 293
Nothing Can Touch It

So these three things remain: faith, hope, and love. But the best one of these is love. Pursue love (1 Corinthians 13:13–14:1).

IMAGINE A COMPETITION WITH ONLY three participants. According to the statistics, all three are equal in ability and giftedness. To come in second or third certainly would not represent defeat or failure; rather, it would highlight the level of mastery at which the competition occurs.

When Paul concludes the chapter in the first letter to the Corinthian Christians that is often thought of as the "love chapter," we see that Paul does exactly this. It was never Paul's intention to put hope and faith on a shelf to collect dust, not to be used to encourage, uplift and bless believers. He enhances the status of them as he gives preeminence to love.

We know that faith without love makes it easy to digress into arrogance or fatalism. As for hope, if it is not accompanied by the power of love, it differs only slightly from wishful thinking or flights of fancy.

No. When love matches grace with faith, it energizes hope in such a way that it gains meaning and purpose. Our existence becomes qualitatively distinct to the degree that we receive and share the love of God.

Love is elevated to premier status among Christian virtues and roots us in the nature of our heavenly Father, who is love (John 4:16), for God is the one in whom we place our faith and who is our everlasting hope!

> **PRAYER:** Father, you not only instruct us on how to live life, but you show us. It is obvious that we need help in order for the world to see that we retain your virtue in its coarse and darkened life and show the evidence of its being and help in making us alive and full of life. Thank you, Father, and may we lead people to elevate the practice of love so that they too can experience the greatest love the world has ever known, even Jesus Christ, in whose name we pray. Amen.

Day 294
Love Me?

Love your neighbor as you love yourself (Matthew 19:19 and 23:39).

I AM APPRECIATIVE OF JESUS' admonition that I should love my neighbor as I love myself. I don't, however like the fact that there is where he left it. No more elaboration on loving myself. How do I love myself? Oh, the scriptures are full of admonishments to love God, to love neighbors, or even to love our enemies and those that persecute us and lie about it. The text in Matthew is the only verse that I have found in the scriptures that expands this idea of love of self and that is the single statement that speaks to or hints at the idea of self-love. And what if the truth is that we do not love ourselves? Or does this mean if we don't love ourselves, we don't love our neighbor; and if we don't love our neighbors, does that mean that we do not love God.

The truth of the matter is that I do not have a feeling of fondness or affection for myself. There are times when I do not even enjoy my own company. So it would appear that "love your neighbor" does not mean, "feel fond of him," or "find him attractive." Do I think well of myself, that I have it all together, that I'm on top of things? I must confess that there are times that I do feel that way. Those times in which I do think myself to be a nice guy usually turn out to be my worst moments, but that is not why I love myself. In fact, it is the other way around: to love myself makes me think of myself as nice, but thinking myself nice is not why I love myself. So loving my enemies does not require that I believe them nice, either. That should bring a lot of relief to a great many people. For these people, the relief is enormous because they imagine that forgiving one's enemies means making out that they are really not such bad people after all, when the evidence speaks to the contrary.

Perhaps we should go a step further. In the times that I am most clearsighted, not only do I believe myself to be a nice man, there is also an undertow that reminds me that I am also a rather nasty man. When recalling some of the things I have done, I see them in horror and loathing. So, apparently, I am allowed to loathe and hate some of the things my enemies do.

PRAYER: Father, grant us the vision to see how we can love our neighbors as ourselves, especially when we have difficulty, at times, loving ourselves. Yet, we know we must have some value because you sent your Son into the world to die in our stead. Thank you! Amen.

⟨◇⟩

Day 295
It's Your Choice; What Will It Be?

Be wise in the way you act toward those who are outside the Christian faith. Make the most of your opportunities. Everything you say should be kind and well thought out so you know how to answer everyone (Colossians 4:5–6).

I DON'T KNOW ABOUT YOU, but I have met some rather brash people in on my journey, folk who seem to be mad at the world and God for whatever reason. They spread their negativism by throwing compassion and thoughtfulness out the window. When they do speak, it is what the world hasn't given them, or has given me, that matters. They haven't been given a fair shake in life, so they strike back in harsh, unkind, and hurtful actions and words. A perfect example of this kind of person I am talking about can be seen in the comedy show of ventriloquist Jeff Dunham. One of his characters, named "Walter," fits this profile perfectly. The attitude and even the expression he has on his face, complete with the corners of his mouth turned down into an expression of anger, represents the folk I am speaking of here.

Then Paul comes along and tells us that we, as believers, are to love these folk. How do you deal with learning to love the unloving? It's easy to love considerate people, but how do we deal, as we must almost every day, with those who are rude and insensitive or who are vulgar and profane in their speech. We must learn to force ourselves to concentrate on the good in those people instead of the words spoken. Everyone is loved by Jesus Christ, who died for the whole world. Observe, try to understand, and in time, some beautiful changes will occur—perhaps not in those miserable people, but in us, as we become more Christlike in our feelings toward others, no matter how they behave.

I use a few little helps for my daily task. Humor is God's aspirin! I look for and usually find a speck of humor in a stressful situation. Laughter is God's gift, and it's a tension-breaker. I also consider the value of people, not their appearances or moods. Remember, "A soft answer turns away wrath" (Prov 15:1). And last, I try to remember that I could make or break a person's day by the way I treat them.

I hope your day is wonderful!

PRAYER: Lord, thanks for sending me where I did not plan to go. Amen.

Day 296
Reaching Our Destination

Go to the land that I will show you. I will make you a great nation (Genesis 12:2).

HOW MANY TIMES HAVE YOU heard the words, "Are we there yet?" from excited children on a trip to their grandparents, an amusement park, or to a friend's house for a play-date? It starts out being sweet and brings a smile to your face as you remember times when you were growing up when that innocent, childhood question was on your lips. You were so excited. But by the 2,145th time, you come to understand your father's action as he turned the radio up full volume. When that didn't work, you and your siblings only got louder. Now you no longer think it is so innocent but rather a full-blown conspiracy. Your once big smile has fallen off your face, and in its place is a frown. Your choice is to pull out your hair or unhook the children's seat belt and open their door while the car is still moving. The unnerving thing about all of this is that you have only traveled about ten blocks.

It would such a relief if they would just sit back quietly and be the little angels that they can be when they act like your side of the family. Wouldn't it be nice to experience the same level of excitement in our dealings with people who have wronged us? Or like the bumper sticker I saw once that read, "God loves you and I'm trying hard to."

It is easy to love someone with whom you have a friendship *and* commonality. You share a hobby or common interests and passions. You might share the same likes and dislikes. And yet there will be times you disagree, get upset, and would like to ring their necks the way my granny would do at Sunday's lunch. Even deep friendships have their ups and downs.

On the flip-side of that deep friendship are those people Jesus encourages us to love in spite of the their unloving. No matter how hard they make it for us, we still are still called to love them. These are the folk who *don't* want to be loved, no matter by what or by whom. They do not care if they make a difficult situation more difficult with such negative attitudes. Jesus not only tells us how to love, but he shows us, as well.

Phillip Larkin was one of the best modern British poets. It was thought for a while that he would be made poet laureate, but he didn't receive that distinction, which must have pleased him because he really didn't want it. In one of his poems, he asks, "What's wrong?" and speaks of the unease that is part of the human condition. He tells us that what is wrong is that we have a sense of life lived according to love and of all that we might have done had we been loved. If we're not loved, we want it. If we have it, we're afraid of losing it, and we never have enough of it. If you love somebody, tell him or her. They need to hear it. They might do great things in the joy of it. It will help to put right what is wrong.

> **PRAYER:** Dear God, you have shown us through your Son, Jesus, that true love—the love that comes from you—makes no distinction between friends and foes, between people who are for us and people who are against us, people who do us a favor and those who don't. Enlarge our hearts to love all your children as you have loved us. Amen.

Day 297
Surprised by Joy

Do not remember the sins of my youth or my transgressions; according to your steadfast love remember me, for your goodness' sake, O Lord (Psalm 25:7, NRSV)!

HAVE YOU EVEN BEEN PART OF A surprise party that caught someone totally off guard with absolutely no idea what was prompting their family, friends, and colleagues' strange behavior? It sneaked up on them and the expression on that person's face was priceless—a "Kodak moment." There is just something about trying to keep it a secret and pull it off that adds so much excitement to the event. You are the hero for the night; you were able to pull it off without a hitch.

And the recipient's reaction makes it even more of a grand happening. As the shock begins to wear off, you realize you haven't been breathing for the past thirty minutes. Once everything is somewhat back to normal, you can mingle and thank everyone for creating a very special memory. In some situations, the surprise turns into a life-changing event. That is what happened to C. S. Lewis, the English writer of the past century.

Lewis spoke of being "surprised by joy." For him, it was aimed at getting his life in tune with God's. Here, I believe, it speaks to the inescapable fact that as we all grow old, we will have to stretch our armies and be guided and led to places we would rather not go. What was true of Peter will be true for us. There is suffering ahead of us—for some, immense suffering—a suffering that will continually tempt us to think that we have chosen the wrong road and that others were shrewder than we.

But we need not be surprised by pain. Be surprised by joy; be surprised by the little flower that shows its beauty in the midst of a barren desert, and be surprised by the immense healing power that keeps bursting forth like springs of fresh water from the depths of our pain.

And so, with an eye focused on the poor, a heart trusting that we will get what we need, and a spirit always surprised by joy, we will exercise the power and walk through the valley of darkness, performing and witnessing miracles.

PRAYER: Father God, the biggest surprise is the surprise that you even want to have a relationship with us. What we could call ourselves would take up so much space, and all the while all you want to do is be with us. Thank you for that love as well as the surprise of joy. Amen.

Day 298

Decisions! Decisions! Decisions!

If you mean yes, say yes. If you mean no, say no. Do this so that you won't be condemned (James 5:11).

IT IS TRUE: MANY OF US feel stress as though we are being pulled apart and split from having to make so many different decisions. It might be because we have never been expected to make a clear-cut decision. Maybe folk do not feel as though a relationship God warrants a hard clear-cut decision. But a clear-cut decision is required. That very basic decision that has to be made is whether or not to follow the Lord Jesus Christ.

Jesus called a hated, despised, loathed tax collector, who was collecting the taxes for the Romans. No one saw anything at all decent in Matthew as he grabbed his filthy profits, but Jesus did. It was understood that a position for a tax collector was bad enough as it was, but the problem was compounded when the tax collector was Jewish. The tax collector was ostracized because the people knew that they were being charged extra so as to line the insides of their own pockets. The Romans knew what was going on, but they didn't care as long as they got their share. Everyone else saw Matthew as only a fallen creature, too low and despicable to be called a man or addressed with any respect.

Jesus saw the importance of confronting Matthew. He stopped on his grand march toward the world's redemption and dealt with poor, despised Matthew. He called upon Matthew to make this first eternal decision. Mathew did not ask where this would lead. Jesus knew that there was something slumbering in Matthew that needed to be awakened, and where the road led was not really the most important matter. What was most important was the question of who was leading, not where the way was leading. Something that dissatisfied Matthew could be satisfied if he followed the Lord. He knew that, and the text suggests that without waiting or thinking about it, Matthew flung his counter and the coins out in the road. Matthew got up and followed.

Matthew was led, as we can be led, to discover that as we forge ahead falling, rising, forgiving, forgetting, and finding, that the way will grow brighter every passing day.

> **PRAYER:** Father, thank you for loving us enough to help us realize that you do not leave us in the trash heaps and garbage piles of our world. You see hope in us and call us to make that very important decision to follow you. May we have the courage to respond, as did Matthew, leaving the trappings of this world powerless and defeated as he immediately followed Jesus, in whose name we pray. Amen.

◇

Day 299
Not Again!

Simon answered, "Teacher, we worked all night and caught nothing. But if you say so, I'll lower the nets." They caught such a large number of fish that their nets began to tear. Jesus said, "From now on you will catch people instead of fish" (Luke 5:6).

WE NEED TO BECOME ACQUAINTED with the floor, because we will be seeing more of it; in fact, we'll even befriend it. Folk with PD have a tendency to fall a lot because of freezing, when one can't get their feet to move or have to deal with weak legs, poor balance, a shuffling of feet, and an awkward gait. It can't be helped, and this freezing robs us of our fluidity of motion to the point that we become more and more clumsy.

We really get frustrated when we fall more than once in the course of a day. While on the floor, you take a quick inventory to see if everything is in working order before trying to get up. Unfortunately after one of my falls, the inventory told me something was not quite right. By the time we got to the hospital, I was in a great deal of pain. X-rays revealed a serious break of the left wrist that would require surgery. I came out of surgery with a metal plate, eight screws, and two anchors. One thing I have learned while spending time on the floor, or the ground, is that I have to get up and try again . . . and again . . . and again.

Jesus' disciples were haggard, disappointed, and were unsuccessful in their fishing one day. They began washing their nets. They had given up, but Jesus told those discouraged men to go back out and try again. If you have tried and failed in your trying, go back and try again.

It means getting up when we fall down. Paul writes, "This one thing I do," which for me means get up. This one thing I do means getting back on track, so with Paul, "I press on." There is a note of doggedness in that word. It has steel for determination in it. There is excitement and there is anticipation in the Christian life. The prize is worthy of every mile of the way, every step of the journey, every tear we shed, every fear we face, every sorrow we endure, every trial we pass through, every enemy we confront, and every fall we rise from.

"I press on." God's love bends low, and his mercy stoops down to help our weary souls. Christ is our companion forever.

> **PRAYER:** Give us a clear vision to our destination, O God, to that shining city on the hill where we will hear, "Well done. Enter in!" But until that time, we will press on with you as our companion. Amen.

Day 300
Live Letters

May the good will of the Lord Jesus Christ be with you (1 Corinthians 16:23).

HOW MANY OF YOU TAKE THE endings of letters for granted? Most of the time, we don't take the time to really read them. We assume that it will just be the typical, "Sincerely" or "Yours truly." We assume that they are just a formality, but to only give them a glance is a bad habit in which to fall. The circumstance that caused this line of thinking was a letter that was received with the ending, "Enthusiastically yours." Reading the letter, one could sense the excitement it contained, to which "Enthusiastically yours" had to be the most appropriate ending.

More often than not, the New Testament letters opened or closed with words that we take for granted. "The grace of the Lord Jesus Christ be with you." Isn't that a blessed promise to hear this priceless echoing in our hearts that can only bring peace and hope? These words are a prayer that the receiver may be filled with the evidence of God's gracious gift of life. They are indeed a blessing of hope. One can see the summary of the good news of our resurrection faith brought on by the resurrection of Jesus Christ.

Our lives are letters—God's letters—to a waiting, wondering world. What word can best describe them? Are they so "grace-filled" that they are a blessing of grace?

The gospel is news that has shape and form. It has choices. Those choices are the ways in which the presence of the risen Christ resounds in us. A grace-filled life is one that reminds us who we are: we are the good news people. We are grace-filled so we may fill others with grace.

So pay attention to the ends of the letters you receive. There just might be a message of which God wants to remind you.

PRAYER: Lord God, grant that our lives may echo with grace and hope. Amen.

Day 301
A Chip Off the Old Block

Then God said, "Let us make humans in our image, in our likeness" (Genesis 1:26).

YOU PROBABLY HAVE HEARD ON many different occasions, as I have, standing by the bassinet or crib of a new born baby that is lying there with both hands and feet moving a hundred miles an hour. "Oh, she has the hands of her mother, don't you think?" asked a relative. "I think she has her father's eyes," another responds.

Now, these relatives did not mean that the newborn baby has the actual hands of the mother or the eyes of the father. What they meant, simply, is that the baby had body parts that reminded them of the parents. We know now that it is all in the genes, the DNA, that captures the likenesses of the parents, which is a miracle in itself. The similarities and looks will change according to the dominant genes as the years go by.

When God made the decision to make humans in the divine image, God was talking about more than our hands and eyes looking similar. The Lord was speaking about our hearts, our essence.

When you think about a world staggering from the effects of war in Iraq, which should have already been brought to a close; Afghanistan, which is beginning a new century of continuing war; and Kuwait and other African nations in civil war, along with the eighty plus areas of fighting around the globe, it is sometimes difficult to believe that after all this and more we are images of the Creator.

I will admit that I have a lot of work to do, because it is difficult for me to accept that human beings created in God's image can do terrible things to other human beings created in God's image, inflicting pain and torturing. Yet, the flip side is much more positive. Where as human beings do terrible things to others, those same human beings can do marvelous things for others. We are so blessed when God awakens our hearts to do good and love is born.

PRAYER: Father God, help all folk we meet to leave us glad that they are related, because we are all made in your image and are part of the same family. In Christ's name, we pray. Amen.

Day 302
Ready to Go, Yet?

As Moses and Elijah were leaving him, Peter said to Jesus, "Teacher, it's good that we're here. Let's put up three tents—one for you, one for Moses, and one for Elijah" (Luke 9:33).

HOW MANY TIMES HAS SOME event carried you to the mountaintop and then, suddenly, you found yourself back down to earth and maybe even in a valley? So many people get hung up on the fact they are back on earth rather than recall the experience they had on the mountaintop. Look what was waiting on Jesus. Jesus took Peter, John, and James up the mountain, now known as the Mount of Transfiguration. While the three disciples slept, Jesus met with Moses and Elijah as they discussed what Jesus was about to do with regard to giving up his life. Would you like to have been a fly on the tree limb and heard those discussions: "How are you feeling Jesus?" "Getting a little anxious?" "What about those three—can't even keep them awake to pray?"

After his words with Moses and Elijah, Jesus and his followers left that holy moment on the mountaintop and walked in on the other disciples squabbling and arguing as to which of them was the greatest. Jesus gave them a powerful response to their question. "You have to come as a child as one of the poor and be a servant to them to be the greatest in my kingdom." I wonder what Peter, John, and James thought after having been on the mountain with Jesus, Moses, and Elijah. Here, they had left the holiness of that encounter on the mount and gone into the room of men who were arguing and wanting to be the greatest of the group.

You see, this journey we all find ourselves on is not about bliss on the mountaintop but about being God's servant and partner in ordinary life. A friend shared with me a title of a book she had just purchased that speaks to this. The title was: *After Ecstasy, the Laundry*. How true to life that is!

The goal is not the glamor of iridescent light but Christ-shaped encounters with others. Rather than thinking that the journey is about getting from this world ourselves into some more glamorous place, it is about getting deeply into this world as God did in Christ.

God thinks you and I are a good idea.

> **PRAYER:** Father, we are all mixed up and some of us are more so than others. It is hard for us to understand the workings of your kingdom. We have thought that to be great in your kingdom we have to earn it, to work for it, so that the one with the most merits wins, All the while not knowing that Jesus' kingdom is under your direction. So with the help of your Spirit we can understand. We all need to become servants, your helpers on our march to the glorious city of yours, O God. Amen.

Day 303
How Do You Live?

Who told you that you could do this (Mark 11:28)?

HUNDREDS OF CHOICES ARE MADE every day. We are keenly aware of some of the deliberate choices being made and unaware of others. Those choices that are set on automatic pilot (like breathing—we don't say over and over, "Breathe now. Breathe now.") are some of the ones whose occurrence we are too often unaware. What follows today is a sampling of choices that we are faced with in our lifetime.

If you put self at the center, you must be prepared to find your outer limits there, and that can be very lonely. If what you are after is power, you had better forget about affection, for it is very difficult. How do you live?

What gives you the right to do these things?

If you really think that life is a rat race, you must not look for any dignity in it. If you have made up your mind that life's purely quantitative, then you had better keep your averages high. If you are a gossip, you must not expect confidences. If it is your practice to confront people, then don't expect them to come knocking on your door when they require tenderness. If what you are really after is security, you had better forget about ecstasy. If you think that your children are among your own private possessions, then you must not look for creative and spontaneous spirits. If you really are a materialist, then don't consult with gurus about spiritual values, for there is very little they have to say to you and even less that you would understand. If you are possessed by your profession, you had better keep one eye on your relationships. If you are only interested in justice and not in mercy, you'd better not make any mistakes. If you are unscrupulously ambitious, you must not expect trustful friends. And if you decide to live by the sword, then by the heavens above you had better carry one, because you are going to need it.

> **PRAYER:** Our God in the heavens and on earth, help us to prepare to meet this world we live in without totally destroying ourselves. We need your guidance and mercy to accomplish such a feat. Help us, O God, for Christ's sake. Amen.

Day 304
Having the Advantage

It's good for you that I go away (John 16:7).

YOU WONDER IF JOHN MIGHT have misunderstood Jesus and left out a word or two. What in the world was he thinking when recording Jesus' words? How could it be to their advantage that Jesus went away? After all he was their teacher, their everything!

Maybe they needed time to think through all that he had said and done. Maybe they needed space to try out their wings. Perhaps Jesus realized that they could not reach their full maturity as long as he was there to make decisions for them and straighten out their blinders. It was for their own good, for the sake of their spiritual development, that he went away.

I believe Jesus meant more than that. The main idea here is that when Jesus went away, he would send the Holy Spirit to be with them. It was to their advantage that the Spirit would come. Jesus was confined to a physical body, but the Spirit was and is not confined. Jesus could be at one place at a time, but the Spirit was and is not limited to space or time. Jesus depended on the ears and eyes of people to deliver his message, but the Spirit worked and works directly on the mind, heart, and conscience.

So, the Spirit could do some things that even Jesus could not do. The Spirit would enable the disciples to understand Jesus more fully and more deeply than Jesus himself. The Spirit could help make them understand him. It was to their advantage that Jesus went away.

The advantage is still ours, because the Spirit that Jesus sent is still with us. Our initial ongoing concern should not be how much of the Holy Spirit that *we* have, but rather, how much of *us* that the Holy Spirit has.

PRAYER: Father, we thank you for sending the Holy Spirit who is our constant companion to us. Let the Spirit open the doors to the richness of your kingdom and for giving us strength to overcome the world rather than the world overcoming us. May the Holy Spirit grant us the knowledge of the known secret of your kingdom for which Jesus died. Send us the Holy Counselor, the comforter who lives within us. Amen.

Day 305
Even Now!

Love each other in the same way that I have loved you (John 13:34).

*E*VEN NOW, JESUS HAS STOPPED IN the shade of the sycamore tree, maybe to catch his second wind or to get some relief from the pressing crowd that was following him. And do you know that the tree Jesus stopped under just happened to be the same one that Zacchaeus has recently climbed into in order to see this preacher from Nazareth.

Even now, Jesus has plans to look up, and call Zacchaeus from the limb he has squirreled himself away on so he could see. Was it he or Jesus who was the short one?

Even now, Jesus is promising him, "I mean to stay with you today." I can picture that when he heard this, Zacchaeus skinned his shins shimmying down that tree.

Even now, Bartimaeus, in the abyss of his blindness, is crying out from his misery, "Son of David! Have pity on me!" The child, born to peasant parents, is even now waiting for the opportunity for Jesus to heal him of his affliction.

Even now, there is a Samaritan woman at a well, who has not yet married "husband number one." Little does she know that she will have five husbands and another man, besides. Even now, Jesus is appealing to the thirst that is in her life, and Jesus promises to satisfy that thirst with the gift of himself.

Just about now the young man, Peter, is beginning to learn how to fish from his father. But even now, Jesus sees him on the seashore and asks him to be fishers of people.

Even now, Jesus is forgiving his sins and calling Peter the "Rock."

Even now, Jesus is silently beckoning us all: Come to me, any of you are tired and those of you that are weary, any of you who find life a struggle and feel the strength drain from your soul: even now Jesus will refresh you. Your souls will find their rest in him. He calls us friend.

Even now, he has come that we might have the fullness and the humble-hearted abundance of life.

Even now, he knows if you are among those people who hunger and thirst, and he says he is the bread of life and the living water, and those who follow him will not hunger or thirst again. He calls us friend—for I am with you always and forever.

Even now he is waiting for your answer.

> **PRAYER**: Father in heaven and on earth, come to us even now, for we know not what the future holds, but we know you hold the future in your hands even now. Even now. Amen.

Day 306
Who Is Praying for Me?

But I prayed for you Simon that your faith will not fail. So when you recover, strengthen the disciples (Luke 22:32).

IN FIRST THESSALONIANS 5:7, WE find the vivid words of Paul encouraging the believers to continue to pray. The Authorized Version says that we should "pray without ceasing," whereas the Revised Standard Version says to "pray continually." The New English Bible says to "pray continually," whereas Moffatt translates, "never give up prayer." Whichever words we employ, it is abundantly clear: Prayer is an area in which our involvement never ends. I don't know about you, but I understand the importance of prayer in the life of a believer. I will confess that I have not arrived at the same level of prayer as a great many prayer warriors in both past and present. I do understand that prayer is not an occasional effort, but a constant experience, day and night. The readiness to pray constantly is important, because whatever we do, or fail to do, the need for prayer is never exhausted. Prayer does not require a particular posture, language, or length to be accepted by God. Rather, prayer is mostly personal. We find ourselves praying, "O God, be with Bob." "Lord, help Ann." When we pray this way we soon discover the need for prayer never ends.

Another thing we soon discover when we pray is that we make use of the word help. This verb, *help*, is almost always central to the prayer experience because it's what we desperately need. We pray sometimes for ourselves; but, far more often, we pray for others. It is a great comfort for me to know that not only am I prayed for by friends and relatives, Jesus and the Spirit are both making intercession for me.

After my mother's death, I was reminded how much I was the object of her prayers and how much I would miss them. But then I was reminded of the "great cloud of witnesses" that surrounds us, encouraging us to get rid of everything that slows us down and to not be restricted in any way from running the race that lies ahead of us. Suddenly, I realized my soul was smiling because I knew beyond a shadow of doubt who one of those witnesses was; and I thank God for reminding me that my mother was still praying for me. Jesus, the Spirit, and my mother praying for me "without ceasing." How could I go wrong? My joy was renewed.

PRAYER: Father, we are grateful that you love us and want to hear our prayers, so much so that you have provided many people to accompany us along life's journey to show and pray us through whatever life throws our way. Thank you, Father. Amen.

Day 307
Things We Do for Love

Greater love hath no man than this: that a man will lay down his life for a friend (John 15:13).

RECENTLY, I WAS CHANNEL SURFING ON the television and stopped at a talk show on which different trends of dating in today's society were discussed. One side argued that there is too much outward expression of sexuality, whereas the other side argued for more openness when it came to methods of dating and sexuality. The discussion progressed to how such trends affected the marriage relationship. The "con" side said that this all contributes to the lack of true commitment, and the "pro" side said that it provides increased commitment because of the openness, trust, and freedom in the relationship. Because I needed to run some errands, I had to I leave before the debate resolved the issue.

My journey found me in a bookstore, where I read many of the titles and a few of the dust jackets. I found, as you might have, that many of our modern novels, self-help books, and bestseller lists read more like sex manuals than stories. No detail is spared us. They are all engineering and mechanics and technique with very little caring or cherishing about them. Not long ago, I overheard a conversation in which a young lady said, "I wish I could meet someone who had more to say to me than, 'Hello, how are you? Would you like to go to bed?'"

Then I recalled a passage in the book of Genesis that reads:

> And Jacob loved Rachel, and said, "I will serve you seven years for her."
> And Jacob served seven years for her, and they seemed unto him but a few days for the love he had for her.

Now, what would you think of that on a Hallmark Valentine card? And what do you think about Laban's tricking Jacob into marrying his older daughter Leah? Jacob's love was boundless toward Rachel because he told Laban he would work seven more years for Rachel's hand. What would you do in this situation?

PRAYER: Dear heavenly Father, you know the true meaning of love and showed us in a concrete manner by the giving of your Son to die for our sins. In his life he defines real love: a love that cares so much that it doesn't matter how long it takes you to obtain it. When you do, you realize it is the greatest of Paul's trio of faith, hope, and love. God, you are the author of unconditional love and we come before you with grateful hearts accepting your pardon. Help us to transform our sin-ridden hearts into Christ's heart. For it is in his name that we pray. Amen.

◄◇►

Day 308
Solitude without Restlessness

Come to me all who are tired from carrying heavy loads, and I will give you rest. Place my yoke over your shoulders, and learn from me (Matthew 11:28–30).

SOMEWHERE IN HIS WRITINGS, Henri Nouwen speaks of the movement from the restless spirit to the restful spirit. He is not saying that we are attempting to escape from ourselves; rather he is suggesting that we find a new center. Just as it is not an escape from ourselves, it is neither an attempt to simply escape the pressures of the world. These are just illusions. This movement is the bringing of our whole selves, with all of our brokenness, fears, pains, and anxieties, to find a new center of inner peace.

We certainly are not advocating attempting to escape the world. Folk with Parkinson's, in particular, need to learn our interior selves and come to acknowledge the inner pain and frustrations we have often covered up over the years. Even more so is the importance and need to recognize our powerlessness to achieve the good and to control our own existence. Yes, we are to act decisively and be responsible for our own choices, and in the same breath we need to be reminded that we are not the masters of our own fate.

These insights should not drive us to despair but make us ready to accept our creatureliness and our need to come to a new center, that center being a relationship with God. That relationship, that new center, is where our strivings are transformed into a new sense of trust. The trust is in the one who not only created us in love but also loved us all the way to the cross and beyond.

When we reach that new center and meet God, we soon discover that God does not necessarily promise neither to relieve us of our burden nor answer all our concerns. But God is the One who embraces us so that our burdens are filled with the Almighty's presence and become light for our journey ahead. And God is sufficient.

PRAYER: God, you are sufficient: sufficient for any need or problem that we must face. Thank you for not giving up on us and providing what we need. In the name of Jesus, we pray. Amen.

Day 309
Complaint Department

My God, my God, why have you abandoned me (Psalm 22:1)?

HOW MANY TIMES HAVE YOU, especially those of you with Parkinson's, ever felt this way? We are aware of the inevitable, but we hang onto the ledge of hope by our bare fingernails, hoping beyond hope that some miracle might occur, that some huge something would happen. Not only have I been there, but also all those who have struggled to keep the lights on rejoice because of the miracle, the miracle being a return to some degree of normalcy. The energy once expended on the struggle with despair and just making it through the day can now be expended on more positive things to continue the victory.

But too many times, in similar situations, we are happy for the moment; but after a while, we start our complaining again, much like the Hebrew people in the wilderness complaining about not enough to eat, not enough to drink, and that that Moses had brought them out of Egypt to die.

Boy, we are complainers aren't we? We pray for God's help, then when God does help, we continue moving down our list, treating God as some kind of "cosmic bellhop," waiting with bated breath eager to jump onto our next complaint. God answers, and we busy ourselves, looking for some other object to show our ingratitude.

We folk with PD wage a daily battle on two fronts: one with PD, and the other with life itself. There are times when I wonder how I will get through the day, what with poor balance and falling over this and that; and then I feel a little tap on my shoulders. Turning around, I see Jesus waving as if to say, "I'm the one that can help, follow me."

We find ourselves on a daily search for God and the Lord's presence and help. Where can God be found? Harry Emerson Fosdick, a renowned preacher of the last century wrote,

> It's easy to find God in heavenly places, but important to find God in hellish ones, as well: in a child's beaming eye but also a beggar's vacant stare, in peals of laughter and in wails of sorrow, in the bosom of our family and in the twilight of our loneliness.

> **PRAYER:** Father, help us to be able to see you in all things small and holy, things that go on to help restore our sanity but give us renewed hope in the future. Amen.

HELLO, GOD—IT'S ME AGAIN

Day 310
Always the Same

Jesus Christ is the same yesterday, today, and forever (Hebrews 13:8).

I WONDER, AT TIMES, IF WE are truly up to the task that lies ahead of us, myself included. How hard is it to remain committed as we traverse the straight and narrow in a world that laughs at those who profess a faith in God?

Not only is the way hard to find sometimes, it also seems that we are unable to conquer it. Everybody, with few exceptions, encounter these predicaments in their personal lives as they face and are overtaken by remnants of old wounds, lingering health battles, troubled relationships, unexpectedly unstable finances, and having come to the end of their ropes, stumble into the heart of darkness. There is a "desperate weariness" that engulfs them and causes the collapse of hope. But life does not have to be lived without the companionship of hope.

I like what G. K. Chesterton's sleuth, Father Brown, once said: "What we dread most is a maze with no center." When faced with life's most unyielding dilemma, the Bible shows us in totally unexpected passages how to get through. Page after page it is recorded how God makes what is impassable by the world's estimation, passable. We are led through the confusion of dead ends into the gracious center of the Lord's own purpose. So we are assured that the most daunting roadblock yields a passage to God; the most impenetrable maze has a center.

Sadly, there is nothing inevitable about the resolution of these apparent roadblocks in our lives. Did not Paul have a word on this? Paul wrote that he asked God to remove what came to be known as the "thorn in the flesh" on three occasions, but God refused. So we work hard on our particular thorns and hope for the grace without which we cannot get through, around, or beyond. We daily face the unpredictable joining of human struggle and God's holy purpose in experiences of what appears impassable, hopeless situations including those mentioned above and even Jesus' death on the cross. Someone once said as his mother was facing the dark night journey of senility, "My heart wants to pound the darkness until it bleeds daylight." As we travel the some-

412

times long and unlit maze of our spiritual journey, I hope we will remember the God who, with a cross, pounded the darkness of sin and death until it bled the daylight of Easter morn.

PRAYER: Father, we are grateful that you are not ever-changing and that we have to work extra hard to see what is on today's agenda to which we have to adapt. What a comfort it is to know of your non-changeableness, which is the same all the time for our deliverance and salvation. Amen.

———◇———

Day 311
Forgiven?

Take heart my son; your sins are forgiven (Matthew 9:2b).

IT IS AMAZING THE UPROAR that these four words cause every time Jesus utters them. The uproar is always from the same groups of people: the scribes and Pharisees. They accused him of blasphemy, but it was not because of the miracle that occurs. It is those four words that he utters each time he performs a miracle. Is it because of their jealousy that Jesus could perform miracles and they could not? Is it because of his rising popularity with the people? Is it because he was taking on the role of God, because after all only God could forgive sin? That is where the real rub is for those learned men of the scriptures. They believe that only God could forgive our sins. And in their eyes this carpenter from Nazareth certainly is not God. He is Mary's son.

Jesus said these words, "Your sins are forgiven," at a time when folk thought being sick, lame, blind, having leprosy, etc., was a direct result of some sin that they or a loved one had committed. He could have easily comforted those who were sick and the others that brought their dying and reminded them of that belief. But, he did more than that: he wanted to restore a normal life to all those with whom he dealt. Take heart. What wonderful words of comfort both to those in his day and those of us today, especially those of us with PD. With PD comes the feeling of having to keep everything moving. Get finished with one thing and then don't waste time, get up, and be about something else. Let's do it. "We're burning daylight." How much more does one with PD need to hear those words: take heart. For our hearts can be heavy with burdens, guilt, and anxiety such that "take heart" would bring so much comfort and free us from all the stuff that weighs us down.

Even today, we say that God forgives sins. But, strictly speaking, sins cannot be forgiven; only people can. It is not our sins that are forgiven; we are forgiven. For our sins are not something other than ourselves, they are not discrete entities that might be pardoned, leaving us untouched. *We* are forgiven. Not only what we *have done*, but what we *are*. And that is the best news in the world. It means that our whole person *dwells in a ceaseless flow of loving acceptance*. It might even enable us to forgive others.

PRAYER: Father, we thank you for your gift of Jesus Christ and for all that he brings with him: his ministry, his death, his resurrection, and his ascension. It all gives us the power to be free and take comfort in hearing you say, "Take heart." Hearing these words settles our hearts. Thank you. Amen.

Day 312
Selective Hearing

Eli realized that the Lord was calling Samuel. "Go lie down," Eli told Samuel. "When he calls you, say, 'Speak, Lord, I'm listening'" (1 Samuel 3:10).

E HEAR SELF-HELP AND SPIRITUAL guru after guru touting their latest new weight loss program or their product that catches all of the fat as you cook or that special berry they found in the jungles of the Amazon with the guarantee that you lose weight, and you do nothing except swallow them (can't get any easier than that). I surfed across one that promised answers to questions you might have about your life as well as you future—have you ever wondered how these psychics never win the lottery? There are as many infomercials as there are channels on TV that have the answer to all the problems of the world. Everything evil can be defeated for a mere $19.95 (plus shipping and handling). For that meager amount you will receive directly all that is needed to evaluate what you are doing wrong and how to come out victorious. They repeat all that you have to do; they only provide you with the tools to succeed.

One of the fundamental wrongs in this is that they advocate our *doing*; if it doesn't work or something goes wrong, it is because of us, our lack of doing. Their program is foolproof. One of our biggest challenges is to resist doing more; rather, we should be practicing the opposite: stillness. We need to be still long enough to evaluate our many activities: activities that drive us to distraction and sometimes exhaustion, but also give us meaning and fulfillment; activities that can give us our routines and our security, but can also block out the "voice" of correction and change. In stillness, we are not doing; we are listening.

We need to recognize that all our constant doing is not always fruitful. It is sometimes mindless. Sometimes it is driven. It can be self-protecting. It keeps us going, when in fact we should be still in order to evaluate and listen into the stillness.

Therefore, a far greater challenge is not to do but to be in the place where we can hear; not to hear the old and familiar, but to hear again what God thinks about our life's direction, priorities, and activities; and to hear again what our hearts are saying. This is often difficult for us. It is a struggle.

The challenge before us is to carefully listen to the movement of our spirit and the struggle that follows when we question: How do I follow Jesus all the way? This is the struggle when we kick in our "selective hearing" because we might not want to hear. This questioning, this groping, will provide an openness that could turn our lives around.

We must hear the new things! Not to hear them is to continue the headlong plunge into the incessant round of activities that are no longer a part of God's direction for our lives and which no longer express our creativity and our central concerns.

PRAYER: Most holy Father, help those of us who have ears to hear to listen. Enable us to live each day with unstopped ears, heeding only your direction and experiencing only your presence. Amen.

-----◈-----

Day 313
Wanting to See God

But you can't see my face, because no one can see me and live (Exodus 33:20).

I am saying that no one has seen the Father (John 6:46).

HOW MANY TIMES HAVE YOU heard people say, "Seeing is believing?" There are times when we wonder how people can think this way, and then there are times we to need to see for ourselves in order to believe. We often feel the way Thomas did. He had been riding a rollercoaster for the past few days. We have no record of what Thomas did or where he went—it is highly probable that he probably moved amid the horde of people. He probably was silently moving in and out amongst the shadows, trying not to draw attention to himself. He might have watched and listened as he saw his dream arrested, beaten, dying on a cross, and later his dead body taken down and laid in a borrowed tomb. Seeing that drama unfold before him, it was no wonder that when the women and the other disciples told Thomas that their master was not dead but alive and that they had even seen him, Thomas was skeptical and said that he would not believe unless he could put his fingers in the master's wounds. Seeing is believing.

There are echoes from the Old Testament of a character who, like Thomas, needed to see the holy one in order to make sure that he was who he said he was. God told the inquiring Moses (as Jesus later told his disciples) that no one could look upon God and live. Seeing is believing. You know the stories as they unfolded: God passed by Moses, who only had a glimpse of the glory of God, and Thomas acknowledged the risen savior without having to place his fingers in the wounds the resurrected Lord.

I would like to broaden the possibilities that other people have seen the holy One and not died.

In Claude-Michael Schonberg's beautiful musical, *Les Miserables*, he concluded that grand work with a line that almost escapes notice if one is not listening closely. He had the company singing the soul-searching words, "To love another person is to see the face of God." During the silence, wondering when it would end, afraid to breathe, I noticed that I had been crying. Those words hit home with a mighty blow. How many times had I asked to see the face of God and because of my excuses only to turn away from the homeless person pushing his grocery cart down the street in his tattered clothes; or the person wanting food; or one just asking for mercy? I turned from them, and by turning from them I turned from the face of God by not loving another person. With those words from the musical still echoing in my soul, I vowed to see God's face in all creatures. Even in my own. How about you?

> **PRAYER:** Blessed Father, we have the invitation to see you by loving another person, but we too often wear blinders and erect walls that prevent us from seeing you. Give us clarity of vision as we look for you in the least of your children. Amen.

Day 314
Grace, Grace, God's Grace

It is certainly true that God's kindness and the gift given through one person, Jesus Christ, has been showered on humanity (Romans 5:16).

*W*EBSTER'S DICTIONARY DEFINES GRACE AS: (a) an unmerited divine assistance given to a person for regeneration or sanctification; (b) a virtue from God; (c) archaic: mercy, pardon; and (d) a temporary exemption, pardon.

What do you think about when you consider the judgment of God? It certainly does not conjure up a lot of warm fuzzies, does it? Usually we think of loneliness, anger, hurt, fear, and suchlike. Yet, thinking about the judgment of God often strikes us with animal terror. Judgment day is "the day of wrath and the day of mourning." Yet the Psalmist longed for God's judgment, and so did Job. I believe it was Plato who said that his soul would run eagerly to its judgment. And Hegel believed that the guilty soul had a right to its punishment. It's clear, then, that however we dread it, the judgment of God is something we should desire, for we know that sooner or later we must be reconciled to truth and goodness, and only the wisdom and mercy of God can be trusted to do it for us.

Near the end of one of her greatest short stories, Flannery O'Connor describes how one of her characters feels "the action of mercy" covering him in acceptance and forgiveness. That's a great phrase, "the action of mercy." It reminds us that love is not only what God is but what God does, that the great words of faith are but an attempt to describe the many forms of love's action. When love sets itself against all that is unlovely, we call it *wrath*. When we call it *mercy*, we mean it is undeserved. And when we speak of *grace*, it is to make love's initiative. God has attributes. But all of those attributes are actions. We know the Lord by what God does.

> **PRAYER:** Father God, we ask and plead with you for mercy, for without it we are surely doomed. Give us this day enough grace to cover all our sins that your grace "shall lead us home." Amen.

Day 315
Love Is Where I Find You

And you shall love the Lord you God with all your heart, and with all your soul, and with all your strength. . . . you shall love your neighbor as yourself (Mark 12:30–31).

HERE CAN GOD BE FOUND? Where can we see our God face-to-face? We begin our looking where we assume is the surest place to find God: the church. But we come up empty-handed, or we just miss the Lord. We look for God in the world, where we might catch a glimpse of where the Almighty has been. We are reminded that even Moses, who asked God if he could see God face-to-face, was placed in the cleft of a rock; his face covered, Moses was permitted only to see the backside, the after-glow of God. Just that glimpse of God changed Moses' face, and it is recorded in the book of Exodus that his face shone so that they put a veil across it so the people would not be afraid. So where is God to be found?

The only true place we find God is where there is love. In love, the gates of our souls spring open, allowing us to breathe the new air of freedom that love brings. Our souls forget our own petty selves and launch us out of our rigid confines of narrowness and the things that make us prisoners of our own poverty and emptiness. In love, all the powers of our souls flow toward God, never wanting to leave the confines of the Lord's love, and we lose ourselves completely in God. Then we remember that the Lord has moved in the inmost center of our heart, closer to us than the breath of our own nostrils.

If we can manage to break out of our narrow circle of self when we love, leaving behind our restless agony of unanswered questions, when our blinded eyes no longer look far away from God's unapproachable brightness, we can allow the Lord to become the innermost center of our lives, where we can bury ourselves completely in the Father.

PRAYER: Incomprehensible God, be my life;
God of my faith, who leads me through the darkness, I enter into
your darkness.
God of my love, who turns your darkness into the sweetness I

crave;

God of my hope, that only you can fulfill;

God of my life, the life of eternal love, be my life and may I be
yours. Amen.

＊◇＊

Day 316

Here We Go Again

*I am forced to deal with a recurring problem. I begged the Lord three times
to take it away from me. But he told me: "My kindness is all you need" (2
Corinthians 12:8).*

ISN'T IT AMAZING HOW THE body compensates for loss? Someone becomes deaf and his powers of concentration increase. Someone loses her eyesight, and the sense of touch increases. It is as though all of the senses are heightened and cranked up another notch. By taking it up another notch, we come to the realization that when God takes something away, the Lord gives us something back.

That was one of the discoveries made by Paul. Some scholars claim that Paul was a sickly man with his thorn in the flesh. There are a plethora of interpretations as to what exactly Paul meant by this.

Whatever it was, this thorn in the flesh caused him great stress. He said he called upon God to remove it, but God denied him. Looking closely, we see that pain and agony were Paul's constant companions throughout the remainder of his life. Through it all, Paul realized that grace that is sufficient for all things and the strength that is made perfect in weakness.

I went to school with a blind man who tuned pianos. What made his ability to tune pianos to perfect pitch was that although he did not have the gift of sight he himself had the gift of perfect pitch with only his hearing. He could tune the pianos perfectly without any mechanical apparatus. That, in my opinion, was God's gift to him for the loss of his eyesight.

When someone gets a gift, a person with a handicap does not think much of it. It's just the way life has been all along. He or she did not think anything unusual about it. It was and is simply counted as a blessing from God.

God always gives compensation.

PRAYER: Gracious God, thank you for providing us with another gift when we lose one. Amen.

Day 317
A Mind Is a Terrible Thing to Waste

Don't become like the people of this world. Instead, change the way you think. Then you will always be able to determine what God really wants—what is good, pleasing, and perfect (Romans 12:2).

*I*BORROWED THE TITLE FROM A marketing blitz of several years ago from the African-American community, which was attempting to encourage the young people to accept the challenge to stay in school and use what they learned to break the cycle of wasting that with which they had been blessed. Paul knew this because he to tried to encourage his people to have the attitude of Christ in them. We should try to learn from Christ and Paul how to live life.

Psychology tells us today that right thinking can produce right behavior because the brain releases endorphins and other chemicals that bring on happy, positive feelings. When our minds are fixed on Christ, we know it will prompt us to lead lives of loving servants.

The flip side of that is: wrong thinking adversely affects our behavior. Chemicals are released when negative thinking occurs, but these chemicals lead one to depression and negative thinking. It is very easy to become a negative thinker. People who are always negative live small and shallow lives.

Paul had neither a medical nor a psychology degree, but he could observe when people were positive, when they were negative, and what both qualities brought with them. He was a witness to how Jesus Christ could change someone's life.

That's why I believe that Paul asked the Philippians to "fill me with joy by having the attitude and the same love. . . . Have the same attitude, or mind, that Christ Jesus had" (Phil 2:2, 5). Paul was a positive thinker. If the Philippians would concentrate on unity, then their disagreements would tend to disappear. Christ unities believers. When we focus on him and on the truth, our differences grow smaller and less significant.

As we experience the Holy Spirit, we who are new creatures in Christ's community are released from the bondage of negative thinking. This, however, requires cooperation. We show our willingness to enter more fully into partnership with Christ by disciplining our thinking. This is hard work, but it could be a great project for the living of our days and no mind or soul will be wasted.

PRAYER: God in heaven, grant us willingness to discipline our thinking. Create in us minds truly renewed by your Spirit, and encourage us as we experience the changes it brings. Amen.

Day 318
The Power of the Weak

The greatest among you will be your servant. All who exalt themselves will be humbled, and all who humble themselves will be exalted (Matthew 23:11–12).

DO YOU REMEMBER WHEN THE showdown was about to take place in the old Westerns? The good guy would always have to go and get his guns for the big showdown because he had chosen to put his colored past behind him; but no matter how hard he tried to conceal his past, someone would stumble upon his identity. He was always found out, and for the peace of the town he had to do go through with the showdown.

A frequent question asked just before the show down occurred at this point. When his past finally caught up with him, he was asked, "What are you going to do now?" All he wanted was to take care of this situation and return to the peaceful life to which he had grown accustomed. But the bad guys went too far, and he chose to confront them, even though the odds greatly favored the bad guys, who usually came as a gang.

Just as the good guy had to decide how to handle his problem, so God's choice as how to take care of the problem between God's self and human beings was in need of attention. God chose to leave the heavenly abode and enter into human history in complete weakness to form the center of what became the Christian faith.

The radical, divine choice is the choice to reveal glory, beauty, truth, peace, joy, and—most of all—love in and through the complete divestment of power. It is very hard, if not impossible, for us to grasp this divine mystery. We keep praying to the "almighty and powerful God." But all might and power are absent from the one who reveals Jesus saying, "When you see me, you see the Father." If we truly want to love God, we have to look at the man from Nazareth, whose life was wrapped in weakness. And this weakness opens for us the way to the heart of God.

PRAYER: Dear God, we don't understand your way of doing things sometimes; if we want to be great, we must be a servant; if we want to be strong we must be weak. That runs in opposition to the world's way of thinking. Help us to learn your way and live accordingly. Amen.

―――――◄○►―――――

Day 319
By Our Side

The king replied, "But look, I see four men. They're untied, walking in the middle of the fire, and unharmed. The fourth one looks like a son of the gods" (Daniel 3:25).

KING NEBUCHADNEZZAR'S ASTONISHED OBSERVATION eclipses the wrath that caused him to plunge Shadrach, Meshach, and Abednego into a fiery furnace when they refused to worship a 90-foot tall statue he had had erected. Most of us have our own fiery furnaces into which we have to walk. God chooses to come into the all-consuming furnace of our world to help us silently, unobtrusively, in the swaddled child of Bethlehem.

There are some very brave people who live with Parkinson's and those who take care of them. As God lends help to the world in little unseen ways, such as a child sleeping in a manger of hay or walking through one's particular fiery furnace, so the Lord helps the caregiver in whatever way he or she is needed.

A caretaker's job is made more complicated when the one with Parkinson's goes into depression. Yes, depression is a disease in itself, is no respecter of persons, and is a deadening of body and soul. It would be wise for the caretaker to be equipped to take time to explore the different dimensions of depression as it comes to play on Parkinson's. Between those two diseases there lies a whole octave of pain. The suffering of life may be tragic; but since Jesus has come into the world, it need never be mortal.

An earlier theologian described God as "our sweet hope." As we taste the sweetness and live by that hope within the mystery of the "already" and the "not yet," we discover the power to overcome depression and to live with God at our side. Our lives become more and more involved in Christ's work of helping those suffering from Parkinson's or whatever other disease with which they have to contend.

If there be any deliverance, it does not begin with caregivers and doctors coming to rescue us, but by arousal from the dead: to get our hardened hearts touched by God's goodness, however dimly perceived, and aroused to the possibilities still undreamt.

PRAYER: Sustain us, O God, through any darkness or fire we are walking through by your being there with us. Amen.

⸺◇⸺

Day 320
The Dream Is Alive

Where two or three have come together in my name, I am there among them (Matthew 18:20).

"THE DREAM THAT IS ALIVE." That is hard for a person with Parkinson's, or their caregivers, to easily swallow. They have watched as the progression of the disease has brought them lower and lower, as well as the dreams they dreamed not being realized.

Jesus was a dreamer. He had a dream that was incredible, and he shared it with his followers. Jesus never tried to whitewash what was happening. He held nothing back. There it was laid open and bare for all to see and respond. He talks about sinful things, what to do when things go wrong in your life, and things that would not matter for the amount of energy put forth for it not to. We all hated the subject because it often brings out the worst in us.

He entrusts his authority with us. We are the objects of his affection, the subjects of his dream. Wow! That's soul shaking. Whatever we bind—that means whatever we admonish or judge—whatever we loose—that means whatever we bless or forgive—these things will be done in heaven. But this is only true if we gather in his name. With him, we are somebodies with a purpose. We are Christ's representatives, his ambassadors, whether we are fighting off a tremor, getting up from a fall, or taking a brisk walk around our neighborhoods.

There is power when one has a relationship with God. But multiply that power by more believers, and you have a power that can literally turn your life—or the world—upside down.

PRAYER: Heavenly Father, forgive our timidity and our self-centeredness as we catch ourselves trying to keep you to ourselves. You are the God of all human beings. Help us all join together the power that you have given us to change and to bless, and let's just see how high our spirits can soar. In the precious name of Jesus, we pray. Amen.

Day 321
Pruning and Shaping

Every branch that bears no fruit, the Father takes away; and every branch that bears fruit, he prunes so that it may bear even more fruit (John 15:2).

WE HAVE JUST COMPLETED THE late winter task of pruning and cutting back the trees and bushes that had been left unattended because my parents were sick for over six years and could not do the task. There was so much underbrush: saw briars, honeysuckle, and English ivy running wild. The look is drastic, but the tree cutter has assured us that it was a necessary task for the health of the trees and bushes. He promised us that they would look fuller and better this spring and summer. In addition to remembering the story and discovering muscles I never knew I had, I took a two-day break to get re-energized. During this period of time, I recalled the story of Jesus regarding the need for pruning and shaping of the vine. I could relate a little to these words.

Jesus' words about pruning and shaping can help us put a new perspective on suffering, especially when we don't understand why it happens to some and not to others. These words help us to think about painful rejections, moments of loneliness, feelings of inner darkness and despair, and the lack of support and human affection we can recognize in our life.

We might say, "Well, we are doing some good here and there, and we should be grateful and content with the little good that we do accomplish." But that might be a false modesty and even a form of spiritual laziness. God calls us to more. God wants to prune us. A pruned vine does not look beautiful, but during harvest time it produces much fruit.

The great challenge is to continue to recognize God's pruning hand in our lives. Then we can avoid resentment and depression and become even more grateful that we are called to bear even more fruit than we thought we could. Suffering then becomes a true way of purification and allows us to rejoice in the fruits with deep gratitude and without pride.

PRAYER: Dear God, you know what's best for us, even if we might think it is too painful and sometimes unfair. Help us to allow your pruning of our lives so that our harvest can be plentiful for your kingdom. Amen.

Day 322
Searching for God

The sacrifice acceptable to God is a broken spirit, a broken and contrite heart.
O God, you will not despise (Psalm 51:17).

I DON'T KNOW ABOUT YOU but there has been one—maybe there have been two times—in which I had to look for something I misplaced: car keys, glasses, wallet, or something else . . . okay, maybe it was more than one or two times. All I know is that I spent a long time searching the same area repeatedly but to no avail. Ready to give up my search, I picked a book up for the seventh time and thumbed through a stack of papers for the ninety-ninth time; and, lo and behold, there was what I was looking for staring up at me as if to say, "You dummy, you should always 'look behind the milk.' I have been here all the time, right where you left me. You have just been looking in the wrong place." But I knew the area to look, because that was the place I always put it.

The fact is that we are always searching for the One who can give our souls rest. We are always trying to discover love and its fullness. Our souls are forever yearning and desiring for the complete truth that tells us that we have already been given a taste of God, God's love, and God's truth. Then the search is on.

We all know the truth, and it is that we can only look for something that we have, and to some degree have already found. How can we search for beauty and truth unless that beauty and truth are already known to us in the depths of our hearts? It seems that all of us human beings have deeper inner memories of the paradise that we have lost. For our purposes here, "innocence" is better than the word "paradise." We are innocent before we started feeling guilty; we were in the light before we entered the darkness; we were at home before we started to search for a home.

Deep in the recesses of our minds and hearts there lies hidden the treasure we seek. We know its preciousness, and we know that it holds the gift we most desire: a life stronger than death and filled with love.

PRAYER: Our dear heavenly Father, we have experienced your love and your provision, and we want it more fully. We search much as

Elijah did in the wind, where you were and are not. We search in the earthquake, as he did, but you are not there. We are about to throw up our hands in defeat, until we hear it: a whisper asking us what we are looking for, even as tears well up in our spirit; we recognize the voice, and we know we have been found by you. In the name of Jesus and out of inexpressible joy and gladdened hearts we pray. Amen.

<hr />

Day 323
Can't Stop Now

I sent messengers to tell them, "I'm working on an important project and can't get away. Why should the work stop while I leave to meet you" (Nehemiah 6:3)?

THERE ARE JEALOUS AND ENVIOUS people who try and sabotage anything positive that a person or a church attempts to do. They can be church-going people, even regular attenders who stay in the shadow so as to deny any involvement. If something arises that they don't agree with, these detractors come up with a plot and meet with like-minded folk who agree with what they are thinking and saying. They also seek the help of the weak-minded people who think that they think as they do. Their actions helped to choke the life out of more than one church, business, or helping ministry.

God promises constant companionship in our work but does not promise that the work will be easy: There will be stumbling blocks to overcome. We will have to contend with ruts, as well as the saboteurs. One of my churches had an expert in this field, to be sure. The local Head Start program's building burned and I was approached to see if they could rent some space in our building in order to continue their programs. An individual—one of the detractors—immediately rallied around himself those who agreed with him. A vote was taken; he lost. The vote passed. Then, this fine Christian person said to all who were there, "We need to tell the janitors to use extra disinfectant when they start. It's no telling what they will bring here every day."

As we continue doing God's work, we will experience tragic events. In these events, God does not remove the tragedy but fills each one with the divine presence. Along our journey, God will give us a task or two to complete.

There have and will always be people with the desire to keep the waters stirred. Nehemiah had an experience that illustrates this point. A group of his neighbors did not like the progress he and his fellow Israelites were making on rebuilding the walls around the city of Jerusalem and Temple. The neighbors were leery of those people who were repairing the walls of the old Temple. They thought up an idea to distract Nehemiah. They tried on more than one occasion to do things that would have caused him to take his eyes off God and stop the work.

Nehemiah's response was priceless. "Can't go with you guys (for coffee and donuts). I am too busy. I am busy with doing a great work for God."

That is the way it is with us, even today. The exception being that we have many more things to distract us and cause us to take our eyes off God. A group comes along and sees our positive great work, and it tries to change the positive work such that it is no longer positive. If we are doing a great work for God, then we can do anything. No matter how distracting others want to be toward us, we busy ourselves doing a great work for God. We are not capable of doing a great work without the help of God.

PRAYER: Father, give us the courage to be like Nehemiah and stand firm and not be distracted. Help us to pray for them that are distracting, and may we keep our eyes on you. Amen.

Day 324
Just One More Time

Jesus looked at them and said, "It's impossible for people to save themselves, but it's not impossible for God to save them. Everything is possible for God" (Mark 10:27).

Jesus astonished not only his disciples but us as well when he said, "You will be my witnesses to testify about me in Jerusalem, throughout Judea and Samaria, and to the ends of the earth" (Acts 1:8).

Go, make disciples of all nations (Matthew 28:19).

At a time when about 120 disciples had gathered together . . . (Acts 1:15).

TO THINK WITH ANY AMOUNT OF logic that Christ and his disciples could make a difference in their world and the generations to come is ludicrous. After all, there were only about one hundred and twenty of them who had the audacity to take Jesus at his word. Even though the task before them seemed quite overwhelming, this small band of followers was outnumbered but had the audacity to accept his call to "try" and was spilled onto the pages of history. Their "trying," in spite of a world that did not share their beliefs or lifestyle, actually turned the world upside down.

One hundred twenty uneducated Jews—except, perhaps, for "Dr." Luke to evangelize the world—is sheer lunacy. They went and tried and did. Remember the story when the disciples had fished all night, caught nothing, and were headed back to the shore empty-netted? As they were rowing on their return trip, tired, dirty, and forlorn, Jesus told them to *try* again. His words struck them as being sort of odd such that Peter and no one chose to debate or question him. When they recognized him, they were reminded that he was just a carpenter and they were professional fishermen. Have you ever wondered what might have happened if they had refused to "try" because they were already tired and frustrated from fishing all night and catching nothing? Nevertheless, they obeyed him and gave it another go. Once they did, a miracle happened. The count was 153 large fish, an outstanding day's haul by anyone's calculation. Their nets did not even tear, though they came close to breaking. It only took Jesus' quiet invitation to try on the other side of the boat and see.

It is easy for folk with PD to feel as if they can't do any more. We can hear Jesus always encouraging us to try. Just look at what took place in the lives of those we looked at earlier when they did try again. Though the odds seemed against them, they were tired, and they were far outnumbered by nonbelievers. They tried and literally turned the world upside down. When things seem hopeless—and sometimes they will—try and see what happens. If there is still doubt in your mind that what this Jesus is telling us is too good to be true, try and see what happens.

Too many times we refuse to say yes, refuse to try again, and lose out on a tremendous blessing from God that we might be able to share with others. When we disobey God, when we take our own way, we are not so much breaking God's law as we are breaking God's heart.

PRAYER: Dear God, our Father, we are very patient when it comes to fishing, be it for real fish or for men and women. We need to persevere more, wait on you, and follow your lead. Help us to be ever faithful. Amen.

Day 325
Don't Forget

I knew that you are a merciful and compassionate God, patient, and always ready to forgive and to reconsider your threats of destruction (Jonah 4:3).

JONAH MUST HAVE REALLY LOATHED THE people of Nineveh. First, he traveled in the opposite direction after God told him to go to there. After the big storm, Jonah's ordeal was not over, for God prepared the big fish for him—and not for Jonah's dinner!

Second, God told Jonah a second time to go to Nineveh and preach to all the people. Can't you just see Jonah walking toward Nineveh, muttering under his breath, kicking a can slowly along the way with his lower lip dragging the ground? He went through the city for one day of preaching, and the 120,000 people that lived there, as well as their king and the animals, responded to Jonah's call for them to turn to God.

Third, Jonah moved east of the city where he was made very comfortable and cool by the shade provided by the plant God caused to grow there. The next day, God caused a worm to attack the plant. Jonah was livid. He finally told God why he headed toward Tarshish rather than Nineveh, where God originally told him to go, as well as why he was so angry at the loss of the shade plant. "I knew that you are a merciful and compassionate God, patient, and always ready to forgive," pled Jonah. Now it was God's turn to remind Jonah of the divine mercy for the people of Nineveh.

Isn't this a comfort to know we don't have to worry about God being vengeful or unforgiving, that God does not hold a grudge, or that God is unloving but rather holds out mercy and hope to us? We need to be careful that we don't get so busy that we forget this key promise from our God.

PRAYER: Dear merciful God, we thank you that you always hold out for us your abundant mercy and hope, and it is always enough for all our sins. Amen.

———◆◇▸———

Day 326
All Things Are Made New

Whoever is a believer in Christ is a new creation (2 Corinthians 5:17).

MAKING ALL THINGS NEW. Why? Is there a need for things to be made new? What's wrong with the old? Jesus says he is making all things new. But that is the very essence of his message. Good news! He has established a new kingdom into which he introduces only new men and women, folk who are new creatures; a kingdom that is entered in a new and living way; a kingdom that has new laws, new customs, new riches, a new charter, and a new king.

Jesus came to take things that were old, dying, and dead and make them new. Is it any wonder then that those who are a part of this new kingdom must be new creatures? Christ does not merely change our outward behavior; he also changes our nature! He comes within us and plants a new person and a new nature such that each of us is a new creation created by God. A new you!

Those with Parkinson's disease look to this time with great anticipation. The chance to be new for us means that our old clumsy bodies and dying brain cells will give way to being made new. We have to take in faith the fact there will be a continual supply of grace within us that the new person begins to grow and become. We have a new love. We love Jesus Christ.

If we become new creatures in Christ, we have new purposes for our lives. How wondrous it is that Christ has come to change us. That day will come when God makes us—and everything God makes—new.

How about it? Have you been changed?

> PRAYER: We want to be remade, to become new creatures. But in the same breath, we must confess our anxiety in the change. We know you say that we should not worry about anything, but we know that to be a new creature we have to change things in our lives, things both new and old with which we are comfortable we have to give up. But you have taken care of that as well. So here we are, O God. Help us to be both willing and ready. In the name of the one who made it all possible, your Son, Jesus. Amen.

Day 327
God's Playtime

He will fill your mouth with laughter and your lips with happy shouting (Job 8:21).

THERE IS A SIGN IN Central Park, New York City, stating that the pond is to be used by sailboats only. My son and I soon became part of group of interested passersby. Some of us paused only briefly to watch the sailboats, whereas others, like us, lingered for a time, chatting with their owners. The sailboats were all different sizes, shapes, and colors, as were the people who owned them. Several times, a comment was made as to how the sailboats captured the personality of their owners: a woman with a colorful sail on her boat wore a matching cap, accompanied by an outgoing and colorful personality; an elderly man built himself or his grandson a yacht; and two young men were making some final adjustments to their schooner. There were also several interesting and funny stories that accompanied the making and sailing of the boats. The owners were of all ages, from an elderly woman and young granddaughter, to a young boy and his dad, a girl and boy who were alone, to the elderly who rounded out the group of would-be players. There were even some "land sailors" who stopped to watch and enjoy the beauty and gracefulness of the boats.

The scenario gave me pause to remember the makeshift boats I had helped fashion as a young boy, then racing them down the old "mill branch" near where we lived. We made our boats out of anything that would not sink. They certainly were not as sleek and sophisticated as those in Central Park.

Then I began to wonder whether such remembrances are pure nostalgia, or if there is always a child in us striving for expression, struggling to be born again and again as part of the divine playfulness of God; that God might be the only child left in the universe; and that the creation is not God's work, but is rather God's play. Maybe this is one of the reasons why Jesus said that to be a part of his kingdom you had to become as a child. I hope God is not the only child left in the universe. Wouldn't you love to fly a kite or sail a model sailboat in Central Park?

PRAYER: Our heavenly Father, thank you for childhood memories. Something jolts the past into the present and we relive those carefree days. Looking back now, we can see where you were working in our hearts and lives then as you do now. Thank you for both good and, yes, even the bad memories, knowing that you were with us through it all. And thank you for the fact that becoming a child is important to you and your kingdom. In the name of Jesus, we pray. Amen.

Day 328
Being Humbly Proud

So if I, your Lord and teacher, have washed your feet, you must one another's feet (John 13:14).

THAT WE NEED TO add to our daily time with God is a constant and honest self-appraisal. As matter of fact, I believe life requires it. In the eighth psalm, the writer reminds us that we are God's most important creation:

> You have made human beings a little lower than yourself. You have crowned them with glory and honor. You have made them rule what your hands have created. You have put everything under their control (Ps 8:5–6).

In contrast, the Gospel of John shows us that if we would follow Jesus' example, we must be willing to perform tasks that many folk feel are too beneath them to perform because they seem to be the most menial of services. To be truthful, the role of a servant does not seem particularly glamorous.

Do we have a tendency to slip ever so easily into an attitude of false pride when it comes to the menial tasks believers should be doing: I'm too educated, have too many riches, live in the right neighborhoods, etc.? These folk are too beneath me for me to work with or associate with, much less do, for them. Or, going to the other extreme of false humility, we fall into the pity-party mode: I can't do anything for anybody, or, I don't have the resources and gifts others have to do such tasks.

As children of God, we should keep our heads high and be unwilling to degrade our minds or bodies. As Jesus' followers, we also will search out opportunities for humble service.

> **PRAYER:** Father, give us this day joy in our relationship to you, but also the desire to serve the unappealing, unloving, and the unlovely. In the name and spirit of Christ, we pray. Amen.

⸺◁◇▷⸺

Day 329
Let God Be God!

Let all the earth fear the Lord. Let all who live in the world stand in awe of him (Psalm 33:8).

HAVE YOU EVER BEEN IN awe of anything? Have you ever had an experience in which the only response you could make was to say, "Ahh?" And, no, I'm talking about going to the doctor's office. Have you ever been caught up in one of those rare moments when you couldn't quite understand what was happening, yet you knew that something holy was going on, and all you could do was be still and bask in its glory?

I am afraid that we are experiencing those moments less and less. We have taken away the holiness of the moment and watering its majesty down by thinking of ourselves as being self-sufficient. After all, we are a sophisticated and intelligent people who can do it all ourselves; we can even explain the unexplainable and rob the moment of all its awe, wonder, and mystery. We believe as though it is necessary for us to water such moments down in order for us to understand them better in order to get a handle on them.

What have we done to God? We no longer live in a time when God is considered powerful, detached, and austere. Rather, we have chosen to go in an opposite direction. Now God is the "man upstairs." Some speak of the weakness of God, and some regard God as an accomplice; others a conversation partner; whereas others understand God to be a part of our understanding of who we are and what we are suppose to do with it all. Even though friendship with God is appropriate, familiarity is not. God is God for goodness' sake. There is a need for us to be put in our place and realize that we are mere mortal creatures and that God is much bigger—and different—for God is the creator God.

Someone left us with an appropriated, practical reminder that reflects an openness and compliance toward God. This person wrote, "Let God use you without consulting you." Doesn't that open up a whole new vista to experience? Here we speak of God's lordship and sovereignty, and as we are in Christ we experience God's friendship and love.

God is Lord. God is not a consultant whose advice we may take or leave. No, we are given the task to live in readiness and availability to do what God wants. And what is it the Lord wants us to do? We are to recover the awe and wonder of a holy God by honoring God and serving others. That is the purpose for which we were put here. That is our reason for living. Can we do it? Do we want to do it?

> PRAYER: Dear God, there is none like you in the entire universe. Help us to recapture the wonder of life with you high and lifted up. Amen.

Day 330
What Do We Get Out of It?

I'm leaving you peace. I'm giving you my peace. I give you the kind of peace not that the world gives. So don't be troubled or cowardly (John 14:27).

A FRIEND AND I WENT TO lunch one day. We were seated next to a table with three men having a wine and a heated conversation as they waited for their entrée to come. We could tell by their expressions and the tone of their voices that something serious had just happened.

"It's just too much; I can't do anymore," we overheard one of the men tell his colleagues. "The bottom line for them is profit, and it doesn't matter who or how they are affected. They just want to turn an acceptable profit."

"I hate it when they cut back because that always means we have to pick up the workload of those who were let go, plus do ours, and do it all without missing a beat." All three of them had been given the clients of those who had been let go, and they were expected to carry on with no complaints: heavier workload, same amount of time in which to accomplish it.

There are times in our spiritual lives when we get all caught up in life. Maybe it is some illness, some problems at work, and some problem in relationships; maybe it is the loss of a much-needed income, or one's life's dreams that are in jeopardy that put on the pressure on our daily living and displace our spiritual lives. Responsibilities pile up, and some of them are unpleasant; and we hate to face them, yet they have to be faced and dealt with. When any of us are told we have some dreaded disease, we immediately start thinking of what all has to be changed. Tough decisions have to be made. We feel insecurity arise in us. Though we don't want to admit it, we wonder if we can do it all. We are present, but even presence starts wearing us down. We need the calmness of God's spirit to dwell in us.

Then friends remind us that God was and is right there with us and that God has not left us at any time now, neither will God do so in the future. The Lord is right where we are and never abandons us. Never.

PRAYER: Dear God, thank you for reminding us of your constant presence and that you are always where we are never leaving us or forsaking us. Help us to say, "Jesus, this moment you are my peace." Amen.

◄◦►

Day 331
A Piece of Cake

Put on the armor that God supplies. In this way you can take a stand against the devil's strategies (Ephesians 6:11).

PUTTING ON CHRIST. NOW, THAT'S A small package with the power of a cluster of nuclear warheads. A large expectation for such weaklings we are. It's bigger than anything, and we are to tackle it. That being the case, we should begin by dressing up as a child of God in order that we might become a real son or daughter. Let's be clear here: This is not one job among many; neither is it a special exercise for special people. It is for all Christianity. The truth of the matter is that there is nothing else that Christianity offers.

We are to go the way of our Lord, and that way is different from the world's and is harder; yet in a peculiar way it is also easier. Christ says, "Give me *all*." It is not our material blessings, our work, or our time; he wants you and me. "It is not my purpose in coming to torment your natural self, but to kill it. No half-measures are any good. It is not my desire to trim a branch here and one there; the whole tree must come down. The whole natural self is what I want. All the desire you believe to be innocent as well as those skeletons in your closet—the ones you believe to be evil. I want the whole caboodle. Don't worry; I will not leave you empty-handed. I will replace your natural self that's been given up for a new self. As a matter of fact, it is myself, my own will to become yours."

Here is the kicker: it is both harder and easier than what we are all trying to do. Let me remind you that Christ himself describes the Christian way as very hard and sometimes as very easy. Remember his words: "Take up your cross"; in other words, it is like going to be beaten to death in a concentration camp. Then he adds his next words, saying, "My yoke is easy, and my burden is light." He means both.

PRAYER: Father, your Holy Spirit is needed by all of us, your children. Only with your help will we able to defeat the devil and live the abundant life offered to us by your Son. Amen.

Day 332
Poverty

Poverty and shame come to a person who ignores discipline, but whoever pays attention to constructive criticism will be honored (Proverbs 13:18).

PARKINSON'S DISEASE HAS A STRESS level all its own: when income and benefits are reduced to disability levels unless a person is wealthy, changes have to be made in one's lifestyle, of which "cutback" is the call word. Even those who made plans are affected because of the recent scandals, bankruptcies, foreclosures, and recession. Who is out there that knows how to fix it if they were allowed?

There are those who have it much worse than I do, such as the poor and homeless. Compared to their situations, I might as well be a millionaire. The poor are all around us. All we need are the eyes to see them. Jesus said, "The poor you will always have with you, but you will not always have me." Was he referring to those that have little or no money? Or could it be that Jesus meant to broaden the definition to include any persons who are not loved, not wanted, or not cared for, in other words, the rejected and forgotten?

This would certainly cause us to have to stretch our thinking. And if that is the case, Jesus is saying that people with real needs are not only in the Third World countries, but they are around us in the First World.

There is great poverty in the First World. All one has to do is walk the streets of any major city, and the evidence is abundantly clear of the plight many people find themselves in the richest nation on the earth; this adds to our shame. But if we put on the eyes of Christ, we would see that poverty goes far beyond not having money and food. The First World countries have other forms of poverty. The warning must be voiced that poverty cannot be thought of simply in physical terms; this list would include poverty of spirit, of relationships, of community. How about when worship and prayer is absent from one's life? Wouldn't that be spiritual poverty?

Yes, there is a danger that this can be an overgeneralization. It is common to note that even though Third World countries are poor materially, they are often richer in relationships and spirituality, whereas in the First World, we find an abundance of material blessings living in a poverty of community and piety.

The point is, knowing that poverty in all of its many and various forms is everywhere with us, there is more to do. There are opportunities and challenges to love, to care, and to give. Yet we remain blinded to what is immediately in front of us. Love is always sought for and love can always be given.

This is by no means to say that all need is the same. But both at home and in other parts of the world, we have opportunities to be God's servants of love and generosity.

> PRAYER: Father, we are in need of seeing through your eyes and love with your heart so as not to miss those in physical and spiritual need. Grant us the wisdom and courage to act with kindness and love with your grace fueling our hearts, minds, and souls, through Jesus Christ, in whose name we pray. Amen.

Day 333
Being Your True Self

David said to Saul, "I've never had any practice doing this." So David took all those things off (1 Samuel 17:39).

CONSIDER THE MARVEL OF HUMAN nature. God has put marvelous life within us. Yet, somehow in our generation, human nature is a problem and a burden and a battle. We have become so encrusted with the weaponry of the world that we are losing our own true selves. The more we lose our true selves, the more frantic we are to discover ourselves. As a result, we live for trivia, and then we say we have an identity crisis. The solution to this is simple: our identity ultimately is found only by making God the center of our lives.

We have flattened people today. We have said, "You are a handicap: you have Parkinson's disease." "You are too old." "You are too young." "You are a man." "You are a woman." "You are not qualified." "You are too qualified." Even the church is guilty: we squeeze people into molds.

Jesus told us to use a child because a child sees everything as plain reality. A child sees something when we do not. Be your own true self. Affirm your own authenticity. Some of us have one talent. Others have more than one. It is far better to be a contented, one-talent person than a neurotic, defeated one-talent person trying to act like a five-talent person. As you go about being your own true self, be careful not to take your signals from the estimates of other people, because their estimates are colored by their own misgivings. David was told to go out "there," that he couldn't defeat Goliath. David's response? "I go in the name of the Lord." And that perspective fully released all the limited talents he had, and he won. He knew his strengths were useful, and he knew his weaknesses were defeating; but he found his central perspective in God.

Don't try to live up to other people's expectations. They have their own battles. They might be projecting their heartaches on you. Be your true self. Your true self is a unique gift that God has given you. Listen to the insights from the Holy Spirit. We are rich, and the Holy Spirit seeks to give us insights and a new and different way of doing things that the world might call foolhardy, such as forgiveness and reconciliation. David shows us how to get back on track. We need more people who, like David, can confront life in the name of the Lord. Then God is able to blend our faults and our imperfections in God's providence and bless us. We emerge with our scars, our disappointments, our heartaches, as well as our glories, our joys, and our triumphs, and we know something about who we are and discover we are content before God.

Then we can turn to life and suffer with those who weep and rejoice with those who laugh. God sent Jesus Christ to die for us; so be your true self, which then allows you to be the redeemed of Christ in the midst of a struggling world. And your Goliath will be defeated.

> **PRAYER:** Our heavenly Father, we stand before another Goliath. Unfortunately, he is of our own making. We have tried to comply with the way the world functions rather than the way you function. Forgive us for thinking that we could face our Goliaths in the world's armor. Call us to trust and have faith in you. Like David, help us to have the determination to confront our Goliaths; because we are on your side, the victory is ours. In the name of the one who won the victory for us, even Jesus Christ, our Lord, we pray. Amen.

Day 334
Feel the Tug

Therefore be not anxious, . . . "What shall we eat?" or, "What shall we drink?" or, "What shall we wear?" But seek first his kingdom and his righteousness, and all these things shall be yours as well (Matthew 6:31–33).

ODAY'S SOCIETY TUGS AT US IN SO many ways. We allow things to command our time and attention: job, children, spouse, home duties, friendships, and relationships. This being pulled away from our inner life allows our outer life to gain strength and control. Even when we try to rest and maybe even go on vacation, we are pulled outward. We make sure that we can be reached, have plenty of books to read, maybe some on tape or eBook. We try to catch up on what we have left undone until now. Time and space for looking inward are hard to find, much less create in our busy world. We need that inner sanctum because that is where we can hear God's voice and direction more clearly. But the difficulty increases because of being pulled outward.

We need to be careful and not restrict our definition of the outward pull to our being busy doing things. The truth of the matter, most times, is that it is but a small part. The major part is the thinking and planning, the worrying, fretting, and the restless seeking of our inner life.

We need to see that not only when we are busy doing things, it is also that we become restless when there is nothing on our immediate horizon. Being in that situation, we have a tendency to be less focused on the inward and more on the outward pull in our lives, even when we have the opportunity to enter the inner sanctuary for refreshment and renewal.

The challenge is more than learning to pace ourselves, set limits, and say "no" without being overwhelmed with guilt. It is not our being able to have more time for ourselves because we are in control. It is a matter of creatively using time for ourselves. Even though such time should be enlightening in the area of our relationships, it should, more importantly, involve inner renewal. The reason for that need is because we deplete our inner resources much more quickly than we realize. Equally important, it should also involve gaining new directions and insights, lest we constantly make the same mistakes and fail to establish patterns that facilitate growth.

A professor was returning home when he came upon a little boy holding the end of a string that reached upward to the sky. The fog was getting thicker and thicker that day in the moor and you could not see the kite. The professor asked the little boy, "What are you doing?"

"I am flying my kite," replied the little boy.

"But you can't see it. How do you know it's up there?" inquired the professor. The little boy said, "Because I can feel the tug of it."

Later one of the professor's students asked him how he could believe in a God he could not see, feel, or touch. The professor said in the words of that young boy flying his unseen kite, "Because I can feel the tug of it." Do you feel the tug of your inner life?

> **PRAYER:** Father, help us to take time with you in the quietness of your holiness. May we be able to say we feel the tug of it in our spirit. Amen.

Day 335
The Danger of Looking Back

Run for your lives! Don't look behind you. . . . Lot's wife looked back and turned into a column of salt (Genesis 19:7, 26).

SOMEONE GAVE SOME GOOD ADVICE when he said, "Don't look back; they be may be gaining on you." As any long-distance runner will tell you, if you look back often to see where your opponents are, it will cost you valuable time and possibly the race. Another drawback to looking back is that some people want to be like the disciples on the Mount of Transfiguration. In the terrific excitement of being with Jesus, Elijah, and Moses, the disciples wanted to build a place for them to stay because the mountainside had been transformed into a holy place. They were certain that these were going to be the best of days.

Not so! Looking back, in order to live what one thinks were the "good ol' days" turns out not to be so. If those who are stuck in the past venture out on occasion but their hearts are stuck in the past, it is risky living, looking back; it causes one's life to grow stale and stagnant.

The danger of looking back can clearly be seen in the escape of Lot and his family before Sodom and Gomorrah's destruction. There was no mistaking the urgency for Lot and his family's leaving: "Run for your life!" the messenger of God cried out. Then the warning: *Don't look back!* Lot and his family escaped from the destruction.

We do not know why, but Lot's wife did not heed the instruction. Perhaps she was curious and wanted to see what was happening; but whatever she was thinking, she was immediately turned into a pillar of salt immediately. But more than likely, that was where her heart was, and she had to turn and look back.

Let's end this devotion on a positive note. Looking back is good and healthy when we look back in order to learn from the past, both the good and the bad. So leave behind what might be hindering you from a life rich with God.

> **PRAYER:** Help us keep our eyes on you and only you, O God. Keep us from looking back when you warn us not to, but to look back in order to grow and not make the same mistakes as before. In Jesus' name, we pray. Amen.

Day 336
Forgiven, Me?

Be kind to each other, sympathetic, forgiving each other as God has forgiven you through Christ (Ephesians 4:32).

OST OF US WHO CLAIM TO BE believers would have no problem with the statement, "I believe in the forgiveness of sin." After all, those who regularly recite the Apostles' Creed speak those words every time they gather for worship. Even though the words are spoken repeatedly, the truth is that forgiveness is not as easy as it might sound. Like a piece of silver that loses its luster if it is not polished regularly, so it is with our forgiveness of sin.

It is hard for me to realize that I can be forgiven by God. When I think about my sins—those which I have categorized as large, and even the small ones that only God and I know about—God is willing to throw even those as far as to the east is to the west, sins both of omission and commission, to remember them no more. What a tremendous promise the Lord gives to us. Not only does God forgive our sins, God remembers them no more and takes us back into the fold.

We believe that our sins, no matter how numerous or bad they are, if confessed to God will be forgiven by God. Jesus expanded that wonderful and disarming truth by saying that unless we forgive other people their sins against us, God will not forgive our sins. He emphasizes the importance of this act by including it in the model prayer (Matt 6:12–14). These words emphatically stated by our Lord leave no room for compromise or exception. He does not give us the choice of not to forgive others their sins depending on the situation, the circumstance, or whether they are too harsh for us to see and know. No, the sins of others are ours to forgive, and we are to forgive them no matter how distasteful, ugly, mean, or horrific. Forgive them all their shortcomings and failures—*all*. If, for some reason, it is not within us to do, we need not expect any of our own sins to be forgiven.

It reminds me of a *Peanuts* cartoon, in which the single frame pictures Lucy and Charlie Brown standing and facing each other. Charlie Brown says to Lucy, "When we were singing 'Jesus Loves Me,' I thought, Jesus loves me. Little ol' me." That says it all, doesn't it?

> **PRAYER:** Father, we are sad to bring our sins before you because we feel ashamed and we believe that we have let you down by making ourselves feel as though we were outcasts. But there you stand with arms opened wide to embrace us and forgive us of whatever sin(s) we have committed. Help us to forgive others their sins toward us so that our sins might also be forgiven. Amen.

Day 337
Trouble Is Our Middle Name

But a person is born to trouble as surely as sparks fly upward from a fire (Job 5:7).

DON'T YOU REALLY RECEIVE A blessing when you see children leading in worship? I am not sure that I have the reason why, but when those young voices start to sing I am on the edge of the pew. Why do they have that affect on us? Is it the simplicity of the moment? Could it be that it is the fear they will lose this simplicity and innocence too soon? If you want to see a church smiling, even the grumps, just watch scowls turn into smiles as the children lead in worship. Sometimes it becomes almost comical. There are usually a couple of them moving to the music, while others sing at the top of their voices. On one occasion, the children were singing a hymn and one little boy's voice carried over everyone else's. He was singing very enthusiastically, but he made a slight alteration to the words of the hymn "Nobody Knows the Trouble I've Seen." With great gusto, his words came out, "Nobody knows the trouble I've *been.*"

Undoubtedly most of us could say the same thing about ourselves. Nobody knows the trouble I've been to my family, to other people, to myself, and most of all to God. At one time or another we have all said things that really were offensive to others or have done stupid things that hurt others. Worst of all, though, in so many ways we have failed to be what God intended for us to be, and in that sense, at least, we do know the trouble we have been.

The faith that centers on Jesus Christ is not at fault, but the followers of Jesus, across the centuries, often have given Christianity a bad name. Thanks be to God, however, we can be forgiven; we can hope in God; we can lead worthy Christian lives.

PRAYER: Father, you are the God of all beginnings. Help us by showing us that we repent of our wrongdoings as we confess our sins and seek to lead lives worthy of followers of Jesus Christ. Amen.

Day 338
It's All a Balancing Act

A time to rend, and a time to sew; a time to keep silence, and a time to speak (Ecclesiastes 3:7). . . .

I AM ALWAYS MESMERIZED WHEN I see people perform a high-wire act. Their concentration is so intense, especially if they are working without a net underneath to catch them in case of a misstep and they lose their balance and fall. The tricks they do are incredible and the audience usually finds itself on the edge of its seats. A huge sigh escapes from the audience at the conclusion of their act. Their balance has to be just right, or the results can be deadly.

Many times people speak of a great balancing act when handling several things. The Christian life is also a balancing act. We emphasize one thing; then ignoring it, we name something else. For example, how many times have you named prayer but failed to work, to serve but fail to be renewed inwardly.

So it is easy to see how holding together spiritual disciplines, priorities, and emphases remains one of our biggest challenges. This is not achieved easily. We are often excited about the particular challenges and often are around only to see them thrown away again. During the times that we are involved, we neglect the disciplines that could have been moderately useful.

People with Parkinson's are masters at their balancing acts. We have to balance our medications. We also have to balance what part(s) of our bodies are working and those that are not. Then once that is determined, we have to engage in prioritizing our findings.

Participating in this, it is easy to recognize that balance and harmony have to be wrestled from our ever-present tendency to find singular solutions and easy answers. There is a need to cease majoring on the minors. We soon realize that it is impossible for us to obtain that balance and harmony in our lives on our own. This balancing act, this harmony, forms the basis of our spiritual life, which we are unable to do alone. Even with others that we add to the list, such as giving and receiving, suffering and healing, prayer and work, these are all part of the mosaic of the inner life. It is when these seeming opposites all blend together to operate in our lives that the quest for balance has begun.

> **PRAYER**: Father of all that is good and holy, we come today seeking your help to keep our balance among people who are staggering totally off balance, causing many around them to lose their balance and fall. Grant to us steady feet and hands and voices tuned to bring the beautiful harmonies that can only come when we are balanced. Amen.

Day 339
God's Challenging Spirit

I wish that all the Lord's people were prophets and that the Lord would put his spirit on them (Numbers 11:29).

THE OLD TESTAMENT PROPHETS PROVIDE A rich challenge to faith and action. At times, their emphasis falls on Israel's sin and the call to repentance. At other times, their message affirms God's faithfulness and the need to trust the Lord. The prophets could be both harbingers of doom and heralds of hope. It did not bother them to bring either; they knew the importance of being faithful to God's direction.

In all instances, however, they did their work in the conviction that they were instruments of God's challenging Spirit. Whatever limitations they might experience were overcome by the power of God's indwelling presence.

The prophets spoke, not out of their own competence, but from a conviction that burned within their bones. They were constrained to declare the word of the Lord. They accomplished this not simply by the spoken word but by acting it out in the example their lives provided for the living of their days.

We, too, might have a sense of inadequacy. We might have no skills at writing letters, preaching sermons, or teaching Sunday school lessons. We need to remember that God's Spirit is not bound by our limitations. God's Spirit can do the unexpected. Another person put it his way, "Not everyone can sing or play an instrument, but everyone can clap."

PRAYER: Gracious God, when we are inclined to limit the work of your Spirit to a select group of prominent people, remind us that you often work in unexpected ways through unassuming individuals. Amen.

Day 340
The Art of Goofing Off

He renews my soul (Psalm 23:3).

WE ALL NEED MORE TIME TO BE quiet with God and to rest in the Lord. There was a elderly man at my church in Goldsboro, North Carolina, who was a frequent visitor to the church office. One day he stopped by, and I was getting ready to go to another meeting when he said, "Preacher, you need to learn how to loaf; you know, to goof off. You are way too busy. I'll tell you what I'll do. I am gong to get some time on your calendar from your secretary and I will come by here, pick you up, and will teach you how this is done."

"We are into Lent which does not leave very much time to do anything extra," said I. My excuses, however, had little affect on his determination to be teacher and for me to be pupil.

"Well," he said, "you leave that up to me and your secretary." I had forgotten the conversation until three weeks later, when my secretary announced his arrival. As soon as he opened the door, he said, "Let the goofing off begin. You ready preacher?" I was somewhat reluctant to go but went anyway. I'll stay about thirty minutes and then excuse myself, I thought.

We drove to his house, and he led me to the back. The landscaping looked like something out of a magazine. Everything was manicured and lent itself to a spirit of tranquility down to the water trickling over the wall into a pool full of fish and lily pads. He excused himself and said he would return. I was stretched out and listening to Telemann's oboe concertos, and then the voice of Diana Krall came over the speakers. I must have dozed off, because I jumped when he cleared his throat. I opened my eyes to see him standing there with plates of cookies and milk. "Preacher," he said, "you are wound too tight. You just need to kick back." We spent the afternoon just sitting, talking, and eating as he gave me a crash course in herbs.

Night was closing in on us as we drove back to the church. I must confess that I was more relaxed and felt less stressed and depressed. Several of the psalms came to mind with a deeper perspective. I most definitely will start goofing off more.

PRAYER: Thank you, Father, for leading us to green pastures and by peaceful waters so we can better hear what you would have us hear. Amen.

―――――◄ ○ ►―――――

Day 341
What a Motley Crew

Come, follow me! I will teach you to catch people instead of fish. They immediately left their nets and followed him (Mark 1:17–18).

WHEN THESE OMINOUS WORDS ARE spoken, we realize that what we had suspected was true: Jesus' agenda was to build his kingdom with ordinary people. Can you feel the urgency in Jesus' invitation? We probably would tell him that we needed to think about it before giving an answer. Facing the unknown future, we all have to think about it. In this case, the disciples had to deal with their readiness for the kingdom's world. Jesus was asking them to give up the only job they knew anything about, the livelihood on which their families depended. Here, the pull of the world stood in sharp contrast to the pull of God's kingdom.

Jesus asks us the same question. We have to answer the question with a question when asked to follow Jesus. We have to wrestle with our usefulness or lack thereof. How would we be useful to God with our disability? Surely God knows what effect it is going to have on us. Thinking on this, I realized one of the very great insights of the Christian faith: namely, Jesus calls us to our representative capacity. You balk at the idea, but can you imagine anything more unpromising than those humble fishermen at their boats on the shores of Galilee? They were an unpromising lot: in education, culture, refinement, and financial resources. In those shortcomings by which we measure worth in our age, they had little. But in the most daring and arduous venture ever on earth, the Master looked at the men and said, "Come with me, and I will make you fishers of men." Oh, what a great call that was! They had an equal audacity: they responded, and they were spilled into history.

Did they automatically come up to the standards of society? No, they didn't. One example was that after Jesus had discoursed on the parables of riches, Peter called him aside and said, "Master, we've left all and followed you. What do we get?" Before we get too tough on Peter, we all need to take a good long, hard look in the mirror: the reflection we see is also guilty of the same question asked about our lives. What do we get out of it all? And the Master replies: "You become children of the Most High." The great reward in following me is not in *getting*; it is *being*. It is not in *having*. It is in *becoming*.

PRAYER: Dear Father, you have called us all to be fishers of people. But in order to catch them, we must know where they are and who they are. Give us your wisdom to go where they are and give them what they need to become fishers of people, too. Amen.

Day 342
The Inward Journey?

Behold I stand at the door and knock; if any one hears my voice and opens the door, I will come in and eat with him and he with me (Revelation 3:20).

ACCORDING TO THE SCRIPTURES, we are created in God's image; and through that image, we find that the kingdom of God is not atop some distant high mountain, on some desert island, or locked away in some dusty back room of a monastery. The kingdom of God can actually be found inside us. This leads us to the fact that if we cannot find the kingdom or meet God within the very depths of our being, our chances of meeting the Lord outside ourselves is lessened a great deal. When the Russian cosmonaut Gagarin returned from his spaceflight in 1961, he made his memorable statement that he never saw God in heaven. Someone recorded the response of one of the priests in Moscow who said, "If you have not seen him on earth, you will never see him in the heavens."

The same can be applied about prayer. If we cannot make a connection with God from within on the small world we call self, the chances are very slight that even if we meet God face to face, we will not recognize the Lord.

I like the advice of St. John Chrysostom, who wrote, "Find the door of your heart; you will discover it is the door to the kingdom of God." So we must turn inward, not outward. Be clear, I am speaking of a difference between what we usually think when someone says we must go inward. I am not speaking of going inward to become introspective or going inward as one would in psychoanalysis. It is not an inward journey into our own inwardness. It is a journey *through* our own selves, a journey through in order to emerge from the deepest level of ourselves into the place where the Lord is, the point at which God can meet us.

PRAYER: Dear Father, we are humbled to know that we are created in your image, but what is just as soul-shaking is that your kingdom is within us and that you have chosen to be with us rather than off in some distant universe. Make us ready for our inward journey, where we will meet you. Amen.

Day 343
How Many Handles?

But I tell you this: Love your enemies, and pray for those who persecute you (Matthew 5:44).

I CAME IN ON A TELEVISION talk show, the topic of which was the mistreatment of children at school by other students. While at school, they were made fun of and called names. Other classmates had lashed out at them, bullied them, and stole their lunch money. It is a growing problem with children today. One ten-year-old girl, when asked why she mistreated her classmates, responded, "All the popular girls in the school do it, and I want to belong to that group."

The question was then asked by the discussion leader, "How would you feel if someone did that to you? Would you like it? Would it make you feel good about yourself?" The entire group joined in unison with a resounding "No." It is such a growing problem that the President of the United States has included $1.4 million in his budget to go toward trying to eradicate the growing problem of bullying in the schools.

This didn't happen overnight and we can argue when the practice of bullying other people raised its ugly head for the first time. That is not for us to ponder today. Let it suffice that the children have had some of the very best teachers: the adults. They have watched as adults said and did hurtful things toward other people. The have witnessed them strike out because of some half-truth or offense, someone spread a rumor, or some act of cruelty and blatant hostility was enacted. They act as though they have never heard the scripture, "'Vengeance is *mine*,' says the Lord." If someone has to respond, no one is any better than Jesus, because he showed us how we should respond to such action(s). Even he had such terrible things aimed his way from invectives to attempted stoning, all because he claimed (and rightly so) that he was one with the Father!

Epictetus, the Stoic, tells us in one of his aphorisms that everything has two handles: by one you can carry an item, and by the other you can't. He gives an example of what he means:

Suppose that your brother has offended you and that you must decide how

you are going to deal with the offense. You may carry it by that handle of offense, but that is foolish and it won't work. If you brood on the offense, your
hostility will deepen and your estrangement will increase.

But there is another handle. You might say, "He has offended me, but he is
my brother," and carry it by the handle of brotherly affection. In this lies the
best hope for reconciliation. What difficulty are you carrying? Are you holding it by the right handle?

> **PRAYER:** Gracious Father, make our heart over to be one that car-
> ries the happenings of life by the right handle, the one of brotherly
> love and mercy. Amen.

Day 344
Hearing the Voice of Grace

My soul is in anguish. How long, O Lord, how long (Psalm 6:3)?

HOW MANY TIMES HAVE WE echoed these words of the psalmist? If
we haven't spoken them, at least we have felt them. If the truth were
known, more of us than not know exactly what the psalmist is experiencing?

Just because a person attends church or professes devotion to God doesn't
mean that he or she is free from trials, temptations, pain, or anguish. Rather,
for many, the church is the place one can go to receive a healthy dose of shame.
But the purpose of the church is to be two-sided. One goes to church to find
healing for shame. That is what the church is meant to be: a place where we
obtain the courage to feel some healthy shame and the grace to be healed of
it.

When one comes to church carrying a load of unhealthy shame, that person's burden becomes heavier, and the unhealthy shame blocks the spiritual

arteries and keeps grace at bay, unable to gain access. To some, the word grace that is hard sounds more like judgment than amazing grace. Then the sweet hour of prayer becomes a sour hour of judgment and condemnation.

We can hear three voices in the church. Each of them, in its own way, feeds the shame we carry with us to church—

> *THE VOICE OF DUTY*: God required me to be perfect before I could be acceptable to the Lord.
> *THE VOICE OF FAILURE*: I was flawed, worse than imperfect, and all in all a totally unacceptable human being.
> *THE VOICE OF GRACE*: By the grace of God, I could be forgiven for all my failures.

PRAYER: Heavenly Father, stop our ears against the world's beckoning attempts to answer questions that only you can. Unstop our ears to hear your promise to be with us and never to leave us. Thank you, O God. Amen.

Day 345
Masks

How horrible it will be for you, scribes and Pharisees! You hypocrites! You are like whitewashed graves that look beautiful on the outside but on the inside are full of dead people's bones and every kind of impurity (Matthew 23:27).

LET'S ALL BE HONEST: We know that each of us, at one time or another, wears a mask. Some of us wear masks all day long. We might wear one in public and another in private. That is what hypocrite literally means: "mask-wearer and actor," and we all have a bit of it in us.

The Greeks and the Chinese took up wearing masks in their dramas to get across the emotions they were portraying. The actors would simply hold a mask up to their face so the audience could understand the emotion being displayed by the actors. They were then confined to that mask until the particular part was finished.

Although we aren't actors and actresses, we still can be found wearing masks and trying to hide our true identities like a masked super hero from a DC or Marvel comic. The comic strip heroes find themselves in turmoil as to whether to remain masked or free themselves from the mask in order to live as normally as they desire. One part wants a different life, whereas another part refuses to change. So they—and we—exist on a seesaw.

There is a key somewhere to the puzzle of us. If we only venture forth from the deep recesses in which that frantic, frightened child dwells and crouch in a safe place to watch the dawn, we could see the child. The child is hungry, longing, and very pale from lack of sunlight. Liberate the child who wants to become an adult.

Liberation is not "easy." It takes a single moment of dying. The child wants to be liberated. The child must either try to become free, or it must ask, even cry out, for help. What we must do is to draw closer to one another. Healing occurs when it is least sought or anticipated. It occurs, in fact, when one has forgotten about being healed and has simply entered into the human condition more fully to be with others and, if possible, serve them.

No matter how tight the mask you place on your face, you can't hide the child's eyes.

> **PRAYER:** Gracious Father, we are reluctant to begin removing the many masks we wear out of fear of what we might find. The most tragic mask we wear is the one that attempts to conceal the child in us. We recall Jesus' words that no one can get into the kingdom without first becoming as a child. So we place our masks on your altar as our eyes sparkle with recognition of your love and power. In the name of Jesus, your child, we pray. Amen.

Day 346
Inner Elegance

That according to the riches of his glory he may grant you to be strengthened with might through his Spirit in the inner man (Ephesians 3:16).

I CAME INTO THE HOUSE after a walk, and the television was on. It was a talk show on one of the cable channels, was made up of several people participating in a panel discussion. I was half watching and listening to the discussion, when one of the panel members spoke of "inner elegance." It stopped me in my tracks. This phrase has fed my soul each time I recall it. It caused me to think about the difference between outer and inner elegance.

For those with PD, inner elegance may be easier to obtain because of the residue that it leaves. Some of the things that PDers have might not be considered elegant by the world. The presence of tremors, garbled speech, dragging one of one's legs, and even drooling run in conflict with outward elegance. Outer elegance is not difficult to find. It can be found on any street whether it is New York City, Los Angeles, Washington, DC, or Lenoir, NOrth Carolina. The storefronts along the streets are decorated with many things that could be considered and seen as outward elegance. There are many beautiful people who exemplify outward elegance, as well. But if our desire is to go deeper, beyond the outer elegance, we move deeper in the Spirit. But the refinement of spirit, sensitivity of soul, a care for moral and spiritual excellence, is harder to find. You can't buy it at Macy's or Saks Fifth Avenue or Rodeo Drive, Belks, or Greenwich Avenue, for that matter.

Philosophers known as the Stoics used to say that as there is clothing for the body, so there is raiment for the soul, ways of doing and being that suit us, that are fitting. They didn't call this clothing "inner elegance," but that's what they meant. It has been a happy experience to think of those among my friends who, whatever their outer vesture, possess an elegance of Spirit.

PRAYER: Our Father, oh how we need your power to help us rid ourselves of the tacky, the profane, the filth, and the obscene conditions we allow our beings to get. Help us to rid our lives of all that is negative and ugly. Then we can live a refined life of inner elegance. Amen.

—◦—

Day 347
Too Fast to Fast?

When you fast, stop looking sad like hypocrites. They put on sad faces to make it obvious that they're fasting. I can guarantee this truth: That will be their only reward (Matthew 6:16).

LATELY, I HAVE BEEN THINKING about the Bible's occasional emphasis on fasting. Fasting has been practiced as a way to purify oneself. Jesus often fasted. You remember how when after John had baptized him in the Jordan River, Jesus was immediately driven out into the desert wilderness where he fasted for an inordinately long time. I was just thinking of the story about Jesus coming down the mountain with Peter, James, and John. They were met by some of the other disciples, who had been unsuccessfully trying to rid a youngster of an unclean spirit. Try as they might, they just couldn't get rid of it. They turned the matter over to Jesus, who said a few choice words, and instantly, the unclean spirit made tracks. "Why couldn't we do that?" they whined. "Because," Jesus said, "such work demands much fasting and prayer."

Fasting has had a long and highly respected position in our religious history. But today with our fast food and overabundant supermarket shelves—do we really need 75 different kinds of breakfast cereal?—we often forget how important fasting can be. If you've been to your doctor recently for a colonoscopy or lower G.I. series, you've probably had to fast the day before. To aid and abet this forced fast, you might have had to drink that wonderful concoction affectionately known as an X-Prep cocktail. Mmm-mmm!

In all the major religions of the world, including Christianity, fasting is seen as a means of purging the body of impurities. Orthodox Jews and Roman

Catholics fast prior to high holy days. This is connected with St. Paul's reminder that our bodies are temples of the Holy Spirit. It is also reflective of the action Jesus took to clear the moneychangers out of the Temple courtyards in order to reinstate the sanctity and purity of that holy worship site.

Thus, fasting helps to purify and prepare us to receive spiritual nourishment. You might recall Jesus' words to his disciples who found him talking to a Samaritan woman at Jacob's Well: "I have food to eat that you do not know about. . . . My food is to do the will of him who sent me and to complete his work (John 4:32, 34). Here, then, is the supreme example of genuine fasting. Fasting isn't so much about not eating as it is to do the work God has given you to do. And you will never grow hungry from that.

> PRAYER: We praise you, O God, for giving us opportunities to truly fast, when we are able to have our souls emptied to receive your spiritual nourishment. Keep us one and all as your children, Lord, and bless us this day and always with the food of your love. In Jesus' name, we pray. Amen.

Day 348
A Lovely Ambition

He told them, "Be satisfied with your pay, and never use threats" (Luke 3:14).

ISN'T IT SAD THAT WE NO longer have heroes? Instead of heroes, we have celebrities. And although the celebrities need a healthy dose of "ambition," such resolve needs to be kept in proper perspective. We live in a world that sees nothing wrong with paying professional athletes millions of dollars, whereas people are surrounded by dilapidated buildings, drug dealers, homeless, and hundreds and thousands of people living in poverty. There is no way any argument that they have is sufficient; they have no legitimate reason. Besides, when you obtain the size of their contracts they receive today, it appears that there might be a little greed and selfishness in it. But this mindset is not unique to professional sports. What about musicians, actors, etc.—oh, and don't let me miss recognizing the garbage we call politicians. Don't the scriptures say something about that (see Luke 10:7)?

Once we have set our sights on who is going to be our celebrity hero, we immediately begin looking and finding their feet of clay. For if our heroes have feet of clay, then the standard will not set too high for us. Thus the bar has been lowered, so everyone passes and is the same. Heaven forbid that anyone come in second or third or worse. We are all successful because no one fails and everything is graded on a curve. Everybody's the same. Every boy and girl is equal.

Stephen Spender wrote a poem called "I Think Continually of Those Who Were Truly Great." One of the things that made them great was that they had what Spender called a lovely ambition. Now, much ambition is not lovely; it is vague and selfish, arrogant, and ruthlessly competitive.

Yet it need not be. It would not be if our ambition were simply to make the most of our gifts and to do our work as well as we could. Someone once asked Hemingway why he wrote one of his short stories thirty-seven times. He replied, "To get the words right."

Now that was a lovely ambition gloriously fulfilled. It reminds us that the best competition is with oneself.

PRAYER: Gracious Father instill in us the fact that we don't always have to win and that a healthy competition with oneself will certainly be a blessing. But most of all, we thank you that we do not have to be perfect in all things for you to accept us and bring us into your loving embrace. Amen.

Day 349
A Melody in the Heart

For great is the Lord, and greatly to be praised (Psalm 96:3).

INDIVIDUAL VOCAL SOLOISTS WORK hard to develop their craft. There are vocal exercises, techniques, placement, and music to learn. Their gift is prepared and made ready for the big night with the orchestra. Now, here is the question: When they perform with an orchestra, do they lose their voice or do they find their voice in an orchestra?

To begin with, I believe that to make good music, you have to submit to the discipline of it. The discipline is not only that in learning the part, but it is also in learning the placement of the voice among the other instruments. One must lose the voice so that one can find a richer, deeper voice with the larger group. What does all that mean? It means that we belong to each other, and our gifts are essential. We are each important, and when we come together to play, we make music that we can't make without each other, each person losing his or her voice only to discover it better, fuller, and more harmonious together.

We are sung into existence by divine melody. Then we find our own little tune amidst the whole. Much to many people's dismay, Jesus is not the composer. During his sojourn on earth, he was constantly pointing us beyond himself to God. Jesus was not the composer. He was the one who heard the tune, caught the melody, and shared it with us.

Do you know what one thing is the sorrow of God? What if the sorrow of God is that we don't hear? Then because when the Lord teaches us to play out of love for us and we still don't play it, that is the sorrow of God.

There is music playing. Why aren't you dancing? Jesus said, "We have piped for you, and you have not danced." Could he have been talking about his life and ministry? I believe he is the music. Someone—I think it was Harry Emerson Fosdick—once said, "The life of Christ was lived like music that was meant to be played over and over again." Jesus heard the music. He took over the music. He took it so into his self that he became the music.

So take this music into yourself, adding your voice to the sacred choir of the ages.

PRAYER: Dear Father, the music you created us to play is so beautiful when we play together in unity. Yet sometimes we try it on our own without any preparation, and we ruin the richness of the music you wrote for us. Thank you, O God, for the music and help us to play it in tune. Amen.

Day 350
Is This Where You Want Me to Be?

"Go home to your family, and tell them how much God has done for you" (Luke 8:39).

HOW HARD IS IT FOR YOU TO share with your family? I know some families that talk about anything, anytime, anywhere. Don't you? And then there are those families who talk only on the rarest of occasions. Even when something good happens, such as a promotion, acceptance of a school or work project, or some type of an award or positive recognition, it might be shared only in passing. In my family history, it has been easy to talk with one another, but the depth that we took a conversation depended on the topic.

There was an incident in the life of Jesus that I find very interesting. Jesus and his disciples had just passed through a violent storm and arrived in the region of the Gerasenes. Before he could get out of the boat and recover his land legs, a man who wore no clothes approached him. He lived among the graves and had been so terribly tormented by demons that every attempt to restrain him failed. Jesus asked the demon his name, and he was told that his name was "Legion," which means anywhere from 3,000 to 6,000. Jesus cast out the demon, sending it into a herd of swine that caused them to run over a cliff to their deaths. The man was clothed in his right mind when the townspeople came to see what was happening.

When Jesus started to get back into the boat for his return trip, the restored man asked Jesus if he could go with him. Jesus gave the man some of what appears to be some rather odd instructions. Jesus told the man to return to his home and tell what God had done for him. The story ends there. We don't know what happened following Jesus' instructions to the man. It is left up to our imaginations.

We do know that this man had been cut off from other human beings. Often, he had been bound in chains, which suggests the fear he stirred in the hearts of those who came near. For such an outcast, returning home to those who knew him would be difficult, to say the least. The easier choice for him would have been to go with Jesus. Yet Jesus himself sent him back to be a witness to his neighbors.

"Return to your home," Jesus said. That was the mission field Jesus chose for this man. It is often the primary mission he chooses for us, too. For most of us, the greatest way we can witness for our Lord is daily to demonstrate to those around us the power Christ has to transform lives. The home front might sometimes be a difficult testing ground of our faith; nevertheless, we are still challenged to bloom where we are planted.

PRAYER: Father God, help us with our Legion, however it manifests itself. We want our actions, and the way we live, to show that you are in control rather than we ourselves, or our Legion. In the name of the one who healed the man of his Legion. Amen.

Day 351
How Amazing Is Grace?

The grace of the Lord Jesus be with you (1 Corinthians 16:23).

G. CAMPBELL MORGAN, ONE OF England's great preachers of days gone by, tells of visiting a parishioner who informed him that she was about to be evicted from her dwelling place because she was unable to pay the rent.

The following Sunday, Dr. Morgan appealed to his congregation on her behalf, and the congregation generously responded. Early Monday morning, he hurried to the woman's residence. Eagerly, he went to her home and knocked on the door. Again he knocked, and again, and yet again, all to no avail. Finally, he turned and walked sadly away.

When he returned, he began asking about her from people who knew her. He learned that the woman had been at home all the time, but fearing it was the landlord coming to collect the rent, she could not bring herself to open the door. She had expected a stern demand to be made of her, when all the while a bountiful gift was being freely offered.

When you think about it, knowing the yearnings on our hearts and how often we fail, it is a miracle in itself that there is any grace at all. Christ is present in our lives, not because of imperial decrees or special merit on our part, but because he offers himself in love and without reservation to all who will receive him. I thank God that he looked beyond our faults and saw our needs, but we have to answer the door. Remember, Jesus promises that if we respond to his knock on the door, he will come in and eat with us. Now, that's grace.

> **PRAYER:** Cast away all fear from our lives and give us the courage to accept and to respond to your call, O God. In the precious name of Jesus, we pray. Amen.

Day 352
The Good Guys Always Win?

You prepare a banquet before me as my enemies watch (Psalm 23:5).

THIS IS A BOLD TITLE when surrounded by so much suffering. Suffering: something every human being experiences sometime in his or her life, either personally or through a friend or loved one. No one is immune from it. We agree that this is one of the few places that PD patients, their caregivers, and those who don't know the first thing about PD have in common. We all might find it in the attempted living of a normal live by one with PD and their caregivers. We might see it in the life of a child, who, with tears streaming down his face, buries his beloved dog. We might see it in the faces of brothers and sisters who are being taken away from their parents, separated into foster homes because of their parents' drug habit. We might see it in a home where the children are huddled, holding each other, hoping and praying that they will not follow their mother, who is being abused by a drunken father. We might see it by the casket of a thirteen-year-old teen that was accidentally shot and killed by his younger brother. We might find it by the bedside of a dying man who has fought the good fight but now is just tired and ready to go home. We might see it in a teen that is afraid to go to school following a shooting spree at her school. All of these and many more attest to the fact that not one of us is free from some type of suffering. The hand of suffering, in some fashion or form, touches all of us.

It is hoped that these words cannot only help us gain perspective but can also help us put a new perspective on *suffering*, especially when we don't understand why it happens to some and not to others. Why does it happen to the innocent and the good people and leave the riff-raff, those who deliberately hurt and cause suffering for others, pass through life unscathed?

I heard Dr. Gardner C. Taylor, a black minister friend of mine, say at my oldest son's memorial service, "Many of you are here for answers, but I am here to tell you that the Bible comes up short when trying to answer our questions of 'why'; but it is filled with 'hows' and sometimes we have to plod along in the 'hows' until God sees fit to give us the answers to 'why.'"

And although I was showing some symptoms of PD at that time, when Dr.

Taylor said those words, immediately the tremor in my right hand stopped, and I felt a peace come over me that I had not experienced in some time. There was peace in my troubled heart. I also realized that even though it appears that the bad guys have won, in the end they are already defeated.

PRAYER: Our gracious Father, help us to wait patiently on your timing. We want the answers to many questions but you, O God, know the best time for us to know. Thank you for the presence your Spirit that helps us through it all. Amen.

Day 353
Facing Up

Jesus started to indicate to his disciples that he must go to Jerusalem and suffer greatly there (Matthew 16:21).

AS JESUS ENTERS VICTORIOUSLY INTO Jerusalem to do his Father's will, he set his face like flint because he knew there would be numerous times over the next few days in which he would be tempted to call upon the legion of angels that were waiting for him to give them the word so they would deliver him from the hands of his captors. I feel sure that during his scourging, the cat-o'-nine-tails tearing through his flesh with each strike to his body and the fatigue that gripped his body from the loss of blood and the lack of sleep and water increased his temptation to call the angels to come and take all the pain, the agony, the and abandonment him from him. But it was not the Father's will for him not to experience the pain and agony to save himself. There would be many opportunities for him to be tried, tested, and tempted to call down those legions of angels.

Nevertheless, Jesus faces his suffering and death directly, and he asks his disciples to face theirs the same way. He does not predict an easy future for himself or his disciples. Jesus went against the human inclination to avoid suffering and death, and his followers realized it was better to face up to the truth. Suffering and death were partners along the narrow road of Jesus. He does not glorify them, or call them beautiful, good, or something to be desired. Jesus does not call for heroism or suicidal self-sacrifice. No. Jesus invites us to look at the reality of our existence and reveals this harsh reality as the way to new life. *The core message of Jesus is that joy and peace can never be reached by bypassing suffering and death, but only by going right through them.*

We can deny the reality of life or we can face it. If we choose to face it, we can do so with the eyes of Jesus; we discover that where we least expect it, something is hidden that holds a promise stronger than death itself. Jesus lived his life in the trust that God's love is stronger than death and that death therefore does not have the last word.

PRAYER: Gracious and loving Father, thank you for allowing us to be a part of the victory you have won over Satan and his forces at an extremely high cost: the death of your Son. Through his sacrifice, all of our sins and shortcomings are forgiven, never to be remembered anymore. Thank you, Father. Amen.

Day 354
You Have Failed. Now What?

Love never comes to an end (1 Corinthians 13:8).

WHEN YOU FAIL AT SOMETHING, what do you do? Dealing with failure challenges us as few other experiences can. Coming to grips with our inadequacies or with desperate situations beyond our control calls for a maturity rarely observed.

Furthermore, failure touches all of life, whether we talk of burned toast, the loss of a job, a failed test, or a failed marriage. No person enjoys immunity from the specter of failure.

Yet when we encounter God in a personal relationship, we suddenly discover a power that transcends our failure! The love of God can conquer our frustrations and pave the way for a life of victory.

Thus, when we are surrounded by failure, we need to turn to the love of God. In so doing, we escape the despair and the hopelessness of defeat. Instead, we take our place in the procession of triumphant believers who have received from Christ Jesus forgiveness, healing, and new hope.

PRAYER: Father, we are grateful that when we fail, it does not mean that we are failures. We know that it would be true if it were not for your sending Jesus into the world to save us from ourselves. Thank you, Father. Amen.

Day 355
It's Cool in the Furnace

If our God, whom we honor, can save us from a blazing furnace and from your power, he will, Your Majesty. But if he doesn't, you should know, Your Majesty, we'll never honor your gods or worship the gold statue that you set up (Daniel 3:17-18).

SOMETIMES, ALL IT TAKES IS A memory of some event in our nation's history that calls forth from us a positive response. Some examples that come to my mind are Joshua's "As for me and my house. . . ." Or how about Henry V of England's "Those happy few, . . ." (speaking of those who fought the French against huge odds and won the battle at Angincourt) or

Patrick Henry's "Don't Tread on Me?" How about, "Remember the Alamo?" These rallying cries steel the will and raise the courage an individual or a nation.

That's what Daniel did. He took a number of floating stories that told of the endurance and ultimate triumph of some of Israel's heroes and set them down in the time of King Nebuchadnezzar, mainly because there arose a ruler who was worse even than Nebuchadnezzar himself. His name was Antiochus Epiphanes ("God Manifest"), or Epimanes, ("the mad"), and he threatened to destroy Israel's faith and culture. The question arose, "How could they stand up to such a man who dealt Israel with unrestrained madness and unspeakable cruelty?" He desecrated their Temple and mocked their God. How were they to stand up to him? The writer of Daniel told them the story of Shadrach, Meshach, and Abednego, who were bound and thrown into a burning fiery furnace heated seven times hotter than usual. The soldiers who threw them into the fiery furnace were consumed because of the heat.

But to the surprise of Nebuchadnezzar, the writer of Daniel records the king said, "But look, I see four men. They're untied, walking in the middle of the fire, and unharmed. The fourth one looks like the son of the gods" (Daniel 3:25).

The king went to the door of the furnace and ordered Shadrach, Meshach, and Abednego to come out of the furnace. They emerged unharmed; the hair on their heads was not singed, and their clothes did not smell of smoke. The Most High God, because of their faithfulness, had delivered them.

It would be advantageous for those of us who have Parkinson's to recall, from time to time, a better day, a positive time in our personal history, such as Israel remembering the characters of their past, their heroes of older days who steeled the will and raised their—and our—courage. Memory steadied the nerves; and good days of the past, called to mind, will be our rallying cry that will furnish hope for our victory to come.

PRAYER: Our God, provider of everything that is good and holy, we come today thanking you for your faithfulness. You promise you will neither leave us nor forsake us in all our fiery furnaces. For this we give you thanks through Jesus Christ, in whose name we pray. Amen.

Day 356
A Fool or a Clown?

Let no one deceive himself. If any one among you thinks that he is wise in this age, let him become a fool that he may become wise (1 Corinthians 3:18).

HERE AGAIN IS ONE OF God's kingdom reversals, which tells us that there are definitely two ways to deal with life when you have Parkinson's. You can wrap yourself up in a pity blanket, confined and limited to live in a kind of bird-unable-to-soar-like-eagles state. You can be so content there—after all you are warm, have a roof over your head, and all the birdseed and water you want—and can take it so seriously that it becomes a burden to you and robs you of your ability to enjoy the life you like. Or, you can accept what you have but continue to live life.

Remember: *You have Parkinson's; Parkinson's does not have you.*

There are definitely two ways at looking at life and the world: through the eyes of the kingdom and through the eyes of the secular world. The world says you have to have power and finish first to be successful. The kingdom says that the last shall be first and to be great you must be a servant. Jesus illustrated the point one time by taking a small child into his embrace and saying, "If you wish to be part the kingdom, you must become as this fragile, harmless, child with all the child-like attributes that come with it." It is total faith, total trust, total dependence, and total obedience to the parent of us all: God himself. Even Paul uses this methodology of opposites when he writes to the church at Corinth. "If you think you are wise," he says, "then you must become a fool for Christ." Another word for fool could be court jester or clown.

Think for a moment of the responsibilities of the court jester. He was the sole person in the court that could be present in the royal family's meetings; he could make light of the king's actions, and by doing so he could have a deep impact on the royal family's decisions and even their demeanor. A good court jester could keep the atmosphere of the court light and jovial.

When believers become fools or clowns for Christ and his kingdom, they come realize that they can fail and not be failures; they can lose and not be losers.

The jester oftentimes would be used to pass along important messages, such as this one from modern day clowns for Christ, "For God so loved the world that he gave his only begotten Son, that whoever believes in him shall have everlasting life."

> PRAYER: In you and in you alone, O God, are we adequate for the task of servanthood that you have given to each of us. Help more of us to see the advantages of being your clowns for Christ's sake. Amen.

------- ◇ -------

Day 357
Just the Thought of You

How precious are your thoughts of me, O God (Psalm 139:17).

PARKINSON'S DISEASE HAS A TENDENCY TO amplify our emotions. When everyone else is crying, you aren't. You are able to weep or celebrate on the inside, but it is difficult to bring those emotions out. What an emotional tidal wave I experienced recently. I came across some of my oldest son, Thomas', favorite baseball cards and some of my younger son, John Arthur's, favorite Pokémon cards. Suddenly, I was jolted back in time. There were my boys, asleep in their Teenage Mutant Ninja Turtle pajamas, their little chests rising and falling to the pulse of their dreams. I remember as if it were today the feeling that I had as I looked into their bedroom: Blessed. I was truly blessed.

That started my pondering this thing we call "blessing." What are blessings? What do you have to do to obtain one? I thought some blessings are fickle at best. For example, just when parents think you are here to stay, you pack your bags and move.

When we are in the midst of blessings, we think it's our due that the blessing will last forever. The next thing you know, we are sitting helpless beside a hospital bed; all we're left with is a name on a wall, a baseball or Pokémon card in a drawer, and memories that haunt our sleep. The memories make my heart swell, and my soul silently whispers words of gratitude to God for two wonderful blessings. Sometimes, we come to gratitude too late. It's only after a blessing passes on that we realize what we had. For Thomas, it was after his death; for John Arthur, it is his moving out and living on his own.

I was jolted back into realty amid the symphony of their snores. We folk who have PD need to let the leaves of our blessed lives fall to the ground, and if we were wise, we would gather them in a pile and keep them safe, lest the winds of forgetfulness blow them away.

We need to fill our mental scrapbook with these blessings and the precious memories that will warm us over and be a blessing in itself.

PRAYER: Gracious Lord, thank you for the memories. Many times, they are all we have and are what sustain us and give us hope. Amen.

Day 358
The Gift of Encouragement

How precious are your thoughts of me, O God (Psalm 139:17).

HERE'S A WORD FOR YOU and me: *Encouragement.* When it's given to you, you immediately become the woman or man of steel ready to take on all the bad guys.

Still, have you ever embarked on a project that seemed at first to be rather overwhelming? Perhaps you began experiencing panic or anxiety. As you were contemplating jumping out of the first story window, out of the blue someone comes up to you and gives you an encouraging word; even Satan could be included. Jesus' ministry kind of started out that way, but Jesus' encouragement came from God himself.

One way in which Paul gave his encouragement, as we see in the letter to the church at Colossae, was by referring to the Christians as "saints" and "faithful." He was also appreciative for their faith, hope, and love.

Encouragement is hard isn't it? But to find fault, now, that's a different story. I know people who, if Jesus himself offered up something, would find something wrong with it. How many good ideas have died from a lack of encouragement? What about the lack of encouragement causing one to put away a worthy idea? Someone shared these words with me when I was coaching baseball: "We can't all perform, but we can all clap."

As adults, we have many opportunities to encourage children. If you need a place in which encouragement is greatly needed, coach a kid's baseball team. Some of the kids have never held a bat or had anyone to take the time to explain and show them the fundamentals of the game. A small boy said to his dad, "Let's go and throw the baseball. I'll throw, and you say 'wonderful!'" In the deep recesses of our soul, we all long for that kind affirmation, though we aren't quite bold enough to ask for it.

PRAYER: Father, help us not to be so ready with our faultfinding. Forgive us for the times we have been quiet and shouldn't have been. Show us clearly the opportunities for sincere compliments to help others and ourselves along. Amen.

Day 359
The Valley of Decision

I have offered you life or death, blessings or curses. Choose life (Deuteronomy 30:19).

"DECISIONS! DECISIONS! DECISIONS!" SOMEONE said to me, expressing that weary feeling that often comes from having to make one decision after another. But after all, that is the way life is. It is inevitable that we are always deciding. We must decide whether or not to get up, and when; whether to go to work or stay at home; and all day long, the need for deciding relentlessly continues. The ultimate, daily question for a person with Parkinson's is, "What will I have to deal with physically today?" What is going to work and what is not, and once deciding what will work, the next step is to move in the strength of God's spirit all day long.

Of course, some decisions are more important than others. Some things get decided as a matter of habit, just willy-nilly. Most of us manage to make enough of the right decisions to get through the day. But then there are momentous decisions to make: decisions that are at the base of life, decisions that will pretty much determine the course, decisions that will pretty much determine the direction and course of many other decisions,

The text reminds us that there is a level on which such decision-making is critical to the very nature of life itself. Once we make this kind of decision, we are set on one track or another. Such decisions are vital. What we decide determines the very fabric of life—even the directions life will take. The truth is that sometimes we are choosing between life and death and good and evil. Our inner self is set on course. We become what we have chosen to be.

Sooner or later, no matter how valiantly we strive to hide or cover-up, we will be revealed for what we truly are at heart. God already knows. We usually know. Others might be fooled for a time, but then, in a moment of stress, under duress, when we are caught off guard, what we are in the inner person suddenly breaks through, and there we are, like the legendary emperor revealed as having no clothes.

Decisions. Yet they are automatic, there are the extraordinary ones, the soul-making ones that are not to be taken lightly. We are reminded that such decision-making is both an awesome responsibility and good news. We can decide to obey or not to obey. We can have a part in deciding who and what we are.

The time for such deciding is always at hand. So long as the choice can still be made, we are extended life's greatest gift. We must never forget that we have so cast the die of our character that choices are gone. The time for deciding is always now, while we can.

> **PRAYER:** There are so many decisions to be made daily, O God, and just as many other voices vying for our attention. They distract us, and we can't handle them alone. So we come asking for your help in making the right decisions for our salvation and the building up of one another and your church. Amen.

⸻◄◦►⸻

Day 360
Poor Little Ol' Me

I have forgotten what happiness is. I said I've lost my strength to live, and my hope is in the Lord. Remember my suffering and my aimless wandering. My soul continues to remember theses things, and is so discouraged (Lamentations 3:17–20).

ONE THING THAT ENTERS THE life of every person with Parkinson's—or the caregiver, for that matter—at one time or the other is a pity party. How long folk remain at the party depends how entrenched they are in the goings on of the event. We can get very tired of the daily disobedience of our bodies and the daily revolts we have to combat with our uninvited guest, for it seems to know our weakest points. Now there is a huge difference between those who have battle fatigue from the fight they engage in during all of their waking hours and those with minor altercations and complain as if no one has experienced what they have.

You know the people that I'm talking about: people who complain habitually to the point that you can no longer say they have a complaint; it is impossible to separate them from their complaining. Those people, who dwell in self-pity, wouldn't know who they were, were it not for their complaining. Their self-pity is not their problem; it is the solution. Others would have no identity if they were separated from their self-pity, their sense of grievance, or their despair. One knows how they will answer any question they are asked and how they will react to anything they have to face. Their pity party has made them unhappily predictable.

It is not a mater of mere thought, will, or emotion. It is not a matter of "mere" anything. It is the whole personality, the full character, and the total being. It is such a part of us that we think it, feel it, and are it.

We can think ourselves into a new way of acting, or we can act ourselves into a new way of thinking. We must allow life to engage the whole person.

If we wanted to push this we could say that it has been an exercise of prayer all along. We might not call it that, but when we seek to understand our difficulties through minds informed by the truth of faith, hearts moved by love, and a conscience quickened by Christian awareness, then whatever we call it, it is the deepest kind of prayer. Prayer is not something we do when we have stopped thinking; prayer is a way of thinking. It is not something we do to avoid the hard choices we have to make, but a way of discovering the wisest choice and finding the strength to make it. Faith is not something separate or different from how we think decide, or act. It informs our choices, directs our decisions, and strengthens our resolve. In other words, it determines the living out of our days.

We can begin to shape and reshape it in this very moment. It begins, as Jesus put it, in faith as tiny as a grain of mustard seed.

PRAYER: Holy God, we want to live lives free of pity parties, but we know that that is almost impossible. So show us your presence that we do not fall into despair. Amen.

Day 361
The Resurrection Conspiracy

After he said this, he breathed on the disciples and said, "Receive the Holy Spirit" (John 20:22).

HERE IS HOW IT ALL BEGAN: Jesus said to his band of unlikely followers, "Receive the Holy Spirit." With that, there was let loose upon the world a new community that was dedicated to the life-giving Spirit of the living Christ and destined to carry the good news the ends of the earth. What happened next, and what maters most today, is infiltration of the gospel into human society, which began as an inner circle of active believers in the crucified and risen Lord who penetrates the world with his life-changing Spirit.

The word *conspiracy* has come to have sinister implications, whereas in a quotation from the wise and witty E. B. White (from a pastoral letter of the Rector of St. Michael's, Fred Hill), he wrote about his wife, Katharine, following her death:

> Katharine was a member of the resurrection conspiracy, the company of those who plant seeds of hope under dark skies of grief or oppression, going about their living and dying until, no one knows how, when, or where, the tender Easter shoots appear, and a piece of creation is healed.

Conspiracy is an exact description of what happened when the Lord commissioned his disciples that evening. The word originally meant "a group of people so closely bound that they literally breathed together." In was in that little room in Jerusalem where the frightened disciples were holed up that the Master's breath created the "resurrection conspiracy." It is great to know in this day of the negative aspects of conspiracy that there is a conspiracy of the followers of the risen. There was, and in spite of the evil plotted against them, they went on witnessing to the resurrection, a conspiracy of love and hope in a community of cruelty and despair. Their activity is summed up in the book of Acts; "With great power, the apostles gave their testimony to the resurrection of the Lord Jesus, and great grace was upon them all" (Acts 4:33).

In a time when life was held cheaply, they cared for the weak and helpless. In a time when fear lay like a cloud over all from the emperors in their palaces to the slaves in the slums, they demonstrated the love that casts out fear. In a time when death was the final terror, they spoke confidently of resurrection.

It is not into a religious club that you and I have been baptized but rather a community that is nourished and empowered by the Spirit of Christ. It is not our own strength that we are going to fight on the side of life and love, but in his.

May that same Spirit breathe on each of us, and on all of us as a family of Christ, joined in this conspiracy of love and life eternal.

PRAYER: Come, Spirit of Christ, and visit each one of us, strengthening us inwardly that as individuals and as a community we may reflect your grace, your life, your love, and your hope. Amen.

⊸◦⊱

Day 362
So Tired; Can't Move

He gives strength to those who grow tired and increases the strength of those who are weak (Isaiah 40:29).

I FEEL WORN SOMEHOW. I can't seem to do one thing that will renew my energies. Someone asked me the other day if I was too tired to run and too afraid to rest. Yes, and I'm confused and ashamed about that, as well as about my seeming inability to take charge of my own life.

Things use to be different; or were they? Once upon time, I had ambition, goals, initiative, drive, dreams, and hope. But lately, they seem to have gone on a sabbatical. It is as if I have resigned myself to the fact that the future is already determined and there is no need to try to make it different. Now my days are spent being "reactive" rather than "proactive." Have I settled for a cut-rate life? Am I truly content riding the waves and not experiencing life to the full? This brings to mind one of my favorite comments whose author I have long forgotten but dare say I will never forget the words. This person wrote, "We have settled to be nibblers of the possible rather than grabbers of the impossible."

Yet there is still an odd sort of apathy present on which I can't quite get a handle. This could be mistaken by outsiders as though I don't care. But that is quite far from the truth. Rather, it's like, "Oh, so what?" I'll try to illustrate.

An event occurs in the day-to-day routine. There has been a mishap and someone has been hurt. It has happened: although you can pray and ask for forgiveness, it's a done deal, you can neither change it nor take it back. So we should get on with it. Stop playing the would've, could've, should've game. Why spend time repeating it over and over, complaining about it day in and day out? What matters is what you are going to do now that it's done. Is that bad? It is if we stay in this condition and dwell on it until we are consumed. Yes, it is unhealthy spirituality, but if we are attempting to give it up, that is indeed a positive move.

PRAYER: Gracious and most loving Father, life's journey can be tiring and difficult at times, and we might want to quit. But with the companionship of your Spirit, we will receive what we need to persevere and continue along that journey. In the name of the one who gives us that strength, Jesus, our Lord. Amen.

Day 363
People of the Gap

I waited for the Lord; He inclined my ear and heard my cry. He drew me up from the desolate pit out of the miry bog and set my feet upon a rock (Psalm 40:1-2).

FROM THE VERY OUTSET, WE are faced with conflict. Our hearts tell us one thing, and reality tells us something else. Our hearts might desire that which is good, positive, and beautiful, but oftentimes they fall short and miss the mark. We want to live life, but we soon come to realize the huge number of obstacles standing there in the way of allowing folk to be where their hearts are. The devil releases all of his angels to vie for our attention. Thus, we join the ranks of the people of the gap.

Whereas this gap can cause great pain for some, for others it becomes an intolerable frustration and burden that causes them to throw away their hopes and dreams. For others, the gap leads to total disillusionment and cynicism.

And then there are the people who see this gap as a discrepancy between desires and achievement; hopes and fulfillment are seen as being very positive and become the means of trying their quality of hope and the depth of commitment. The delay between the wish and the fulfillment becomes the opportunity to evaluate whether this is really what we desire, whether this is worth struggling and working for.

Seeing the gap, we come to the stark realization that we cannot achieve our dreams on our own. There are a few things that must be addressed in front of God in order for the Lord to heal and close the gap. These are the essentials:

> We need the miracle of God's participation.
> We need the gift of patience.
> We need the grace of perseverance.
> We need to work hard to make things happen.
> More urgently, we need God's guidance, sustenance, and help.

Thus, our experience of the gap can drive us to prayer and humility as well as to persistence and faithfulness.

PRAYER: Our gracious heavenly Father, where we want to be and where we find ourselves are more often than not worlds apart. You knew that was going to be the case, so you went the extra mile and let Jesus leave his home in glory to come and live among us mortals and help us fight the raging battle with the powers of evil. Another reason for his coming was to disclose you to us and that we could believe him. Your unconditional love made it so. Thank you. In the name of Jesus, we pray. Amen.

⊸◦⊷

Day 364
Don't Act out of Anger

Also get rid of your anger, hot tempers, hatred, cursing, obscene language, and all similar sins (Colossians 3:8).

"SEEING RED," "ABOUT TO BLOW his stack," "She's about to erupt," "Lose your cool," "So mad, I could eat nails." These are just a few of the ways in which our society expresses anger with words. Those of us with PD can relate to this emotion quite well. You might finally have made it as a concert pianist or been on the verge of a private practice as a surgeon, or you might have been an up-and-coming pulpiteer. All the hard work, time, study, and sacrifice appeared to be paying off; things started looking up. Then this disease made its presence known and crippled your career. Anger? That's putting it mildly! Some of us live every day angry, and with each passing day we find ourselves getting more and more angry.

Is there some advice we could perhaps implement to help us to stave off this damaging emotion? Anger is somewhat similar to "feeling sorry for ourselves." In both situations, we feel very upset or angry; our tendency is to lash out, to condemn, or to take revenge. Some advice for this reaction would be to try waiting before reacting. Remember, count to ten—I know with some folk you need to count to 101. It would be good for you to talk to yourself. "Don't act, don't make decisions, don't do anything right now, even if makes you vengeful." Lashing out pulls you away from your true identity as a forgiving and loving believer.

You also know that you might regret your "felt" reaction. This is a time to wait, not to act. Give yourself time to remember who and whose you are. Take time to get things back into proportion and to realize that you don't always feel this way. Learn to wait and to listen from the communication experience you have with the Father. Learn to become like the God who loves you with all of your darkness and with all of your beauty. Stop and go within to allow the Spirit, the breath of God, to touch you and transform your dark thoughts and feelings. You are only a child, and you need help to act and react as a true child of light.

> **PRAYER:** Our heavenly Father, your children hear you say, "Vengeance is mine; I will repay." Only you can help us to hold our tongues and negative reactions at those times we are tempted to return hurt for hurt, pain for pain, ugliness for ugliness. Help us to show love and compassion instead. In the name of Jesus, we pray. Amen.

Day 365
The Bible in Fifty Words

Ezra, standing higher than all the other people, opened the book in front of all the people. As he opened it, all the people stood up (Nehemiah 8:5).

HAVE YOU EVER BEEN IN A bookstore, only to notice the plethora of books and pamphlets that are designated as Bible "helps." There's the popular *One Year with the Bible*, which is nicely tidy and compact enough to fit in a Bible slip-case or even between the pages without doing too much damage to the binding of the good book. As its title indicates, it is designed to help folks read through the Bible in a year.

Then there are the Lectionaries, common and not so common alike. These touch on major portions of the Bible, sometimes thematically or topically, but usually in accordance with the old high and low feast days of the liturgical calendar year that begins with Advent and ends with Christ the King Sunday. This particular Bible "help" covers several cycles of readings over a course of three years.

There are even Bible "help" software programs for computer users! Some of them are well-packaged, complete with suggested ways to read through the entire Bible in a year, commentaries, extra-biblical literature—even devotional readings! Other similar software packages force you to buy cheap and make toll-free phone calls to ask for alphanumeric codes to unlock portions of the software—for a donation, of course.

Many of these Bible "helps" require a sizeable investment of time, which is especially difficult for people who are in a hurry or whose attention spans require frequent stimuli. I recently received a bit of help from a friend to overcome this dilemma. So if you haven't had time to read the Bible, here it is in fifty words:

God made, Adam bit,
Noah arked, Abraham split.
Jacob fooled, Joseph ruled,
Bush talked, Moses balked.
Pharaoh plagues, people walked.
Sea divided, Tablets guided,

Promise landed.
Saul freaked, David peeked,
Prophets warned,
Jesus born.
God walked, love talked,
Anger crucified, hope died.
Love rose, spirit flamed,
Word spread, God remained.

Here endeth the lesson. Thanks be to God!

PRAYER: Gracious God, we thank you for this day, still full of opportunity to share in the word that you have given us. We praise you and glorify your holy name. Bless us and be graious to us in this time together as we share and hope and dream. In Jesus' name, we pray. Amen.

Day 366
I Need a Break!

Jesus replied, "You unbelieving corrupt generation. How long must I be with you? How long must I put up with you" (Mathew 17:17)?

A GREAT NUMBER OF YOUNGER KIDS today have no knowledge of the legendary cartoon character, Wile E. Coyote. Each episode has him pitted against the known speedster, the Road Runner. In each installment, instead of animal senses and cunning, Wile E. Coyote uses absurdly complex contraptions and elaborate plans to pursue his quarry. He obtains these complex and ludicrous devices from a fictitious mail-order company, the Acme Corporation, which he hopes will help him catch the Road Runner. The devices invariably fail in improbable and spectacular ways. Whether this is a result of operator error or faulty merchandise is debatable. The coyote usually ends up burnt to a crisp, squashed flat, or at the bottom of a canyon—some shorts show him suffering a combination of these fates. Even with all the failure and frustration, Wile E. continues his daily hunt.

As a matter of fact, we can learn from Wile E., particularly with regard to frustration and anguish. Everybody who has Parkinson's or has anything to do with the care of PD folk can feel the muscles in the shoulders, neck, and face begin to tighten at the mention of the word, "frustration." There is no doubt that we have all experienced it varying degrees: first, frustration; then anguish; then maybe even despair, which I hope is less the case than the first two. The plethora of stories that could be told about these twins, frustration and anguish, and how they are dealt with would be an excellent resource for us to have.

Each person with Parkinson's will experience these feelings at some time or another and at different levels. It is how we manage them that really makes the difference in moving us to deal with frustration and anguish. The sad part is that oftentimes, we don't recognize it is invading our space until it has progressed to the critical stage. We have to understand that it is another outcropping of Parkinson's and we have to deal with it. We might have to face it on more than one occasion, but we can do it. It can be defeated. And if you get frustrated, remember Paul's words to press on, as well as seeing Wile E. preparing for another attempt to capture the Road Runner; for no matter the numerous times he failed, he did not let the frustration and anguish get the best of him. When one of his plans failed, it was back to the drawing board to get ready for another chance to have Road Runner for lunch.

Can frustration and anguish (as well as despair) be overcome? Yes! But it takes a great deal of understanding, patience, and love to get us through. If you start feeling this way, go and watch some Looney Tunes.

> **PRAYER:** Father, we are in need of your help and encouragement in causing us not to be frustrated or in anguish, but be filled with the hope that yes, there is a way out, and that out is with you beside us. In Jesus' name, we pray. Amen.

A Parkinson's Disease Glossary
(not exhaustive)

*T*his glossary of terms and phrases about PD covers some of the typical medical and scientific terms, as well as healthcare, disability patients, and their families encounter as the disease progresses.

ACETYLCHOLINE: A chemical in the brain (neurotransmitter) that regulates movement, memory, learning, and emotions.

APNEA: Cessation of breathing.

AUDITORY HALLUCINATIONS: State of hearing voices or sounds that are not real.

AGONIST: A drug is an agonist if it attaches itself to a cell in such a way as to make it act or work as it usually acts when it is normally stimulated by chemicals within the body or brain. In the case of Parkinson's disease an agonist (such as bromocriptine) stimulates a specific neurochemical cell or receptor to produce more of its natural product (dopamine).

ANTIOXIDANT: A substance that protects cells from oxidative damage.

AKINESIA: *A-* means "without" and *kinesia* means "movement," so akinesia means "without movement."

ANTIOXIDANTS BODY: Body chemicals that scavenge for and neutralize free radicals.

ATAXIA: Loss of balance and coordination.

ACTIVITIES OF DAILY LIVING (ADL): Self-care task such as grooming, dressing, walking, speaking, keeping house, cooking, etc.

BRADYKINESIA: A term reflecting the slowness seen in patients with Parkinson's disease.

BRADYPHRENIA: A term reflecting a slowness in one's ability to think and process information and is often seen in Parkinson's disease.

BASAL GANGLIA: Of the mid-brain responsible for controlling movement and is linked with emotional and thinking centers of the brain.

BLEPHAROSPASM: Forces eye closure (quenching); maybe a side effect of the anti-Parkinson's medication, levodopa.

CARDIO-PULMONARY RESUSCITATION (CPR): Combined techniques of basic life support for a person who has stopped breathing or whose heart has stopped beating.

CENTRAL NERVOUS SYSTEM: The brain and spinal cord.

CHOREA: A type of dyskinesia (abnormal movement) characterized by repetitive dance-like, levodopa therapy.

CHRONIC ILLNESS: A physical or mental condition that conditions or recurs over a long period of time.

COGNITIVE: Related to memory, thinking, and language.

COGNITIVE FLUCTUATIONS: Frequent changes in thinking ability, level of attention, and alertness commonly seen in patients with dementia or with Lewy bodies (change can last for minutes or weeks).

COGWHEEL RIGIDITY: A "ratchet" type of muscle rigidity, notable at the distal extremities (e.g., the wrists).

DEEP BRAIN STIMULATION (DBS): A type surgery to treat the symptoms of PD.

DELIRIUM: A state of altered awareness with agitation, hallucinations, and confusion.

DELUSIONS: Fixed thoughts or ideas that are not based on reality.

DEMENTIA: Chronic loss of mental capacity due to an organic cause; typically involves progressive changes in memory, behavior, personality, and motor function, and might also be associated with psychological symptoms, such as depression and apathy.

DEMENTIA WITH LEWY BODIES (DLB): A progressive degenerative disease or syndrome of the brain that shares symptoms of both Alzheimer's and Parkinson's disease and is characterized by fluctuating cognition, hallucinations, and Parkinsonism.

DEPRESSION: A feeling of sadness or loss of interest or pleasure, usually with negative thinking.

DOPAMINE: A chemical in the brain that regulates movement and emotion.

DYSARTHRIA: A group of speech disorders caused by disturbances in the strength or coordination of the muscles that produce speech as a result of damage to the brain or nerves.

ESSENTIAL TREMOR: A common diagnosis sometimes confused with early Parkinson's disease. Also known as familial tremor, onset is usually in young adulthood or midlife, and might involve voice and head tremors as well as a fine bilateral tremor of the hands.

EXTRAPYRAMIDAL SYSTEM: Nerve cells, tracts, and pathways that connect the cerebral cortex, basal ganglia, thalamus, cerebellum, and spinal neurons; regulates reflex movements such as gait and balance and is impaired in Parkinson's disease.

FESTINATION: Short, shuffling steps and an involuntary speeding up of gait.

FLEXION: A bent, curved posture of the spine or a limb.

Freezing: Common term for akinesia (qv); temporary involuntary inability to move; being "stuck in place" as if feet were glued to the floor.

Free radicals: Toxic substances that are continuously produced by all cells of the human body.

Frontal lobe: Region of the brain responsible for complex thinking and also involved with emotions.

Genetic: Related to heredity or family genes.

Gustatory hallucinations: State of tasting a substance that is not real or present.

Hallucinations: Deceptions or tricks played by the brain that involve the body's senses (seeing, hearing, tasting, feeling, and smelling),

Hypomimia: Decreased facial expression due to rigidity of facial muscles.

Idiopathic: Meaning a disease with no known cause; the most common form of Parkinson's.

Lewy bodies: Abnormal "clumps" of protein that accumulate in the cells of the brain and nerves and are often seen with PD and dementia with DLB (qv).

Micrographia: Change in handwriting, with script becoming very small.

Motor fluctuations: Sudden, unpredictable changes in the ability to move.

Motor symptoms: PD symptoms that affect movement, including tremor, rigidity, bradykinesia, and postural instability.

Neurodegenerative disorder: A disease or condition that is caused by the death or degeneration of nerve cells in the brain or spinal cord. Parkinson's disease, Alzheimer's disease, and amyotrophic lateral sclerosis are examples of neurodegenerative disorders.

Neuroprotective: Slowing or stopping the death of brain cells.

Neuron: A cell that conducts electrical neural impulses from one part of the body to another.

NEUROTRANSMITTER: A chemical substance found throughout the body that transmit nerve impulses from one cell to another cell.

NON-MOTOR SYMPTOMS: Secondary symptoms associated with PD that are not related to changes of the motor system (i.e., pain, numbness, anxiety, sadness, restlessness, drooling, sweating, urinary changes, heart palpitations, dizziness).

OROPHARYNX: Region back of the throat.

PALSY: A paralysis of a muscle or group of muscles. An old-fashioned word for Parkinsonism; Parkinson's disease was originally known as the "shaking palsy."

PARKINSONISM: Broad term used to describe Parkinson-like symptoms (resting tremor, slowness, poor balance, walking problems.

PATHOLOGY: The study of a disease process, including what is affected, and what it looks like under a microscope.

POSTURAL INSTABILITY: Difficulty with balance; unstable balance; a tremor that increases when hands are stretched out forward.

RETAIN INSIGHT: The ability to understand reality despite current hallucinations or delusions.

RIGIDITY: Increased resistance noted to the passive movement of a limb.

SEROTONIN: A neurotransmitter that regulates mood, emotion, sleep, and appetite.

SHUFFLING: Small, baby steps or the sliding of feet.

SIALORRHEA: Medical term for drooling.

SOCIAL AVOIDANCE: Avoiding social situations due to feelings of anxiety, fear, or embarrassment around others.

STEREOTACTIC SURGERY: A technique in which surgeons enter the brain through a small burr hole in the skull, and use three-dimensional coordinates to locate specific targets in the brain. Examples of stereotactic procedures are pallidotomy, thalamotomy, and deep brain stimulation.

SUBSTANTIA NIGRA: A region of gray matter in the brain where dopamine cells deteriorate and cause Parkinson's disease.

TACTILE HALLUCINATIONS: State of feeling a sensation that is not real or present

TREMOR: Involuntary shaking of a body part.

VISUAL HALLUCINATIONS: State of seeing a person or object that is not real or present.

VISUAL ILLUSIONS: State in which a real object is misperceived as a different or altered object.

VISUAL-PERCEPTION SKILLS: The ability to process and understand visual information (i.e., distance between objects).

CPSIA information can be obtained
at www.ICGtesting.com
Printed in the USA
FFOW04n1650050314
4063FF